RETHINKING THE SYLPH

Titles in Print
   Looking at Ballet: Ashton and Balanchine, 1926–1936
   The Origins of the Bolero School
   Carlo Blasis in Russia
   Of, By, and For the People: Dancing on the Left in the 1930s
   Dancing in Montreal: Seeds of a Choreographic History
   Balanchine Pointework
   The Making of a Choreographer: Ninette de Valois and "Bar aux Folies-Bergère"
   Ned Wayburn and the Dance Routine: From Vaudeville to the "Ziegfeld Follies"
   Rethinking the Sylph: New Perspectives on the Romantic Ballet

A STUDIES IN DANCE HISTORY BOOK

RETHINKING THE SYLPH

New Perspectives on the Romantic Ballet

edited by Lynn Garafola

WESLEYAN UNIVERSITY PRESS
MIDDLETOWN, CONNECTICUT

Published by Wesleyan University Press, Middletown, CT 06459
www.wesleyan.edu/wespress
© 1997 by Wesleyan University Press
All rights reserved
Printed in the United States of America   5   4   3   2
CIP data appear at the end of the book
ISBN for the paperback edition: 978–0–8195–6326–2

Cover: Kimberley Glasco as Giselle
Photo by Cylla von Tiedemann. National Ballet of Canada.

Contents

Illustrations   vii

Acknowledgments   xi

Introduction   1
LYNN GARAFOLA

National Dance in the Romantic Ballet   11
LISA C. ARKIN AND MARIAN SMITH

Feminism or Fetishism: *La Révolte des femmes* and Women's
Liberation in France in the 1830s   69
JOELLEN A. MEGLIN

Marriage and the Inhuman: *La Sylphide*'s Narratives of
Domesticity and Community   91
SALLY BANES AND NOËL CARROLL

Redeeming *Giselle*: Making a Case for the Ballet We Love to Hate   107
JODY BRUNER

Women of Faint Heart and Steel Toes   121
JUDITH CHAZIN-BENNAHUM

Blasis, the Italian *Ballo*, and the Male Sylph   131
GIANNANDREA POESIO

Ballet Dancers at Warsaw's Wielki Theater   143
JANINA PUDELEK

The Arrival of the Great Wonder of Ballet, or Ballet in Rome
from 1845 to 1855   165
CLAUDIA CELI

Salvatore Taglioni, King of Naples   181
LAVINIA CAVALLETTI

Jules Janin: Romantic Critic   197
JOHN V. CHAPMAN

Appendixes

National Dance in the Romantic Ballet 245
LISA C. ARKIN AND MARIAN SMITH

Ballets Performed in Rome from 1845 to 1855 at the
Teatro di Apollo and Teatro Argentina 253
CLAUDIA CELI

Ballets by Salvatore Taglioni 259
LAVINIA CAVALLETTI

Bibliography 263

Contributors 275

Index 277

Illustrations

Marie Taglioni performing the cachucha in *La Gitana*.   12

Fanny Elssler performing the cracovienne in *La Gipsy*.   15

Marie Taglioni in *La Gitana*.   16

Carlotta Grisi and Lucien Petipa(?) performing the polka in *Le Diable à quatre*.   17

The different forms of polka, with a portrait of Cellarius.   19

Fanny Elssler in *La Tarentule*, *La Sylphide*, *La Gipsy*, *La Gitana*, and in a zapateado.   28

Fanny Cerrito performing the lituana.   37

Fanny Elssler and James Sylvain in a "*Pas Styrien*."   40

Sofia Fuoco in a tarantella.   41

Fanny Cerrito in the ballet *La Fille de marbre*.   41

Fanny Elssler in her "favorite dances."   47

Giselle, Act II.   50

"Conquer or Die."   71

Costume design for Mina.   73

Feminism or phallic fetishism? Costume design for Zulma.   77

More gender ambiguity: Zéir, the King's page.   79

Marie Taglioni in *La Sylphide*.   93

La Sylphide.   94–98

Kimberly Glasco in Giselle's adagio.   111

Albrecht answers the siren's call of Giselle's adagio.   112

Kimberly Glasco prays for Albrecht's safety.   113

Margaret Illmann prays for Albrecht's safety.   113

Karen Kain, as Giselle, dancing her first exuberant variation.   116

Giselle's death.   117

Kimberly Glasco and Aleksandar Antonijevic in the ballet's
final moments.   118

Isaac Cruikshank, "The Graces of 1794."   121

Adam Buck, "Two Sisters."   121

"La Folie du Jour."   122

Baron Gérard, "Madame Récamier."   122

Jean-Simon Berthélémy, costume sketch, *Proserpine.*   122

P.L. Débucourt, "La Dansomanie."   123

"Costume de Bal," 1805.   123

Early nineteenth-century corset.   124

Early nineteenth-century dress shoe.   125

Marie Taglioni's pointe shoe held by Dame Alicia Markova.   125

Amalia Brugnoli and Paolo Samengo in *L'Anneau magique.*   125

"Les Coulisses de l'Opéra."   126

Emilie Bigottini in *Clari, ou la Promesse de mariage.*   127

Bridal gown, 1819.   127

Costume design by Auguste Garnerey for a female soloist in
Aladin, ou la Lampe merveilleuse.   127

Costume design by Hippolyte Lecomte for Marie Taglioni as
Zoloe in *Le Dieu et la Bayadère.*   127

Paris fashion plates.   128

Marie Taglioni as Flore.   129

Portrait of Carlo Blasis.   131

A dancing couple in classical dress.   133

Portrait of Claudina Cucchi.   134

Claudina Cucchi as Giselle.   139

Mathilde Kchessinska and her father Felix Kchessinsky in a mazurka.   144

Konstancja Turczynowicz and Felix Kchessinsky in *Cracow Wedding.*   149

Portrait of Roman Turczynowicz.   151

Design for a memorial tableau for Roman Turczynowicz's jubilee.   151

Konstancja Turczynowicz and Aleksander Tarnowski in
Le Diable à quatre.   153

Cracow Wedding.   161

Fanny Cerrito and Arthur Saint-Léon performing the Aldeana in *La Fille de marbre*. 169

Domenico Ronzani in *Ezzelino sotto le mura de Bassano*. 171

"Ronzani's Grand Ballet Troupe." 173

Lucile Grahn in the title role of *Catarina, ou La Fille du bandit*. 174

Giovannina King, "*prima ballerina assoluta* of the Teatro Valle." 176

Francesco Penco, "*primo ballerino assoluto* of the Teatro Valle." 177

Raffaella Santalicante Prisco, "*prima mima assoluta*," in *Renato d'Arles*. 177

Ottavio Memmi and Pia Cavalieri. 178

Salvatore Taglioni, lithograph by Luigi De Crescenzo. 182

Portrait of Salvatore Taglioni. 185

Lise Noblet in a zapateado. 211

"The danseur who prides himself on having preserved the noble traditions of Vestris." 215

Marie Taglioni as the Sylphide. 216

Jules Perrot in *Zingaro*. 218

Fanny Elssler as Lauretta in *La Tarentule*. 219

"Dances of the *haute école*." 223

Portrait of Lucile Grahn. 229

Carlotta Grisi in *Le Diable à quatre*. 232

"Come Away to the Glen." 233

Portrait of Lucien Petipa, the first Albrecht. 235

Adèle Dumilâtre, the first Myrtha. 236

Hilarion meets his end. 237

Carlotta Grisi as Giselle. 239

Acknowledgments

I am deeply grateful to the authors whose essays follow. Without their patience, generosity, and intellectual fellowship, this volume would never have materialized. I am also grateful to the Studies in Dance History editorial board for its enthusiastic support of the project, Suzanna Tamminen of Wesleyan University Press for welcoming it to one of this country's most distinguished dance publishers, and Joan Greenfield for designing it with her usual unerring eye and sense of movement. The staff of the Dance Collection, New York Public Library for the Performing Arts, was unfailingly helpful in locating material for illustrations. I am indebted to Gordon Hollis of the Golden Legend, Inc., who kindly allowed a Daumier caricature in his possession to be reproduced, and to Joan Erdman, who brought a historian's sensibility to the excellent index. Finally, I wish to thank my husband, Eric Foner, for generosities too numerous to mention, and my daughter, Daria Rose, who first went up on pointe as these pages were edited.

—L.G.

Editorial note: Where material from more than one division of the Bibliothèque Nationale, Paris, is cited in the endnotes, the abbreviation "BN" is used along with a shortened form of the division name: hence, "BN-Musique" (for the Département de Musique) and "BN-Opéra" (for the Bibliothèque de l'Opéra).

RETHINKING THE SYLPH

LYNN GARAFOLA

No era has done more to define the image and essence of ballet than the Romantic decades of the 1830s and 1840s. Indeed, it was in these years, which coincided with the liberal July Monarchy in France and a rising tide of nationalism elsewhere, that ballet as we know it first came into existence. Although individual elements, from the theme of the supernatural to the all-important use of pointe, predated Romanticism, it was only in this period that they crystallized into a new, coherent whole. The result was ballet's reinvention as a modern art.

To a far greater degree than its predecessors, the Romantic ballet was an international movement. It flourished from Naples to New York, Buenos Aires to St. Petersburg, thanks in part to the peregrinations of its stars, who dazzled audiences on tours that sometimes lasted for years, and the far-flung engagements of its ballet masters, who remounted in theaters of the periphery works originally produced in the ballet capitals of Paris and London. But there were at least two other sources of this international commerce, and both were distinctly untraditional. One was the service offered by the Paris Opéra—as the Académie Royale de Musique was popularly known—whereby theaters and opera houses could acquire annotated scores for ballets they wished to duplicate on their own stages. This implied not only the existence of a repertory that crossed national boundaries, but also the then new idea that music was as crucial to a ballet's identity as the story. It is hardly accidental that the earliest ballets that survive even in bastardized form in today's repertory—*La Fille Mal Gardée*, *La Sylphide*, *Giselle*—date to the Romantic period.[1] For the first time, a ballet was seen as entailing a set combination of texts rather than being solely identified by its libretto.

Another sign—and source—of the internationalism of the Romantic ballet was the widespread dissemination of its iconography. Lithography, invented in the closing years of the eighteenth century, gave a great boost to printing and the production of multiple, relatively cheap images. "In the printing arts," writes George Chaffee, one of the great twentieth-century collectors of nineteenth-century ballet prints,

> the Romantic Era was one of the greatest periods in all history. Never before or since have so many "presentation books" poured from the presses—albums of pictures with or without text; gift-books ("Keepsakes" was the happy and homespun English expression), richly dight as a

mediaeval Book of Hours....The vogue,... rising in the 1820's and becoming a rage from 1830 on, resulted in an alliance, a collaboration between artists and poets never before known.[2]

Of all ballet prints the most highly esteemed were French. Although many of the artists were foreign, the capital of this flourishing print industry—like the capital of the Romantic ballet—was Paris. It supplied the home market and was also, as Chaffee notes, a great export center. Indeed, the quality of French workmanship was so high that foreign designs were sometimes sent to Paris to be drawn on stone and printed.[3] The images themselves were immensely varied, offering action studies, scenic designs, costume plates, technical illustrations, caricatures, portraits, and ensemble scenes. And they were everywhere—in books, albums, portfolios, and magazines, on sheet music covers, and decorating the walls of lower-middle-class homes. Marie Taglioni never danced in the United States, but she could be seen on sheet music covers published in Philadelphia and New York—an international celebrity created in part by technology.

Although Romantic prints could be varied in subject matter, they belonged above all to the ballerina. She haunts them, as she haunts the writing of the era, an icon of femininity, graceful, teasing, mysterious. With her soulful gaze and airy skirts, she inhabited a world remote from home and hearth, the secluded valleys, misty lakesides, secret glades, and wild heaths that in ballet as in fiction, poetry, and opera extolled a Romantic idea of nature even as they coded her as an exotic dwelling on the periphery of European civilization. (One reason such landscapes were so popular on the ballet stage was their novelty: the invention of gaslight had only recently made them possible.) Often she was shown in flight, eluding the arms of an expectant lover. Or she might stand demurely on a scallop shell, a vision as tantalizing in her nearness as in her appearance of chastity. Whatever the guise, she exuded charm. It was there in the incline of her head, the delicate rosiness of her cheek, the slenderness of her waist, the pointes skimming a path strewn with flowers. Even when depicted in company, she was always different.

The image of the ballerina as a creature apart, an embodiment of beauty, desire, and otherness, did not die with the Romantic era. It persists even today, despite huge changes in taste and periodic challenges by homosexual radicals beginning with Serge Diaghilev, who sought to invest her attributes in a new, androgynous breed of male star. Today's ballerina, to be sure, no longer looks like her Romantic forebear: she is sleeker, suppler, faster, leggier—an acrobat with the flexibility of a rubber band. But she remains the embodiment of the fashionable body, slimming down or adding flesh as this ideal changes: an hourglass figure during the fin de siècle, Twiggy-thin in the late 1960s, a marvel of muscular prowess today. Although her body has changed and she sometimes dons unitards, bicycle shorts, and bell-bottoms, her basic garb remains what it first became during the Romantic period—the tutu. This, as Judith Chazin-Bennahum shows in her photo-essay "Women of Faint Heart and Steel Toes," was initially an adaptation of the fashionable ballgown of the late 1820s, just as the prototype for the pointe shoe was the era's fashionable dress slipper. These prototypes underwent enormous changes, but unlike the shoes and dresses that preceded them, which were also based on contemporary models, they henceforth became the ballerina's badge of identity. No matter if a tutu is long (as in *Giselle*, *Les Sylphides*, or *Serenade*), short (as in *Swan Lake* or *The Sleeping Beauty*), or of the "powder-puff" variety favored by George Balanchine, it is still her timeless uniform, just as the pointe shoe, whether darned (as it was initially) or blocked (as it became in the 1860s), whether soft, hard, or deshanked, is her distinctive footwear.

Of course, there was more to the Romantic ballet than tutus and pointe shoes, even if these were the most obvious of the ballerina's new attributes. As Lisa C. Arkin and Marian Smith point out in their essay, "National Dance in the Romantic Ballet," the 1830s and 1840s coincided with a veritable craze for folk-derived forms on the stage and dance floor alike. At the Paris Opéra, the official headquarters and disseminator of ballet Romanticism, national dance figured in over three-quarters of the house offerings, operas as well as ballets, while at public balls, regardless of whether they catered to an elite or popular clientele, polkas, mazurkas, and that earlier "ethnic" import, the waltz, dominated the proceedings. Although France did not lack for folk traditions, the overwhelming majority of national dances on the French stage came from Europe's underdeveloped periphery—southern Italy, Spain, Scotland, the Tyrol, eastern and central Europe: they represented a primitive "other" that the march of French colonialism would later identify exclusively with the Middle East. Still, even then, the depiction of national dances revealed the existence of an exotic-erotic hierarchy. With its seductive curves and Arab influences, Spanish dance represented the Orient nestling in the bosom of Europe itself.

Like costumes, national dances were also markers of authenticity and suppliers of local color. However, in the hands of a choreographer of the stature of Jules Perrot, they could serve a narrative as well as decorative end. In *Eoline*, which was set in the Polish region then known as Silesia, he conceived one of the ballet's key scenes—when the heroine succumbs to the hypnotic power of the evil Rübezahl—entirely in the idiom of the mazurka, the great Polish national dance. As the authors note, this was one of several national *pas* choreographed by Perrot in which an important psychological or emotional transformation occurred during the dance itself. Later, this kind of transformation would be expressed solely in the classical idiom.

Today, it is virtually impossible to imagine the centrality of such material to Romantic-era ballet, since much of it was either eliminated or divested of its dramatic and narrative function when works such as *Giselle* were revived by Marius Petipa in the late nineteenth century. Indeed, Romantic ballets filtered through the Russian imperial tradition—as well as original works such as *The Sleeping Beauty* and *Swan Lake*—treated national dances as interchangeable divertissements. At the same time, the dances themselves became increasingly codified, the source of their originals, with the exception of Spain, virtually confined to the Tsarist empire and its immediate neighbors to the West—Hungary, home of the czardas, and Poland, birthplace of the polonaise no less than the mazurka.

Although national dances were a key part of the Romantic ballet, it was the *ballet blanc*—the ballerina in virginal white replicated en masse by the ensemble—that was radically new. Unlike scenes based on national dance forms, the *ballet blanc* was conceived in classical style, that is, in the international—or supranational—lexicon of the danse d'école. Originating in the French court, the danse d'école underwent rapid development in the aftermath of the French Revolution, when heeled shoes and cumbersome skirts were discarded in favor of sandals and tunics. The change in costume made possible the multiple rotations, bounding leaps, dramatic extensions, acrobatic lifts, and high relevés that now entered the ballet vocabulary, celebrating the heroism of the newly liberated body. In the eighteenth century, the division between theatrical and social dance forms was not always clear. By the 1830s, the shared territory had largely vanished, except for national dances. Moreover, with the widespread adoption of pointe, female technique entered a period of unprecedented growth and unimagined virtuosity. If the Romantic period was the first to reap the fruits of the technical advances of the previous forty years, it was also the first to create a universal ballet "language" comparable to the elite forms of French and Italian that were beginning to supplant local dialects. The craze for national dances notwithstanding, it was during the Romantic period that the Spanish bolero school and the Italian *grotteschi* tradition—vital eighteenth-century dance idioms—became a kind of local peculiarity that could exist internationally only as a form of exoticism.

A universal and universalizing phenomenon, the new danse d'école was also strictly gendered. Eighteenth-century technique did not noticeably distinguish between the sexes. This changed, however, with the technical advances of the early nineteenth century, which initiated a process of differentiation that eventually transformed ballet into an art about women performed by women for men. By far, the most dramatic example of this was pointework, which became not only a uniquely female utterance (although, theoretically, the technique could have been used by men) but also a metaphor for femininity—the Romantic ballet's true subject. But pointe was not the only weapon in the ballerina's growing arsenal. She usurped the adagio, once the province of the danseur noble, and made its harmonious poses and gently unfolding movements her own. Her dancing put lightness and grace at a premium, qualities that softened the appearance of force in movements that required it. With male roles increasingly played by women dressed as men, the Romantic ballet not only feminized the representation of maleness but also made men themselves redundant. As critic Jules Janin's intemperate words on the subject of the male dancer demonstrate, nothing was more alien to the Romantic ballet than the strapping muscles and vigorous movements of real men. His reviews, selected and translated here by John Chapman, reveal that if Marie Taglioni changed the way people danced, she also changed the way people like Janin perceived and looked at dance.

Although a pan-European phenomenon, the feminization of ballet occurred earlier and more completely in France than elsewhere. In Italy, as Giannandrea Poesio reminds us in "Blasis, the Italian *Ballo*, and the Male Sylph," men held their own, even those who specialized in French-style dancing. Blasis, the author contends, was far more a man of the Enlightenment than an exponent of Romanticism, even if his career overlapped with the latter. Although he trained the first important generation of La Scala ballerinas, all of whom displayed exceptional proficiency in pointework, his technical manuals treated the male body as the norm and all but ignored the female. Like August Bournonville in Copenhagen, Salvatore Taglioni in Naples, and other ballet masters whose careers unfolded outside the orbit of the Paris Opéra, Blasis remained loyal to the late eighteenth-century French tradition of male dancing—that is, to a style unaffected by Romanticism and a technique that had yet to reflect the radical changes precipitated by pointework.

The position of the danseur was not the only difference between French and Italian versions of ballet Romanticism. As Lavinia Cavalletti points out in her essay on Salvatore Taglioni, Marie's uncle and the ruling eminence at the Teatro di San Carlo in Naples for nearly half a century, Italian audiences never wholly yielded to the seduction of the supernatural. In Naples, as in Milan or Rome, historical themes—drawn from antiquity, the Renaissance, or eras as recent as the eighteenth century—retained an importance that distinguished the Italian expression of Romanticism from its French counterpart. This is not to say that Romantic elements did not seep into works by Taglioni or Blasis, or that audiences south of the Alps remained in the dark about the repertory in the making to the north. Marie Taglioni may never have danced for her uncle in Naples, but her seasons at La Scala were greeted with acclaim. In Rome, the subject of Claudia Celi's essay, Fanny Elssler's appearances at the Teatro Argentina prompted an outpouring of wild, impetuous enthusiasm. Almost as successful were Lucile Grahn's in *Catarina, ou la Fille du bandit*, now renamed *Caterina degli Abruzzi*, set in the mountainous region due west of Rome: what was exotic in London, where the work had premiered, was now only a day's ride away. Northern imports were frequently adapted for Italian sensibilities. Antonio Cortesi's *Giselle*, which he staged for La Scala, had five acts; Domenico Ronzani's production at the Teatro Argentina had three. It also had a "happy" ending, with Giselle and Albrecht (or Alberto, as he was now called) pledging their troth beyond the grave.

Just as the definition of the exotic shifted with locale, so, too, did the meaning of national forms of expression. To the cosmopolitan audiences of Paris or London, dances such as the bolero, mazurka, or tarantella served a largely decorative purpose, providing local color, authenticity, and a mild dose of primitivism. Elsewhere, however, the same dances could become a patriotic statement, an expression of the desire for national self-determination. Thus, in a country such as Poland, which had long since ceased to exist as a national entity, a work such as *Cracow Wedding* asserted the continued vitality of a culture daily threatened with suppression or subjected to the "Russification" described by Janina Pudełek in her essay on Warsaw's Wielki Theater. Similarly, in Russia, with its Francophile elite, *The Little Humpbacked Horse*, albeit staged by a Frenchman to entertain that elite, coincided with nationalist stirrings in painting and music. Sometimes, a patriotic subtext was read into works with exotic or historical settings and subjects. Thus, in a Rome yet to be delivered from the yoke of the French, the crowds exploded with patriotic enthusiasm when the all-female regiment of *bersagliere* at the end of *Bianca di Nevers* marched smartly from the wings in the plumed hats of Garibaldi's army of national liberation.[4] Although seldom viewed in this context, the Romantic ballet was a contributor to the rhetoric of nineteenth-century nationalism, which it also helped disseminate.

This rhetoric, like the other discourses on which the Romantic ballet impinged, was voiced, so to speak, in a language and an art ever more closely identified with the feminine. Not only did women dominate the stage in terms of numbers, but they also overwhelmed it as the stars of ballets with titles such as *Betty*, *Ondine*, *Catarina*, *Giselle*, and *Esmeralda*. If the protagonist of the vast majority of ballets was female, the Romantic ballet itself was a meditation on femininity—its mystique, elusiveness, unattainability, and innumerable avatars. The critic Théophile Gautier spoke of "Christian" dancers and "pagan" dancers, the first exemplified most famously by Taglioni as the Sylphide, the second, by her great rival, Fanny Elssler, in the fiery cachucha that became her trademark.[5] But this is too simple a categorization for a sorority that displayed so many different faces. Moreover, it overlooks the *danseuse en travesti* or travesty dancer, that strange creature who donned the garb of princes, sailors, soldiers, or lovers, and in many places drove men from the stage until the twentieth century. Like pointe, travesty work was a specialty act transformed during the Romantic period into a convention explicitly associated with the representation of gender. However, where pointe ushered women into a realm of perpetual maidenhood, an idealized version of the separate female sphere, male dress, with its leg-revealing tights, announced their sexual availability.[6] Indeed, in the Romantic period, when family-centered training largely gave way to institutionalized training in academies, the connection between ballet dancers and certain forms of prostitution deepened. This occurred not only in major pleasure capitals such as Paris, but also in minor ones such as Warsaw, where, as Janina

Pudełek shows, ballet dancers welcomed the protection of rich men, even when they were Russian.[7]

Many of these themes came together in *Le Révolte au sérail*, the harem ballet that Filippo Taglioni choreographed for his daughter Marie only a year after *La Sylphide*. The work, as Joellen A. Meglin reveals in her essay, echoed the feminist discourse of the Saint-Simonians while displaying considerable amounts of leg as the harem captives of Mahomet, the Moorish King of Granada, don warrior garb to fight for their freedom. The military maneuvers performed by the ballet's Amazon regiment were hugely successful, launching a genre that persisted on the music hall stage into the twentieth century. The theme of domesticity and its relationship to the "inhuman," which Sally Banes and Noël Carroll explore in an essay on *La Sylphide*, also survived the Romantic era. Indeed, with Petipa, the contrast between the two became an organizing principle, a metaphysical girding, and even a basis for tragedy. It also links the Romantic ballet to contemporaneous efforts in opera, where themes of marriage and madness appear as well. How to account for the enduring attraction of *Giselle* and reconcile a postmodernist distaste for the ballet's politics with an "incorrect" pleasure in its art are questions that Jody Bruner sets out to answer in an essay that draws on the ideas of the psychoanalyst and literary critic Julia Kristeva. Analyzing the contradictions that abound in the ballet, she shows that an accommodation is indeed possible.

With the Romantic era began the great feminization of ballet as a social practice. For reasons that are not altogether clear, the phenomenon began earliest and lasted longest in France. Here, by the 1830s, the corps had become almost wholly female and leading men the object of sustained and bitter attack. By the late 1840s, the handwriting was on the wall for leading men such as Lucien and Marius Petipa, who either fled the country (the case of Marius, who went to St. Petersburg in 1847) or found offstage managerial positions (the case of Lucien, who became principal ballet master of the Paris Opéra in 1860). Jules Perrot, who spent most of the 1840s and 1850s working abroad, ended his career teaching women at the Paris Opéra, the balding, white-haired gent painted by Degas. Unsurprisingly, few French danseurs of even middling quality emerged in the decades that followed. At the school attached to the Paris Opéra, the number of boys plummeted, as it did at La Scala, although the Italian prejudice against male dancers was never as thorough-going as its French counterpart.[8] Even at the Imperial Ballet in St. Petersburg, where men retained an onstage presence throughout the century, the danseur noble was threatened with obsolescence. Indeed, until the late 1890s, when Enrico Cecchetti's pedagogical efforts began to bear fruit, successors to Pavel Gerdt, Petipa's aging, eternal Prince Charming, conspicuously failed to materialize.

Since ballet itself continued to flourish (especially on the popular stage), it was only a matter of time before a shortage of male labor developed. Beginning in the 1850s, jobs once held by men began to be occupied by women. Chief among them was teaching. When Marie Taglioni took over the class of perfection at the Paris Opéra in 1858, she inaugurated a trend that continued virtually without interruption until the Second World War. Women taught the other classes as well, creating an all-female sphere within the framework of the Opéra's all-male administration. Moreover, the immediate post-Romantic period witnessed the emergence of the first important group of women choreographers. Among them was Marie Taglioni, who staged *Le Papillon* for the Opéra in 1860; Elizabetta Menzeli, who choreographed the dances for the first *Aida* (sung in Cairo in 1871); Madame Mariquita, who served as ballet mistress at the Folies-Bergère and Opéra-Comique; Katti Lanner, who served in a similar capacity at the Stadt-Theater, Hamburg, and the Empire Theatre, London; and Giuseppina Morlacchi, who adapted any number of Romantic and post-Romantic ballets for American audiences.[9] While their work was far from original and, with the exception of Taglioni's ballet, created for popular, provincial, or less prestigious venues, their very existence challenges the idea that women choreographers were an invention of the twentieth century and of modern dance in particular.

The growing presence of women as choreographers, a phenomenon that continued apace throughout the nineteenth century, did anything but enhance the artistic status of ballet. If anything, it diminished it, associating ballet with second-class citizenship in the artistic polity. Indeed, the modernization and "gentrification" of ballet precipitated by Diaghilev's Ballets Russes in the 1910s and 1920s, insofar as it entailed the displacement of women associated with the "old ballet" and their replacement by men identified with the "new," was at least partly intended to "correct" what was perceived in many quarters, especially Russian ones, as a severe gender imbalance. Even if the ballerina's "phallic pointe" (in Susan Foster's provocative phrase)[10] remained a source of envy, ballet was now too important an art to leave to mere women.

However powerful the reaction against the gender conventions of nineteenth-century ballet, they continue to shadow the present. Indeed, neither politics nor special pleading has managed to turn back the clock to a time when men reigned supreme over the ballet stage. Although the Paris Opéra was founded long before the advent of Romanticism, it was only during the era of sylphs that ballet, perhaps its most celebrated progeny, acquired the "classical" lexicon and gendered identity of the art we know today. The first truly international dance movement, the Romantic ballet witnessed the introduction of artistic and social practices and ideologies whose influence continues to be felt on the threshold of the twenty-first century. Dancers today may not emulate Marie Taglioni (except possibly in the second act of *Giselle*), but they can still draw inspiration from the era's ballerina sisterhood, whose mute poetry seduced the imagination of an entire age through the sheer power of performance.

Notes

1. Although *La Fille Mal Gardée* was first produced in 1789, it was the Paris Opéra revival in 1828 to a new score by Ferdinand Herold that became the "original" of the work and the forebear of Lev Ivanov's 1885 St. Petersburg revival (to music by Peter Ludwig Hertel), from which most modern productions descend. The genealogy of *Giselle* is more complicated. The ballet premiered at the Opéra in 1841, remaining in repertory until the late 1860s. However, modern productions trace their origin to Marius Petipa's 1884 revival for the Imperial Ballet, St. Petersburg. It was this production (with the addition of a few dances by Michel Fokine) that the Ballets Russes presented at the Paris Opéra in 1910 and that Nicholas Sergeyev set on the Paris Opéra company in 1924, the Camargo Society in 1932, and the Vic-Wells Ballet in 1934. Although Petipa's brother Lucien was the original Albrecht, it is unclear to what extent Petipa was reviving the ballet's original choreography or revising it, especially in the "old-fashioned" second act. The Ballets Russes program credited the dances and mise-en-scène to Petipa, and the libretto to Vernoy de Saint-Georges, Théophile Gautier, and Jean Coralli, who was not a librettist but one of the ballet's two original choreographers. (The other and more important, Jules Perrot, went unmentioned.) The most celebrated of all Romantic ballets, *La Sylphide* premiered at the Opéra in 1832 and, like *Giselle*, did not survive the 1860s. In 1892, Petipa revived the work, although it never became the "holy" ballet that *Giselle* did in Russia. Most of today's productions date to the version mounted by August Bournonville in 1836 for the Royal Danish Ballet. The work has remained in that company's repertory ever since.

2. George Chaffee, "Three or Four Graces: A Centenary Salvo," *Dance Index*, 3, nos. 9-11 (Sept.-Nov. 1944), pp. 141-142.

3. *Ibid.*, p. 157.

4. The *galop delle bersagliere* was choreographed by Paul Taglioni for the ballet *Flik e Flok*, then tacked on to *Bianca di Nevers* by the Roman impresario Vincenzo Jacovacci. For a discussion of the political aspects of the Taglioni ballet, see Claudia Celi and Andrea Toschi, "Alla ricerca dell'anello mancante: 'Flik e Flok' e l'Unità d'Italia," *Chorégraphie*, 1, no. 2 (Autumn 1993), pp. 59-72.

5. For his 1834 review of *La Tempête* where this formulation first appeared, see *Gautier on Dance*, ed. and trans. Ivor Guest (London: Dance Books, 1986), pp. 15-16.

6. For a fuller discussion of the subject, see my article "The Travesty Dancer in Nineteenth-Century Ballet," *Dance Research Journal*, 17, no. 2 (1985-1986), pp. 35-40.

7. For a discussion of the economic conditions that made occasional prostitution a virtual necessity for dancers of the Paris Opéra during the same period, see Louise Robin-Challan's article "Social Conditions of Ballet Dancers at the Paris Opéra in the 19th Century," *Choreography and Dance*, 2, no. 1 (1992), pp. 17-28.

8. According to Nadia Scafidi, in 1838 there were thirty-two girls and eight boys enrolled at the school attached to La Scala. In 1853 the figures were twenty-eight and two; in 1868, thirty-nine and zero ("La Scuola di ballo del Teatro alla Scala: l'ordinamento legislativo e didattico nel XIX secolo," pt. 1,

Chorégraphie, Spring 1996, p. 62.

9. For Menzeli, see Ann Barzel, "Elizabetta Menzeli," *Dance Chronicle*, 19, no. 3 (1996), pp. 277-288; for Lanner, see Ivor Guest, *Ballet in Leicester Square: The Alhambra and the Empire 1860-1915* (London: Dance Books, 1992), pp. 93-96; for Morlacchi, see Barbara Barker, *Ballet or Ballyhoo: The American Careers of Maria Bonfanti, Rita Sangalli and Giuseppina Morlacchi* (New York: Dance Horizons, 1984), pp. 122-167.

10. "The Ballerina's Phallic Pointe," in *Corporealities*, ed. Susan Leigh Foster (London: Routledge, 1996), pp. 1-24.

National Dance in the Romantic Ballet

LISA C. ARKIN AND MARIAN SMITH

Historians have long acknowledged the surging interest in folk culture that exerted a potent effect upon artists and scholars in the nineteenth century as the old influences of classicism and Francophilia finally began to be eclipsed. In such disparate works as Edvard Grieg's *Peer Gynt*, Sir Walter Scott's *Rob Roy*, Smetana's *The Bartered Bride*, and Victor Hugo's *Les Orientales,* one may see a burgeoning pride in the folk culture of one's own region and a fascination with that of others.

Much of this new enthusiasm for indigenous folk cultures was inspired by the writings of Johann Gottfried von Herder (1744–1803), the highly influential historical philosopher who in the late eighteenth century had posited that the evolving concept of nationhood was dependent upon a sense of shared tradition among a homogeneous assemblage of folk. Central to his way of thinking was the belief that the collective consciousness of a nation resided in its religion, language, and folk traditions, and that to honor these home-bred forms of cultural expression was far more desirable, more natural, and more fundamentally human than to embrace the mechanical, artificial ideology of the so-called Enlightenment. He extolled the sweetness of one's own native soil and the beauty of the primitive folk expression that projected the soul of a people. At the same time he promoted the then-radical notion that no one culture was inherently superior to others, but that the various peoples—each possessing a unique and worthy *Volkgeist* (folk spirit)—should coexist and learn from one another, and, moreover, that such pluralism was a fundamental condition of humanity.[1]

The writings of Herder engendered a new and profound respect for folk culture that permeated European literature, painting, and the performing arts in the nineteenth century. And while the creative impact of folk forms upon writers, artists, and composers of that period has long been an important subject of scholarly investigation, its effect upon ballet has not yet been fully explored. For, though the type of dance referred to variously as "national," "folk," "character," and "ethnic" is acknowledged to have constituted a part of the Romantic ballet, it is still generally treated only as a marginal adjunct in scholarly investigations of the subject, a lesser cousin to classical dance, a folkstyle that provided an occasional means of injecting "local color" but was peripheral to the genuine aesthetic of Romantic ballet.

This viewpoint, we argue, conflicts with the evidence. Indeed, an

Marie Taglioni, in Spanish costume, performing the cachucha in the ballet La Gitana. *This image appeared on the cover of a sheet-music piano arrangement published in New York. Dance Collection, New York Public Library for the Performing Arts, Astor, Lenox, and Tilden Foundations.*

examination of primary source documents shows that national dance played a far more prominent role in the Romantic ballet than is generally acknowledged today, both in its theory and its practice. And ballet's spectators during the period deemed Romantic (that is, roughly 1830–1850) were actually much more likely to encounter national dance than they were the ethereal *ballets blancs* now so strongly associated with that period. We believe that the presence of national dance in the Romantic ballet was so great, in fact, as to merit a scholarly exploration far wider in scope than an article-length study can possibly hope to cover. Not only is a straightforward factual chronicle of its existence in order (for national dance is known to have flourished in all of Europe's most important opera houses), but so, too, is an investigation of how national dance was related to the broader social, political, and artistic trends of the nineteenth century. For the marginalization of this idiom in much dance historiography has not only left a lacuna in the study of Romantic ballet per se, but also made national dance virtually inaccessible to scholars in other disciplines who could no doubt draw analogies between its contributions to ballet and the manifestations of folk-derived expression in the other arts. Indeed, a fuller treatment of this topic by dance historians will doubtless lead to its integration into the scholarly discourse of nineteenth-century cultural studies in general.[2]

But in the meantime we are faced with a strange conundrum. National dance played an enormous role in ballet and was considered a salient force within it. Yet, despite its very high visibility on the ballet landscape of the nineteenth century, many representations of that landscape have shrunk its proportions considerably. That is, it has suffered something of the same fate as the "juste-milieu" paintings and the *colporteur* literature of the same age, which were extremely well known to the nineteenth century but until fairly recently were marginalized as unworthy of serious consideration.[3]

In the present article, we hope to make a step toward bringing national dance closer toward the mainstream of scholarly research, both in and outside the discipline of dance history. We focus on Paris, a city often regarded as the cradle of balletic Romanticism, although by no means the only venue that warrants close study in this regard.

Our approach is a varied one. We first discuss the popularity of national dance, both on the stage and on the social-dance floor. We then discuss the nature of the Romantic narrative ballet, and how character dance was situated within it. (Please note that we use the term "national" and "character" dance interchangeably in this article, as writers of the nineteenth century frequently did.)[4] We also delve into the rather difficult matter of "authenticity," weighing the words of ballet theorists and critics of the time in an attempt to discern how folk dances were brought to the stage. Then, after discussing the work of Jules Perrot, we discuss the false dichotomy of character dance versus the *ballet blanc*. Finally, we raise the subject of dance historiography, suggesting that it has been easy to apply twentieth-century performance practice and aesthetic preferences to our assessments of the past, and that this has hindered our attempts to determine what the Romantic ballet looked like in its heyday.

The Popularity of National Dance

Simply put, national dance was performed regularly and frequently in the opera houses of Europe during the Romantic period. It figured prominently within both operas and ballets, and in some theaters was featured in independent danced divertissements as well.[5] Indeed, it must be recalled that audiences were accustomed to great abundance and variety: an evening's entertainment could even consist of a complete opera and a ballet. And national dance was very likely to comprise part of the performance.[6]

Consider the case of the Paris Opéra. From about 1835 until well past mid-century, national dance seems to have occurred in over three-quarters of the performances given there, regularly appearing in both ballets and operas. In May 1841, for example, it was featured in twelve (and possibly more) of the fourteen performances given:

Mon., May 3	*Don Giovanni* (opera, set in Seville) Spanish dance during the ball scene (Act II)
Wed., May 5	*La Favorite* (opera, set in Castile) Spanish dance during the victory celebration (Act II)
Fri., May 7	*Les Huguenots* (opera, set in Paris) Gypsy dance to celebrate the day of rest (Act III)
Sun., May 9	*La Favorite* (opera, set in Castile) Spanish dance during the victory celebration (Act II)
Mon., May 10	*Le Diable amoureux* (ballet, set in Italy and Persia) Saltarella, cachucha, mazurka[7] *Le Philtre* (opera, set in the Basque region) Evidence is unclear.[8]

Wed., May 12	*Guillaume Tell* (opera, set in Switzerland) Tyrolian dance by peasants forced to perform for the tyrant Gesler (Act III)
Fri., May 14	*La Favorite* (opera, set in Castile) Spanish dance during the victory celebration (Act II)
Mon., May 17	*Robert le Diable* (opera, set in Italy) Evidence is unclear. The *pas de cinq* in Act II, performed by five men portraying Sicilian peasants, may have been a *pas de caractère*.[9]
Wed., May 19	*La Favorite* (opera, set in Castile) Spanish dance during the victory celebration (Act II)
Fri., May 21	*La Muette de Portici* (opera, set in Spanish-dominated Naples) Spanish and Neapolitan dances (Acts I and II)
Mon., May 24	*Les Huguenots* (opera, set in Paris) Gypsy dance to celebrate the day of rest (Act III)
Wed., May 26	*La Juive* (opera, set in the city of Constance) No evidence of national dance.
Fri., May 28	*Guillaume Tell* (opera, set in Switzerland) Tyrolian dance by peasants forced to perform for the tyrant Gesler (Act III)
Mon., May 31	*Le Philtre* (opera, set in the Basque region) Evidence is unclear.
	Le Diable amoureux (ballet, set in Italy and Persia) Saltarella, cachucha, mazurka[10]

So character dance was quite a familiar sight on the Opéra's stage. It became so pervasive, in fact, that one eulogist on the occasion of Pierre Gardel's death in 1840 could lament that "the dance [is now] composed of *only* so-called *pas de caractère*."[11] Théophile Gautier even hyperbolically implied that the character *pas* was the only type that a danseur should perform (as opposed to the classical *pas*): "A male dancer performing anything other than *pas de caractère* or pantomime has always seemed to me something of a monstrosity. Until now I have only been able to support men in mazurkas, saltarellas, and cachuchas."[12]

In the offhand comments and customs of ballet's habitués across Europe, too, one may find countless expressions of the notion that character dance was commonly considered a normal part of ballet. In the London publication, *The Natural History of the Ballet Girl*, a description of the daily routine of the typical corps dancer finds her hastily changing her costume in the dressing room "between the *pas de fées* of the opening scene and the villagers' *mazourka* of the closing one."[13] A contingent of male dancers from the Paris Opéra (including Lucien Petipa, the first Albrecht) was invited to take part in a polka competition with several highly skilled members of the social-dance elite (the polka being considered a complex folk-derived dance at the time), and knew the dance so well that they were able to beat their opponents handily.[14] Michel Saint-Léon, in the Württemberg court, taught both classical and character *pas* to the royal princes and princesses.[15] Manufacturers of ballet souvenirs—statuettes and lithographs, for example—sold images of ballerinas both in "classical" and "character" garb. Young ballet students in St. Petersburg were sometimes granted scholarships on the basis of their character dancing.[16] And so on.

It is also crucial to recall that, though the sight of the corps performing character dance was a familiar one—critics often described ensembles of coryphées performing perhaps a mazurka or bolero—the greatest ballerinas and premiers danseurs of the Romantic period performed national dances as well. That is, national dance was not the province of lesser dancers, nor of those whose body types precluded their excelling in the danse d'école style. Nor was it ceded strictly to those (like Fanny Elssler) who found it particularly congenial to their talents. It was an art that the highest-ranking soloists were fully expected to perform, along with mime and classical dance. Lucile Grahn, for example, the first Danish Sylphide and a dancer renowned for her steadiness on pointe and her lightness, made a great impression with her tarantella in

Fanny Elssler performing the cracovienne in La Gypsy, *1839. Notice the tiny spur on her left shoe and the martial costume, and in the background a view of Edinburgh and its castle.*
Dance Collection, New York Public Library for the Performing Arts, Astor, Lenox, and Tilden Foundations.

the divertissement *Le Pêcheur napolitain*.[17] Carlotta Grisi and Jules Perrot, who together helped create the role of the ethereal Wili Giselle, also performed many a character dance both separately and together, including the zapateado at the close of the Viennese season in 1838 and an "original *Tarantella* directly imported from Naples" (to name only two of their joint triumphs).[18] Lise Noblet, another dancer known for her lightness and the elegance of her poses, also delighted audiences with her Spanish dancing. With her sister Félicité she performed a Spanish dance in *La Muette* and achieved a triumph that Gautier describes as follows:

> The great success of the evening was the Spanish dance by the Mmes. Noblet. Their entrance was eagerly awaited. They appeared in white satin basquines, threaded and bespangled with silver, with roses in their hair, and wearing the high ceremonial combs—in fact, the whole fantastic costume of Dolores Serral. Then, to the strains of a melody that was as naive as all folk tunes are and fragmented into equal divisions by the babble of

Marie Taglioni, wearing a gypsy costume, in the ballet
La Gitana, *1840. Dance Collection, New York Public
Library for the Performing Arts, Astor, Lenox, and Tilden
Foundations.*

the castanets, they danced the most daring and brazen *pas* ever to have been seen at the Opéra. It was phenomenal, outrageous, unimaginable, but it was charming. Imagine swaying hips, spines arching back, arms and legs thrown into the air, the most provocatively voluptuous movements, a hot-blooded fury, and a diabolical attack—truly, a dance to awaken the dead.... The two sisters were applauded as never before, and...they were called back and made to start the *pas*, *El Jaleo de Jerez*, all over again.[19]

And Marie Taglioni "enchanted the world" with her Spanish dancing as *La Gitana*, a role which also called for two gypsy dances (one of them danced to music in which bottles, cauldrons, glasses, and saucepans were used as instruments).[20] This ballet, which Taglioni performed dozens of times to great acclaim beginning in 1838, including four seasons in Russia and three in London, generated a Taglioni souvenir iconography second in richness and variety only to that of *La Sylphide*.[21] It also firmly established her reputation as a solid character dancer, a reputation that has been largely forgotten, perhaps because historians have so strongly emphasized her triumphs as the sylph.

Social Dance. Rhapsodic assessments of character-dance performances liberally dot the newspaper review of ballets and operas of the Romantic period, and it is clear that audiences of the day were no less demonstrative when it came to character dance than they were for opera and danse d'école. Sometimes, in fact, character dance struck observers as even more exciting than the other types of opera-house fare. Heinrich Adami suggests as much in his résumé of Fanny Elssler's eight-performance season in Vienna in the summer of 1837:

> In eight performances, Fanny danced the *Cachucha* twenty-two times, yet who can boast that he knows this dance completely or can say that the twenty-second performance was not just as interesting as the first. That this should be so is the finest victory of natural grace over art, just as a rose, though seen a thousand times, is still a rose and the queen of flowers.

I have been present at many a stormy evening in the theatre, but I have never witnessed such general and unrestrained excitement as at the last appearance, and particularly after the *Cachucha* had been performed a third time.[22]

Yet shouting approval, applauding wildly, demanding encores, and throwing flowers onto the stage (as audiences were wont to do) was not the only way that members of the public could express their enthusiasm for national dance. They could also dance it themselves, fitting foreign dance styles to their own bodies, much as they donned costumes to wear to public balls.

In the 1830s and 1840s, in fact, there was a veritable national-dance craze on Europe's public dance floors. Amateur dancers flocked to dance studios to take lessons in national dancing. They rented and purchased national costumes to wear to public balls.[23] They purchased sheet music for character dance arranged by composers for amateur consumption, and books on the subject of national dance (one of which featured the mazurka, the cracovienne, the polonaise, the tarantella, the anglaise, the bolero, the cosaque, the fandango and the pas russe).[24] They even danced quadrilles—a type of social dance normally constructed of classical steps—that had been stylized according to national tastes.[25] One dancing master, for example, concocted the so-called "Empire Quadrille," in which each section of the dance imitated a different national style. Another adapted the Polish mazurka "after the laws of the French quadrille" so that the "inconveniences" of its complexity and improvisatory nature could be "obviate[d]."[26] His quadrille-mazurka provided a "sample, a foretaste of the mazurka"; "a sort of compromise" between the characteristic freedom of the Polish dance and the French inclination toward the incorporation of classical steps and familiar sets of spatial figures.[27] A Parisian journalist addressed this idea of contrast between traditional social dances and the newly popular national dances, writing in 1833, "the banal and fastidious contredanse will be definitively put to rest [at the Opéra balls]

Carlotta Grisi and Lucien Petipa(?) performing the polka in the ballet Le Diable à Quatre. *The man's costume is in the Cracow style, and features coins on the belt, striped pants, a feather in the cap, and embroidery on the coat. Dance Collection, New York Public Library for the Performing Arts, Astor, Lenox, and Tilden Foundations.*

to leave room for this variety of dances that are executed in Russia, Italy, and Germany—the polonaise, the fandango, the waltz, the mazurka [that] will become acclimated to Parisian soil."[28] Indeed, one can imagine that these character dances did allow those who danced them a greater range of movement than did the "fastidious contredanse." As another observer put it, social dancers "understood the happy alliance that could be forged between stiff French dance and loose Andalusian dancing."[29]

So powerful was the popularity of national dance in the ballrooms of Paris during this period, in fact, that it attracted the attention of humorists, one of whom wrote a vaudeville (entitled "Les Souvenirs de jeunesse") in which overzealous choristers doing the galop push the main character into a chair and then sing these lyrics:

Rédowons, schotischons,	[Let's redowa and schottish,
Fillettes et garçons,	girls and boys,
mazourkons	Let's mazurka
et polkons	and polka
Aux doux bruit des chansons.[30]	To the sweet sound of songs.]

Another humorist wrote somewhat sarcastically of the national dance craze in the satirical journal *La Musée Philipon*:

In 1842 the Grande Chaumière [a public dance studio] shone with an unaccustomed brightness, and was more than ever the meeting place for all true lovers of national dance....[A] multitude of dances, each one newer than the next, were tried, censured, approved, or prohibited; because needless to say, it is only at the Grande Chaumière that one may find the true traditions of elegance and beautiful manners.

The author also lampoons Spanish dance:

Among the choreographic...creations which distinguish the offerings of last summer, we must especially mention the *pas des taureaux indomptés* [the dance of the untamed bulls]. This way of moving, or rather of hurling oneself around, seems to us to have a particular cachet. [An illustration depicts a man in a tall silk hat, charging like a bull his unsuspecting female dance partner, who is bowing so deeply that she does not see what is in store for her.]....We have it on good authority that the notables of Carnaval are preparing, for the Opéra balls of 1843, new and different *pas de caractère* that will bring about a general revolution in all of Paris and, I do not fear to say, in all of Europe.[31]

Of further significance are the public ball divertissements—that is, the entertainments presented during public balls for the enjoyment of the revelers. Entertainers customarily appeared at some point during the evening and performed in a space cleared for them on the dance floor, as the ball's attendees stood by and watched. When the entertainment ended, the ballroom dancing resumed. Among the many acts hired for the Paris Opéra's carnival season balls were "mirliton" acts and ballet dancers from the Opéra itself—including coryphées performing quadrilles and soloists performing ensemble numbers with titles such as "The Four Sea-

The different forms of polka danced in 1844, with a portrait of Cellarius at the center. This anonymous French lithograph published by Lemercier indicates the extraordinary popularity of the polka as a social dance. Gaston Vuillier, La Danse *(Paris: Hachette, 1898), p. 247.*

sons."[32] And, after the sensational success of the four Spanish dancers—Dolores Serral, Mariano Camprubí, Manuela Dubinon, and Francisco Font—hired in January 1834 to appear both at the Carnival balls and in the opera *La Muette de Portici*, the Opéra's leading ballerinas were sometimes enlisted to perform character numbers as well. As *Vert-Vert* reported in December 1834:

> the great success obtained at the last Carnival gave rise to the idea of seeking a new success with an array of national dances of the different peoples

of Europe, and in some local dances from our southern provinces. Thus we will see the execution, in turn, by the principal ballet dancers of the Opéra, with Mlles Taglioni and Elssler leading, of the *pas styrien*, the mazurka, boleros and fandangos from Andalusia, the tarantellas of Naples, and dances of the Languedoc region—*las Treias* and *lo Chibalet*.[33]

The sensation caused by the Spanish visitors during the 1834 ball season also paved the way for Elssler's success with the cachucha in *Le Diable boiteux* in 1836, and apparently helped propel an existing fondness for national dance into an uproarious popular phenomenon.[34] Indeed, while theater audiences at the Paris Opéra had seen Polish, Italian, Hungarian, and Spanish national dances in pre-Romantic ballets, there can be no doubt that the visiting Spanish dancers who so inflamed Paris in 1834 contributed greatly to the new and growing popularity of national dancing in the mid-1830s.[35]

In any case, the public ball divertissements are significant in any consideration of the reception of national dance for three reasons. First, they show that classical and character *pas* were deemed equally appropriate as popular entertainment for ball guests. Second, they serve as a reminder that social and theatrical dance were closely bound together and that a complete reception history of national dance must accommodate both venues. Third, they demonstrate that the viewing of professional character dancing (sometimes at quite close proximity) was an activity that was quite in keeping with real-life experience for many members of the Parisian public. Thus, staged scenes of national dancers entertaining onstage characters (as in the ball scenes in *Don Giovanni* and *La Jolie Fille de Gand*, for example, and then later in the century in *Swan Lake* and *The Nutcracker*) actually mirrored the events of a real-life public ball. This imparted a certain immediacy and an air of reality to the staged divertissement that is lacking today.[36]

National Dance in the Narrative Ballet

Clearly, national dance was a popular form of entertainment, and it held a prominent place both in public festivities and in staged versions of such festivities. However, it must be noted that national dance was not only a popular form of divertissement but also lent itself to the narrative ballets (often called ballet-pantomimes) that were so popular during this period.

Before we proceed further, a digression on the subject of these ballets is in order. For it is important to reimagine what these works looked like—forgetting for a moment the modernized versions of Romantic ballets on today's stages—in order to understand how national dances fit within them.

First of all, mime and action scenes typically constituted as much as half of an entire ballet: indeed, it was not unheard of for entire scenes of a ballet (sometimes two in a row) to be devoid of dancing.[37] It is more accurate, in fact, to conceive of these ballets as mimed dramas that called for dancing from time to time, which is quite different from today's revivals, in which narrative ballets are presented as danced works with only occasional mime scenes. The proportions of the nineteenth-century productions may be seen readily in annotated répétiteurs (rehearsal scores) of Romantic ballets, which distinguish plainly between mimed and danced segments, and give an excellent indication of how much actual time was devoted to each.[38] The ratio of dance to mime and action scenes in the original *Giselle*, for instance, was roughly equal—fifty-four minutes of mime and action, and sixty minutes of dance (though the dancing has now been supplemented and the nondancing scenes shortened or eliminated to suit modern tastes).[39] And even the most perfunctory perusal of newspaper reviews of ballets from this period shows quite plainly how important a role mime played in these works. For the mime was not only necessary to convey the story; when executed well it accounted for much of the spectator's delight and pleasure in ballet. Of Fanny Elssler in *La Gipsy*, Gautier wrote, she "rises to the most sublime heights of dramatic art; a noble pride in innocence, energy, tears, grief, love, intoxicating joy, she runs through the whole gamut of human emotions."[40] Another observer, describing Pauline Duvernay in *La Révolte au sérail*, wrote that during the military maneuvers of the corps de ballet she performed one of the principal roles "with the wittiest pantomime, the most expressive and passionate gestures, represent[ing] all the incidents of an animated discussion and giv[ing] an idea of the council of war held by the women. A general laugh, and unanimous applause is earned by this gay and comic scene."[41]

The reason, of course, for the far greater prominence of mime and action scenes and the circumscribed role of dance (when compared to today's ballets) was that these Romantic ballets were designed to impart a story to the audience. Ballet was considered first and foremost a dramatic genre, like opera and the spoken play. Castil-Blaze even went so far as to say in 1831 that "most modern ballets are operas or dramas that have been translated into the mimic language."[42] And another observer described ballet as a genre in which "actors neither speak nor sing, but dance and execute a pantomime."[43] Indeed, the emphasis placed upon the plots of these ballets, both in the press and in performance practices, can scarcely be understated.

It was customary, for instance, for the plot of any new ballet to be recounted in detail in newspaper reviews of the premiere and in souvenir books as well.[44] The plot was told in even more detail in printed ballet libretti made available to spectators for purchase. Ballet libretti were generally from fifteen to forty pages long, and they explained the action of a ballet scene by scene, often including actual lines of dialogue—sometimes in quotation marks—to be mimed by the characters. Spectators at the ballet were also accustomed to seeing actual words displayed onstage—on banners and memorial tablets, for instance—helping them follow the plot.[45] It was also customary for the music of each new ballet to be closely coordinated to the pantomime gestures, helping make them as accessible as possible to the audience. In the opening scene of *Giselle*, for instance, Hilarion pointed to Giselle's cottage as sweet music was played, as if to say "here lives the one I love." With a menacing gesture, he then pointed to his rival Albrecht's cottage as sinister music was played.[46] The effect of these lengthy and frequent mime and action scenes, with music that followed the actors' movements and gestures moment to moment, was probably akin to that of the melodrama of the boulevard theaters.[47]

The evidence also suggests that some of the physical movements called for in the Romantic ballet might seem somewhat stilted and stylized according to today's tastes. Among such movements were the dramatic gestures that were sometimes performed in unison. In the ballet-pantomime *La Gipsy*, for example, thirty-odd Bohemians mimed the words "But who are you?" by "throwing their forearms" (as one unsympathetic critic wrote).[48] And the actors often froze in tableaux or "pictures," sometimes at moments of high drama in the middle of a scene, sometimes just before the fall of the curtain.[49] So typical was this as a curtain-closing device that audiences hardly could do without it. "The ballet," wrote *The Times* about *La Tarentule*,

> should end more effectively; a postilion walks in to tell the doctor that his carriage is ready, and the curtain falls without anything like a *groupe* being formed. This was a kind of damper, the audience scarcely knew whether all was over or not, and for fear of applauding in the wrong place, at first did not applaud at all.[50]

Critical commentary of the period also demonstrates that in ensembles the choreography was often intended to delight the eye more by the design and placement of groupings than by active, kinetic movement. Groups, in fact, are frequently mentioned by critics as one of the key visual features of a ballet. ("You can't describe this ballet," wrote a critic about *La Fille du marbre*, "you must see the groups";[51] another, reviewing *La Fille du Danube*, insisted that there was "not an elegant grouping or elegant tableau" in the entire ballet.)[52] Another important choreographic category, both for soloists and for corps dancers, was the pose, which warranted frequent mention in libretti and reviews. Thus, according to the libretti, the poses of the Wilis in *Giselle* were "voluptuous"; Urielle's in *Le Diable amoureux* were "ravishing," and Miranda's in *La Tentation* were sometimes decent, sometimes voluptuous.[53] And choreographers often sought a kaleidoscopic effect by presenting a series of successive "pictures," such as the bathing scene in *La Révolte au sérail*, described in the libretto as follows:

> Zulma and her friends sport in the water. Slaves burn perfumes; others prepare to dress the king's wives. Zulma emerges first and is enveloped in a light veil behind which she makes her toilet. Soon her companions follow her example and dress in the same manner. Then the women dance and admire themselves in mirrors, forming a succession of the most captivating pictures that center upon the beautiful Zulma.[54]

Ivor Guest describes another example in the first act of *Lalla Rookh*:

> The ambitious nature of the dance was indicated by the titles of these fig-
> ures: Hermes, The Shell, The Kiosks, The Cage, The Mirror, The Harp,
> The Framed Picture, The Morning Breeze, The Stars, The Pineapple, The
> Car of the Rising Sun, The Butterflies, The Sun's Rays, and The Living
> Statue and its Pedestal. *The Times* declared that the *pas symbolique* was
> "one of the most elegant scarf dances ever contrived" and showed "what
> new combinations are possible in a style apparently so hackneyed." No
> words, in the opinion of the *Morning Post*, could do adequate justice to
> the groups: "in every movement there was poetry, every group was picto-
> rial, as if it had stepped forth from the canvas of Boucher or the still
> greater Guido."[55]

Some choreographers went so far as to imitate specific paintings, in the
manner of tableaux vivants, such as Perrot's representation of Léopold
Robert's celebrated "La Fête de la Madonne" in his ballet *Ondine*.[56] And
Gautier declared that a "ballet should be a picture before being a drama,"
that "the best combination for the production of a fine theme for a ballet
[was] a poet explaining his ideas to an artist who expresses them in
sketches." Clearly, a strong pictorial sense often lay behind both the
design and the appreciation of the Romantic ballet.

Finally, let us turn to the matter of the realism of the physical mise-en-
scène. For ballet, like opera and the spoken play, was subject to the new
Romantic trend that called for sets, costumes, props, and special effects
that were as realistic as possible. (As Gautier said, "we are no longer living
in a time when the inscription 'magnificent palace' nailed to a post suffices
for the illusion of the spectators.")[57] In the late 1820s the Paris Opéra
came to be especially well known for the opulence and detail of its elabo-
rate settings, and its ability to transport the audience to whatever historical period or distant land a libretto might call for.

Pierre-Luc Charles Ciceri, for example, in charge of sets at the Opéra,
was sent to Switzerland and to Italy so he could have the immediate experience that would make it possible for him to create an aura of authenticity in his stagings of *Guillaume Tell* and *La Muette de Portici*.[58] He even,
on occasion, oversaw the recreation of real-life buildings. For instance, an
actual cloister—supposedly that of Montfort-l'Amaury—was replicated
for the ballet of the nuns in the third act of the opera *Robert le Diable*.[59]
And the magnificent waiting room of the royal palace in Stockholm was
recreated for the opera *Gustave III*. "All this sumptuous dwelling," wrote
one critic, "is transferred to the stage with unbelievable exactness. It is so
accurate that the French Ambassador to Sweden who was sitting near us
said that for a moment he thought he had returned to his post."[60]

Realism was also the order of the day in the Opéra's costume department, where careful attention was given to making costumes that looked
appropriate to the time and place of an opera's or ballet's setting. (Indeed,
the costume inventory was cross-listed historically and geographically,
and included costumes for a wide variety of regional characters, including

"Bayadères, Basques, Bohemians…Créoles, Chinese…Indian slaves, modern Indians,…Provençaux.")[61] The labors of the period's costumers did not go unnoticed by critics. In the case of *La Juive*, which was set in fifteenth-century Constance, much praise was heaped upon the painstaking attention to detail in the costumes for the Act I procession scene:

> Nothing is missing in this prodigious resurrection of a distant century. The costumes of the warriors, civilians, and ecclesiastics are not imitated but reproduced to the smallest details. The armor is no longer pasteboard; it is made of real metal. One sees men of iron, men of silver, men of gold! The Emperor Sigismund, for instance, is a glittering ingot from head to foot. The horses, no less historically outfitted than their riders, prance and turn.[62]

Composers, too, did their part to create a sense of place. As one musical lexicographer put it in a definition of ballet music: "As for the dance airs, they must be characteristic and analogous to the place where the action takes place; thus, the dance airs of the Indians, Scots, or Hungarians must have the character of the music of their countries."[63] This prescription was well heeded. The Scottish setting of *La Sylphide*, for instance, was brought to life by this jig by Schneitzhoeffer:

Jig from La Sylphide *(from manuscript conductor's score, A.501, BN-Opéra).*

Rossini's Tyrolian chorus from *Guillaume Tell* (to which Marie Taglioni danced the tyrolienne) imitates the sound of yodeling:

Tyrolian chorus from Guillaume Tell
(from full vocal/orchestral score published by Troupenas, Paris, n.d.).

The mazurkas composed by Adolphe Adam for *Le Diable à quatre*, a ballet set in Poland, follow the custom of accenting the second or third beat of the measure and of resting on the third beat at the ends of phrases; this one, for example, places the accent on the second beat:

Mazurka from Le Diable à quatre
(piano sheet music arranged by J. Herz and published in Paris, 1845).

For *Le Diable boiteux*, Casimir Gide provided a good deal of Spanish-sounding music, including this piece for the opening ball scene which makes use of Spanish rhythms and imitates the sound of the strumming of the guitar (marked by "x"):

Opening ball scene from Le Diable boiteux
(from manuscript répétiteur score, Mat 19e [314-9], BN-Opéra).

We also know from Michel Saint-Léon's pedagogical manuscripts from the Württemberg court that, at least in his case, appropriate folk music was used for the teaching of character steps. He used this melody for the Cracovia:

Cracovia from Michel Saint-Léon manuscript (Rés. 1137, BN-Opéra).

This is closely related to the melody "Na krakowska nute" that is still danced in Poland today:

Krakowiak from a performance by the Janusz Kazmierzak's
Folk Orchestra (mid-1970s).

Of course the efforts to create a convincingly realistic theatrical illusion sometimes fell short. Gautier, for instance, chided the Opéra for using a South American set to depict a North American subject (and for using "rocks that are to be found nowhere in the world and ought not to appear at the Opéra").[65] And Jules Janin suggested that the composer Gallenberg had done a poor job of creating musical verisimilitude in *Brézilia*, opining that though the action was set in the New World, the score sounded like it was from the Other World.[66] But whether in the practice or in the breach, the rule is clear: costume and set designers and composers were expected to make their productions seem plausibly authentic to the spectator.

To summarize: the narrative ballet of the Romantic period emphasized the conveying of a story and featured numerous, lengthy mime scenes to do so. The music followed the miming closely to make it more palpable and also helped set the scene by providing "ethnic" music when necessary. The choreography often included poses and groupings. And the mise-en-scène endeavored to present the locale in which the action took place with as much verisimilitude as possible. So how did national dancing fit into these ballets?

First, national dance was considered a valuable tool for establishing the setting of ballets as well as operas. Character choreography usually did not exist as a thing apart, but worked together with the music and the mise en scène to create a convincing sense of place. Thus, the corps de ballet became a human landscape, a moving backdrop that offered spectators the satisfying illusion that they had actually glimpsed some foreign place. (Critics often remarked upon the success of this approach. The tarantella danced by the corps in *Ondine*, for instance, was praised for being "as spirited and characteristic as if it were danced on the *chiaja* by real *contadini*.")[67]

In the same vein, national dance could help characterize a ballet's protagonists, a contribution of major importance, since these ballets so strongly emphasized the story. And since many of the main figures in these stories had a distinct ethnic heritage—indeed, ballet of this period put a premium on such figures—national dance was an potent dramatic tool as well as a key means of demonstrating the character's identity to an audience. Escudier stresses this double function in a review of Elssler's portrayal of the Calabrian peasant Lauretta, the lead female character in *La Tarentule*: "Mlle Elssler...dances a tarantella that gladdens and excites you. In turn coquettish, fiery, and witty, she portrays with wonderful intelligence that ardent character which is only found on the volcanic soil of Italy."[68]

Likewise, by dancing the mazurka in *Le Diable à quatre*, Carlotta Grisi's young Polish heroine (aptly named Mazourka) not only delighted the audience with the charm of the dance, but also revealed and affirmed her identity to them. Leila, the Egyptian slave girl in *La Péri*, did the same when she performed the "pas d'abeille," or bee dance, which according to Gautier one could see "performed in Cairo in its native purity by almehs."[69] Occasionally, the ballerina even made her first entrance with a national dance, thus immediately conveying to the audience a crucial element of the character she was portraying.[70]

It is true, of course, that character dances were occasionally inserted in operas or ballets without a dramatic rationale. Carlotta Grisi, for example, in the title role of *La Péri*, substituted a Spanish manola for the Egyptian bee dance, arousing the objections of Gautier, who said that "Spanish dance has nothing at all to do with the action or intention of the work."[71] And the Hungarian dance performed on at least one occasion in *Don Giovanni*, an opera set in Seville, drew a sardonic response from Jules Janin:

> There were at least a dozen men dressed as Hungarians (yes, Hungarians) who devoted themselves to striking pleasing poses. They came, went, raised their arms, slapped their calves, passed under each other's arms, held each other by the left thumb,... and laughed, with those who had any, showing their teeth.[72]

But if the sheer popularity of character dance sometimes led to its inclusion in operas and ballets in incongruous ways, the libretti did officially call for dances that matched the physical setting of the work in question.[73]

Character dance was also held to be inherently expressive. Some observers even went so far as to imply that national dance had an expressive capacity that the classical *pas* lacked. The author of *Read's Characteristic National Dances*, an "elegantly illustrated" gift book published in London in 1853, hints that national dance could express true feeling better than more "artificial" forms of dance:

> Thus far, the sounds of feet echo the feelings in the heart; when science interferes the muse no longer haunts the wood-beamed kitchen of the farmer's home, or the bounteous revels of the baronial hall. Bedecked in the bright but insubstantial garb of opera display, her artificial grace is, perhaps, no longer the language of a buoyant heart within. Art may lend attractive graces to the form, and study give vast brilliance to the step; but upon the confines of the artificial it is not the province of our little work to trespass.[74]

And though national dances were indeed performed in opera houses, the writer's preference for naturalism over artifice was very much in keeping with the tenets of the new Romantic drama and its rejection of outworn theatrical conventions. Authentic expression, according to this new way

American sheet music cover showing Fanny Elssler in La Tarentule *(center),* La Sylphide, La Gipsy, La Tarentule, La Gitana, *and in a zapateado.*
American Antiquarian Society.

of thinking, could not spring forth from the restrictive forms of eighteenth-century classicism.

Indeed, the connection between the rise of character dance in the narrative ballet and the loosening of old classical strictures in spoken drama during this period is one that is well worth noting. Just as playwrights were beginning to forsake the rules of verse drama and put everyday words into the mouths of its characters (a process that sent shock waves through the old guard of Paris and led to near-riots at the Comédie Française), so did choreographers welcome the opportunity to present ballet characters who expressed themselves in ways that looked more natural and made them seem more like real human beings.[75] August Bournonville may have been referring to this idea when he extolled the virtues of national dance (or "native dance," as he called it) as an expressive tool in the Romantic ballet:

> Forty to fifty years ago [the true French school] was divided into fixed classes: *sérieuse*, *demi-caractère*, and *comique*, and the dancers were content to excel in one particular genre.... Now, however, it is the music that determines character; the *style de perruque* has given way to the Romantic,... and though bravura dancing, like bravura singing, is in eternal conflict with the dramatic element, *the latter has won an important victory by the acceptance of native dances as an integral part of the art.*[76]

The matter of contrast between mimed and danced scenes in the Romantic ballet, finally, must also be considered in any attempt to discern how national dance fits into such works. For any sort of *pas*, whether it was in classical or character style, surely drew special attention to itself simply by the fact that it provided such a distinct and obvious contrast to the mime scenes. That is, any given *pas* was probably more striking to the eye than it would have been if performed in a work that was danced throughout.

This is not to say that mime necessarily occupied a rung of lesser prestige in the Romantic ballet than dance (as it does today), nor that it was considered intrinsically dull (quite the contrary!), but rather that the contrast between the danced and mimed scenes could have been deployed as a powerful narrative tool. It seems likely, in fact, that the ebb and flow between the dancing and miming may have been akin to that between the aria and the *scena* (the dramatic scene consisting largely of recitative) in opera, and that skillful choreographers, like skillful opera composers and librettists, could make the most of the dramatic possibilities that this built-in contrast between kinesis and stasis supplied.[77]

By the same token, the varying voltages of the *pas* that were choreographed for any given narrative ballet also supplied interesting contrasts, making it possible for any particularly energetic *pas* to stand out. So, national *pas*, which were often characterized by driving rhythms, speedy footwork, and partnering that privileged rapid turns over stately arabesques, sustained poses, and adagio movements, in some cases probably struck spectators as especially kinetic, adding, as Gautier once expostulated in a fit of pique, "spice to the deadly boring framework of ballet."[78] And though it would be quite wrong to suggest that character dance was, across the board, more energetic than the danse d'école, one must nonetheless bear in mind that certain of the Romantic ballet's relatively static qualities (its pictorial emphasis and use of the frozen tableau, for example) could make any sort of allegro dancing stand out. And in many cases the allegro *pas* that made the strongest impression were national dance ones.

The deep sense of contrast that the spectators may have perceived between classical and character dancing in the 1830s—a time during which Gardel's choreographies were still well known—is expressed by Gautier, who (especially when intoxicated with Hispanophilia) was capable of making broad comparisons detrimental to classical dance:

> A woman who appears...to pose before your opera glasses in the glare of eighty footlights with no other purpose than to display her shoulders, bosom, arms, and legs in a series of attitudes that show them off to best advantage seems amazingly impudent if she is not as beautiful as [the Graces]....Dolores [Serral] and [Mariano] Camprubí have nothing in common with our own dancers. They have a passion, a vitality, and an attack of which you can have no idea....There is nothing mechanical in their dancing, nothing that appears copied or smacks of the classroom.[79]

And in 1839, recalling Serral's debut in Paris, he wrote:

> We explained how superior were her suppleness, vivacity, and Andalusian passion to the geometrical poses and the right-angled *écarts* of the French school. At that time people of taste found [her] dancing...bizarre, alien, incompatible with the traditions of good schooling and the rules of good taste. The very mention of the word *cachucha* made wigs stand on end and set the *pochettes* [pocket violins] of ballet masters screeching.[80]

And, as hyperbolic as these comments are, they convey the sense of stark contrast between old and new that many balletgoers undoubtedly experienced at this time of transition between the "style de perruque," in which the principal characters performed in the noble style, and the new, more expressive Romantic ballet, in which they were likely to perform national dance.

"Authenticity": Theory and Practice

Like Herder, many ballet theoreticians of the late eighteenth and nineteenth centuries expressed a keen interest in the authentic, "true," and "natural" folk expressions of various nations. For example, Giovanni-Andrea Gallini, in a treatise published in 1772, provides "A Summary Account Of various kinds of Dancers in different Parts of the World," including Spanish, French, Flemish, Italian, Tyrolian, Hungarian, Polish, Russian, Chinese, Turkish, and Mexican dancers. In this section, he also states that the expressive arts embody the "genius" of a nation and should render their subject matter in as convincing a manner as possible:

> Where dances are well composed, they may give a picture, to the life, of the manners and genius of each nation an each age, in conformity to the subject respectively chosen. But then the truth of the costume, and of natural and historical representation must be strictly preserved. Objects must

be neither exagerated [sic] beyond probability, nor diminished so as not to please or affect.[81]

Gennaro Magri, in his 1779 *Theoretical and Practical Treatise on Dancing*, likewise insists that an authentic rendering of a nation's expressive arts requires knowledge of its distinct cultural attributes. He suggests further that the application of this knowledge was required of the professional dancer. The *ballerino*, he writes, should study

> geography in order to know the rites, climates, places, customs, abuses, Islands, seas, Cities of different Nations, especially those of African, Asiatic, and American ones, not known to us, so as to stage properly and express the character in a natural way, if wishing to put one of these Nation's dances into a spectacle. These are all necessary things, without which one cannot succeed as a first-rate ballerino.[82]

Carlo Blasis also wrote about the expression of national identity through dance. Indeed, as his long career progressed, the passages on character dance in his various treatises became lengthier. In the earliest, *Traité élémentaire, théorétique et pratique de l'art et la danse*, published in Milan in 1820, Blasis devoted less than one page to the subject, suggesting in the chapter on "Dancers: Serious, Demi-Caractère and Comic" that

> All dancers of the comic roles should study characteristic steps. They must devote themselves to a correct representation of national idiosyncrasies and imbue each step and pose with the style and spirit of the peoples whose dance they are performing. The best known character dances are the Provençal, the Bolero, the Tarantella, and the Russian, Scottish, German, Tyrolian, Cossack, etc. national dances.[83]

However, with the breakdown of the traditional genres of dancers in the 1820s, national dances came to be adopted into the repertory of principal dancers and featured with increasing frequency in ballets and operas. This heightened interest in character dance is reflected in Blasis's next treatise, *The Code of Terpsichore* (London, 1828), in which he devotes a major portion (twenty pages) of the opening section to character dancing, especially dances of the Spanish type. He justified his attention to the subject with this comment: "As an investigation and minute description of these [Spanish] dances seems requisite with the nature and subject of the present work, I feel myself called upon to present them to my readers. They will behold in these pastimes—these imitative exercises of the Spaniards—depicted a transcript of their character and their taste."[84]

Blasis continued to expand his treatment of national dances. Nearly twenty years later, in *Notes Upon Dancing* (London, 1847), he devoted thirty-two pages to the subject, discussing the history, style, expressive qualities, music, and steps of over fifteen national dances, as well as an etymology of some of their titles. He also calls national dance "a principle [sic] charm of the Ballet," and admonishes professional dancers to "study characteristic steps and render themselves servile imitators . . . of dancing peculiar to different countries, giving their attitudes and movements the true national stamp of the dances they are performing."[85]

In what seems to have been his last theoretical treatise, *Tantsy voobshche, baletnye znamenitosti i natsional'nye tantsy* (Dances in General, Ballet Celebrities, and National Dances), published in Moscow in 1864 and little known outside of Russia, Blasis devotes seventy pages to national dances in the chapter "The Theater (Stage Presentations)." He covers more than fifty-two dances, stressing the importance of accuracy in bringing such dances to the stage:

> The mechanism by which dances are created is a result of the very essence and nature of the human being. And, thus, the musician and choreographer must study the vast array of national music and dances and through their work must make visible those mutual relationships that exist between songs and dances. And, on the other hand, they must also point out the differences between nations, judging by their dance and music cultures.[86]

There is also evidence that Blasis intended to write a book devoted entirely to national dance. The book was advertised as follows in *Notes Upon Dancing*:

NATIONAL DANCES

Prospectus already printed—National Dances still in use in various countries. Containing a description of the steps, attitudes, costumes, peculiar characteristics, with original music, of the principal National or popular dances, as practised by various classes of society. This description will be accompanied by artistical and philosophical remarks upon the beauties peculiar to each species of dancing, shewing that the true spirit and plan of construction is closely connected with, and derived from, the tastes and habits of the different countries where they were invented.[87]

This advertisement goes on to say that Blasis planned to describe over one hundred and twenty-three dances in what he called "the first [work] of the kind that has appeared." Although there is no record of the volume being published, the obvious attention given to national dances by this foremost classical theoretician is nonetheless striking.

Equally notable is the way his discussions of national dance resonate with Herderian thought. Like Herder, Blasis writes explicitly of how the distinctive traits of a particular nation are communicated through the expressive mode (which for Herder is spoken language and for Blasis the language of movement):

> *Herder*: Each nation speaks in the manner it thinks and thinks in the manner it speaks.[88]

> *Blasis*: Each nation has its own dances and the dance characterizes that nation.[89]

Too, both men see pluralism as the basis of the human condition and assert that a people's physical surroundings inform its expressive culture:

Herder: Each nation must be considered on its own merits, with regards to its situation and its own distinctive features; arbitrary selection or rejection of this or that characteristic, of this or that custom, do not render its history.[90]

Climate, water, air, food and drink, they all affect language.... Viewed in this way, language is indeed a magnificent treasure store.[91]

Blasis: The physical strength, agility, and flexibility of every nation is in close accord with the climate. That is why gestures and unpleasant movements that may be acceptable to one nation are completely unacceptable to others. Taking into account the differences in gesture, dances should be as various as nations.[92]

Both Herder and Blasis view language and dance (respectively) as developing from a people's deepest experiences and, thus, serving as an embodiment of its soul:

Herder: What is the whole structure of language but a mode of development of man's spirit, the history of his discoveries?[93]

Blasis: The mechanism of making dances arises from the very essence and nature of the human being.... Dances could be defined as the true picture of man's condition.[94]

Putting Theory into Practice. How did this theoretical fascination with the diverse cultural expression of nations manifest itself in the practical realm? For Herder, it meant learning languages and oral traditions, something that he clearly felt passionate about, as his comments about Greek indicate:

I wish I could...get to Greece...to learn to speak like a born Greek. How many thousand small distinctions there are in constructions, tenses, particles, pronunciation, which one hears only through the living speech!...Oh, if I could read Homer as I do Klopstock! If I would not have to scan him mechanically, what a different poet he would be for me! If I knew how to scan him for passion and spontaneous nature, how much more would I hear then! What intensification, what suspensions, what tremulousness, what agitation, etc.![95]

Herder was indeed recognized for his ability to assimilate foreign literature and to appreciate it "from the inside out," as it were. As George Bancroft has written, Herder "knew how to enter upon the study of a foreign work as if he had been of the country and time for which it was originally designed, and he was able to transfer into his own language the lighter graces, no less than the severe lessons of foreign poets."[96]

Blasis, too, took it upon himself to make a study of foreign culture, asserting that he had "studied the character, customs and habits of various nations, succeed[ing]...in the composition of national dances, [by] strictly preserv[ing], defin[ing] and illustrat[ing] all native peculiarities."[97] Doing so was not merely a matter of learning how to apply various types of stylistic varnish; it was—as studying languages was for Herder—a means of tapping into the essential qualities of various nations.

To what extent did choreographers and dancers follow Blasis's advice during the Romantic period? What care was taken to heed the words of the theoreticians and "devote themselves," as Blasis put it, "to a correct representation of national idiosyncrasies"?[98] We do know that some of the greatest artists of the Romantic ballet sought out instruction from native dancers. Marie Taglioni learned her mazurka from a well-known dancer in Warsaw and had an authentic mazurka costume made in Cracow. (Eugène Desmares reported in a letter that "Marie learned the mazurka here, not the one that you know a little, which is not exact. It's a delicious *pas* that she keeps for her friends; she had a national costume made for herself in Cracow, which is the city where the mazurka is danced the best.")[99] And after she was criticized in St. Petersburg for her performance of a Russian-style *pas de caractère*, she worked with a Russian dancer before attempting such a number again. Her biographer Léandre Vaillat describes her subsequent success:

> A great artist always tries to learn lessons. With the meticulousness that had characterized everything about her dancing career, Taglioni prepared. At her father's benefit performance,...she reappeared in the divertissement in *La Gitana*, dressed this time as a true Russian. The public was surprised to see her again with all the gestures and character of a Russian dancer. The incomparable Mons. August, a veteran of the corps de ballet, served as her partner. Despite his advanced age, he had some truly beautiful moments. He had given his young comrade advice from which she had justly profited. She danced this time in Russian style, and all hearts beat with joy.[100]

Perhaps having learned from Taglioni's misadventure, Fanny Elssler also studied with a Russian teacher, Nikita Peshkov, before dancing a national *pas* during her engagement in Russia in January 1851. Wearing a sarafan and kokoshnik, she impressed the critic of the *Moskovskie vedomosti* with her convincing rendition of Russian style: "[t]o understand even the slightest nuances of the national character that are expressed in our dance and to master them can be done only by an artist of genius such as Fanny Elssler. Her shoulders spoke; she glided like a swan...and in every way resembled a real Russian maiden."[101] Elssler also took care to learn her czardas in Pest itself.[102]

August Bournonville, too, directly benefited from his work with native dancers. Performing under the tutelage of Camprubí and Serral in Denmark in 1840, he marveled that "before my imagination there now appeared a whole new world of character dances which I had indeed suspected but had not fully understood."[103] And Marius Petipa, when commissioned to choreograph a Caucasian lezghinka for the opera *Russlan and Ludmilla*, brought in four Caucasians from the Russian army to instruct him in this unusual dance before making any attempt to stage it. He also turned to native sources when asked to provide a dance for the opera *Carmen*: "I became familiar with Spanish dances first hand, at the source," he wrote in his memoirs. Thus, "I inserted [a] genuine, original fandango in the opera *Carmen*.... [I]t was not my invention, but the national dance that I had learned when I was in Madrid."[104]

It is also possible that professional ballet dancers gained knowledge of native folk dance by attending performances in popular theaters and other venues. Fanny Elssler, for instance, is known to have seen a troupe of *devadasis* from a Vishnu shrine near Pondicherry at the Théâtre des Variétés in 1838.[105] Gautier, too, went to see the troupe and predicted that "[i]nevitably, the very un-Indian bayadère of the Opéra will merge with the *devadasi* of Pondicherry."[106] Much research remains to be done on the impact of native dancers who toured European cities and performed in popular theaters, ballrooms, fairgrounds, and other venues. But it seems plausible that their dancing helped critics and spectators establish a standard of "authenticity" by which they judged the character *pas* performed by professional ballet dancers. In any case, one may see in the following two critiques by Gautier that reviewers did raise the question of authenticity, tending to object when a dancer was believed to lack the flavor and stylization of the original:

> All the movements of the arms and legs are irreproachable, but the backs and the hips are a little lacking in suppleness. The proud, arched bearing of the Andalusian has not quite been caught. The feet and the hands are Spanish, but the torso is still too French. All southern peoples dance with their bodies as much as their legs, and so it is necessary to give the torso more suppleness and mobility to achieve a perfect imitation.... Mme A[lexis] Dupont does not always know how to temper her frenzy. The manner in which she shakes her head is too abrupt, like the frisking of a lamb, and more suitable to a Styrian dance.[107]

> In the second act, Mlle Plunkett danced with some partner or other a very lively and exaggerated sort of bolero.... By performing many frenetic and fantastic things that the dancers of Seville, Granada, and Cadiz would never have permitted themselves to attempt, she displayed qualities of flexibility and suppleness which, had they been more controlled, could have created a greater impression.[108]

The Process of Choreographing Character Dance. While it is true that many artists of the Romantic ballet availed themselves of opportunities to observe and study authentic forms of national dance, it would be naive to suggest that choreographers of the period made a regular practice of transferring the folk dances of the countryside to the professional stage without modification. So the question inevitably arises: to what degree did choreographers of Romantic ballet truly strive to preserve the original vocabulary and characteristic style of folk dances? It seems highly likely that original folk dances were distilled to a certain repertory of steps, poses, and gestures that were recognizably associated with a particular culture—with technical virtuosity and the choreographer's own artistry being then added to the mix. Blasis suggests as much in *The Code of Terpsichore* when he admonishes dancers to study the "characteristic steps,...attitudes, and movements"[109] of various national dancers and ballet masters to "remark the customs and manners peculiar to different countries, even to their particular features, and whatever other mark of distinction is remarkable between them."[110]

A certain repertory of markers, then, was sufficient to function emblematically, reinforcing the spectators' sense that they were somehow gaining access to the essence of a culture or nation. And the high significative value attached to these markers was bolstered by the well-entrenched Herderian notion that folk arts were a pure form of expression, springing from "the very essence and nature of the human being."[111] Thus, a character *pas* created by a choreographer but replete with distinctive markers characteristic of a certain style of folk dance would have offered the viewer, in Blasis's words, "a kind of picture or transcript of the taste, feeling and character" of a particular nation.[112] So, character dance was not truly expected to reproduce authentic folk dance in the modern-day ethnographic sense, but instead was distilled, its salient features thereby thrown into high relief and presented to the audience in a way that gave the impression of a well-wrought verisimilitude.

Yet, while he insisted upon noting "mark[s] of distinction," Blasis also found it reasonable to generalize about the *resemblances* that could be "traced between the manners of certain nations."[113] He categorized manners according to the broad geographic regions of the North and South, positing that the opposing temperaments of these two regions informed their dancing with certain fundamental distinguishing traits. He wrote in 1847 that:

> those graceful, attractive, picturesque and poetic dances of the Southern climates, in which the heart indulges without reserve in its emotions, and the various movements are dictated by a glowing imagination....[T]he dances of the Northern countries, where reserve, mixed with elegance and energy, and a kind of restrained gaiety, clearly indicate the character of the people with whom such dances are most in use.[114]

Thus, unsophisticated as this may seem to us today, Blasis associated temperament with place and painted the distinctions between regions with very broad strokes. A similar approach was taken by Bournonville, though he held that there existed three (not two) categories of temperament, and he attempted to trace each category historically and geographically. Bournonville wrote in 1848:

> The native or so-called national dances with which we are familiar may be divided into three types: the chaste, the voluptuous, and the martial. Among the first ought to be classed the earlier Italian, Spanish, and French dances which, like the Nordic, were performed to the accompaniment of romances, heroic poems, and elegies. They moved quite slowly and

demanded great dignity on the part of both the man and woman. These dances were those of civilized nations. . . . I would call them *classical*.

The second kind stems from Hindustan, where female dancers are raised in temples. They are called *Devadasis* (in Portuguese *balladeiras*; in French *bayadères*); from them come the Egyptian *almées*, the Moorish and later Spanish and Italian dances whose central motif is the ecstasy of love and whose performance is, for the most part, left to women. This is the *Indian* genre.

Lastly, those dances wherein the masculine grace and strength are particularly displayed, and where the female dancer is more subordinate, have their origins in northern Asia and known throughout Russia, Poland, Hungary, and Bohemia, to Germany and the entire north, by the names of polska and waltz. . . . These are the *Slavic* dances.[115]

For both Blasis and Bournonville, it seems that this approach was a way of organizing, of setting up a general paradigmatic structure within which the specific markers could be situated. Furthermore, it appears that a partnership was held to exist between the movement marker and its corresponding temperament, and that together the two elements shaped a national style. This, we suggest, constitutes the styling that is the hallmark of the character dancer. Temperament is regarded as an essential quality, a natural identifying expression. For example, the quality of "voluptuousness" when applied to a dance step (for example, a pas de basque) served to signify a distinctive place and people. And "voluptuousness" was first understood as a depiction of regional temperament and its associated dance styles, and secondarily may also have been appreciated for its sensual effect. Consider, for example, Gautier's impression of the "purity" of Dolores Serral's voluptuousness: "Her talent has a character all its own. In the most exaggerated *écarts* of this unrestrained and animated dance she is never immodest. She is full of passion and voluptuousness, but true voluptuousness is always chaste."[116]

Bournonville's delineation of these broad categories is borne out with striking vividness in extant eyewitness accounts of ethnic-derived dancing from the Romantic period—as performed both by native dancers and by academically-trained ballet dancers. In the following descriptions, in fact, one may not only gain a clear idea of what

Fanny Cerrito performing the lituana, 1840. Dance Collection, New York Public Library for the Performing Arts, Astor, Lenox, and Tilden Foundations.

these markers looked like; one may also see that the stylistic affinities between the individual national dances in each of the three categories as posited by Bournonville—the martial, the voluptuous, and the chaste—were clearly perceived by the spectators.

"THE MARTIAL TYPE"

Polish Dances

Mazurka: "The Heel-strokes, which are interspersed with the various steps of the mazurka, and which are even amongst the necessary accompaniments of the dance, must be given in time and with a certain energy.... I have remarked that the Poles make an inclination of the head on the first step, and reraise it on the second with a sort of decision full of grace.... The mazurka is composed, at once, of impulse, majesty, unreservedness, and allurement. It has something of the proud and the warlike" (Cellarius).[117]

"It would be difficult indeed to accurately describe the characteristics of this dance; in fact to fully appreciate its beauties one must have seen it executed again and again by accomplished dancers. The Mazurka is a combination of exalted pride and martial boldness, knightly gallantry and the most graceful devotedness.... The music of the Mazurka is in either 3/4 or 3/8 measure, of which the second syllable is accented, as shown by a point or an accent placed above it; by the regular accent of the first syllable is also observed.... Here [in the striking steps] also the syllable is audible, and although this attribute is agreeable to the dancers, and quite in harmony with the character of the Mazurka (especially if the dancer wears spurs)" (Zorn).[118]

Mazur,[119] as performed by eight native Polish dancers in St. Petersburg, 1851: "[O]n stage rushed four nimble couples of dancers.... The mazur started, passionate and full of enthusiasm, a fiery mazur adorned with all of its various figures and poetic poses, full of grace or ravishment, sometimes on the edge of true bravery and even debauchery. The skillful danseurs cleverly stamped their feet, and the pretty ladies passed among them full of enthusiasm. Wonderful! Extremely beautiful!" (*Sankpeterburgskie vedomosti*).[120]

Cracovienne, as performed by Fanny Elssler in *La Gipsy,* Paris, 28 January 1839: "[T]he Pas de la Cracovienne affords her [Elssler] a triumph which will make the ballet's fortune. She dances in the most coquettish and roguish costume that could be imagined: an officer's tunic sparkling with buttons and a *vivandière's* skirt, boots with steel spurs, and a black necktie framing a delightful chin—the whole crowned with a triumphant, sprightly little plume, the prettiest you ever saw. It is impossible to describe this dance: it is rhythmic precision mingled with a charming ease, a muscular and bounding agility which cannot be imagined; the metallic clicking of the spurs, a kind of castanets on the heels, emphasises each step and gives the dance a quality of joyous vivacity which is quite irresistible. This *pas* is encored every evening" (Gautier).[121]

Varsovienne, as performed by Fanny Cerrito and Mlle Camille at Cerrito's benefit, London, 21 July 1842: "[A] pretty bit of eccentricity.... Cerrito infuses such a spirit into these characteristic pas, they seem such natural outbursts of delight that nothing can be more fascinating. On she went bounding along, admirably supported by the clever little Camille, and accompanied by the plaudits of the audience, which were renewed as the two danseuses advanced along the lamps, saluting them in military fashion" (*The Times*).[122]

Other Slavic and Germanic Dances

Hongroise, as performed by the Danseuses Viennoises, 1845: "[T]he *hongroise* [was] interpolated into the ball scene of the second act.... Half the troupe, dressed in male costume, served as partners to the others. You cannot imagine the rapidity and daring of these little Hungarians, the majesty with which they clicked the silver spurs on boots...the determination with which they slapped their thighs...decorated with rich trimmings, and the swagger with which they wore the Uhlan bonnets on the sides of their heads. You know full well that a feeling for tempo, an energetic and free rhythm, and a calculated allure are indispensable qualities for these national and popular dances. Every beat must be stressed with heel taps or the clatter of spurs, so that the slightest error would be noticed at once" (Gautier).[123]

Lituana, as performed by Fanny Cerrito in a divertissement at Her Majesty's Theatre, London, 2 May 1840: "[O]ne of those eccentric, wild, playful, semi-masculine pas, in which the danseuse sports a military hat and boots, and goes through soldier-like gestures...[performed] with extraordinary rapidity...[and]...all the dash and sportive prettiness which constitutes the charm of the dances of this kind" (a London critic).[124]

Styrienne, as performed by Fanny Cerrito and Auguste Albert in a divertissement at Her Majesty's Theatre, London, 12 August 1841: "[Q]uite a unique dance: the lady appears altogether at the mercy of the gentleman who sometimes twirls her round like a teetotum, sometimes pushes her uncourteously from him....An inferior dancer could have made nothing of it, but Cerrito entered fully into its humour" (a London critic).[125]

"THE VOLUPTUOUS TYPE"

Spanish Dances

General: "They dance with their whole body, they arch their backs, bend sideways, and twist their torsos with the suppleness of an almeh or a grass snake. In *poses renversées* the dancer's shoulders almost touch the ground; her arms, dreamy and passive, have a flexibility and a limpness like that of a loosened scarf.... [T]his voluptuous languor is succeeded by leaps of a young jaguar.... Spanish male dancers...always appear to be passionately in love.... [T]hey possess a certain ferocious grace, a particular allure, insolently holding their bodies back, which is theirs alone" (Gautier).[126]

"She [Dolores Serral] is full of passion and voluptuousness....She weaves her arms as though swooning from love, and bends back her head.... Her body curves with a nervous shiver...then she sinks down, brushing the floor with her arms while still playing the castanets, only to

Fanny Elssler and James Sylvain in a "Pas Styrien." American Antiquarian Society.

spring up, quick and alert as a bird, darting a sparkling laugh at her partner" (Gautier).[127]

Cachucha: "[T]he Cachucha is a national dance of a primitive character....It is a charming poem written in the twisting of the hips, sidelong expressions, a foot advanced and then withdrawn, all joyfully accompanied by the chatter of castanets and having more to say on its own than many volumes of erotic verse.

There is one position that is ravishingly graceful. It is the moment when the dancer, half-kneeling, with back proudly arched, head thrown back, a large red rose unfolding in her beautiful half-loosened black hair, arms dreamily extended and only gently shaking the castanets, smiles over her shoulder at the lover who is approaching to steal a kiss....He is supple, precise, sinuous and lively as a young jaguar" (Gautier).[128]

Cachucha, as performed by Fanny Elssler in *Le Diable boiteux*, Paris, 1 June 1836: "Those swayings of the hips...those provocative gestures... and, above all, Elssler's sensuous grace, lascivious abandon, and plastic beauty were greatly appreciated by the opera-glasses of the stalls and boxes" (de Boigne).[129]

Double Cachucha, as performed by Fanny Cerrito and Jules Perrot, in a divertissement at Her Majesty's Theatre, London, 14 July 1842: "[N]ever in our remembrance is there a pas de caractère so beautiful as the *Double Cachucha* danced by her [Cerrito] and Perrot.... [W]hen the cachucha really does begin, it is an inspiration; she is a creature of fire. It is in the Spanish spirit of defiance that she and Perrot dance *at* each other. The fury, as it were, of this part of the dance is beautifully relieved by those exquisite attitudes, where Cerrito falls on one knee and leans back with languishing expression, while Perrot stands over her" (*The Times*).[130]

Italian Dances

Tarantella: "It is gay and somewhat voluptuous displaying in its music, steps, attitudes, the taste and temperament of those who invented it. Love and pleasure are conspicuous throughout every movement. Each gesture and motion are full of seductive grace...the woman tries, by the life and rapidity of her motions to excite the love of her partner, who, in turn endeavors to win her favour by his agility and his elegance, and tender gestures. The two dancers now unite, then separate, return, fly into each other's arms, again bound away, and by means of a great variety of gesticulations, they exhibit alternatingly love, hatred, indifference, disdain, coquetry and inconstancy....Sometimes they hold hands, or the man kneels whilst the woman dances around him; he then rises, when she starts away, and he eagerly pursues" (Blasis). [131]

Sicilienne, as performed by Fanny Cerrito and Arthur Saint-Léon in London, 1845: "*Pas* more felicitous, more beautiful, more admirably suited to their charming inventor were never devised.... [A]ll that pursuit and flying, that coquetting and tantalizing in which Cerrito is inimitable.... The drop upon Saint-Léon's arm as for a pose, and then the hopping in of the two together, preserving the attitude, produced a most novel effect...genuine merriment and...perfect naturalness" (*The Times*).[132]

"Indian"/"Moorish"/"Egyptian"

Indian: "The special class of Indian woman...are supposed to sing and dance in front of shrines...[an] Oriental pantomime. While they are getting ready to dance, their looks, postures, and figures tell the public 'Come, the fire of passion is already burning in my blood'" (Blasis).[133]

Pas de Chibouque, as performed by Fanny Cerrito in *Lallah Rookh*, London, 11 June 1846: "Cerrito dances such a variety of steps and baffles all description—now

TOP: *Sofia Fuoco in a tarantella.* Raffaele Carrieri, La Danza in Italia, 1500-1900 *(Milan: Domus, 1946), p. 56.*

BOTTOM: *Fanny Cerrito in the ballet* La Fille de marbre. *Dance Collection, New York Public Library for the Performing Arts, Astor, Lenox, and Tilden Foundations.*

executing exquisitely small twinkling steps, at the next moment bounding like an antelope. There was in this dance the characteristic movement, as well as measure, of the dances of the East—of that Eastern world which, through the Moors, conveyed the premature form of the bolero, cachucha, guaracha, etc., to Spain" (*Morning Post*).[134]

Le Parfum et les Echarpes (Perfume and Scarves), as performed in the work *Le Saïs*, at the Théâtre de la Renaissance: "Four almées...throw scarves in the air while opening their arms to make a grand crown. They repeat [this] three times...do a *saut de basque* dragging the foot on the floor, bending at the hip *au dedans...pas de bourrée dessous-dessus*...while changing the épaulement, [then do] a waltz turn while carrying the hands behind the head....Repeat three times" (H. Justament).[135]

"THE CHASTE TYPE"

Fewer examples of this type of dancing are to be found in newspaper reviews during the Romantic period, since this category is by definition pre-Romantic (or indeed, far older, as Bournonville seems to imply). But one can at least discern from these reviews that representations of classical Greek figures onstage did seem to subscribe to this type as Bournonville describes it. Furthermore, it is clear that a certain dignity and nobility were imputed to the minuet, and that its overall effect, too, seems to be in line with Bournonville's "chaste" category.

Minuet, as performed by Fanny Elssler in *La Gipsy*, 1839: "[T]he minuet [is] danced by the heroine....Few things have been seen more fearful than the cold and measured grace of Mdlle. Fanny Elssler in this juncture, than the manner in which every step was watched, every gesture allowed its right time, so that neither flurry nor faltering might be detected" (Henry Chorley).[136]

Minuet, performed in *La Péri*, Paris, 1843: "As for the French woman [dancing a minuet], all varnished with bad make-up, all curled, all covered with powder in the style of a field marshall's wife: 'By Allah!' said Achmet, 'I am tired of Louis the XV...this imprisoning rouge, this powder suffocates you'" (*Le Journal des Débats*).[137]

Minuet, as performed by Fanny Cerrito and Lucile Grahn in *Un Bal sous Louis XIV*, London, 1845: "[The] demure posturings [of the minuet were executed] with becoming reserve and formality" (*Morning Post*).[138]

Ancient/Classical: "The chief *pas* was a *Diane Chasseresse*....The slow movement is very beautiful, its chief characteristic being given by the series of classical attitudes into which the dancer falls. The gracefulness with which Fleury poised on one toe, bent forward with extended bow, and in that attitude slowly revolved, was very striking" (*The Times*).[139]

Iconography of the period also provides valuable affirmation that characteristic positioning of the torso, arms, head, and feet served to "mark" national origin. Consider the stylistic similarities between the cracovienne and the lituana, both Slavic dances: one hand positioned at the waist or hip, the opposite arm curved above the shoulder, and the extended foot that created rhythmic patterns when "'spotted' lightly" against the floor.[140] These same stylizations are also called for in Michel Saint-Léon's notations of the krakovia and the mazurka, in which the arms assume the Slavic stylization of one arm at the hip and the feet alternatingly "beat" ("frappe") a rhythmic pattern.[141]

These samples of nineteenth-century prose accounts and pictures, of course, provide only a small glimpse into the vocabulary of markers that helped define particular national dance types to the audience. But they do indicate that there existed a palpable set of signs that audiences could "read"—heel clicking, hands positioned on the waist, and head-tossing in the Slavic types; turning and partnering in the Germanic types; hopping and fast footwork in the Italian types; bending, twisting, and kneeling in the Spanish types. Thus, much as the spectators understood the significative value of pantomime gestures (which could indicate such concepts as "marriage," "death," "pretty," and "night") and musical types (jigs for Scotland, yodeling music for Switzerland, cymbals for Turkey, etc.), they also became accustomed to national movement idioms. And they could rely on all three sets of signals to help make sense of the action and the characters of the somewhat complex narrative ballets of the Romantic period.

Unfortunately, however, while it is clear that choreographers relied upon these vocabularies of steps and gestures, there is a regrettable lack of documentation of how they actually brought this material to the stage. Indeed, the frustrating silence of the sources when it comes to specific information about Romantic-era choreography poses quite a daunting problem to all historians of the period, whether they are seeking insight into classical or character *pas*.[142] But it does seems safe to assert that the Romantic choreographer was faced with the challenge of remaining true both to the "authentic" signature of the national dance and to his or her creative impulse at the same time.[143] As Bournonville wrote of his own experience in composing Spanish *pas*:

> I was not blind to the pretty and romantic qualities to be found in the Spanish character. But here, as in everything else, it was a matter of determining what had a right to be put on stage, of making the proper choice of material, then finding the most suitable way of using it. I wished to show, without depriving the picture of its national physiognomy, one could idealize it and draw it into the dramatic sphere.[144]

Critics sometimes even referred specifically to the successful combining of a well-known style with a fresh new idea. Gautier, for instance, notes that in a tarantella choreographed by Saint-Léon, "[t]here is a moment that is delightfully graceful and original, when he [Saint-Léon] places his foot against hers [Fanny Cerrito's] and they move together as one, as though joined at the toes."[145] But until more choreographic and anecdotal evidence is unearthed, we must remain largely ignorant of precisely how various choreographers went about the task of creating national *pas*, how they negotiated between their own original ideas and the standard movement vocabularies of the various styles.

Jules Perrot

In the case of Jules Perrot, the dearth of choreographic evidence is particularly frustrating. For many nineteenth-century critics clearly admired him not only for his gift for using dance as a means to advance the drama in narrative ballets, but also for his notable character dance choreography. And it seems that he combined these two talents in an intriguing way. Though, again, the lack of choreographic evidence prevents us from offering an in-depth discussion of his choreography, we believe it would be remiss of us not to mention him. For descriptions of his ballets do allow us a glimpse into the process by which at least one artist combined folk-derived material and his own creative ideas in a dramatically affecting way.[146]

Three threads seemed to run through Perrot's career that are of particular importance to the history of character dance. First, critics clearly regarded him as a great innovator whose choreography epitomized a new approach to ballet. "The old historical ballet of action seems to have for ever departed," wrote the *Morning Post* in 1847 in a review of Perrot's *Les Eléments*. "In lieu of the fabled gods of the Pantheon we have the imaginings of Victor Hugo and Henri Heine choreographed; where strode stalwart zephyrs, we now have the elements symbolized, if not etherealized....The aged deem this rebellion; the youthful, revolution."[147] Second, as Gautier pointed out, he drew successfully from both classical and character idioms.[148] And while he was justly celebrated for his classical choreography, it is noteworthy that the vast majority of his ballets called for national dance.[149] Third, Perrot conceived of new ways to use national dance as a means of helping advance the story in narrative ballets, perhaps integrating it more fully into the action than some of his peers. In *Ondine*, as Guest explains, he

> made the most imaginative use of Italian material. His tarantella was an impressive set-piece for the corps de ballet, but its interruption for the evening prayer was a masterly stroke which doubled the effect of the reprise that followed, while, later in the ballet his adaptation of a saltarello to convey Ondine's faltering strength was a prime example of the use of dance to advance the narrative.[150]

Perrot also seems to have had the capacity to tap into the deep and inherently expressive force of folk dance in a way that worked well on the stage. In *Eoline*, for example, which was set in Silesia (now a region of western Poland), Perrot brought the driving, captivating impetus of the Polish mazurka to his sensational *mazurka d'extase*, where Eoline is drawn under the spell of the evil Rübezahl. "You can sense the supernatural force that dominates the will, overcomes the resistance, fascinates like a snake, and draws its victim to the abyss," wrote Gautier in a review of the St. Petersburg production of the ballet:

> Hypnotized by his glance, Eoline rises to her feet and begins to dance with him. She is like a dove...feathers ruffled, wings aquiver, terrified yet fascinated. It is obvious that Eoline has no love for Rübezahl, yet this magical dance benumbs and intoxicates her. An insidious languor softens her movements, her head droops, her eyes become misty, and her lips part in a smile as her breathing quickens. Half fainting, she falls into Rübezahl's arms.[151]

The critic for the London *Times* was equally impressed by this mazurka, which "exhibited mental qualities worthy of the greatest names of the profession.... It is the best thing of the sort that has been done since the *Valse de Fascination* in *Alma,* and is marked by greater profundity of thought than that."[152] Indeed, this is one of several national *pas* choreographed by Perrot in which the character performing it underwent an important psychological or emotional transformation during the course of the dance itself.

One testament to the great merit of Perrot's character dance choreography is that Marius Petipa "borrowed" it. A well-documented instance of this occurred in 1861, when he interpolated Perrot's "La Cosmopolitana" into *Le Marché des Innocents,* a minor work restaged by Petipa for his wife's benefit performance at the Paris Opéra.[153] A long, complex number, "La Cosmopolitana" had been choreographed by Perrot in 1853 for the ballet *Gazelda.* According to Ivor Guest, the *pas* was "intended to convey the nomadic nature of gypsy life by introducing a succession of national dances—Moorish, Tyrolese, Spanish and English."[154] To Petipa's surprise, Perrot withheld permission for the dance to be performed. Although Petipa gave him full credit on the program, Perrot filed suit against him for breach of copyright. The judge ruled in favor of Perrot, stating that "a *pas* from a ballet composed of national dances from different countries, but combined in such a way as to form a particular and distinct composition, constitutes an intellectual work that is protected by the law of literary and artistic property."[155] Thus, the judge explicitly acknowledged that a choreographic composition based on national dance material could be deemed a unique artistic property.

The "Ballet Blanc" and National Dance

Gautier's famous distinction between Marie Taglioni as a Christian dancer and Fanny Elssler as a pagan one has left an indelible mark on ballet historiography, encouraging the idea that the *ballet blanc* belonged to a different species of ballet than works featuring national dancing; that the palpable contrast between the styles of these ballerinas might somehow be viewed as a paradigm for two types of Romantic ballet—a white variety, and a more colorful, earthy sort.[156] But, in fact, the two were not mutually exclusive. Indeed, there seem to have been few, if any, "white ballets" that remained "white" throughout. And the sort of ethereal dancing we associate with "white" ballets such as *La Sylphide* and *Giselle* was often performed in tandem with national dancing. Thus, in *La Sylphide* the highland corps danced Scottish jigs, and a corps of sylphs performed classical *pas*. In the title role of *Ondine* Fanny Cerrito danced a moonlit *pas de l'ombre* in one scene and a lusty tarantella in the next. In Act III of *Pâquerette* she appeared "in a haze of white gauze, shimmering with golden spangles"; in Act IV, "she wore a smart Hungarian jacket [that] cl[ung] tightly to her trim figure, and boots with resonant heels [that] imprison[ed] her pretty feet."[157] Marie Taglioni, in *La Fille de Danube* (the ballet Janin called "the very poetic sequel to *La Sylphide* [except] that the supernatural resides no longer in the ether but in the depths of the waters")[158] danced beneath the surface of the Danube (as an undine), then returned to land with a mazurka, possibly in the costume made for her in Poland in 1838.[159]

In some houses, a *ballet blanc* might be followed by a work in character style: Cerrito, for instance, at the Théâtre de la Monnaie in Brussels in 1844 played the title role in *La Sylphide*, then launched into a performance of *La Gitana*. (One critic praised her for appearing truly to have become a sylphide in the first ballet, and for displaying in the second a "provocative pride...more in the spirit of Spanish dancing" than Elssler's "coquettish[ness] and captivating...softer manner.")[160] Two weeks later at the same house she danced *Giselle* and followed it with a *cachucha*—garnering thunderous applause for both.[161] And Carlotta Grisi, at a London benefit performance in 1842, performed the second act of *Giselle*, followed by the rousing tarantella from *Le Pécheur napolitain*.[162]

This leads to the subject of *Giselle*, today the most famous and widely performed of all the ballets created during the period under scrutiny here. Though *Giselle* is not generally regarded as a ballet that reflects the Romantic taste for national dancing, a closer examination of the documents generated at the time of its first production reveals that it originally did so. Recall that much was made in the press of its German setting and that the names "Gisela" (gallicized as "Giselle") and "Albrecht" would have struck Parisian audiences as decidedly German. Like Carl Maria von Weber's opera *Der Freischütz*, which had premiered at the Opéra only three weeks before, *Giselle* did much to satisfy the appetite for German folklore whetted in 1833 by the publication in France of Heine's *On Germany* (or *De l'Allemagne*), with its tales of "delicious apparitions... encountered in the Harz mountains and on the banks of the Ilse, in a mist softened by German moonlight" that Gautier later acknowledged were his inspiration for the ballet's libretto.[163] Adolphe Adam admirably performed his duty of providing music "characteristic and analogous to the place where the action takes place,"[164] including two excellent waltzes for the heroine, the waltz being a dance very strongly associated at the time with German-speaking peoples. (Any German character appearing in a ballet divertissement, in fact, was likely to perform a waltz, just as French characters in such divertissements tended to dance a minuet. For example, when four European women are introduced into the harem in Act I of *La Péri*, the Scot dances a jig, the German a waltz, the Frenchwoman a minuet, and the Spaniard a bolero.)[165] This may seem odd, since the ethnic connotations of the waltz have all but disappeared in the twentieth century. Yet European audiences of the Romantic period would have instantly recognized its "German-ness." This is why Adam gave Giselle a waltz as her entrance music and why he wrote the now-famous "Giselle Waltz" for the scene later in Act I in which Giselle leads her fellow peasants in a dance. Of this waltz, Adam said rather proudly, that it had "all the German color indicated by the locality,"[166] an idea echoed by critics. Escudier, for example, called it "an enchanting waltz, in the Germanic spirit of the

American sheet music cover depicting Fanny Elssler in her "favorite dances."
The center oval shows her in La Tarentule, *the corner ovals (starting at the upper right and moving clockwise), in the cracovienne from* La Gipsy, *in* La Sylphide, La Tarentule, *and* La Gitana. *American Antiquarian Society.*

subject."[167] It was also said that Adam's score demonstrated the "grace, the suavity, and the vaporous poetry of the Germanic deities that inspired the composer."[168]

Nineteenth-century audiences, moreover, would have recognized the ethnic references in the brief snippets of Spanish and "Eastern"-sounding music that Adam wove into what he called the "fantastic ball" scene of Act II, presumably to accompany the foreign Wilis as they executed what Adam called "the figures of their native dance."[169] Gautier described these foreigners in his libretto:

> Several Wilis present themselves, alternately, to their sovereign. There is Moyna, the *odalisque*, executing an oriental dance; next Zulma, the bayadère, displaying her Indian poses; then two Frenchwomen, dancing a kind of fantastic menuet; then some German women, waltzing among themselves. Finally they are joined by the whole band of Wilis.[170]

When one listens to the music closely, one can plainly hear an eight-measure phrase of Spanish-sounding music, followed by music (beginning with an oboe playing in a minor key) surely intended for the odalisque and the bayadère.[171]

Spanish and Bayadère/Odalisque music from the "Wili's Fantastic Ball" scene in Giselle (reduced from manuscript conductor's score, A.533, BN-Opéra).

And shortly thereafter one can hear music that might be interpreted as the minuet and waltz danced (respectively) by the French and German Wilis.[172]

German music from the "Wili's Fantastic Ball" scene in Giselle.

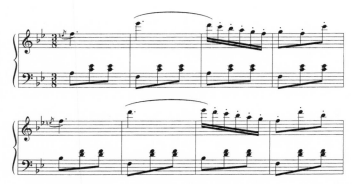

French "Minuet" from the "Wili's Fantastic Ball" scene in Giselle.

(It is something of a tour de force that Adam managed to work all of these ethnic connotations into the framework of a waltz—Spanish rhythms, an oboe playing in a minor key to suggest the "East," the "oompah" effects of a German waltz, and a more delicate and slightly more fussy melody in what I am suggesting is the "minuet." Note, too, that of these four melodies, only the German one recurs. This of course is in keeping with the setting of the ballet.)

The presence of the Spanish music can surely be attributed to the fact that Gautier had told Adam of his earlier idea of including a Wili in Spanish dress who arrives "with the rattling of *castañets* and a swarming of white butterflies." (Adam even wrote the words "groupe général de Wilis—papillons" in the score at the beginning of the scene in which the Wilis arrived.) Recall Gautier's initial inspiration for the second act of *Giselle*:

At a certain time of year, in a forest glade, the Wilis gather on the banks of a pond where large water-lilies spread their leaves on the viscous waters which have opened up to receive the drowned dancers. Moonbeams shine between the black cut-up hearts which seem to float like dead loves. Midnight sounds, and from every point on the horizon, led by will o' the wisps, come the ghosts of girls who died dancing. First, with the rattling of *castañets* and a swarming of white butterflies, wearing a large comb cut in the latest style like the interior of a Gothic cathedral, silhouetted against the moon, comes a cachucha dancer from Seville, a gitana, twisting her hips and wearing a skirt which is tight with flounces of cabalistic signs; a Hungarian dancer in a fur bonnet, making the spurs on her boots, like teeth, chatter in the cold; a *bibiaderi* in a costume like that of Amani, a bodice with a sheath of sandalwood, gold lamé pants, a belt and necklace of mirror-bright metal plates…bizarre jewels, rings in her nose, bells around her ankles; and then the last, showing herself timidly, a small student from the Opéra in practice clothes, with a handkerchief around her neck, her hands in a little furry muff. All these costumes, exotic and otherwise, are discolored and they take on a sort of spectral uniformity. This solemn assembly takes place and ends with the scene in which the dead girl leaves her tomb and seems to come back to life in the embrace of her lover who believes he can feel her heart beating alongside his.[173]

Though Gautier's original idea of putting the Wilis in character costumes was discarded, the evidence of the music and the libretto strongly suggests that a handful of solo Wilis—the odalisque Wili, the bayadère Wili, and the German and French Wilis who *were* included in the final version of the libretto—did perform a few measures of character steps during this

A hand-painted lithograph of Giselle, *Act II. The figure on the right has long wavy hair and is wearing a costume that seems intended to look Indian. Bibliothèque de l'Opéra.*

fantastic ball scene, and perhaps a Spanish Wili did so as well; her presence is certainly suggested by the music.

Further evidence that some of the Wilis were presented as "character"
Wilis may be found in a nineteenth-century French lithograph depicting
an Indian Wili. Unlike her sister Wili (on the left), the Indian Wili's hair is
long and wavy, and instead of being fastened up in a bun, it falls to her
shoulders. She wears a cloth draped diagonally across her torso in the
manner of a sari, and in the hand-colored copy of the lithograph, she is
even given dark skin.[174] This is not to say, of course, that the lithograph
depicts the costumes of the Wilis accurately. In fact, the costume and production lists compiled at the Opéra at the time of *Giselle*'s premiere give
no indication that the Wilis were not costumed identically.[175] Yet, the
mere fact that a nineteenth-century depiction of *Giselle* could include a
character Wili at all bolsters the more substantial evidence of the libretto
and score that some of the Wilis were presented to the audience in a way
that visually and aurally suggested particular ethnicities. In any case,
these three sources—libretto, score, and lithograph—by imputing ethnic
characteristics to the Wilis, Romantic ballet's quintessential shades, con-
tradict the notion that national dance and the *ballet blanc* were conceived
in the nineteenth century as existing in opposition to one another.

Historiography

Many twentieth-century historians have given short shrift to character
dance in the Romantic ballet. Here, for example, is a twentieth-century
definition of "Romantic ballet" that leaves out character dance entirely:

> *[R]omantic ballet*, term used for the type of ballet introduced during the
> Romantic period. It represented a fundamentally different approach from
> anything that had gone before. The idea of representing a dream world
> and fairy tales brought about the development of new techniques, espe-
> cially for the ballerina, who rose on her toes for the first time in an
> attempt to represent ethereality and "other-worldliness." Music and decor
> were carefully planned to portray character and atmosphere, and the stan-
> dard white costume was adopted for the ballerina. There was a temporary
> decline in the importance of the male dancer. The poet Théophile Gautier
> (1811–1872) gave considerable impetus to the movement in his writings
> and with his work on the libretto of the most famous romantic ballet of
> all, *Giselle* (1841), which successfully fused all the romantic elements.[176]

And here is a late twentieth-century definition of character dance that
indicates its present lowly status:

> *Character Dance.* General term for all kinds of theatrical dance outside the
> bounds of the classic-academic dance, deriving from traditional, national,
> or folklore sources—also the dance of the artisans and guilds, the comic
> dance and the dance which is representative of a certain type of character.
> Dancers who are not tall enough, or in technical respects are not ideally
> gifted for the academic dance often prefer the character dance.[177]

Both of these definitions would undoubtedly come as a great surprise to the nineteenth-century ballet spectator, who was likely to be acquainted with a good many works that had nothing to do with the dream world and to know quite well that the greatest ballet dancers of the day were equally at home in "classic-academic" style and in character dance.

Yet, when considered in the light of *today*'s performance practice, both definitions seem quite reasonable. This is because the hierarchy implied in the definition of character dancing—a hierarchy that clearly prioritizes the danse d'école over character dance—does exist today in many quarters. In fact, few of today's classically trained dancers study or perform character dancing as extensively as did their nineteenth-century counterparts. Moreover, the two ballets from the Romantic period most widely performed today—*Giselle* and *La Sylphide*—do seem to fit the much-proclaimed model of the "other-worldly" quite well (at first glance, at least).

Today's performance practice, however, can be deceptive in terms of offering a reliable model for the past. Indeed, in the last fifty years, there has been a pendulum swing away from narrative toward pure-dance forms of ballet. This has affected today's Romantic repertory—both the way it is constituted and the way it is performed. And this, in turn, has affected the historiography of nineteenth-century ballet.

For some twentieth-century critics, "pure dance" has taken something akin to a moral precedence over narrative and any sort of dance that expresses or portrays something outside itself. André Levinson, perhaps the most influential twentieth-century critic in this regard, insisted that in *La Sylphide*:

> the dance, instead of being subservient to expressive gestures, itself became the interpreter of the emotions and their symbolic equivalent. . . . In a constant approach to a geometric purity of design, making a pattern in space of straight lines and sweeping perfect curves, idealizing the dancer's body and dematerializing her costume, the *ballet blanc* is able to transmute the formal poses of the slow dance movement—the *Arabesques* of the *Adagio*—as well as those aerial parabolas outlined by seemingly imponderable bodies (technically known as the *grands temps d'élévation*) into a mysterious and poetic language.[178]

Indeed, Levinson posits that it was through Marie Taglioni and *La Sylphide* that dance was finally able to come "into its own again" roughly a half-century after Noverre had contributed to its becoming (in Levinson's words) "simply...a means to an end; [and]...no longer an end in itself. Its independence, its intrinsic aesthetic value had been sacrificed to the expression of character and sentiment."[179] Levinson also suggests that ethnic-derived dances, too, are subject to the principle that confers a higher aesthetic value upon abstract dance. For such ethnic-derived dances, he implies, are unsophisticated and artless unless they are "completely transformed by style": only an inclination "toward abstraction" can elevate them.[180]

Though Levinson's view of the ipso facto superiority of the abstract ballet is not universally held today, it has nonetheless exerted a powerful influence in our century, creating a climate supportive of the pure-dance aesthetic. In any case, there is no doubt that Romantic ballets such as *Esmeralda*, *Le Diable à quatre*, *La Gitana*, and *Le Diable boiteux*—works that relied chiefly upon character idioms to tell their story—would make little artistic sense to audiences reared on modern versions of *La Sylphide* and *Giselle*. Moreover, it would seem that definitions such as those quoted above that equate the Romantic ballet with white tutus and ethereal dream worlds are based on the tiny fraction of works that have survived in today's repertory rather than on the wide variety of ballets actually performed during the Romantic period.

Moreover, even ballets that trace their descent to the Romantic period give only a very imperfect idea of how they were danced in the Romantic period. Today's *Giselle*, for instance, differs markedly from its 1841 original: the proportion of dancing is far higher than in the original production, as is the amount of pointework; the mime and action scenes are fewer and shorter, and the roles for nondancing characters have been much reduced. The second act, in fact, has become much more of a "white" act dominated by the Wilis and Albrecht, by dint of the elimination in most productions of the mime and action scenes involving Wilfrid, Bathilde, and various peasants, huntsmen, and nobles. Moreover, the semiotic significance of the ethnic and mime music has been so effaced that it now goes unheard by choreographers, performers, and audiences. So, *Giselle*, which in 1841 gave roughly equal attention to dance and mime/action scenes while making considerable use of character dance, has become much more abstract, less focused on narrative, less grounded in the details and techniques of storytelling, and more a vehicle for pure dance (particularly in the second act). Thus, it has found great success over a hundred-and-fifty-year period, but only by being reinvented to accommodate new tastes. And its updated version much more aptly reflects these latter-day tastes than the aesthetics of the period in which *Giselle* was conceived.[181]

Conclusion

There is ample and compelling evidence that national dance was perceived as a powerful imaginative force in ballet during the Romantic period, and that dancers, choreographers, and audiences welcomed it, quite simply, as an intrinsic part of the art of ballet. We believe that a recognition of this state of affairs must inform the ongoing work of those writing the history of Western theatrical dance.

Important steps have already been taken to fill in some of the gaps left in the historiography of Romantic ballet by the long neglect of character dance. Deborah Jowitt, in her book *Time and the Dancing Image*, has drawn attention to the women who inhabited ballet's "fictional East."[182]

Janina Pudełek has studied the ways in which Polish folk dances played an active role in the productions of the Warsaw Ballet.[183] In 1939, three teachers from the Leningrad Ballet School, including Alexander Shiriaev, who had worked closely with Petipa in the 1890s and early 1900s, published a treatise documenting the history of national dance and codifying character dance technique.[184] Knud Arne Jürgensen has reconstructed the cracovienne, one of the most popular solos of the Romantic era, from Bournonville's original choreographic record.[185] Joellen A. Meglin has specifically addressed of the ways in which Spanish character dancing projected a kind of apparent sexuality that was used as a foil in the ballet *Le Diable boiteux* to underscore French middle-class values.[186] Lynn Garafola has shone a retrospective light upon character and folk-derived dance by analyzing its renewal in Fokine's *genre nouveau*.[187] And Ivor Guest, in his invaluable chronicles of the Romantic ballet and its most famous artists, has provided readers with a vast wealth of material about the performance and reception of character dance, attesting to its popularity and pervasive presence in the era.

Yet the image of the sylph as the Romantic era's "most popular figure" stubbornly persists, as does the idea that representing "a dream world and fairy tales" was the overriding force behind the Romantic ballet.[188] (One writer has even gone so far as to say that "Elssler cannot be counted, strictly speaking, as a pure Romantic ballerina," whereas Taglioni does qualify because "[she] can hardly be imagined except as poised ethereally in a swirl of Victorian tutus.")[189] And few of the great artists of the Romantic ballet are remembered for their dancing or choreography in the character idiom, save Fanny Elssler. In a recently published reference work on ballet, in fact, the entry on Perrot makes no mention of character or national dance, and could easily leave the uninformed reader with the impression that all of his dancing and choreography was in the classical style.[190]

Thus, we face the dual challenge of more fully integrating existing scholarship that touches upon national dance into broad historical surveys of Western theatrical dance, and at the same time carrying out new primary research on the topic as well. The areas of inquiry that suggest themselves, indeed, are many and various. One path to pursue is the matter of ballet's place within colonial politics, considering on a case by case basis how ballets with national dance, or even individual dances, could be used to advance a given colonial or anticolonial agenda or fuel existing antagonisms between European powers. (How, for instance, did balletic images of French and English colonial subjects—Egyptians, Indians, and Algerians, for instance—mirror official government policy toward these peoples?[191] Did ballet, like opera, serve to fan the flames of rebellion in the Italian peninsula during the tumultuous years of the Risorgimento?)[192] Another approach would be to scrutinize the relationship between classical and character styles, and attempt to discern how they may have influenced one another. (Anecdotal evidence suggests that folk dances were "balleticized"; could the danse d'école have remained utterly unaffected by the various approaches to nationally-styled épaulement and port de bras that dancers and choreographers knew so well?)[193] A related question concerns the effects of character training on performance. Though a definitive answer would be hard to come by, it would be intriguing to investigate whether training in character styles had any impact on a dancer's performance in noncharacter roles. This idea was raised by Alan Jones in a *New York Times* story in 1983: "The self-assurance, pride, and daring that come with character training are often reflected in the quality of a dancer's other roles. Mr. [Mikhail] Baryshnikov says: 'Many of the best classical dancers, from Alexandra Danilova and Felia Doubrovska to Rudolf Nureyev, had character training. They get to cheat, play with the audience, because they are so sure of what they are doing.'"[194]

Another profitable endeavor would be to examine the use of character dance in the pre-Romantic ballet and to learn more about the various reasons (aside from Elssler's cachucha) for the burgeoning popularity of character dance in the 1830s.[195] Another would be to follow the composer's paths, assessing musical techniques of depicting various national types as they evolved in the ballet scores of the nineteenth century. Yet another would be to focus on the oeuvre of several popular nineteenth-century choreographers—Perrot, Saint-Léon, Joseph Mazilier, Petipa, Lev Ivanov—comparing (to the extent that the evidence permits) their approaches to character dance and their ways of integrating it with classical dance within a single dramatic work. Petipa's achievements, perhaps, are of particular interest today, not only because a number of his ballets remain extant but also because he has been credited with revealing "pure choreographic meaning"[196] and with contributing to the twentieth-century revival of the pure-dance aesthetic.[197] How did these achievements intersect with his achievements as a character dancer and choreographer? Did Petipa himself conceive of classical revivalism and character dance as wholly unrelated? As Oleg Petrov has pointed out, "In putting classical dance first Petipa did not turn away from the ballet theater's other means of expression—character dance and mime."[198] If he foretold the abstract works of Balanchine, he was also a man of his own time steeped in the tradition of character dance and keenly aware of its dramatic power. An integrated study of his work, following the paths of classical and character styles as well as endeavoring to understand the overlap of the two, will contribute greatly to our understanding of Petipa's genius, the Imperial Russian tradition, and its legacy in our century.[199]

In fact, a twentieth-century performance history of character dance in Russian ballets of the late nineteenth century would make a fascinating study in itself, for the material has been subjected to such widely varying interpretations. Compare, for example, two variant (and equally interesting) versions of the Spanish pas de quatre in *Swan Lake*, as performed in the past few decades by the Bolshoi Ballet. In one version, two couples (making frequent eye contact and dancing in close proximity to one

another) make deep backward extensions of the spine and perform zapateado as well as other rapid allegro footwork.[200] The other version is radically different. It features only one dancer, a woman, who wears pointe
shoes instead of character shoes. Her spine remains straight throughout,
never arching backward, and instead of remaining close to the floor she
leaps frequently into the air and takes several poses on pointe.[201] What
forces—political, aesthetic, or otherwise—dictate such varying interpretations? How are shifting tastes in the twentieth century reflected in such
choreography? Might the balleticization of the second version of this pas
de quatre be read as a form of abstraction congruent with Levinson's sentiments that folk-derived dances can only be elevated by an inclination
"toward abstraction"?[202]

A careful assessment of the place of character dance within the dramaturgy of nineteenth-century ballet is perhaps one of the most important scholarly undertakings that awaits us. The fact that nearly all the
character dance audiences see today in the nineteenth-century ballets
seems irrelevant to the drama because it is relegated to "entertainment"
scenes—the celebration on Clara's behalf in the Kingdom of the Sweets in
The Nutcracker, the diversion for the guests in the ball scene of *Swan
Lake*—has made it easy to forget that character dance could be deployed
in ways that served a variety of functions.[203] One such function (as noted
above) was to help characterize a ballet's principal figures. Another, as
Baryshnikov has pointed out, was to "build the dramatic excitement of
the ballet."[204] Another related function was to introduce contrast—not
only at the most obvious level but also to convey deeper meaning and to
fulfill a larger structural purpose. For instance, as Alan Jones has pointed
out, the Hindu dance in *La Bayadère* was a means not only of showing
various caste types to the audience, but also of establishing symmetry,
while addressing in an abstract way the fundamental conflict of the plot:

> The Hindu dance is perhaps unmatched among Petipa's creations for its
> wild, bacchanalian abandon.... The omission of the Hindu Dance defeats
> Petipa's stated desire to represent in the betrothal divertissement all of
> India's castes as he imagined them. More crucial, the omission weakens
> the suggestion of profane sensuality in the union of Solor and Gamzatti
> and the contrasting effect that this act was intended to give to the serene
> classicism of the "Kingdom of the Shades" scene that follows.[205]

Even the impact of the famous "Kingdom of the Shades" scene, then, is
diluted if its counterpart is withdrawn. The Hindu Dance is not simply
decorative, but stands as a crucial component within a well-conceived
configuration of events and images, invented by a choreographer lauded
for his keen sense of structural design.

Clearly, there is no lack of territory to cover in the study of the history
of character dance in ballet and the aesthetic theories that have attended
it. The practical challenges, of course, are not to be underestimated. The
task of compiling factual information about character dance, for instance,
will require following Ivor Guest's example of combing through newspa-

per reviews, libretti, costume drawings, scores, letters, office correspondence, and the personal papers of composers, dancers, and choreographers, and doing so in dozens of archives. Too, the language gap between Russia and the West must be bridged so that we may better integrate Russian scholarship with that written in the West. Yet by overcoming these challenges, and broadening the scope of historical inquiry to include character dance on a more systematic basis, we will achieve a fuller and more balanced understanding of the creative forces that shaped the Romantic ballet. At the same time, we will become better able to situate the art of theatrical dance within the broader social, political, and artistic movements in nineteenth-century Europe.

We are indebted to Ivor Guest, without whose scholarship this article could never have been written. We also wish to thank him for so generously sharing with Marian Smith one of his research files. Original research for this article was carried out under University of Oregon Summer Research Grants awarded individually to Lisa C. Arkin and Marian Smith.

Notes

1. See, for instance, Johann Gottfried von Herder, *Selected Early Works 1764–1767*, ed. Ernest A. Menze and Karl Menges, trans. Ernest A. Menze with Michael Palma (University Park, Penn.: Pennsylvania State University Press, 1992), and Frederick M. Barnard, *Herder's Social and Political Thought: From Enlightenment to Nationalism* (Oxford: Oxford University Press, 1965).
2. We borrow the term "folk-derived" from Lynn Garafola, specifically her discussion of Fokine's *genre nouveau*. See Garafola, *Diaghilev's Ballets Russes* (New York: Oxford University Press, 1989), pp. 9–14.
3. See John Chapman, "An Unromantic View of Nineteenth-Century Romanticism," *York Dance Review*, no. 7 (1978), pp. 28–40, and James Smith Allen, *Popular French Romanticism* (Syracuse, N.Y.: Syracuse University Press, 1981), pp. 2–3.
4. Thus, we restrict the use of the latter term to its narrowest sense, meaning "folk," "national," or "ethnic." The term "character dance" is more inclusive than "national dance" because it can also include rustic dance, dances by older characters, and dances that show a character's occupation (e.g., dances of shoemakers, bakers, sailors). Our use of the term "character dance" or *"pas de caractère"* in this article, however, is restricted to national dance unless otherwise indicated.
5. Among the theaters that regularly featured independent character divertissements were Her Majesty's Theatre in London, the Théâtre de la Monnaie in Brussels, and La Fenice in Venice. Divertissements *within* operas or ballet-pantomimes were sets of dances that took place during respites from the forward motion of the plot. The dramatic rationale for divertissements included wedding celebrations, masked balls, and harvest festivals.
6. See Marian Smith, "'Poésie lyrique' and 'Chorégraphie' at the Opéra in the July Monarchy," *Cambridge Opera Journal*, 4, no. 1 (1992), pp. 1–19.

7. It is unclear, from the libretto, which of these dances occurred in which acts (except for the bayadère dance, which took place in Act III). These dances are, however, mentioned by critics. See Cyril W. Beaumont, *Complete Book of Ballets* (London: Putnam, 1937), pp. 205–215, and Ivor Guest, *The Romantic Ballet in Paris*, 2nd ed. rev. (London: Dance Books, 1980), pp. 192–195.

8. According to the costume lists (AJ13/214 and AJ13/215, Archives Nationales), dancers were featured in this opera. But no choreographer is listed in the libretto, and it is unclear what dances—if any—they performed.

9. *Robert le Diable*, libretto, "nouvelle edition" (Paris, 1834).

10. Calendar de l'Opéra, BN-Opéra Réserve.

11. The emphasis is ours. "[W]hen time has rolled on and the good things of the past acquire a new interest the best ballets of Gardel will be revived and people will be amazed at the imagination, taste, delicacy, skill, and versatility of their choreographer. Then the dance will no longer be composed of only so-called *pas de caractère*, performed exclusively by women in accordance with the ridiculous idea of excluding male dancers, as though one sex alone could anywhere claim a monopoly of this pleasure" (*Courrier des Théâtres*, 10 and 14 Nov. 1840, quoted in Guest, *The Romantic Ballet in Paris*, p. 94). It was common for corps dancers, half of them dressed as males, to perform character dances.

12. *La Presse*, 2 Mar. 1840, quoted in Iver Guest, *Jules Perrot: Master of the Romantic Ballet* (New York: Dance Horizons, 1984), p. 57.

13. Albert Smith, *The Natural History of the Ballet Girl* (London: D. Bogue, 1847; rpt. London: Dance Books, 1972), p. 96.

14. "A great number of artists, painters, sculptors and men of letters, *les gentlemen riders les plus chocnosophes*, and a host of pretty women were present at this solemnity, at which M. Cellarius and M. Eugene Coralli were to meet face to face and polka to polka." See Philip J.S. Richardson, *The Social Dances of the Nineteenth Century in England* (London: Herbert Jenkins, 1960), p. 83.

15. *Cahier des exercises de 1829, Cahier d'Exercises Pour L. L. A. A. Royalles les Princesses de Württemberg 1830*, and *2me Cahier Exercises de 1830* (also containing material entitled "Exercises de 1831"), Rés. 1137, BN-Opéra. For a discussion of these manuscripts, see Sandra N. Hammond, "A Nineteenth-Century Dancing Master at the Court of Württemberg: The Dance Notebooks of Michel St. Léon," *Dance Chronicle*, 15, no. 3 (1992), pp. 291–312. We would like to thank Sandra Hammond for her discussions of these manuscripts with us.

16. Anna Petrovna Natarova, "From the Recollections of the Artiste A.P. Natarova," in *A Century of Russian Ballet: Documents and Eyewitness Accounts, 1810–1910*, ed. and trans. Roland John Wiley (Oxford: Oxford University Press, 1990), p. 137.

17. This divertissement was performed in April 1845 in London.

18. See Guest, *Jules Perrot*, pp. 35, 47, 51. *Zingaro* was composed by Uranio Fortuna for the Théâtre de la Renaissance, Paris.

19. *La Presse*, 2 Oct. 1837, in *Gautier on Dance*, ed. and trans. Ivor Guest (London: Dance Books, 1986), pp. 17–18. The Spanish dancing in this opera had been one of its more popular features since its premiere in 1828, but it seems likely that the Spanish dance performed at this revival was new. Lise

Noblet, one of the most famous ballerinas in Europe, danced at the Opéra from 1818 to 1841. Her sister, Mme. Alexis Dupont (*née* Félicité Noblet), danced at the Opéra from 1826 to 1841. See Guest, *The Romantic Ballet in Paris*, p. 57.

20. N. P. Willis, *Famous Persons and Famous Places* (London, 1854), quoted in Beaumont, *Complete Book*, p. 112. See also Léandre Vaillat, *La Taglioni, ou la Vie d'une danseuse* (Paris: A. Michel, [1942]), p. 405. *La Gitana*, choreographed by Filippo Taglioni for Marie Taglioni, was first performed at the Bolshoi Theater, St. Petersburg, 23 Nov./5 Dec. 1838.

21. Edwin Binney III, *Longing for the Ideal: Images of Marie Taglioni in the Romantic Ballet* (Cambridge: Harvard Theatre Collection, 1984), p. 29.

22. Quoted in Ivor Guest, *Fanny Elssler* (Middletown, Conn.: Wesleyan University Press, 1970), pp. 80–81.

23. "Un vilain masqué," *Physiologie de l'Opéra, du Carnaval, du Cancan et de la cachucha* (Paris, 1842), p. 52. People could dress as Armenians, Turks, Tyrolians, and hussars, for instance. The powdered wig was also considered a good complement to any costume. See also Victor Sorel, "Costumes des bals parisiens 1837 à 1850" (Paris, n.d.).

24. This book is mentioned in Mons. Albert, *L'Art de danser à la ville et à la cour. Un nouvelle Méthode des vrais principes de la danse française et étrangère* (Paris, 1834).

25. See, for example, Carlo Blasis, *The Code of Terpsichore* (London, 1828), pp. 495–502. See also E. A. Théleur, *Letters on Dancing* (London, 1831; rpt. *Studies in Dance History*, 2, no. 1 [1990]), p. 100.

26. Henri Cellarius, *La Danse des Salons* (Paris, 1847), p. 68. This was translated and published in London in 1847 as *Fashionable Dancing*.

27. *Ibid.*, p. 69.

28. *La Revue et Gazette Musicale*, 28 Dec. 1833, and *Le Ménestrel*, 28 Dec. 1833, quoted in François Gasnault, *Guinguettes et Lorettes: Bals publics et danse sociale à Paris entre 1830 et 1870* (Paris: Aubier, 1986), pp. 74–75.

29. *Histoire chronologique, philosophique et morale du Cancan*, in *La Musée Philipon* (n.d.), AID 3460, BN-Opéra.

30. GD 8°/39782, BN-Arsenal.

31. Interestingly enough, this writer attributes the rise of the national dance craze to the cholera epidemic: "[Because of the cholera epidemic] Parisians felt the need to distract themselves by any means possible...[and] sought to find pleasure and novelty from dancing. This tendency was singularly favored by the appearance at the Opéra of Spanish dancers who introduced the French public to all the charms and abandon of the cachucha....The student understood the happy alliance that could be forged between stiff French dance and loose Andalusian dancing. A choreographic conservatory [the Grande Chaumière] was soon established at the Boulevard Montparnasse" (*Histoire chronologique, philosophique et morale du Cancan, op. cit.*). The Grande Chaumière's address was No. 13 Boulevard Montparnasse. Lessons in national dancing constituted an important part of its offerings, and other types of dancing were taught there as well.

32. AJ13/182, Archives Nationales. "Mirlitons"—shepherds and shepherdesses—are listed among the acts hired for the Opéra balls. There is no information about the identities of these performers.

33. *Vert-Vert*, 24 Dec. 1834.

34. Among the pieces in which Spanish dance had appeared were *Le Sicilien* (1827) and *La Muette de Portici* (1828). Also, premiers danseurs from the Paris Opéra, such as the great Louis Duport, were reported to have performed Spanish divertissements as early as 1812. See Jan Cieplinski, *A History of Polish Ballet, 1518–1945* trans. Anna Ema Lesiecka (London: Veritas Foundation Publication Centre, 1983), p. 32.

35. See Guest, *The Romantic Ballet in Paris*, chs. 1 and 2; Knud Arne Jürgensen, *The Bournonville Heritage* (London: Dance Books, 1990), p. 57; and Marian Hannah Winter, *The Pre-Romantic Ballet* (London: Pitman Publishers, 1974).

36. Among the many examples of staged works that included ball scenes in which onstage revelers could observe danced entertainments were *Le Diable amoureux*, *Gustave III*, *La Jolie Fille de Gand*, *Don Giovanni*, *Le Diable à quatre*, *Ozaï*, and *Paquita*. Other types of festive occasions, too, sometimes lent themselves well to the conceit of having dancers provide entertainment to other characters on stage. In *Eoline*, for example, a noble party is entertained by miners performing the silésienne to celebrate a wedding.

37. See, for example, Gautier's comments on *La Gipsy* in *La Presse*, 4 Feb. 1839, in *Gautier on Dance*, p. 65.

38. These scores offer detailed instructions for the mime scenes and simply label the danced segments as such (using interchangeably the words "divertissement," "pas," or "ballet"). The existence of such scores was brought to the attention of Marian Smith by David Day, who is currently cataloguing the collection of the Brussels municipal archives. We owe him many thanks for allowing her to view these rare and fascinating scores before their being made available to the public. There also exists, in the Theater Museum, St. Petersburg, a Parisian annotated répétiteur of *Giselle* that appears to describe the first production of this ballet.

39. This calculation was made by reading the annotated *Giselle* score referred to in the previous note and using the timings of Richard Bonynge's performance of *Giselle* (Decca, 1987, released on CD by London as 433-007-2). See also Marian Smith, "The First Production of *Giselle*: A Preliminary Report on a Parisian Manuscript" (*Dance Chronicle*, forthcoming).

40. *La Presse*, 4 Feb. 1839, quoted in Beaumont, *Complete Book*, p. 203.

41. Véron, quoted in Victor de Bled, *Le Ballet de l'Opéra* (Paris, n.d.), p. 303.

42. *Le Journal des Débats*, 20 July 1831.

43. Peter Lichtenthal, *Dictionnaire de Musique*, rev. ed., trans. Dominique Mondo (Paris, 1839), p. 114. This was first published in Milan as *Dizionario e Bibliografia della Musica* in 1826.

44. This was often true even for ballets that were "translations" of operas or plays, though critics at times did declare that a description of the plot was unnecessary since it was already familiar to the reader.

45. To name two examples among many: in *La Révolte au sérail*, a pivotal development in the plot is explained by means of a large parchment unfurled by one of the king's officers (Act II, Scene 5) on which can be read, "à la demande du vaillant Ismaïl, le Roi rend la liberté à toutes ses femmes....Zulma seule restera captive" (*La Révolte au sérail*, libretto [Paris, 1833]). In *L'Orgie* (Act II, Scene 1), a placard with the words "Fête patronale du village" is affixed to a stake (*L'Orgie*, libretto [Paris, 1831]).

46. *Giselle* répétiteur. The music remains the same in this scene but the gestures are no longer carried out.

47. On the melodrama, see Emilio Sala, *L'opera senza canto. Il mélo romantico e l'invenzione della colonna sonora* (Venice: Marsilio, 1995).

48. *La France musicale*, 3 Feb. 1839. A comparison of the blocking and movements of opera and ballet characters is given in Marian Smith, "Staging Practices at the Paris Opéra: The Operatic Livrets de mise en scène and the Ballet-Pantomime," *La Realizzazione Scenica dello Spettacolo Verdiano*, ed. Pierluigi Petrobelli (in press).

49. These tableaux were sometimes characterized in libretti and (in the case of opera) staging manuals as "lugubrious tableau," "religious tableau," "sad tableau," and the like. On the dramatic technique of "shock" (*éclat*) and the tableau, see Carl Dahlhaus, *Nineteenth-Century Music*, trans. J. Bradford Robinson (Berkeley: University of California Press, 1989), p. 126.

50. *The Times*, quoted in Beaumont, *Complete Book*, p. 155.

51. Review of *La Fille du marbre*, *La France Musicale*, 24 Oct. 1847.

52. Review of *La Fille du Danube*, *La Presse*, 26 Sept. 1836.

53. *Giselle*, libretto (Paris, 1841); *Le Diable amoureux*, libretto (Paris, 1840); *La Tentation*, libretto (Paris, 1832). See also Gautier's description of Indian dancers "stopping abruptly in their tracks," *La Presse*, 20 Aug. 1838, in *Gautier on Dance*, pp. 39–46. Note further that in the *Giselle* libretto, the Wili Zulmé is described as a Bayadère who "displays Indian poses."

54. *La Révolte au sérail*, libretto (Paris, 1833), in Beaumont, *Complete Book*, p. 94. This ballet, with music by Théodore Labarre and choreography by Filippo Taglioni, was first performed at the Paris Opéra on 4 December 1833.

55. Guest, *Fanny Cerrito: The Life of a Romantic Ballerina* (London: Dance Books, 1974), p. 104. This ballet, with music by Cesare Pugni and choreography by Perrot, was first performed at Her Majesty's Theatre on 11 June 1846.

56. Note also that critics often likened sets to paintings, and dancers to statues. To name three examples among many: Ciceri's sets for *Manon Lescaut* (1830) are called "exact reproductions of Boucher and Watteau" (*Le Constitutionnel*, 5 May 1830, quoted in Guest, *The Romantic Ballet in Paris*, p. 97); Fanny Elssler is likened to a "figure by Bendemann, the painter of *Jeremiah*" (*La Presse*, 2 Oct. 1837, in *Gautier on Dance*, p. 19); the Festival of the Piedigrotta in *Stella* "immediately recalls an old painting of a Neapolitan Fair" (*Journal des Théâtres*, 27 Feb. 1850, quoted in Beaumont, *Complete Book*, p. 336).

57. Gautier, *Histoire de l'art dramatique en France* (Paris, 1858), 2, p. 67, quoted in William Crosten, *French Grand Opera: An Art and a Business* (New York: King's Crown Press, 1948), p. 68.

58. M. Elizabeth C. Bartlet, "Grand opéra," in *New Grove Dictionary of Opera* (London: Macmillan, 1992), 2, p. 514. As Bartlet points out, Ciceri also studied first-hand how La Scala had staged a volcanic eruption in its version of Pacini's *L'ultimo giorno di Pompei*. Ciceri served as *peintre en chef* from 1816 until 1848, sharing the title with Ignazio Degotti from 1816 to 1822, and with Louis-Jacques-Mandé Daguerre from February 1820 until 1822. Nicole Wild, *Dictionnaire des Théâtres Parisiens au XIXe Siècle* (Paris: Aux Amateurs de Livres, 1989), p. 317.

59. See Crosten, *French Grand Opera*, p. 52.

60. *Le Temps*, 4 Mar. 1833, quoted in Crosten, *French Grand Opera*, p. 64.

61. AJ13/215, Archives Nationales.

62. *Le Courrier Français*, 27 Feb. 1835, quoted in Crosten, *French Grand Opera*, p. 65. Extant sketches of flags, armor and other props, as well as costumes, attest to the designers' diligence. See D.216, *La Juive*, BN-Opéra.

63. Lichtenthal, *Dictionnaire*, 1, pp. 115–116. Newspaper reviews, too, occasionally refer to both types. "The dramatic part was treated very well by [Halévy]...the dance airs are pretty" (*La Revue Musicale*, review of *Manon Lescaut*, 1830, pp. 11–15).

64. This *krakowiak* was transcribed from a performance by the Janusz Kazmierzak's Folk Orchestra from Lodz on the recording entitled *Tance Ludowe Z Polski* (Folk Dances from Poland), vol. 2, "presented by Ada and Jas Dziewanowski." This *krakowiak* is identified on the recording as a national Polish dance, not a regional one. Another close variant of this melody may be found in measures 142 ff. of "La Cracovienne," in Jürgensen, *The Bournonville Heritage*, p. 64.

65. *La Presse*, 11 July 1837, in *Gautier on Dance*, pp. 10–11.

66. *Le Journal des Débats*, 13 Apr. 1835.

67. *Morning Post*, 14 Aug. 1843 and 23 June 1843, quoted in Guest, *Perrot*, p. 102.

68. *La France Musicale*, 30 June 1839.

69. *La Presse*, 25 July 1843, in *Gautier on Dance*, p. 119.

70. The gypsy Esmeralda, for instance, enters dancing, "bound[ing] on...stage with the tambourine" (*The Times*, quoted in Beaumont, *Complete Book*, p. 299).

71. *La Revue et Gazette de Théâtres*, 13 Apr. 1845; *La Presse* 31 Mar. 1845, in *Gautier on Dance*, p. 162. See also Deborah Jowitt, *Time and the Dancing Image* (Berkeley: University of California Press, 1988), pp. 64–65. Jowitt posits that Carlotta Grisi objected to the bee dance because of its immoral nature.

72. *Le Journal des Débats,* 17 Mar. 1834.

73. In many cases, character-variety divertissements were performed, but were carefully rationalized as an entertainment for onstage characters, and thus did not violate the strictures of realism. Typical examples may be found in *Ozaï* (in which the "four parts of the world" perform as the "musicians play the national airs of each country" at the French ball in Act II) and in *La Péri* (in which native dances of the Scottish, French, Spanish, and German women are performed for the pleasure of Achmet in Act I). A more famous character-variety divertissement is that staged in *The Nutcracker* to celebrate Clara's heroism. See the original libretto in Roland John Wiley, *Tchaikovsky's Ballets* (Oxford: Oxford University Press, 1985), pp. 333–337.

74. This book contains detailed color lithographs of twelve national dances in national costumes and characteristic poses, accompanied by descriptions of character, geography, and history and a folktale from that country. See *Read's Characteristic National Dances* (London: Read Publishing Company, 1853).

75. See Marvin Carlson, "Hernani's revolt from the tradition of French stage composition," *Theatre Survey*, 13, no. 1 (1972), pp. 1–27. It is surely no coincidence that Théophile Gautier, who proved to be one of the greatest

champions of character dance in ballet, also led the charge of the new Romantic forces at the Comédie-Française.

76. Our emphasis. August Bournonville, *My Theatre Life*, trans. Patricia N. McAndrew, foreword Erik Bruhn, introd. Svend Kragh-Jacobsen (Middletown, Conn.: Wesleyan University Press, 1979), p. 9.

77. On compositional conventions in nineteenth-century Italian opera and the ways they determined the structure of the libretto, see these very important essays: Philip Gossett, "Verdi, Ghislanzoni, and *Aida*: The Uses of Convention," *Critical Inquiry*, 1 (1974), pp. 291–334, and Harold Powers, "'La solita forma' and 'The Uses of Convention,'" *Acta musicologica*, 59 (1987), pp. 65–90.

78. Gautier, *La Charte de 1830*, 18 Apr. 1837, in "Théophile Gautier on Spanish Dancing," ed. and trans. Ivor Guest, *Dance Chronicle*, 10, no. 1 (1987), p. 19.

79. *Ibid.*, p. 17.

80. *La Presse*, 28 July 1839, *ibid.*, p. 31.

81. Giovanni-Andrea Gallini, *A Treatise on the Art of Dancing* (London, 1772), p. 135.

82. Gennaro Magri, *Theoretical and Practical Treatise on Dancing*, trans. Mary Skeaping (London: Dance Books, 1988), p. 55. This was originally published in Naples in 1779.

83. Blasis, *Traité élémentaire, théorétique et pratique de l'art de la danse*, trans. by Mary Stewart Evans (New York: Kamin Publishers, 1953), p. 64.

84. Blasis, *The Code of Terpsichore* (New York: Dance Horizons, [1976]), p. 32.

85. Blasis, *Notes Upon Dancing* (London: M. Delaporte, 1847), p. 144, and *The Code of Terpsichore*, pp. 91–92.

86. This treatise is not listed in the entry on Blasis *The Concise Oxford Dictionary of Ballet* (London: Oxford University Press, 1977), pp. 76–77. Many thanks to Roland John Wiley for bringing this treatise to our attention and for generously supplying us with a photocopy of it; thanks also to Elena Bogdonovich for the translations from the Russian.

87. Blasis, *Notes Upon Dancing*, p. 143.

88. Johann Gottfried von Herder, *Sämtliche Werke*, 33 vols. (Berlin: B. Suphan, 1877–1913), 2, p. 18, and 1, p. 420; translation in Barnard, *Herder's Social and Political Thought*, p. 56.

89. Carlo Blasis, *Tantsy voobshche, baletnye znamenitosti i natsional'nye tantsy* (*Dances in General, Ballet Celebrities, and National Dances* (Moscow, 1864), p. 142.

90. Herder, *Sämtliche Werke*, 18, p. 248; translation in Barnard, *Herder's Social and Political Thought*, p. 61.

91. *Ibid.*, 5, pp. 125–136; translation in Barnard, *Herder's Social and Political Thought*, p. 57.

92. Blasis, *Tantsy voobshche*, p. 142.

93. Herder, *Sämtliche Werke*, 5, pp. 51–90; translation in *J.G. Herder on Social and Political Culture*, ed., trans., and introd. F.M. Barnard (London: Cambridge University Press, 1969), p. 142.

94. Blasis, *Tantsy voobshche*, pp. 142–143.

95. Herder, *Sämtliche Werke*, 4, pp. 354–364 and 401–445; translation in Barnard, *J.G. Herder on Social and Political Culture*, p. 107.

96. Quoted in Robert T. Clark, Jr., *Herder: His Life and Thought* (Berkeley: University of California Press, 1955), p. xi.

97. Blasis, *Notes Upon Dancing*, p. 114.

98. Blasis, *Traité élémentaire*, p. 64.

99. Vaillat, *Taglioni*, pp. 394–395, 398.

100. *Ibid.*, p. 407.

101. Quoted in Guest, *Elssler*, p. 245.

102. *Ibid.*, p. 217.

103. Bournonville, *My Theatre Life*, p. 84.

104. Marius Petipa, *Russian Ballet Master: The Memoirs of Marius Petipa*, ed. Lillian Moore, trans. Helen Whittaker (London: Adam and Charles Black, 1958), pp. 70–71, 15.

105. *La Presse*, 27 Aug. 1838, in *Gautier on Dance*, p. 50. The troupe of *devadasis* was engaged in Paris by the impresario E.C. Tardival.

106. *La Presse*, 20 Aug. 1838, *ibid.*, p. 39.

107. *La Presse*, 28 July 1839, in "Théophile Gautier on Spanish Dancing," p. 36.

108. *La Presse*, 31 Mar. 1845, in *Gautier on Dance*, pp. 161–162.

109. Blasis, *Code of Terpsichore*, pp. 91–92.

110. *Ibid.*, p. 180.

111. Blasis, *Tantsy voobshche*, p. 142.

112. Blasis, *Code of Terpsichore*, p. 32.

113. *Ibid.*, p. 180.

114. Blasis, *Notes on Dancing*, p. 143.

115. Bournonville, *My Theatre Life*, pp. 8–9.

116. *La Presse*, 2 Oct. 1837, in "Gautier on Spanish Dancing," p. 22.

117. Cellarius, *Fashionable Dancing*, pp. 55, 61.

118. Friedrich Albert Zorn, *Grammar of the Art of Dancing* (Boston, 1905; rpt. Dance Horizons, 1976), pp. 253–257. According to the author's statement in the preface, this volume was written around 1885 and based on "fifty years of experience" (p. xi).

119. Janina Pudełek and Joanna Sibilska write that they "prefer the original Polish form 'mazur' to the more common Western 'mazurka' or 'little mazur.'" See Janina Pudełek with Joanna Sibilska, "The Polish Dancers Visit St. Petersburg, 1851: A Detective Story," *Dance Chronicle*, 19, no. 2 (1996), p. 171.

120. I.M., "Petersburgskaia letopis," *Sankpeterburgskie vedomosti*, 6/18 Feb. 1851, quoted *ibid.*, p. 178.

121. Gautier, quoted in Beaumont, *Complete Book*, pp. 202–203.

122. *The Times*, quoted in Guest, *Cerrito*, p. 45.

123. *La Presse*, 20 Jan. 1845, in *Gautier on Dance*, p. 156.

124. Quoted in Guest, *Cerrito*, p. 24.

125. Quoted *ibid.*, p. 36.

126. *Voyage en Espagne*, ch. 12, in "Gautier on Spanish Dance," p. 7.

127. *La Presse*, 2 Oct. 1837, *ibid.*, p. 22.

128. Gautier, *La Charte de 1830*, 18 Apr. 1837, in *Gautier on Dance*, p. 7.

129. Charles de Boigne, *Petits Mémoires de l'Opéra* (1857), quoted in Beaumont, *Complete Book*, p. 147.

130. Original emphasis. *The Times*, quoted in Guest, *Cerrito*, pp. 44–45.

131. Blasis, *Notes Upon Dancing*, pp. 34–35.

132. Quoted in Guest, *Cerrito*, p. 96.

133. Blasis, *Tantsy voobshche*, p. 175.

134. *Morning Post*, 11 June 1846, quoted in Guest, *Cerrito*, p. 105.

135. H. Justament, "Ballets pantomime de M. H. Justament," manuscript, C.891 (1–9), BN-Opéra. Many thanks to Carol Marsh for alerting us to the existence of this manuscript.

136. Henry Chorley, *Thirty Years of Musical Recollections* (London: H. F. Chorley, 1862), 1, pp. 66–67, quoted in Beaumont, *Complete Book*, p. 204.

137. *Le Journal des Débats*, 19 July 1843.

138. Quoted in Guest, *Cerrito*, p. 96.

139. *The Times*, quoted in Beaumont, *Complete Book*, p. 193.

140. Jurgensen, *The Bournonville Heritage*, p. 57.

141. Saint-Léon, *Cahier des exercises*, ff 28v–29v and ff 25v–27v.

142. An important exception is the cracovienne. See Jürgensen, *The Bournonville Heritage*, pp. 57–66, and Jürgensen, "Reconstructing *La Cracovienne*," *Dance Chronicle*, 6, no. 3 (1983), pp. 228–266. Note also that Sandra Noll Hammond has brought to light a great deal of crucial detailed information about ballet classes, giving us an excellent idea of the technical level of the nineteenth-century dancer. See for instance, Hammond, "Ballet's Technical Heritage: The *Grammaire* of Léopold Adice," *Dance Research*, 13, no. 1 (1995), pp. 33–58.

143. Note that it was not only the important male choreographers and dancers of the day who created character *pas*, but some of the leading female dancers as well. Fanny Elssler, for instance, arranged her own cachucha in *Le Diable boiteux*, and Fanny Cerrito composed a number of character dances including tarantellas, a varsovienne, a sicilienne, and the *pas espagnol d'Andalousie* in *Alma*.

144. Bournonville, *My Theatre Life*, p. 176

145. *La Presse*, 25 Feb. 1850, in *Gautier on Dance*, p. 224. The critic for *Journal des Théâtres* also wrote of Saint-Léon's ability to blend character and classical styles: "Saint-Léon is a great fancifier who does not wish to follow well-trodden paths; he creates a style and seems to blend all that the dances of Europe possess in the way of piquant originality and dainty coquetry, while conforming to the traditions of the French School. There are suggestions of Spain, Sicily, Calabria, and Moscow in his compositions, of which he alone has the secret; rejuvenated memories brought to perfection which, in truth, are inventions" (27 Feb. 1850, quoted Beaumont, *Complete Book*, p. 410).

146. We are indebted to Ivor Guest's analysis of Perrot's choreography in *Jules Perrot: Master of the Romantic Ballet*.

147. Quoted in Guest, *Cerrito*, pp. 114–115.

148. Writes Ivor Guest: His "mastery as a choreographer was many-sided.... [H]is palette contained a rich variety of dance material from the formal enchaînements in the classical technique to national dances" (*Perrot*, p. 105).

149. Among Perrot's ballets and divertissements featuring national dance numbers were *Die neapolitanischen fischer* (1838), *Alma* (1842), *Ondine* (1843), *La Esmeralda* (1844), *Eoline* (1845), *Kaya* (1845), *Catarina* (1846), *Lallah Rookh* (1846), and *Faust* (1848).

150. Guest, *Perrot*, p. 105.

151. *Journal de St. Pétersbourg*, 11/23 Nov. 1858, quoted in Guest, *Perrot*, p. 312.

152. *The Times*, 10 Mar. 1845, quoted in Beaumont, *Complete Book*, pp. 303–304.

153. Guest, *Perrot*, p. 320. See also Petipa, *Russian Ballet Master*, pp. 39–41.

154. Guest, *Perrot*, p. 271.

155. Trib. Civ. Seine, 11.7.62, aff Petipa. Pataille 73,234, quoted in Guest, *Perrot*, p. 323.

156. See *La Presse*, 24 Sept., 1838, in *Gautier on Dance*, pp. 47–55.

157. *La Presse*, 20 Jan. 1851, in *Gautier on Dance*, 225–226.

158. See Cyril W. Beaumont, *Marie Taglioni* (1930; rpt. London: Dance Books, 1977), p. 57.

159. The evidence that she danced the mazurka in *La Fille de Danube* is in the score (Mat 19 [294 (22)], BN-Opéra). It is unclear whether she included this mazurka from the time of the work's premiere in 1836, or if she added it after studying the mazurka in Poland in 1838.

160. This performance took place on 1 April 1844. See Guest, *Cerrito*, pp. 77–78.

161. This performance took place on 16 April 1844. See *ibid.*, p. 78.

162. Guest, *Perrot*, p. 83.

163. Gautier, *Histoire de l'Art Dramatique* (Paris, 1858), 2, p. 133, quoted in Cyril W. Beaumont, *The Ballet Called Giselle* (London: C.W. Beaumont, 1944), p. 18. *De l'Allemagne* was published in *Europe Littéraire* in 1833 and appeared the same year in German as *Zur Geschichte der neueren schönen Literatur in Deutschland*. It was published in book form in 1835.

164. Lichtenthal, *Dictionnaire*, 1, pp. 115–116.

165. *La Péri*, libretto (Paris, 1843).

166. Adolphe Adam, letter to Jules-Henri Vernoy de Saint-Georges, in Serge Lifar, *Giselle: Apothéose du Ballet Romantique* (Paris, 1942; rpt. Paris: Editions d'Aujourd'hui, 1982), app.

167. *La France Musicale*, 4 July 1841.

168. *La France Musicale*, 17 Aug. 1845.

169. *Giselle*, libretto (Paris, 1841).

170. *Giselle*, libretto (Paris, 1841).

171. The Spanish segment is sixteen bars long if the repeats are taken.

172. In the "Second Night" of Heine's *Les Nuits florentines*, the storyteller recalls his obsession with a beautiful woman he had seen dancing on Waterloo Bridge: "Was it some national dance from the South of France of Spain? These were recalled by the violence with which the dancer threw her body to and fro, and the abandon with which she tossed back her head like a bold bacchante....Her dancing had a spontaneous and intoxicating quality, something darkly inevitable or fatalistic, for she danced like Fate itself" (quoted in Guest, *Perrot*, p. 66).

173. Gautier, *Histoire de l'art dramatique*, pp. 137–138. A group of Indian dancers, including Amani-Ammalle, made a great impression on Gautier when they performed in Paris in 1838. See his articles in *La Presse*, 20 and 27 Aug. 1838, in *Gautier on Dance*, pp. 39–50.

174. An unpainted version of this picture is reproduced in Guest, *The Romantic Ballet in Paris*, fig. 66.

175. See AJ13/510, Archives Nationales. These memoranda indicate that the Wili costumes were the same, though Myrthe's wings were sky blue and Giselle's were white.

176. Ferdinand Reyna, *Concise Encyclopedia of Ballet*, trans. André Gâteau

(Chicago: Follett Publishing Co., 1974), p. 193.

177. Horst Koegler, *The Concise Oxford Dictionary of Ballet*, 2nd ed. (Oxford: Oxford University Press, 1982). Quoting Ninette de Valois, Koegler goes on to define the demi-caractère dancer as being distinguished by "great academic virtuosity, as opposed to the grace and lyrical qualities of the purest classical [dancer]—e.g. 'The Blue Bird.'"

178. André Levinson, "The Idea of the Dance: From Aristotle to Mallarmé," in *André Levinson on Dance: Writings from Paris in the Twenties*, ed. and introd. Joan Acocella and Lynn Garafola (Middletown, Conn.: Wesleyan University Press, 1991), p. 80. See also Stanley J. Rabinowitz, "Against the Grain: Akim Volynskii and the Russian Ballet," *Dance Research*, 14, no. 1 (1996), pp. 3–41.

179. Levinson, "The Idea of the Dance," in *André Levinson on Dance*, p. 79.

180. Levinson, "Argentina," *ibid.*, p. 97.

181. The *La Sylphide* created in Paris in 1832 has also undergone radical transformations. The version usually performed today is based on Bournonville's version of the Parisian original (using the score by Løvenskjold instead of that by Schneitzhoeffer). The version staged by Pierre Lacotte using Schneitzhoeffer's music, too, departs from the original in significant ways, as an examination of the manuscript scores demonstrates.

182. See Deborah Jowitt, "Heroism in the Harem" in *Time and the Dancing Image*, pp. 49–66. See also John Chapman's valuable "An Unromantic View of Nineteenth-Century Romanticism," *op. cit.* Chapman's study does not pertain to national dance per se but does call into question several received notions about the historiography of the Romantic ballet.

183. Janina Pudełek, "The Warsaw Ballet under the Directorship of Maurice Pion and Filippo Taglioni, 1832–1853," *Dance Chronicle*, 11, no. 2 (1988), pp. 219–273.

184. Andrei Lopoukov, Alexander Shirayev, and Alexander Bocharov, *Character Dance*, trans. Joan Lawson (London: Dance Books, 1986). This book was first published in Leningrad in 1939.

185. Jürgensen, *The Bournonville Heritage*, pp. 57–66.

186. Joellen A. Meglin, "*Le Diable Boiteux*: French Society Behind a Spanish Façade," *Dance Chronicle*, 17, no. 3 (1994), pp. 263–302.

187. Garafola, *Diaghilev's Ballets Russes*, pp. 9–14.

188. See Roger Copeland and Marshall Cohen, *What is Dance?* (New York: Oxford University Press, 1983), p. 18, and Reyna, *Concise Encyclopedia of Ballet*, p. 193.

189. Alexander Bland, *A History of Ballet and Dance* (New York: Praeger, 1976), pp. 56, 61.

190. "Jules Perrot," *International Dictionary of Ballet*, ed. Martha Bremser (Detroit: St. James Press, 1993), pp. 1106–1108.

191. On the topic of the representation of people of color in French ballet, see Joellen Meglin's forthcoming study; her paper on the subject, "Beauties and Benefactresses, Barbarians and Buffoons: Representations of Blacks in French Ballet 1779–1806," was presented at the 1996 conference of the Society of Dance History Scholars held in Minneapolis. On the subject of exoticism and the appropriation of Spanish dance in French Romantic ballet see Lisa C. Arkin, "The Context of Exoticism in Fanny Elssler's Cachucha," *Dance Chronicle*, 17, no. 3 (1994), pp. 303–325; on Orientalism in opera, see

Ralph Locke, "Constructing the Oriental 'Other': Saint-Saëns's *Samson et Dalila*," *Cambridge Opera Journal*, 3, no. 3 (1991), pp. 261–302.

192. For instance, what was the climate at La Fenice in Austrian-dominated Venice when *La Vivandiera ed il Postiglione*—which featured an interpolated sicilienne performed by Fanny Cerrito and Saint-Léon—elicited patriotic demonstrations and was banned by the police in January 1848? (See Guest, *Cerrito*, pp. 123–124.) How was Perrot's use of a saltarella as a diversion allowing Abruzzian bandits to outwit uniformed soldiers in *Catarina* (1846) understood by English audiences who, on the whole, favored Italian resistance to Austrian and French rule over Italy? (See Guest, *Perrot*, pp. 159–164.)

193. Marina Keet has suggested that the arm movements of traditional Spanish dance may have contributed to classical port de bras. Marina Keet, "Ballet's Debt to Spanish Dance: Some Regional Dances of Spain," *Proceedings of the Society of Dance History Scholars* (1991), p. 105, and Marina Keet, personal communication with present authors, 7 July 1996.

194. Alan Jones, "Character Dance Returns with Panache," *The New York Times*, 19 June 1983, sec. H, p. 20.

195. See Jürgensen, *The Bournonville Heritage*, p. 57.

196. Oleg Petrov, "Russian Ballet and its Place in Russian Artistic Culture in the Second Half of the Nineteenth Century: The Age of Petipa," trans. Tim Scholl, *Dance Chronicle*, 15, no. 1 (1993), p. 54.

197. Acocella and Garafola, "Introduction," *André Levinson on Dance*, pp. 1–2. See also Tim Scholl, *From Petipa to Balanchine: Classical Revival and the Modernization of Ballet* (London: Routledge, 1994).

198. Petrov, "Russian Ballet," p. 47.

199. Elizabeth Souritz, in a comparative study of Petipa's Moscow and St. Petersburg productions of *Don Quixote*, notes that the Moscow version called for far more character dance than the St. Petersburg one. Her analysis (when it is published in its final form) will provide valuable information about the exigencies affecting Petipa's use of character dance at various times in his career. See the summary of her "Marius Petipa's Don Quixote," in *Proceedings Society of Dance History Scholars* (1991), p. 250.

200. Video recording of *Swan Lake*, performed by the Bolshoi Ballet, distributed by Kultur (1988). The film on which this video recording is based was produced in 1957; the stage production, however, dated to 1937 and retained Alexander Gorsky's 1920 choreography for Acts I and III.

201. Video recording of *Swan Lake*, performed by the Bolshoi Ballet, distributed by Kultur (1984). This production was first staged by Yuri Grigorovich in 1969.

202. Levinson, "Argentina," in *André Levinson on Dance*, p. 97.

203. Comparisons of the dramaturgy of nineteenth-century ballet and opera would no doublt prove enlightening. Important studies of the dramaturgy of Italian opera include Carolyn Abbate and Roger Parker, *Analyzing Opera: Wagner and Verdi* (Berkeley: University of California Press, 1989) and Pierluigi Petrobelli, *Music in the Theater* (Princeton: Princeton University Press, 1994).

204. Jones, "Character Dance," p. 20.

205. *Ibid.*, p. 21. See also Carl Dahlhaus's discussion of visual dramaturgy in *Nineteenth Century Music*, pp. 124–131.

Feminism or Fetishism?
La Révolte des femmes *and Women's Liberation in France in the 1830s*

JOELLEN A. MEGLIN

La Révolte des femmes (The Revolt of the Women) or *La Révolte au sérail* (The Revolt of the Harem), as it is better known today, has been called one of the few feminist ballets of the nineteenth century.[1] Choreographed by Filippo Taglioni as a vehicle for his daughter Marie, the work premiered at the Paris Opéra in 1833, only a year after the creation of *La Sylphide*. Just how feminist was *La Révolte au sérail*? One way to answer this question is to consult the feminisms of the day. In Paris in the early 1830s the Saint-Simonians, utopian socialists, offered a new vision of social regeneration in which woman was to figure prominently. From this movement, founded by a group of disciples of Claude-Henri de Rouvroy, Comte de Saint-Simon, and led by Prosper Enfantin, emerged an autonomous women's movement that truly addressed the condition of women. By comparing the libretto of *Révolte* with written documents and accounts by historians of this early movement to champion the cause of women, it is possible to locate the ballet within the feminist *mentalités* of its day.[2] A close reading of the libretto of *Révolte* shows that, while its rhetoric bore superficial resemblances to the rhetoric of contemporary feminisms, the reason for introducing the woman question seems to have been to make the ballet topical, titillating, and good theater, rather than to make a statement of political conscience.

Nonetheless, there are some intriguing similarities between this balletic fiction and the historical facts of women's liberation. In the libretto, for instance, the women of the court (ladies of the harem) band together with the women of the people to protest the tyranny of men. As Zulma leads her harem rebels to freedom, they encounter a group of working women. "Come," she cries to them, "come join us! It is the cause of women that we defend—your cause. It is time to free yourselves from the despotism of men."[3] Exactly how these subtle ideas were communicated in pantomime is difficult to imagine. But that may have been beside the point; the rhetoric resembles an appeal for association in the first issue of the *Tribune des femmes*, a journal created in 1832 by young proletarian women connected to the Saint-Simonian movement:[4] "Let us no longer form two camps, one of women of the popular classes and another of women of the privileged classes. Let our common interest bind us together."[5] And indeed, this philosophy lent itself well to dramatic and scenic effect. The last tableau of the ballet's second act found the women of the harem and "their new allies" fleeing across the river in boats, while the King, his

69

court, and the men of the people raged in frustrated pursuit behind a golden gate.

Many parallels between the make-believe world of the ballet and the utopian world of the Saint-Simonians can be drawn. The Saint-Simonian social platform harshly criticized what it called the "old" Christianity.[6] In the ballet Ismael, the hero, vanquishes the Christians, thus creating a topsy-turvy world where alternative social visions can reign. Later, the Spirit of Womankind, a female figure recalling the Saint-Simonians' Woman Messiah, a symbol of social redress, reverses the defeat of Zulma's legions. In fact, the Saint-Simonians declared 1833 the "Year of the Woman," and a group of Saint-Simonian men, calling themselves "Compagnons de la Femme," actually went to the Middle East in search of the new Messiah.[7] Historical fact begins to sound more and more like balletic fiction, and balletic fiction more and more like historical fact. Indeed, two years later, reviewing *Brézilia* (another Taglioni ballet), Jules Janin observed: "[Monsieur] Taglioni has returned to his favorite idea, *the emancipation of women*. This ballet, the tribe of women, is altogether the counterpart of *La Révolte au Sérail*. [Monsieur] Taglioni, these are the doctrines of Saint-Simon elevated to the demonstration of the pirouette and the entrechat."[8] So the Saint-Simonian echoes in the ballet were perceived by at least some members of the Paris audience.

The Oriental mysticism pervading both the social movement and the ballet was a reflection of the larger vogue for mysticism among Romantic artists and writers of the 1830s. Moreover, the use of Orientalism to criticize French social mores was part of a time-honored tradition in French letters, one that dated at least as far back as Montesquieu's *Lettres persanes* (Persian Letters), published more than a century before. Nor was anticlericalism particularly new after the scathing critique of Enlightenment thinkers such as Voltaire, to say nothing of the violent persecution of priests and nuns during the French Revolution. Indeed, *Révolte* recast numerous eighteenth-century discourses in terms that reverberated with concerns of its own period—the July Monarchy.

The female warrior was another familiar archetype. There was Joan of Arc, for instance, a powerful symbol in French society invented anew for each age and cause.[9] Even more potent were the female images of Liberty, commonplace since the Revolution, that Zulma's role as a female liberator would have evoked. In *Marianne into Battle: Republican Imagery and Symbolism in France, 1789–1880*, Maurice Agulhon demonstrates that allegorical representations of Republican ideals most often took the form of women.[10] Without a doubt, Taglioni would have seen "The Departure of the Volunteers" (1792) by Rude, one of the four bas-reliefs on the Arc de Triomphe. We may infer from Agulhon the impassioned feelings a female hero might arouse:

> [T]he yelling woman brandishing her sword and with spread wings is—in theory—the Spirit of War. As is well known, the episode that is evoked (1792), the remarkable surging movement that animates the group and the

"Conquer or Die," proclaim the members of the "New French Army of Saint-Simonian Women" (in the words of a post-World War I caption writer) in this 1832 print, illustrating a "proclamation addressed to the army...by their general." L'Art vivant, 2, no. 32 (15 Apr. 1926), p. 294.

visibly emitted cry from her gaping mouth resulted in the statue being interpreted as 'the Marseillaise.'[11]

After the Revolution of 1830, which brought Louis-Philippe to the throne, a growing number of female Liberties expressed the resurgence of Republican ideals. In 1831 the Salon exhibited Eugène Delacroix's "Liberty Leading the People at the Barricades" (1830) as well as several other lesser known works in plaster whose subjects were Liberty.[12] Poetry also celebrated the female figure of Liberty:

> The truth is that Liberty is not a countess
> From the noble Faubourg Saint-Germain,
> A woman who swoons away at the slightest cry
> And who wears powder and rouge.
> She is a strong woman with thrusting breasts,
> A harsh voice and a hard charm,
> Who, with her bronzed skin and her flashing eyes...
> Takes her lovers only from among the people[13]

In *Révolte* the women of the harem made the transition from powder and rouge to sun-bronzed skin quite literally. Moreover, Zulma's rejection of the King for a man of the people clearly placed her in Liberty's camp and in opposition to the tyrannical state. The immense popularity of the ballet may, in fact, be partially accounted for by its undertones of Republican fervor in a repressive time. For, as Agulhon points out, Louis Philippe's régime carefully avoided the female imagery that "would have provided the Republican opposition with rallying points tailor-made for whipping up Republican fervour."[14] In the ballet Republican sentiments could be safely reaffirmed behind the hypothetical and remote case of a women's war.

Such thinking leads to the speculation that, as part of a larger cultural system of symbols, the female liberation figure in the ballet evoked ideas of class liberation far more than equality between the sexes. At a time when male dancers were rapidly declining in importance, a revolt of the women would have been an innocuous vehicle for the affirmation of liberty, equality, and fraternity. The Moorish setting clinched it: the Orient versus the Occident, polygamy versus monogamy, a decadent old régime versus an enlightened new one, tyranny versus liberty—so the dichotomies stacked up, leaving little doubt that the discourse was more Republican than feminist.[15] In fact, the vacillation between the ballet's titles, *The Revolt of the Women* and *The Revolt of the Harem*, may have been in itself a sign of competing subtextual meanings.[16]

What Republican and Saint-Simonian imagery shared was "the glorification of a woman in the guise of a secular allegory quite distinct from—indeed opposed to—Christianity."[17] The Woman Messiah sought by the Compagnons was to have been an Eastern woman whose love, empathy, and preeminence among women marked her as a deliverer of womankind. Filippo Taglioni's Zulma, reserved for an outstanding fate because of her singular beauty, courage, and love, approximated this ideal. The public adulation and reverence surrounding Marie Taglioni and the messianic light in which she was cast by her father worked together to mythologize a new idol in Romantic terms.

Taglioni *père* could have read about the activities of the Saint-Simonian missionaries abroad in the group's *Livre des actes*.[18] He might have stumbled upon a copy of the journal *Tribune des femmes* (also published under other titles, such as *La Femme libre*), which circulated between 1832 and 1834,[19] and been intrigued by possible themes for a new ballet. In the very first issue of the journal he would have read: "We want marriage with equality.... Better celibacy than slavery!"[20] Indeed, this was close to the theme of the ballet, with the harem of the Moorish King of Granada symbolizing women's lack of matrimonial freedom in French society.

However, what the ballet scenario critiques, ultimately, is the lack of freedom in choosing a spouse, not inequality between spouses. Here, the tyrant is not so much the husband as the father. The domineering father who, oblivious to his children's desires, arranged marriages for them based on money brought another figure to mind: the monarch out of touch with the needs of his subjects and only concerned with his power base in the bourgeoisie. The stern, doddering family patriarch was an old theme in French literature dating back at least as far as Molière's works. In the nineteenth century the Napoleonic *Code civil* legally enshrined the father's exclusive control over his children's marital alliances, which meant that marriage was often based on consolidation of family assets rather than passion. Such thinking suggests that *Révolte* was more of a veiled protest against absolute patriarchal power than against inequality between the sexes and that economic or class issues were at the heart of the protest.

* * *

Révolte is set during the Moorish domination of Spain. Mahomet, King of Granada, honors Ismael, Commander of the Army, "the bravest of the sons of Granada, the deliverer of his fatherland."[21] Ismael has vanquished the Castilian Christians and enters triumphantly, followed by a large cortege. As a popular, conquering hero of the people, he resembles Napoleon. Mahomet, on the other hand, bears comparison, in his tyranny and polygamous lifestyle, with French monarchs of the old régime.

The harem dances before the King and his court. The basic conflict of the ballet is set up with the revelation that the King's favorite, Zulma, is also Ismael's beloved. As arbitrary rule is pitted against true love, the symbolism becomes clear: submission to kings is tantamount to slavery, while true love is synonymous with liberty. Zulma performs for the court, dance becoming a symbol of both enslavement and captivation. What could be more seductive? Like a kept woman, the slave is the ultimate enchainer of desire. Ismael returns at the head of a parade, and a throng of people tries to enter the palace with him. "The King orders [Ismael's guards] to permit everyone to enter, and men, women, and children rush all at once pell-mell into the room. Noisy tableau animated with popular joy."[22] Here is another subliminal identification of Mohamet with the Bourbon kings who allowed the popular classes to enter Versailles.

Another character of interest is introduced in the first act—Mina, Zulma's faithful Negress, who watches after her mistress's interests throughout the drama. Mina's self-effacing loyalty, her lack of any identity of her own, is ironic in the face of the ballet's message of liberty. However, since the liberal 1780s, the black female companion had been something of a stock figure in French ballet.[23] In *Révolte*, Mina's loyalty seems intended to authenticate Zulma's humanity. The scenario indicates that Mina was played by "Madame Elie," almost certainly the Louise Launer Elie who created the role of Old Madge the Sorceress in *La Sylphide* and specialized in matronly character parts.[24] The rendering by Maleuvre suggests that makeup, accoutrements, costume, and possibly even posture were used to represent blackness.

The second act of the ballet opened with a scene in the harem baths, a columned pavil-

Costume design for Mina (in the role of a "Negress") engraved by Maleuvre in the series Petite Galerie dramatique. *Beginning in the 1780s and continuing throughout the romantic period the black slave was a key figure in ballets about freedom from despotism. Dance Collection, New York Public Library for the Performing Arts, Astor, Lenox and Tilden Foundations.*

ion surrounding a white marble pool draped in gold. Women frolicked in the water with voluptuous abandon. The scene recalled, on one hand, the marble and gold fountains and statuary of Versailles; on the other, paintings by Ingres such as "Grande Odalisque" (1814) and "Interior of a Harem" (1828), which depicted a reclining odalisque and bathers in a harem.[25] Marilyn R. Brown has argued that Ingres's harem paintings recast the classical mythology of Venus into a new orientalist mythology, hinted at the popular imagery of contemporary Parisian prostitution, and implied "notion[s] of control consistent with then-current ideologies of the Orient and of womankind."[26] Similarly, *Révolte*, wrapped in a veil of Oriental mysticism, alluded to a contemporary urban phenomenon and played out a scenario of women's liberation that can only be described as highly ambiguous.

The bathers dressed behind a transparent gauze that augmented the scene's erotic interest. No doubt the many onstage costume changes indicated by the scenario coincided with notions about the female dancer's off-stage character. As Dr. Louis Véron, director of the Opéra from 1831 to 1835, once remarked: "It is perhaps to the young ladies of the Opéra particularly that one could apply that unpleasant and unmerited definition which someone has written of women in general: 'Woman is a creature who primps, babbles, and disrobes [*s'habille, babille, et se déshabille*].'"[27] In this scene of scantily dressed women (how were they clothed?), frolicking in the water and dressing and dancing amid burning incense (did they actually burn incense in the theater?), we can imagine a delicious blend of all-female eroticism and exoticism perfectly suited to a Romantic sensibility.[28] The Orient converged with female private space to create a pretext for racial and sexual voyeurism. However, the obsession with dress has a familiar French ring:

> As soon as she is dressed, each bather mingles in animated dances and surrenders herself with abandon to all the capricious attempts of coquetry. Some admire their beauty in portable mirrors; others, in various poses, form gracious tableaux, in the middle of which shines above all the lovely Zulma; at last, lacking nothing to seduce, their toilette is accomplished.[29]

The voyeuristic frame for this scene (similar to the first-act slave parade and the third-act pantomime, where the women bedeck themselves with rich fabrics and jewels) brings to mind a scene from *Lettres persanes*. Zachi reminds Usbek of the "famous quarrel between his women":

> Each of us pretended herself superior to the others in beauty. We presented ourselves before you after exhausting all that the imagination could furnish in dresses and jewels. You saw with pleasure the miracles of our art; you admired to what extremes we took the ardor to please you.... it was necessary to appear before you in the simplicity of nature. I didn't concern myself at all with modesty; I thought only of glory. Happy Usbek, what charms were spread before your eyes! We saw you wandering for a long time from enchantment to enchantment...you carried your curious

regards in the most secret places; you had us pass in a second into a thousand different situations: always new commandments and always a new obeisance.[30]

As in *Révolte*, the harem women of Montesquieu's epistolary novel revolt against their social condition. However, as this quotation makes clear, it was the imagery of female bodies obedient to the whim of male desire that made the novel's lengthy philosophical tracts palatable. In fact, the work was really Montesquieu's treatise on the flaws of coercive government and regulation of will; in his mind, oppressive bonds between humans were maintained equally by Oriental polygamy, lack of divorce in France, and monarchical absolutism. Abby R. Kleinbaum has pointed out that Montesquieu used the confinement of women in harems as a metaphor for the absence of male liberty under despotic governments.[31]

Now, a little women's history will tell us that what was happening here was that the *querelle des femmes*—women's quarrel, starting in the fifteenth century and continuing through the eighteenth, with men's deprecation of women[32]—was being commuted into a *querelle entre les femmes* (or quarrel among women). This theme was even more evident in Marivaux's *La Colonie* (1729), where a women's revolt degenerated into petty quarrels and contests of vanity, reassuring its patrons that women were constitutionally incapable of assembling for the purposes of self-determination.[33] Meanwhile, eighteenth-century ballets had their share of stock scenes of jealousy in the harem: the entrée "Les Fleurs, Feste persane" ("The Flowers, Persian Festival") from Rameau's opera-ballet *Les Indes galantes* (The Gallant Indies) (1735); Noverre's *Les Fêtes, ou Les Jalousies du sérail* (The Festivities, or Jealousy in the Harem); and Sébastien Gallet's *Les Circonstances embarrassantes* (Embarrassing Circumstances) (1796), to name a few.[34] What was so riveting about Taglioni's 1833 harem ballet was the way it combined old themes of women's vanity, competition for the place of favorite, and revolt against despotic tyranny with new themes of militarization and class consciousness that reflected the historical experience of two revolutions. Yet, while championing the general revolutionary spirit, *Révolte* distorted, trivialized, and transformed into escapist fantasy the reality of women's political activity during the 1789 Revolution and in Paris of the 1830s.

Darlene Levy has proposed that, in the period from 1789 to 1793, women used clothing as a form of political discourse; their gestures in dress were intended to proclaim their desired political identity as citizens. Levy has offered examples in terms of jewelry, arms, and headdress: a delegation of *femmes artistes* offered their jewels to the nation as a gift to reduce national debt; a deputation led by Pauline Léon demanded the right of women to bear arms; the Republican Revolutionary Women lobbied for a decree requiring all women to wear the tricolor cockade. In each case, women attempted to parlay the symbolic vestments of power into real political power. Responses to such efforts were ambivalent, as popular visual representations indicate, with some stressing patriotic fervor and others treating the entire discourse with parody.[35]

Révolte resumed this 1790s discourse in dress, preserving elements of both its serious and mock tones and adding its own Romantic-age fascination with gender ambiguity.[36] Scenes that were memorable to audiences and critics capitalized on the play of gender signs. "They deny us liberty," cries Zulma, "well then, it is necessary to conquer it!"[37] Lances appear with a wave of a magic bouquet. The women arm themselves and brandish their weapons with "a menacing air and express the bellicose ardor inspiring them in a warrior dance." But when Myssouf, the Chief Eunuch, returns with guards, "the lances change into lyres, and the warrior dance gives way suddenly to a graceful one."[38] Overabundant female sexuality seeps through ascetic male surface. The "voluptuous dances" fool the guards, who depart, leaving only Myssouf. Suddenly, upon a signal from Zulma, the women tie him up with their scarves; the lances reappear. Zulma fixes her bouquet to the end of her lance with her scarf, "whose folds float at the mercy of the wind like a flag."[39]

The ballet catered to the Romantic taste for androgynous depictions of women. As voluptuous courtesans were transformed into ascetic warriors, costumes and choreography hinted at hermaphroditic and polymorphous pleasures. Woman's sexuality rather than her liberation was the subject here. Ironically, as objects of seduction (lyres, scarves, flowers) became instruments of war (weapons, manacles, flag), seductiveness and menace were intertwined. The metaphor of women's coquetry as a weapon harked back to Jacobin rhetoric for stripping women of political rights.

Mixed gender signs were also conveyed by the visual images appearing on the title page of the scenario and on a handbill. The title page contains a figure that is a melange of turban, sword, drapery, shield, bow, arrow, and long tresses. Objects lay on top of each other, jutting out in opposing directions, suggesting both gender crossing and conflict between the sexes. The handbill has two lances piercing outward, arrowheads exposed, from a center lyre. Around the base of the lances are twining stems with flowers, leaves, and grapes.[40]

Act II ends with a scene of class alliance—the harem women fleeing in boats with the women of the people. Act III moves from the interior rooms of the palace, where the harem has been confined, to a military encampment at a "wild and picturesque" site in the Alpuxares mountains. Here, with "bivouac fires"[41] burning from mountainside to mountainside, the warrior women are equipping themselves for battle. Female rebels or bandits in the mountains or other remote, uncivilized regions were a popular theme in the Romantic period.[42] In *Révolte*, as in other ballets, the sex role reversal created a sense of surprise and awe: the inversion of the natural was good theater. The audience saw women building palisades around the camp, standing watch, guarding rifles that stood in piles under the moonlight. At the sound of a march, detachments of women emerged from all directions. Female commanders gave orders, and female platoons placed themselves in battle formations, horizontals that invoked—and contradicted—the usual female position during intercourse. (Somewhat later, courtesans would be called *les grandes horizontales*.) The symmetry of the inversion—women doing everything men did—relied upon the asymmetry of gender roles in French society for its effect. Moonlight enhanced the sense of a dreamy, unreal realm.

Zulma is the general-in-chief of this army, which, in the words of the libretto, "renders her military honors."[43] She passes through the ranks and inspects the troops, correcting posture and carriage of arms (more male signs in movement and gesture performed by female bodies that depended upon anomaly or displacement of the normal for their theatrical effect). The women's shawls and scarves serve as bedding, enhancing the sense of escapist fantasy, a magic never-never land. A second handbill, subtitling the work a *ballet-féerie* or fairy ballet, emphasized even more the magical, unreal tone.[44]

When Ismael enters, he tries to coax Zulma into escaping with him and allowing him to be her protector. But Zulma will not be a coward and violate her oaths to her loyal followers. Ismael removes her helmet and arms, and Zulma is about to yield...when the sound of

Feminism or phallic fetishism? Costume design for Zulma, Act III, engraved by Maleuvre in the series Petite Galerie dramatique. *Dance Collection, New York Public Library for the Performing Arts, Astor, Lenox and Tilden Foundations.*

bugles recalls her to duty. Thus, Zulma sways back and forth between male and female roles—disarmed and rearmed in another play of gender imagery. The scene is predicated upon an additional reversal of gender roles, for in Western literature it is the female seductress who weakens the will of the male warrior.

Mahomet has sent an emissary to propose peace. He wants to reestablish "harmony between the two sexes,"[45] a phrase evocative of Saint-Simonian rhetoric. He offers the olive branch. At this, according to the libretto, "[t]he general [Zulma] assembles her lieutenants, has them form a circle as for a council of war, and deliberates with them."[46] In his memoirs, Véron recalled the amused reception of this scene:

> In *La Révolte au Sérail*, during the corps de ballet's military maneuvers, a council of war with the commanding officers assembles onstage. The program offers no further explanation. When Mademoiselle [Pauline] Duvernay was entrusted with one of the principal roles, by the most subtle kind of pantomime and the most expressive and impassioned gestures, she suc-

ceeded in conveying the picture of an animated discussion and in giving an idea of a council of war held by women. A general laugh and bursts of applause greeted this cheerful and amusing scenic play. By her mime, the young dancer had added the happiest and liveliest touch to the scenario.[47]

Véron's reminiscence corroborates the idea that the spectacle of women performing military maneuvers and formations reserved for men was received in a light-hearted vein.

As a condition of peace, the demand that the women put forth—that "[a]ll women...be free"—appears radical enough. However, the message of the ballet becomes clearer when we learn the meaning of this freedom: women "will be able to give their heart to the lover who pleases them" and marry the man they love.[48] Thus, *Révolte* continued a theme popular in ballets of the 1820s: the triumph of true love over corrupt power, be this of parents, aristocrats, or the dictates of society.[49]

Moreover, instead of ending here on a note of strategic victory, the ballet resorts to the old antifeminist stereotype of women's vanity. When the King presents the rebels with sumptuous fabrics and chests of jewels, they drop their arms and break ranks as "[c]aution gives way to coquetry":

> Some grab rich fabrics which they drape around themselves gracefully; others prefer necklaces and bracelets and crowd around to choose those they like best....[W]ho will be the most beautiful...who, by her lustre, will eclipse her rival? During this assault of coquetry, the King's guards slip furtively behind the women and skillfully seize their arms.[50]

From female vanity, the stereotypes multiply: the compulsive desire for luxury, coquetry, disarmed availability.[51] And as sorority succumbs to female rivalry, the men retake their legitimate domain. Again, the scenario shows its intent to use gender sign switching as sensuous theatrical device rather than as serious social statement.

Now, after thunder, lightning, and a darkening of the stage, the Spirit of Womankind (*Génie des Femmes*) and her Court appear. A dazzling light illuminates this tableau. The Spirit orders the King to consent to the marriage of Zulma and Ismael and forbids him from oppressing women in the future. Finally, the Spirit points out the advantage of having two armies instead of one. The ballet ends with Zulma taking her army through military maneuvers. It is telling that women have won this rebellion through spiritual or magical means rather than by force or military know-how.

Exactly what have they won? The right to bear arms? Tossed in at the end, this has not been a point of contention until now. The handling of rifles has merely provided a touch of phallic fetishism. Maleuvre's rendering of Zulma's costume in Act III fetishizes and phallicizes the ballerina's breasts and groin area, thus reinforcing the idea that this has been the point of the ballet all along. Truly, this is the visual image of the "assault of coquetry"; woman's power is strangely undone by the refusal to see it in anything but sexual terms. The moral of the story has been woman's right to chose her marriage partner, not her right to defend her liberty with arms.

Révolte, like Saint-Simonianism, challenged women's lack of freedom with regard to sexual choice. This, however, was largely defined in male terms: a woman should love a man freely so he would be loved truly and without ulterior motive. Nevertheless, the Saint-Simonians did believe that women were oppressed by restrictive sexual mores and that greater sexual freedom would ameliorate their lot. In this, they clearly challenged the monogamous ideal. The ballet, on the other hand, ended in monogamous coupling, virtuously exclusive. And while the revolt in the ballet was directed against the slavery of living in the King's polygamous establishment, the most liberal leaders among the Saint-Simonians advocated a kind of free love that allowed for multiple sex partners. They believed that some people were inconstant by nature and should be free to act upon their changing desires. (In some ways, utopian socialism was a sequel to eighteenth-century libertinism, in which political freethinking was linked to sexual license.) Yet, the plot of the ballet was propelled by the utter constancy of the heroine. Indeed, it was less about liberating female sexuality from male control, than about overthrowing a corrupt established power. And paradoxically, just as Saint-Simonian men exploited the increased availability of sex from Saint-Simonian women, the ballet exploited displays of available women under male domination.

More gender ambiguity: Zéir, the King's page, was played by a woman dancer, Pauline Leroux. Costume design engraved by Maleuvre in the series Petite Galerie dramatique. *Dance Collection, New York Public Library for the Performing Arts, Astor, Lenox and Tilden Foundations.*

The harem had a long history in French ballet by the early nineteenth century. Its illicit sexuality conveyed multiple meanings: the promiscuous lifestyle of the *ancien régime*; the middle class system for sexual outlet—kept mistresses, extramarital affairs, a thriving brothel industry; and finally, the degradation of women workers forced to prostitute themselves (see below). The harem was a symbol that the time was out of joint; something was rotten in France. In 1808, Charles Fourier, architect of Fourierism, another brand of utopian socialism, published his scathing critique of bourgeois society.[52] Fourier equated social progress with the progress of women toward liberty. In his scheme, society passed through stages—Barbarism, Civilization, and Harmony—that were defined by women's sexuality, whether this was experienced in harems, monogamous marriage, or free love.[53] He saw the hypocrisy and fraud of monogamous marriage, with its "secret insurrection" of adultery, as a measure of a society in collapse.[54]

As suggested earlier, the slavery of the harem could also be read as a symbol of loveless, arranged, bourgeois marriage. This last analogy leads us back to Saint-Simonianism. Indissoluble marriage was a prime target of its social critique. In the ballet, as in utopian socialist discourse, marriage stood for some larger social critique. In fact, as a symbol of arranged marriage of convenience (for economically corrupt ends), it represented a working-class critique of the bourgeoisie. True love, allied to the social mores of the people, was a symbol of social regeneration.

Several contextual factors affected how *Révolte* worked as a class critique. One was the economic context of the unrestricted growth of capitalism and the proletarianization of the working class. Another was the symbolic use of marriage, family, and working women to convey class viewpoints and wage class struggle. In the midst of this economic climate and these larger symbolic systems, the Romantic ballet had a symbolic coherence of its own: here, true love and marriage of interest had special meanings. Finally, the harem heroines in the ballet mirrored the economic condition of ballet dancers, who belonged, for the most part, to the working class. I will consider each of these factors in turn.

Joan Wallach Scott discusses the proletarianization of workers in the Parisian garment trades in the 1830s and 1840s.[55] Traditionally, tailors, dressmakers, and seamstresses were skilled workers, learning their trades in studios, workshops, or shops (*ateliers*) under the supervision of masters. This organization of work provided them with training and decent wages. With the growth of the ready-made clothing industry, garments were mass-produced in standardized sizes. Craft expectations declined; home work became widespread; wages fell. Custom tailors and dressmakers could not compete with the new manufacturers, who purchased raw materials in bulk and paid unskilled workers meager wages. The 1830s and the 1840s saw numerous strikes, as workers protested the ruthless competition that forced them out of shops and into their homes to work endless hours and earn below-subsistence wages.

Images of the family in the period's working-class literature of protest registered bitter criticism of capitalism. Ideal love was pitted against loveless bourgeois marriage for gain. While concerns of dowry, wealth, and inheritance underlay bourgeois family relationships, working-class marriage was simply based on affection.[56] Indeed, during Louis Philippe's "bourgeois monarchy," marriages allied family enterprises in business, administration, and technology, leading to a concentration of wealth at the upper end of the social scale and the pauperization of the working class at the lower end.[57] Thus, marriage became a symbol of the social fabric, signifying either the rapacious greed of capitalism or the working-class ideal of social reorganization. Harmony (between the sexes and

between classes), association (cooperative, regulated economic relationships), and fraternity (brotherhood of skilled workers) were key words of
the working-class polemic.[58]

Was the revolt of the harem an exposé of prerevolutionary aristocratic
sexual license and corrupt, decadent monarchy? Or did the ideal love of
the protagonists and the dismantling of the harem offer a critique of middle-class self-aggrandizement and exploitation of the working class and
the female sex? I think to some extent the ballet straddled these two perspectives, reflecting the diverse class viewpoints of its audiences. However, three kinds of further evidence convince me that economic discourse
(and class struggle) was indeed at the heart of the ballet's subtext.

The first is found in the wider symbolic system of the Romantic ballet.
If we reconsider *La Sylphide* (1832) in terms of economic analysis, the
theme of ideal love or love without material interest in opposition to
mundane bourgeois marriage becomes apparent. In *Le Diable boiteux*
(1836) the devoted grisette, a working-class figure, is held up as the ideal,
in contrast to the fickle ballerina, a courtesan figure, and the scheming
middle-class widow, who seeks a marriage of interest. And in *Giselle*
(1841), the acme of the Romantic ballet, a peasant girl's love for an aristocratic libertine is destroyed by his family, intent on marrying him off to a
social equal. The powers that be are corrupt because of their association
with personal gain, while ideal love is the force of social regeneration. The
discourse of liberation here was distinctly working class. The Romantics
appropriated this discourse to express their disenchantment with the
materialism and philistinism of bourgeois life.

Révolte also invoked the discourse of the vulnerable female wage earner,[59] a figure recalled again and again in the pages of the working-class *Tribune des femmes*:

> [Prostitution] is with that unhappy young woman who fights against mis-
> ery by obstinately holding down a job that does not, however, pay enough
> to relieve her from the hunger that devours her, until she sells herself to
> the vulture—who watches for her moment of distress—for a piece of
> bread that, sobbing, the girl brings home to her old, sick mother.[60]

Elsewhere, the writer argued that privileged women were equally prostitutes, because their fathers forced them to marry for money. Her purpose
was to expose male hypocrisy, rehabilitate women in the eyes of society,
and champion female equality in a new social order. The theme of the
defenseless female wage earner was also invoked much earlier, during the
Revolution, for a variety of political purposes. Appearing in petitions to
the government written by women, it was intended to improve their economic condition.[61] However, when used by political economists in the
1840s and 1850s, the image of the miserable woman worker would serve to
advocate regulation of capitalism along with familial control of women.[62]

For the purpose of analyzing the subtextual meanings of *Révolte*, the
connection between prostitution and women living and working outside

the domain of the family is important. Issues of encroaching capitalism were of far more immediate concern to French society than issues of morality in Moorish harems. On a superficial level one could read into the harem the decadence of prerevolutionary aristocratic society, with its promiscuity and publicly displayed libertinism. This put the critique at a distance, although the fears it addressed were also remote. On a deeper level, the harem represented the exploitative forces of capitalism that unleashed women's sexuality in a society that measured order by its control of women's sexuality.[63] Thus, the harem slave symbolized the working woman who lived outside the protection of the family. She was a *femme isolée*, the miserable and vulnerable woman worker who fell into prostitution to make ends meet.

What the ballet shared with the political-economic polemic was the "metaphoric use of female sexuality" to narrate class relations.[64] In other words, prostitution, with its display of the degradation of women, served as a symbol of other social evils, thereby deflecting attention from its root cause in women's oppressed economic condition. Obscuring women's economic plight, the metaphor invited restructuring of class relations along with patriarchal safeguards to control women's sexuality. The ballet's implied resolution, Zulma's marriage of love to a hero of the people, safely contained and set right female sexuality.

Next, consider this harem ballet vis-à-vis the economic circumstances of the ballerinas who performed as harem slaves. The members of the corps de ballet were generally from the working class.[65] In his memoirs, Véron goes on at length about the easy virtue of the Opéra dancers, comparing them to the courtesans of Rome.[66] But mingled with this old archetype of decadence is a more recent one—that of the easily seduced woman worker:

> In the corps de ballet, on the other hand, as I have already indicated, one encounters at once the deepest misery followed by sudden wealth complete with steady incomes, carriages, and diamonds. In backstage parlance, every income, every annuity, is called a "paper." And a young dancer, to excuse her first fall from virtue, will tell you with pride, "But I have a paper." One cannot imagine the privations, suffering, fatigue, and courage of those poor girls on whom fortune has not yet smiled. Hope alone sustains them. They say to themselves, laughingly, "I suffer today, but perhaps I shall be rich tomorrow".... I paid many compliments to one mother on her young daughter, whose beauty was growing every day. "We are very unfortunate, nonetheless," she told me, "and I have to give her to whoever wants her, just to have enough to eat."[67]

The irony, of course, is that Véron profited twice from this situation—first as director of the house, then as scandalmonger. For what he does not mention is that he created the management policy that openly abetted liaisons between the ballerinas and season subscribers by giving the latter access to the Foyer de la Danse.[68] Then he used his privileged role as an inside observer to regale the public with the immodest ways of the ballerinas.

Audience members who mingled with the dancers in the Foyer de la Danse would surely sense the underlying rightness of casting them as courtesans who danced for the pleasure of the court: it made the performance that much more titillating. Ivor Guest describes these gallants as "young men-about-town...for the most part members of the Jockey Club, [who] acquired the habit of looking on the *coulisses* of the Opera as their private seraglio."[69] Albéric Second, in *Les Petits Mystères de l'Opéra* (1844), observed: "The Opéra provides them with their amorous pleasures, just as the Pompadour stud-farm provides them with their equestrian pleasures; they consider it as a storehouse for remounts, no more."[70] After all, Véron had believed that the Opéra would become the Versailles of the bourgeoisie.[71] In a ballet like *Révolte*, art certainly held a mirror to reality.

A third type of evidence, although indirect, supports the argument that *Révolte* contained an economic subtext. This is a one-act "burlesque ballet opera" performed in England entitled *The Revolt of the Workhouse*. Written by Gilbert Abbott à Beckett, it opened at the Fitzroy Theatre on 24 February 1834,[72] exactly nineteen days after *La Révolte au sérail* premiered in England at the Theatre Royal, Covent Garden.[73]

The characters of the burlesque rather obviously caricature those of the original work. Mahomet Muggins, Master of the Workhouse, is the counterpart of Mahomet, King of Granada; Ismael Skullcrack, Beadle-in-Chief, corresponds to Ismael, Commander of the Army; and Myssouf Sheepshanks, Clerk to the Establishment, takes the place of Myssouf, Chief of the Eunuchs. The harem slaves have become female paupers, market women put out of business by ruthless forces and now confined to the workhouse. There is even a "pauper Negress," played as a dame role by a Mr. Oxberry, presumably in blackface. Zulma is replaced by two characters: Araminta, betrothed to Skullcrack, and Moll Chubb, Commander-in-Chief of the Female Revolters (played, again *en travestie*, by a Mr. Mitchell).

The bath scene was replaced by a "washing room" scene. Instead of a white marble pool, "an enormous pump" was at center stage, and the paupers played with soapsuds.[74] The scene where lances became lyres received an equally pedestrian translation: the beadles' staves became brooms. Here, as in the ballet, male symbols were feminized in the process of concealment: the beadle's stave, a symbol of public order, was converted into a symbol of household order. The burlesque worked by juxtaposing indigence with the sumptuousness of the ballet's setting:

> [Sally.]   Because, if dirt but constituted lands—
>
> Judy.   You'd have a whole estate upon your hands![75]

Hints of sexual harassment by male workhouse sultans also link the ballet and the burlesque:

[Muggins.] Well, valiant Skullcrack, don't the paupers' charms
         Make one disposed to seek their precious arms?[76]

Moll.   They soap us first; and when they closer gather us,
         Who knows but they may also want to lather us?[77]

By replacing the harem revolt—something fantastic and escapist—with a workhouse "row"—which reflected real social conditions—the burlesque mocked the apparent naiveté and thin Moorish facade of the original. And it identified the real issue at stake—worker exploitation (put in terms of the sexual harassment of women)—thus exposing the economic subtext of the ballet.

Ten years later, in *Condition of the Working Classes in England*, Friedrich Engels would use the harem as a symbol of worker exploitation put in terms of female degradation: "most of the prostitutes of the town," he wrote, "had their employment in the mills to thank for their present situation.... If the master is mean enough,... his mill is also his harem."[78] Thus, like the French political economists, Engels used woman as a central symbol in the critique of capitalism. Similarly, in the ballet, the revolt of the harem symbolized Republican/working-class liberation. By 1833, France was no stranger to worker unrest. The revolt and harsh suppression of the Lyon silk workers in 1831 prompted a wave of sympathy for Republican opposition to the Orleanist regime.[79] There is more than a coincidental likeness between Mahomet, with his false edicts, and the wholesale merchants who signed a minimum wage agreement they later refused to honor.[80] Moreover, in 1833–1834 male labor unrest was growing because large numbers of women were entering the work force to operate the steam-powered machinery.[81]

The harem was a symbol with a long history in the ballet that had particular meanings in the 1830s, though these were ambiguous and could be read from middle-class or working-class perspectives. Nonetheless, what is clear is that Taglioni's harem revolt represented class struggle rather than women's liberation. Women earning their keep outside the family symbolized anomie, displacement, and corruption. True love or the restoration of the family was the implied solution.

As the final and perhaps most crucial test of the feminism of *Révolte*, let us place it beside ideas of women's liberation as they were voiced by women themselves. In 1832, two Saint-Simonian women founded the *Tribune des femmes*, a journal with the express purpose of publishing articles only by women:[82] "[W]hat we want above all is for women to shake off the state of restraint and discomfort in which society holds them, and to dare to say from the complete sincerity of their heart what they foresee and want for the future."[83] In their writings these women revealed a "totally feminine consciousness."[84] They deliberately sought to avoid male influence, encourage the expression of diverse opinions, and to act according to their "own free will."[85] To emphasize their freethinking, they signed their writings with only their first names.[86] Hence, their writings are a valuable source for a feminist analysis based on women's voices in France of the 1830s.

In these texts women's economic dependency was a central concern. Marie-Reine (Reine Guindorf, one of the journal's founders) clearly enunciated the connection between women's lack of material independence and her lack of freedom: "As long as a man provides us our material needs, he can also demand that in exchange we submit to whatever he desires, and it is very difficult to speak freely when a woman does not have the means to live independently."[87] The women who wrote for the *Tribune* saw the right to earn money in the workplace as basic to any sort of social equity. The moral question—the freedom to mate according to one's desire—paled next to the importance of the economic one. Some women hinted that the Saint-Simonian emphasis on true love was actually a detour on the path to equality.

These utopian socialist women viewed association between women as the key to economic independence. Women would be emancipated by association "because their means of existence [would] no longer depend on their fathers or their husbands."[88] Thus, the cure for sexual degradation was a social restructuring that would provide a stronger economic base for women. Their vision of women finding strength in union, work, and property ownership was a far cry from a return to the protection of the patriarchal family.

Moreover, they attacked the very foundations of the monogamous, patriarchal family unit—rights of inheritance and private property, legal definitions of the marital relationship, paternal authority over children, the double standard regarding extramarital sex, indissoluble marriage, women's performance of household and maternal duties without recompense. They challenged the subjugation of a wife to her husband's will. The feminists who emerged from the Saint-Simonian movement wanted, above all, a world in which a woman's "first love" was not her "whole destiny"[89]—the very state of affairs idealized by *Révolte*.

Yet the reason Saint-Simonian ideas had attracted these women (and the essence of their hope for liberation) was the promise of "the rehabilitation of stigmatized flesh."[90] For it was the bondage of shame that most held women in thrall. The feminists of the *Tribune* saw through the disparagement used to control women, a disparagement to which working-class women were particularly susceptible. They saw through the hypocrisy of men who made women bear the burden of shame for the injustices they themselves had inflicted. "For a long time our protectors have taken advantage of the power they obtain from this title only to seduce, judge, and condemn us."[91] Even if a working woman managed to remain chaste in a world that offered her little more than starvation and constant danger, it did not matter; she would still be perceived as fallen simply because she was downtrodden. "Because this world even associates shame with poverty and makes people feel they have to apologize for being poor."[92] An end to social prejudice that oppressed women by degrading them in the eyes of the world: this was what the feminists of the 1830s sought.

Yet *Révolte* was subtly premised upon woman's shame—her sexual-economic bondage. Even though the plot showed Zulma liberating herself from immoral chains, the production elements of the ballet trumpeted images of female sexuality and prostitution. Grounded in female shame and ending with a return to the traditional family unit, *Révolte* cannot be considered a feminist ballet. At best, it delivered mixed messages with regard to women's liberation. By invoking a discourse of class liberation in which the working woman was a symbol of sexual exploitation, the ballet actually skirted the issues. Like the political and socialist agendas of the period, it shifted the focus toward solutions that, far from alleviating the plight of nineteenth-century women, led to their continued repression and hardship.

The author would like to thank Judith Chazin-Bennahum and Madelyn Gutwirth for their many valuable comments.

Notes

1. See Cyril W. Beaumont, *Complete Book of Ballets* (London: Putnam, 1937), p. 118: "*La Révolte au sérail* is the first and, for a century, remained, the only ballet to deal with the emancipation of women."
2. For an excellent collection of documents, see Claire Goldberg Moses and Leslie Wahl Rabine, trans. and eds., *Feminism, Socialism, and French Romanticism* (Bloomington, Ind.: Indiana University Press, 1993); for an excellent historical account, see Claire Goldberg Moses, *French Feminism in the Nineteenth Century* (Albany, N.Y.: State University of New York Press, 1984).
3. [Filippo] Taglioni, *La Révolte des femmes: ballet en trois actes*, 2nd ed. (Paris: J.-N. Barba, 1934), pp. 28–29. Translations from the French are my own.
4. Moses and Rabine, p. 282.
5. Jeanne-Victoire [Jeanne Deroin], quoted in Moses and Rabine, p. 283.
6. For further elaboration on the stages of the Saint-Simonian movement and the "new Christianity," see Moses, pp. 42–45.
7. *Ibid.*, p. 50; Moses and Rabine, p. 234n.
8. [Jules Janin], review of *Brésila, ou Brésilia*, by [Filippo] Taglioni, in *Le Journal des Débats*, 13 Apr. 1935. See also Erik Aschengreen, *The Beautiful Danger: Facets of the Romantic Ballet*, trans. Patricia N. McAndrew, *Dance Perspectives*, 58 (1974), p. 17.
9. See Charles Wayland Lightbody, *The Judgements of Joan: Joan of Arc, A Study in Cultural History* (Cambridge, Mass.: Harvard University Press, 1961).
10. Maurice Agulhon, *Marianne into Battle: Republican Imagery and Symbolism in France, 1789–1880*, trans. Janet Lloyd (New York: Cambridge University Press, 1981).

11. *Ibid.*, p. 45.

12. *Ibid.*, p. 39.

13. Auguste Barbier, "La Curée," quoted *ibid.*, p. 40.

14. *Ibid.*, p. 46.

15. For some connections between East/West and gender symbolism see *ibid.*, p. 41.

16. Jules Janin's review of the ballet published on 6 December 1833 in *Le Journal des Débats* calls it *La Révolte au sérail*, as does the review published in *Le Moniteur* on the same date. *Le Constitutionnel* (6 December) clears up the confusion by mentioning that while the playbill promises a ballet entitled *La Révolte au sérail*, the libretto announces *La Révolte des femmes*. According to this critic, the second title is worth more, because it makes the sex of the mutineers known. He suggests that the pantomime leaves him in doubt as to what caused the revolt.

17. Agulhon, p. 57.

18. This journal appears to have been available in 1833. See Moses and Rabine, p. 228.

19. *Ibid.*, p. 282.

20. *Ibid.*, p. 283.

21. Taglioni, p. 10.

22. *Ibid.*, p. 18.

23. She appeared, for instance, in *Mirza* (1788) and *Manon Lescaut* (1830). See Judith Chazin-Bennahum, *Dance in the Shadow of the Guillotine* (Carbondale, Ill.: Southern Illinois University Press, 1988), p. 143, and [Jean Aumer], *Manon Lescaut, ballet-pantomime en trois actes*, (Paris: Bezou, 1830), p. 31. Interestingly, Marie Taglioni played the part of the slave Niuka in *Manon*.

24. See Beaumont, *Complete Book*, pp. 77, 94, 104. However, he lists "Mlle. Elie" as playing the role of Mina (p. 111); the libretto I consulted (2nd ed.) had "Mme Elie" listed.

25. See *Musée National du Louvre: Peintures école française XIXe siècle* (Paris: Editions des Musées Nationaux, 1960), 2–3, pls. 398, 400, 404, and pp. 5–7 of the "Catalogue Sommaire."

26. Marilyn R. Brown, "The Harem Dehistoricized: Ingres' *Turkish Bath*," *Arts Magazine*, no. 61 (June 1987), p. 59.

27. Quoted in Victoria Huckenpahler, "Confessions of an Opera Director: Chapters from the *Mémoires* of Dr. Louis Véron," Pt. 2, *Dance Chronicle*, 7, no. 2 (1984), p. 198. Huckenpahler's work includes translations of excerpts from Dr. Louis Véron, *Mémoires d'un bourgeois de Paris* (Paris: Librairie Nouvelle, 1857).

28. Lynn Garafola says "[t]he fantasy of females at play for the male eye is a staple of erotic literature, a kind of travesty performance enacted in the privacy of the imagination." See "The Travesty Dancer in Nineteenth-Century Ballet," *Dance Research Journal*, 17, no. 2, and 18, no. 1 (1985–1986), p. 39.

29. Taglioni, p. 19.

30. Charles de Secondat, Baron de Montesquieu, *Lettres persanes* (Paris: Flammarion, 1992), pp. 21–22.

31. Abby R. Kleinbaum, "Women in the Age of Light," *Becoming Visible: Women in European History*, eds. Renate Bridenthal and Claudia Koonz (Boston: Houghton Mifflin, 1977), p. 221.

32. See Joan Kelly, "Early Feminist Theory and the *Querelle des Femmes*, 1400–1789," *Signs: Journal of Women in Culture and Society*, 8, no. 1 (1982).

33. Pierre Carlet de Chamblain de Marivaux, *La Colonie: Comédie en un acte et en prose*, *Théâtre complet* (Paris: Editions Gallimard, 1949), pp. 639–671.

34. [Jean-Philippe Rameau], *Les Indes galantes, ballet héroïque* (Paris: Ballard, 1736); [Jean-Georges] Noverre, *Lettres sur la danse et les arts imitateurs* (n.p.: Editions Lieutier, 1952), pp. 243–248; Chazin-Bennahum, pp. 141, 149.

35. Darline Levy, "Do Clothes Make the Women? Gender, Dress, and Civic Virtue," paper presented at National Endowment for the Humanities Summer Seminar: Women's Place: Women, Marriage, Sex, and Reproduction in Eighteenth-Century France, State University of New York, Stony Brook, 6 Aug. 1996. See also Darline Gay Levy, Harriet Branson Applewhite, and Mary Durham Johnson, trans. and eds., *Women in Revolutionary Paris 1789–1795* (Urbana, Ill.: University of Illinois Press, 1979).

36. Théophile Gautier would give prime examples of the Romantic taste for gender ambiguity in his hermaphroditic descriptions of Fanny Elssler (1838) and in his novel *Mademoiselle de Maupin* (1835). See *Gautier on Dance*, trans. and ed. Ivor Guest (London: Dance Books, 1986), p. 32.

37. Taglioni, p. 26.

38. *Ibid.*, p. 27.

39. *Ibid.*, p. 28.

40. "La Révolte au sérail, Ballet-pantomime en trois actes" [handbill], BN-Opéra.

41. Taglioni, p. 30.

42. For sources of the bandit milieu and female banditry in painting, comic opera, and drama, see Susan Au, "The Bandit Ballerina: Some Sources of Jules Perrot's *Catarina*," *Dance Research Journal*, 10, no. 2 (1979), pp. 2–5. Au explains the Romantic fascination with the female bandit as follows: "The fascination with bandits and their lawless lives may have grown out of the Romantic restlessness and desire to escape from the conventions and restrictions of daily life. Women in particular were constrained by the implicit rules and regulations imposed upon respectable wives and mothers; thus, the image of a female bandit seemed doubly liberating" (p. 3).

43. Taglioni, p. 31.

44. "Analyse de La Révolte au sérail, Ballet-féerie en 3 actes" [handbill], BN-Opéra.

45. Taglioni, p. 35.

46. *Ibid.*

47. Quoted in Huckenpahler, p. 210.

48. Taglioni, p. 36.

49. See John Chapman, "An Unromantic View of Nineteenth-Century Romanticism," *York Dance Review*, no. 7 (1978), pp. 39–40.

50. Taglioni, p. 37.

51. Regarding the stereotype of the woman disarmed, see Kelly, p. 28.

52. See Jonathan Beecher, *Charles Fourier: The Visionary and His World* (Berkeley: University of Califorma Press, 1986), pp. 425–430.

53. Charles Fourier, "Théorie de Quatre Mouvements," in *Design for Utopia: Selected Writings of Charles Fourier*, ed. Charles Gide, trans. Julia Franklin (New York: Schocken, 1971), p. 77.

54. Charles Fourier, "Amorous Anarchy," *The Utopian Vision of Charles Fourier: Selected Texts on Work, Love, and Passionate Attraction*, eds. and trans. Jonathan Beecher and Richard Bienvenu (Boston: Beacon Press, 1971), p. 172.

55. Joan Wallach Scott, "Men and Women in the Parisian Garment Trades: Discussions of Family and Work in the 1830s and 1840s," in *The Power of the Past: Essays for Eric Hobsbawm*, eds. Pat Thane, Geoffrey Crossick, and Roderick Floud (New York: Cambridge University Press, 1984), pp. 67–93.

56. *Ibid.*, p. 85.

57. André Jardin and André-Jean Tudesq, *Restoration and Reaction, 1815–1848*, trans. Elborg Forster (Cambridge: Cambridge University Press, 1983), pp. 170, 174–176.

58. See Scott, p. 67.

59. See Joan W. Scott, "'L'Ouvrière! Mot Impie, Sordide...': Women Workers in the Discourse of French Political Economy, 1840–1860," in *The Historical Meanings of Work*, ed. Patrick Joyce (New York: Cambridge University Press, 1987), pp. 119–142.

60. Christine-Sophie, *Tribune des femmes*, in Moses and Rabine, p. 288.

61. See Levy, Applewhite, and Johnson, pp. 19, 69.

62. Scott, "'L'Ouvrière! Mot Impie, Sordide...,'" p. 126.

63. *Ibid.*, p. 131.

64. *Ibid.*

65. John V. Chapman, "The Paris Opera Ballet School, 1798–1827," *Dance Chronicle*, 12, no. 2 (1989), p. 207. See also Huckenpahler, pp. 210–211.

66. Quoted in Huckenpahler, pp. 198–203.

67. Quoted *ibid.*, pp. 210–211.

68. See Victoria Huckenpahler, "Confessions of an Opera Director: Chapters from the *Mémoires* of Dr. Louis Véron," Pt. 1, *Dance Chronicle*, 7, no. 1 (1984), p. 54. Huckenpahler says: "Véron of course alludes to this behind-the-scenes traffic, but he does not acknowledge that it was he who, through redecoration, a good publicity machine, and a relaxation of old rules, abetted the practice. Perhaps he felt such an admission would have been too strong for the readers of 1857!"

69. Ivor Guest, *The Romantic Ballet in Paris*, rev. ed. (London: Dance Books, 1980), p. 28.

70. Quoted *ibid.*

71. See Aschengreen, p. 6.

72. Gilbert Abbott à Beckett, "The Revolt of the Workhouse: A Burlesque Ballet Opera, in One Act," in *Miller's Modern Acting Drama* (London: John Miller, 1834).

73. Beaumont, *Complete Book*, p. 118.
74. Beckett, p. 15.
75. *Ibid.*, p. 16.
76. *Ibid.*, p. 10.
77. *Ibid.*, p. 16.
78. Friedrich Engels, *Condition of the Working Classes in England*, quoted in *Not in God's Image*, ed. Julia O'Faolain and Lauro Martines (New York: Harper and Row, 1973), p. 299.
79. Jardin and Tudesq, p. 294.
80. *Ibid.*, p. 293.
81. *Women, the Family, and Freedom: The Debate in Documents*, 1 (1750–1880), ed. Susan Groag Bell and Karen M. Offen (Stanford: Stanford University Press, 1983), p. 200.
82. Moses and Rabine, p. 282.
83. Marie-Reine [Reine Guindorf], *Tribune des femmes*, quoted *ibid.*, p. 287.
84. Suzanne Voilquin, *Memories of a Daughter of the People*, quoted in Moses, p. 87.
85. Suzanne Voilquin, *Tribune des femmes*, quoted in Moses and Rabine, p. 301.
86. Jeanne-Désirée [Désirée Veret] expressed the rationale for this in another context: "We should...take our [names] only from our mothers and God....If we continue to take the names of men and doctrines, we will be slaves without knowing it of the principles they have engendered and upon which they exercise a kind of paternity to which we will have to submit in order to be consistent with ourselves" (*Tribune des femmes*, quoted *ibid.*, p. 296).
87. Marie-Reine [Reine Guindorf], *Tribune des femmes*, quoted *ibid.*, p. 315.
88. Angélique and Sophie Caroline, *Tribune des femmes*, quoted *ibid.*, p. 299.
89. Suzanne Voilquin, *Tribune des femmes*, quoted *ibid.*, p. 308. Stéphanie Jullien, a middle-class woman, describes marriage as woman's only option in order to have "*a lot in life.*" Letter reprinted in *Victorian Women: A Documentary Account of Women's Lives in Nineteenth-Century England, France, and the United States*, ed. Erna Olafson Hellerstein, Leslie Parker Hume, and Karen M. Offen (Stanford: Stanford University Press, 1981), p. 148.
90. Claire Démar, "My Law of the Future," quoted in Moses and Rabine, p. 188.
91. Jeanne-Désirée [Désirée Veret], *Tribune des femmes*, quoted *ibid.*, p. 285.
92. Angélique and Sophie Caroline, *Tribune des femmes*, quoted *ibid.*, p. 299.

Marriage and the Inhuman:
La Sylphide's *Narratives of Domesticity and Community*

SALLY BANES AND NOËL CARROLL

La Sylphide, a ballet originally choreographed by Filippo Taglioni to music by Jean-Madeleine Schneitzhoeffer and given its premiere at the Paris Opéra on 12 March 1832, is generally considered to be the first major Romantic ballet. Its themes of the supernatural, exotic folklore, and the quest for the ideal were skillfully realized in the union of scenic effects, diaphanous costumes, shadowy gas lighting, and above all, the expressive use of dance technique, in particular the pointework and lightness of the female dancer. According to the dance historian Ivor Guest, "*La Sylphide* sealed the triumph of Romanticism in the field of ballet"; it was, he wrote, "as momentous a landmark in the chronicles of Romantic art as 'The Raft of the "Medusa"' and *Hernani*."[1]

La Sylphide spawned a range of imitations and variations on the theme of the supernatural. It served as a template, ushering in a period, as the French critic Théophile Gautier remarked, when "the Opéra was given over to gnomes, undines, salamanders, elves, nixes, wilis, péris—to all that strange and mysterious folk who lend themselves so marvelously to the fantasies of the *maîtres de ballet*."[2]

But it was not only the formal qualities, or even the content of these ballets that set the tone of the Romantic era in ballet. The economic and social conditions of ballet production and reception in France had shifted after the 1830 revolution, for the Opéra was converted from a state-owned and operated institution into a state-subsidized but privately run commercial enterprise. At the same time, the class makeup of the Opéra audience diversified, and the new, predominantly bourgeois audiences—many of them raised on the phantasmic and exotic spectacles of Paris boulevard melodramas—exerted an unprecedented box-office power.[3] In the 1830s and 1840s, the Romantic ballet flourished, especially in Paris, but also in other European capitals, including London, Milan, Vienna, St. Petersburg, and Copenhagen.

La Sylphide was a benchmark in ballet history, and it was also a turning point in the career of Marie Taglioni, the choreographer's daughter and best student.[4] For Taglioni *fille* created the title role of the airy sprite who seduces a Scottish farmer away on his wedding day, into the mystical forest. The ballet showcased the dancer's mastery of technique, her special ability to mask the effort of physical virtuosity in order to appear suitably imponderable and ethereal. Gautier compared her to "an idealised form, a poetic personification, an opalescent mist seen against the green obscurity of an enchanted forest."[5] When she toured Russia in 1837, a critic marveled that "it is impossible to describe the suggestion she conveyed of aerial flight, the fluttering of wings, the soaring in the air, alighting on flowers, and gliding over the mirror-like surface of a river."[6] The role catapulted Taglioni to international stardom, and she became indelibly identified with the character of the Sylphide.

The scenario for *La Sylphide* was written by Adolphe Nourrit. A tenor at the Opéra in Paris, Nourrit appeared in the leading male role in Meyerbeer's opera *Robert le Diable* in 1831, playing opposite Marie Taglioni in a spectral Ballet of the [Dead] Nuns. Earlier, Nourrit had been inspired to write the scenario for *La Sylphide* upon reading Charles Nodier's 1822 novella *Trilby, ou le Lutin d'Argail*, set in an ancient Scottish landscape of lochs, mists, and highlands, in which a fisherman's wife falls in love—lethally—with a male elf.[7] Nodier himself was influenced by Sir Walter Scott's fantastic evocations of a medieval Scotland populated by goblins, witches, and sorcerers.

Although Nourrit's scenario is often referred to as an adaptation of Nodier's story, it is also usually said that the two narratives have very little in common, besides the Scottish setting. For one thing, the gender relationships are reversed in *La Sylphide*. For another, *La Sylphide* makes no reference to religion, while *Trilby* involves an exorcism, a pilgrimage, and a ruined cemetery.[8]

What is not usually acknowledged is that the core theme of Nodier's novella—the fatal subversion of marital relations—becomes even more evident in the ballet. In fact, the transgendered representation of the elf as a supernatural female figure in *La Sylphide* also recalls Scott's novels and poems, for both the Sylphide, as a seductive enchantress, and the witch, as a soothsayer with mysterious demonic powers, are reminiscent of Scott's women.[9] The very structure of the choreography in *La Sylphide* emblematically narrates the regulation of sexuality through marriage by the community. Indeed, if *Trilby* exacts one thousand years of estrangement for infidelity, *La Sylphide* stands as a cautionary tale, admonishing men on pain of death to marry *inside* their own community and not to be lured *outside* their own folk into a world portrayed as other and inhuman.[10]

La Sylphide, that is, is based upon a radical opposition of love, sexuality, and matrimony within the group—an event that is portrayed as occurring *inside* a cavernous farmhouse—versus love *outside* the folk—love literally outdoors, in the forest regions of the sylphs.[11] Moreover, this difference is further presented as a choice between humanity (the folk), on the one side, and the inhuman (the Sylphide), on the other. Just as Taglioni herself and ballerinas in general might be seen as seductively drawing gentlemen away from their hearths and the heart of their families, and into the Foyer de la Danse, the Sylphide seduces young James away from his wedding into a realm that he barely understands and that he only inhabits at the cost of self-destruction.[12]

In 1834, the Danish choreographer August Bournonville saw Taglioni's

Sylphide in Paris. He created his own version in 1836 in Copenhagen, to new music by Hermann Lovenskjold. It is Bournonville's version that we will analyze here, because we believe that, although it has been altered in obvious ways, it is still the closest we can come to the original Taglioni version.[13]

La Sylphide is a ballet in two acts. The first act takes place in a commodious farmhouse where James Reuben lives with his widowed mother. It is his wedding or betrothal day.[14] But just before the entrance of Effie, his fiancée, and the wedding guests, James, dozing by the fireplace, is visited by a gossamer vision—the Sylphide.[15] She hovers over his chair, dances out her love for him, kisses him, and then, when he wakes and approaches her, disappears up the chimney. Gurn—James's friend and rival—arrives, then the bride, with her women friends. When James notices Madge, the witch, warming herself at the fireplace, he angrily tells her to leave. But she offers to read the eager young women's futures in their palms. Notably, considering the major theme

Marie Taglioni in La Sylphide, *lithograph by Alfred E. Chalon, 1836. Dance Collection, New York Public Library for the Performing Arts, Astor, Lenox, and Tilden Foundations.*

of *La Sylphide*, all of Madge's predictions concern marriage and procreation: the first young woman, Madge predicts through pantomime, will bear many children who will all flourish; the second, children who will die. The third fortune-seeker is a child, who is slapped for her effrontery: she is too young for such stories. The fourth young maiden is surprised to discover (she mimes embarrassment as she touches her abdomen) that she is already pregnant. Madge tells Effie, the fifth maiden, that her happiness lies with Gurn, not James. Marriage stories, it seems, preoccupy the women in this ballet.

Effie goes upstairs to get ready for the wedding ceremony; the guests leave, and suddenly the Sylphide appears again, this time in the window. She tells James she loves him and dances with him flirtatiously. She wraps his scarf around herself and seems to beg for his protection. Gurn watches as James kisses the sprite. When it is time for the others to return, the Sylphide hides in James's armchair, and he covers her with a plaid. Gurn tells the others what he has witnessed, and pulls the plaid aside, but the Sylphide is gone. All that remains is a bundled scarf. The rest of the guests arrive and dance in various formations, as the Sylphide, visible only to

James, flits among them. As the bridal couple is about to exchange rings, the Sylphide snatches Effie's ring from James's hand and dashes out of the house. He runs after her, leaving the wedding guests stunned.

The second act takes place in a misty forest. Madge summons the other witches, who dance around a boiling cauldron, out of which Madge pulls a scarf. The mist clears, and the Sylphide and James appear. She shows him how she lives and introduces him to a bevy of other sylphs. But as they dance together, she constantly escapes his grasp. James seeks advice from Madge, who gives him the scarf and advises him to wrap it around the Sylphide. This, she explains, will make the Sylphide's wings fall off. But when he captures her, the loss of the Sylphide's wings also marks her death. The sylphs carry her aloft, while the wedding procession of Effie and Gurn crosses the stage. As James falls to the ground, grief-stricken, the witch rises over him triumphantly.[16]

Commentators have often interpreted *La Sylphide* as an allegory of the search for the ideal, as represented by the Sylphide.[17] And such an interpretation is surely borne out in the searching, yearning movements of James, who is so often late in arrival, the sylph having fluttered elsewhere. Yet, we feel that there is also a darker design that is compatible with the incidents of the ballet. It is the story of marriage, of socially licensed sexuality, and of what is possible and impossible, sanctioned and forbidden, with respect to courtship.[18]

The theme of whom one may marry, of course, is a recurring one in Romantic ballet, although it appears as early as the pre-Romantic ballet *La Fille Mal Gardée* (1789). It appears, for example, in the major works like *Ondine*, *Alma*, and *Giselle*, as well as in *La Sylphide*. In *Giselle*, the theme of whom one may *not* marry is portrayed most realistically and straightforwardly. One must stick with one's own social class or risk destruction. In *La Sylphide*, perhaps the sylphs represent an aristocratic station to which James ought not aspire. They are certainly *higher* than

La Sylphide, *as seen by Jules Collignon, V. Beaucé*, et al. Les Beautés de l'Opéra *(Paris: Soulié, 1845).*

he, considering their aerial capabilities (not new to this ballet, but nevertheless symbolically potent here). In any case, they, along with the tribe of witches, stand for the other, for some literally alien group outside what is given as James's natural and appropriate network of affections—so often portrayed as a ring of joyous, folkish dancers.

Within the farmhouse, James is surrounded by his people. And the ballet literalizes the ethnocentric proclivities of peoples to identify themselves as the People and, in consequence, to regard outsiders as not quite human, or, in the case of *La Sylphide*, as downright inhuman—as bewinged creatures sometimes marked by insectile movement and even more generally by "unnatural" movement (i.e., balletic movement which, parenthetically, also connotes aristocratic movement).[19] The action of the ballet, in turn, mobilizes this association of the inside/human/folk in order to cast marriage to outsiders and nonfolk—to sylphs, foreigners, and other nonhumans—as destined to go badly.

So, in terms of its plot, *La Sylphide* is fundamentally about whom one should marry and whom one shouldn't marry. But it advances this theme in its very structure, not simply in its plot. Symbolically, the ballet presents two options: marriage *inside* the group, which is depicted as human and as sanguine, and marriage or love *outside*, which is portrayed as union with the inhuman and as inevitably tragic. In short, freely borrowing from Lévi-Strauss, we might say that *La Sylphide* is a myth about the regulation of marriage—i.e., it is about whom it is appropriate to marry. Working out the inappropriateness of marrying one of *them* instead of one of *us*—the inhuman rather than a human; the other rather than a member of the community—not only supplies the thematic motivation for the plot development in *La Sylphide*. It also serves as the basis for the articulation of an overarching choreographic structure of studied and highly connotative contrasts. This is developed in terms of contrasts

between the endogamous marriage—within the population of Scots—and the exogamous marriage—between a Scots and a sylph.

In order to analyze the choreographic structure, it will be useful first to discuss the movement structures for the three salient groups in the ballet (the Scots, the witches, and the sylphs). Then we will analyze the choreography for the key individuals (the Sylphide, Effie, James, and Madge) and for their interactions.

In terms of the myth of marriage regulation, the audience is presented with three "tribes," only one of which it is appropriate for humans to marry into, since of the three groups only one is human. Although they have aspects and even steps in common, each of these tribes is marked off by distinctive movement qualities. Even if a particular gesture or step is replicated from one group to another, it does not always have the same look or significance. The same step may be performed in disparate styles, taking on an entirely discrete identity (for instance, both Effie and the Sylphide do ronds de jambe en l'air, but in one case it signals precision and closure, while in the other it suggests weightlessness and porosity). Or, it may be clear that a member of one group is "quoting" the movement as well as the style of another group (as when Gurn flaps his arms and then poses à la Sylphide to show the Scots what he has seen, i.e., the Sylphide, or when, in the forest, the Sylphide gestures in the Highland Fling shape and style similar to that seen among the Scots in Act I—right arm held shoulder height, left arm curved solidly over the head—to signal to James her desire to marry him and her willingness to join his clan).

The initial group, the Scots, have two dances in Act I: first, there is the entry of Effie's women friends, and then a dance of the whole community, including both males and females. Each dance is done in a distinctive folk-dance style, with allusions to Scottish dances like the highland fling. The women's dance is a brief, brisk ceremonial entry. Two phalanxes of four young women, led by a ninth female dancer, hold their left arms jauntily

akimbo in the style we soon come to recognize as characteristic of the Scots. Their right arms, however, hold either the hems of their kilts (suggesting a curtsey) or a gift. They nod their heads or turn them smartly on the beat of the music, and they kick their feet forward as they step, like frisky colts. After the fortune-telling episode and the pas de deux between James and the Sylphide, the women enter in the same formation as before, followed by two phalanxes of men playing bagpipes. Now the entire community dances, making more complex floor patterns, forming and reforming lines, circles, and squares, and dividing up sometimes into couples and sometimes into single-gender groups. Their ability to form these dance figures cooperatively signals their social cohesion.

The dominant movement qualities of the two Scottish dances—earthbound energy, dexterity, and strength contained within limited, hemmed-in spaces—indicate that this is sturdy farming stock. Both men and women wear utilitarian shoes, and the men and women often dance identical steps close to the ground, side by side or facing one another, with arms intertwined or crossed as in a skating formation. At the same time, many of their dance figures are reminiscent of children's games, suggesting a playful spirit of celebration.

We have already seen the delicate Sylphide, wearing a white tulle dress and satin slippers (pointe shoes resembling the dress shoes for evening wear fashionable in the 1830s), dancing alone in a distinctly ethereal, balletic style. When she has danced with James, the two contrasted sharply, and they never touched. Therefore, the folk dance style here, performed by hearty, earthy people wearing bright jackets and plaid kilts and scarves, strongly connotes, first, that the Sylphide does not belong; their movement, in Labanalysis terms, is bound, while hers is free. And that contrast, taken literally, perhaps explains why James has become obsessed with her, for she seems to represent a realm outside of, and free from, social constraints. Second, the folk dance style signals that this is a community that

dances to the same beat and whose steps and hands intricately interlock—metaphorically, a community with shared values, knowledge, and behavior.

Older adults, marriageable youth, and children all take part in the second folk dance. The designs of the choreography emphasize both the theme of matrimony and reproduction within a closed group and the countertheme of the runaway bridegroom. Almost all the participants in the dance, even the widowed older adults, are potential brides and grooms. In their dance, they not only celebrate the upcoming nuptials of James and Effie, but also show off their own prowess as prospective mates. That there are several generations in the dance promises continuity; through dancing, the children learn the courtship rituals and are initiated into the community. Moreover, various dance figures seem to symbolize matrimonial union sanctioned by and enclosed within the community, as repeatedly couples are formed and reformed out of small groups as well as the whole. When lines of couples cover the space in crisscross patterns, or when they break apart to form neat rows, images of domesticated landscapes, plowed fields, and the multiplication both of crops and of human progeny arise. When all join hands to form a large circle, the community as a whole contains, but does not subsume, individuals, couples, and families. But within this image of equality and unity, something is amiss. For when the group moves into a quadrille, and Effie changes partners, coming "home" she ends up alone, since James, who has run after the Sylphide, is absent from the "home" position.

The second group to appear are the witches, at the beginning of Act II. More a gang than a community, they dance in a circle but, unlike the humans, make no physical contact with one another. Their gestures are angular, asymmetrical, and mechanical; their hands are perennially twisted and splayed, and Madge's fingers are preternaturally long. Although the witches, too, are strong and earthbound, they are shown as the oppo-

site of the agile humans. Their movements are jerky and spasmodic as they greet one another, crouch by the cauldron, pass around cups of infernal brew and bolt it down. Snakelike, they press their bellies to the ground. Although they live in nature, they are anything but natural (in the sense of wholesome). Rather, resembling the grotesque figures in Renaissance antimasques, they are monstrous inversions of humanity.

The third "tribe" are the sylphs. Like the witches, they live in nature in a single-sex community, where there can be no reproduction. In fact, the sylphs seem undifferentiated in many respects besides gender. Their movements are not only identical, but extremely symmetrical. They are dressed identically. They look so much alike—as if they were clones — that James can't find his beloved Sylphide when she disappears within the group. If the farmers and the witches are earthbound, the sylphs are airborne. If they are strong, the sylphs are lighter than air. Moving up onto pointe and back down again, taking small vertical jumps and mincing steps (bourrées) that make them appear to hover in place and skim rapidly along the ground, they are more like hummingbirds or moths than women. Their arms float upward weightlessly. The music they dance to has no beat, and its instrumentation—a solo flute and harp—sounds wispy and feminine. In contrast to the humans, their gestures and steps are airy and open; their bodies seem boundaryless and permeable.

The contrast among these three groups is even more starkly drawn in the individual members of the groups whose fates are intertwined in the drama and the ways those individuals interact choreographically. The first character we see dancing is the Sylphide. Her motions are as mercurial as her moods. When the curtain opens, she kneels at James's armchair, in the dainty, contemplative pose—her chin resting on her right hand, her right elbow resting on her left hand—from the well-known painting by Lepaulle of the original French version of the ballet. She is by turns gracious, cautious, confident, loving, mischievous; she moves forward and back from James's chair as if to embody some ambivalence about revealing herself to him; she begins with low, small-scale footwork and then opens into space-devouring leaps; above all, she is never fixed in one place. Her back is flexible, and her movement sequences are extremely fluid. And when she dances in her own habitat, in the second act, her hovering (with the help of some unobtrusive stage machinery) turns into flight. In both spaces, James has trouble catching her or finding her (unlike a wife, who's always at home). In contrast to Madge, who often gestures powerfully downward, the Sylphide's tendency is to move up—into chimneys or trees.

Moreover, it is important to note that the Sylphide has a special relationship to the apertures of the house (the chimney, the window, the door), and that Madge, too, is first sighted at the hearth. Both are liminal figures, who straddle cultural boundaries—inside/outside, natural/supernatural. The Sylphide is not only ambivalent, she is also ambiguous. For although she is childlike, seemingly innocent, and fragile, she also has a seductive, perhaps even demonic side. The Danish dance historian Erik Aschengreen has noted that in certain interpretations of the ballet, the Sylphide "was directly related to the witch Madge," and that the French critic Jules Janin had found the character "both dangerous and enchanting."[20] That the Sylphide and Madge are never simultaneously present onstage may suggest that they are mysteriously related as reverse images.

After the Sylphide vanishes up the chimney, Effie and her friends enter. Although her part largely involves mime, Effie has one small solo dance, which she does to welcome her wedding guests. Where the Sylphide was tentative, Effie is perfectly at home. She plants herself firmly in the center of the room and, as she opens first her right arm, then her left arm in a wide, open gesture of welcome, she turns to each side to survey the room. In an echo of the opening scene, she too kisses James, who has once again fallen asleep in his chair. But he is startled, rather than enchanted, when he wakes this time. After Effie's friends offer her gifts, she dances. Slowly and deliberately placing her left hand on her hip and her right hand overhead, she performs a few steps of some fancy footwork. Although her leg gestures are similar to the Sylphide's, they seem more mundane. Her crisp delivery, the way her raised foot crosses at her knee or ankle, her tight turns, and her sharp changes of direction all give the dance a folkish air. And when her dance ends, she again performs her wide embrace, one arm opening out at a time to include all the guests.[21]

Dancing for her guests, Effie is outwardly directed, presentational in her gestures. Her dancing has a social purpose, just as her sexuality will be channeled toward social reproduction. In contrast, the Sylphide, in her first dance, seems to play by herself and for herself. She touches herself both protectively and provocatively when James approaches her, and although in her second dance she communicates her need for him, it is not clear what form her desire could take. Effie is potentially a mother; the Sylphide certainly is not. In some ways, Effie is sweet and innocent, but she can also be tenacious. She has definite plans for her future, and they include marriage. Furthermore, she will not be a wife entirely dominated by her husband; when James brutally seizes the witch's arm, she calms him down, insists that Madge be given a drink of liquor to warm her bones, and begs James to let the witch tell the maidens' fortunes.

A moment before we suddenly see the witch crouching to warm herself at the hearth, James wraps Effie ceremoniously in a plaid scarf, the tartan of his clan. (This scarf, of course, foreshadows another scarf—the poisoned one that serves as the instrument of the Sylphide's death.) When the witch and the guests leave, and Effie goes upstairs to change, the Sylphide returns to the farmhouse, this time through the window. And now, James kneels at *her* feet. At first she mimes her sadness at James's marriage. But she brightens as she invites James to come home with her to the forest, and her dancing becomes flirtatious. Or perhaps her powers of enchantment are magical; twice she seems to pull James toward the door, but each time he, remembering his vows, resists. She wraps herself in the same portentous scarf that James had wrapped around Effie and looks at him coyly as if to implore him to put her in his fiancée's place during the wedding ceremony. The wedding guests return, do their folk dancing, and the wedding ritual begins, only to be broken when James rushes out the door to follow the Sylphide.

In a sense, James has two broken nuptials. And although each interrupted ceremony takes place in a completely different realm, his two solo dances in the two acts are very similar. He seems literally to jump for joy. And not only does he jump; he jumps high and wide, moving across the stage and taking up so much space that he presses the Scots (in Act I) and the sylphs (in Act II) to the very perimeters of the stage. James also turns while he jumps, executing the most complex steps in the entire ballet.[22] As well, he does rapid, detailed footwork, beating his ankles together and performing entrechats (changing the positions of the feet, by crossing one in front and then in back of the other, while jumping).

However, even though the steps James performs in each solo are similar, they have different meanings in the two different circumstances. In Act I, his solo takes place just after the entry of the wedding guests. It is almost a ritual display of the bridegroom's favorable qualities. As he holds his arms in a circle above his head (a high fifth port de bras) and then moves the circle downward (a low fifth port de bras), he seems to frame his head and torso, presenting himself as if in a portrait, as if to say "Look how handsome I am, and see how heroic my uplifted chest is!" When he jumps high and turns in midair, the community can observe his strength and coordination; when he dispatches his entrechats, they can take stock of his ability for detailed precision, as well as the speed with which he works. His consumption of space signals a distinctively male drive to control territoriality, which in turn connotes power.[23]

In Act II, James performs certain steps slightly differently; for instance, the beats of his ankle resemble the fluttering steps of the sylphs more than the bold, highly controlled footwork of his earlier dance. And he even adopts some of the sylphs' steps. This solo, unlike the solo in the farmhouse, is segmented, its parts alternating with responses from the Sylphide; thus it is really part of a pas de deux, which, in turn, is sandwiched between group dances by the sylphs. Thus in the second solo, James seems less to be demonstrating his strength and skills than to be introducing himself, having a challenge dance with his beloved, and then being incorporated into the group.

If James is powerful, here in the forest his nemesis, Madge, proves to be even more so. Crouching by the fire, bending over her cane, or limping toward a seat, in Act I she looks like a helpless old woman, gnarled and crippled. But in the opening scene of Act II, she is in her element. Her arms weave strange incantations over the cauldron's brew. She beckons commandingly for her sister witches to join her. And when they do, her gestures become elated and expostulatory. She thrusts them strongly upward, outward, and downward. She seems, with her arms, to be ranting like a mad scientist or hysterical dictator. The same powerful thrusting gestures later in this act shove Gurn to his knees to propose to Effie, and James to *his* knees to beg for Madge's help. When James asks Madge's forgiveness for his rude treatment of her in the farmhouse, she draws herself up, gesturing both the pride of one whose dignity was insulted and the exultation of one who will never forgive, but will ultimately achieve her revenge. After the Sylphide's death, the witch lifts her arms above her head and seems to tower over James, showing that she is literally above him.[24] But merely to kill him would not suffice; she pulls him back into semiconsciousness to make him suffer more deeply as he watches the Sylphide's funeral. In the final tableau, she lifts her arms triumphantly as she crouches by James's prone body.

On the one hand, *La Sylphide* operates, in a broad sense, like a cautionary tale, warning that romance and sexual passion outside one's social circle risks destruction and death. But on the other hand, *La Sylphide* indulges forbidden wishes, allowing James to gambol with the woodland sylphs for the best part of the second act before he is killed. In this way, the ballet is reminiscent of so many crime stories whose final moral lesson—that crime does not pay—is preceded by waves of gratifying violence and mayhem. Similarly, *La Sylphide* admonishes against courtship outside the group, but only after painting it in idyllic colors, thus in the last instance taking back with one hand what it has lavishly entertained with the other.[25]

Marriage, of course, has always been an important social theme in Western dancing. In the Renaissance, amateur ballets were mounted at royal wedding ceremonies, whereas with the professionalization of dance in the late seventeenth and early eighteenth century, representations of weddings were made part of the ballet itself.[26] With *La Sylphide*, however, an important turn is taken, one which profoundly marks the direction of the Romantic ballet. For in *La Sylphide*, as in many of its progeny, the theme of marriage is introduced, only to be subverted in various ways. If eighteenth-century ballets represent wedding ceremonies, Romantic ballets so often show them undermined. Rather than a celebration of the incorporation of the community, *La Sylphide* explores society's anxiety toward the other, toward sexuality, and perhaps toward the institution of marriage itself.

We would like to thank Erik Aschengreen and his students, as well as Mary A. Brennan, Judith Chazin-Bennahum, Susan Cook, Lynn Garafola, and Cathryn Harding for their helpful comments on this article.

Notes

1. Ivor Guest, *The Romantic Ballet in Paris*, 2nd ed. (London: Dance Books, 1980), pp. 114, 5.
2. Théophile Gautier, "Farewell Performance of Marie Taglioni," in *The*

Romantic Ballet as Seen by Théophile Gautier, trans. Cyril W. Beaumont (1932; rpt. New York: Dance Horizons, 1973), p. 73.

3. See Guest, pp. 4, 22, 30, 105–108.

4. On Taglioni's life and career, see André Levinson, *Marie Taglioni*, trans. Cyril W. Beaumont (London: Imperial Society for Teachers of Dancing/C.W. Beaumont, 1930; rpt. London: Dance Books, 1977); Léandre Vaillat, *La Taglioni, ou la Vie d'une danseuse* (Paris: A. Michel, 1942).

5. Théophile Gautier, "Revival of 'La Sylphide' (1844)," in Gautier, *The Romantic Ballet*, p. 70.

6. Quoted in Selma Jeanne Cohen, ed., *Dance as a Theatre Art*, 2nd ed. (Princeton, N.J.: Princeton Book Company, 1992), p. 67.

7. An English translation has recently been published. See Charles Nodier, *Smarra and Trilby*, trans. Judith Landry (Sawtry, Cambs: Dedalus, 1993).

8. Erik Aschengreen, however, compares *La Sylphide* to *Trilby* and argues that the similarities between the two should be examined. One example he gives is that both Jeannie (the heroine of *Trilby*) and James (in *La Sylphide*) first meet their supernatural loves in a half-waking state at the hearth, while dreaming or fantasizing about unattainable erotic desires (Erik Aschengreen, "The Beautiful Danger: Facets of the Romantic Ballet," trans. Patricia N. McAndrew, *Dance Perspectives*, no. 58 [Summer 1974], p. 13).

9. See Nancy Moore Goslee, "Witch or Pawn: Women in Scott's Narrative Poetry," in Anne K. Mellor, ed. *Romanticism and Feminism* (Bloomington: Indiana University Press, 1988), pp. 115–136. Gautier notes that in the part of the Sylphide, Marie Taglioni "resembled unmistakably those fairies of Scotland of whom Walter Scott speaks, who roam in the moonlight near the mysterious fountain, with a necklace of dewdrops and a golden thread for girdle" ("Revival of 'La Sylphide,'" p. 27).

10. In *Ballet and Modern Dance* (New York: Thames and Hudson, 1988), Susan Au notes that *La Sylphide* "might be interpreted as a cautionary tale" (p. 51). But her interpretation differs from ours, in that she finds the Sylphide "such an appealing figure" that the cautionary aspect is undermined.

11. The forest is a crucial symbolic site in which various psychological transformations—including falling in love and coming to maturity—take place, not only in fairytales like Red Riding Hood but in other literary genres (including several Shakespeare plays).

12. The hearth is also a multivalent image that is internal to *La Sylphide* itself; we will discuss it further below, in note 15.

13. Our examination of the ballet here is necessarily limited due to space. For an extended analysis, see Sally Banes, *Dancing Women* (London: Routledge, forthcoming).

14. According to Guest (p. 113) and Cyril W. Beaumont (in *Complete Book of Ballets* [London: Putnam, 1937], p. 95), the ballet takes place on James and Effie's wedding day. However, according to the Bournonville scenario (in Cohen, p. 79), it is their betrothal day.

15. It should be noted here that in many fairytales, the fireplace or hearth is the dwelling place of fairies or spirits. The fairies conjure with the embers, often in ways that prove troublesome for humans. (See, for instance, "My Own Self," an English fairytale retold by Joseph Jacobs, in *The Book of Virtues: A Treasury of Great Moral Stories*, ed. William J. Bennett [New York: Simon and Schuster, 1993], pp. 30–32.) But at the same time, the hearth is first and

foremost a symbol of comfort and domesticity. Perhaps this perfectly contradictory signification has to do with the liminal status of the hearth—its indeterminate status as a threshold (limen) between inside and outside the home, a symbolically charged space in terms of the ritual and social process. (See Arnold Van Gennep, *The Rites of Passage* [Chicago: University of Chicago Press, 1960], pp. 20–21.) We will discuss the use of liminal spaces in the choreography of *La Sylphide* below.

16. The formal analysis of the ballet here follows the Bournonville version, since the original Taglioni choreography has been lost. Our analysis is based on the 1988 made-for-TV film, directed by Thomas Grimm and produced by the National Video Corporation in association with Danmarks Radio, of a performance of *La Sylphide* by the Royal Danish Ballet at the Royal Theatre in Copenhagen. The cast includes: Lis Jeppesen (The Sylph), Nikolaj Hübbe (James), and Sorella Englund (Madge).

17. See, for instance, Guest, p. 114; Aschengreen, "Danger," p. 9.

18. Aschengreen points out that it is James's erotic contact with the Sylphide in Act II that causes her death (and, eventually, his). This is not only symbolized by his wrapping her in the scarf, but also (in Bournonville's scenario) directly stated: "In his outburst of joy [James] gives her a thousand caresses." Aschengreen notes that "the harmony and happiness James has experienced in the woods are shattered the moment the sensuous and sensual are admitted" ("Danger," p. 9).

19. Gautier wrote that "the theme of this very poetic pas [in which the Sylphide loses her wings] is almost certainly borrowed from the natural history of insects. Virgin ants shed their wings after the love-flight" ("Revival of 'La Sylphide' [1844]," p. 70).

20. Aschengreen, "Danger," pp. 7, 11.

21. Effie's solo was added to Bournonville's original choreography by Hans Brenaa. Nevertheless, we include it in our analysis because it is perfectly in tune with the rest of the choreography and with Effie's character in the ballet.

22. In this respect, of course, the Bournonville ballet may differ from the Taglioni version. For Bournonville, a strong dancer himself, often created more technically demanding, powerful male roles in his ballets than was the current practice in France, where men were seen as unwelcome interlopers into a graceful, distinctively female province. However, since (as noted above) the Taglioni version has been lost, we do not know how complex a role Taglioni *père* created for Joseph Mazilier, who originally danced the part of James.

23. See Erving Goffman, *Relations in Public: Microstudies of the Public Order* (New York: Basic Books, 1971), ch. 2, and Nancy M. Henley, *Body Politics: Power, Sex, and Nonverbal Communication* (Englewood Cliffs, N.J.: Prentice-Hall, 1977), ch. 2.

24. Originally, like many old-women roles in ballet, Madge was danced by a man, and in some companies that perform the Bournonville ballet today, she still is. But in Copenhagen, the tradition changed when Henning Kronstam became artistic director of the Royal Danish Ballet in 1979, since—as in the version we analyze here—he preferred to cast a woman in the role of Madge (Conversation with Erik Aschengreen, Copenhagen, 23 Oct. 1995).

25. Aschengreen notes that in general, Bournonville did not approve of this kind of gratification. He points out that Bournonville was criticized by the Danish

naturalist critic Edvard Brandes for discouraging eroticism in his female dancers and for "fear[ing] the passionate," and he quotes Bournonville's own statement regarding the goal of ballet: "[To] intensify thought, to uplift the spirit, and to refresh the senses." In looking at the choreographer's entire oeuvre, Aschengreen concludes that ultimately Bournonville upheld the Biedermeier ethos, which, he states, differed from French Romanticism in that it "was willing to delight and to refresh, but never by toying with the provocation of the senses." According to Aschengreen, Bournonville strongly held "the deep and, at that time, common concept that eroticism could endanger man's peace of mind," and therefore the choreographer deliberately softened the original French production's eroticism, as well as its demonic qualities. However, Aschengreen's assessment of Bournonville's general point of view does not undermine our argument, since Aschengreen still considers *La Sylphide*—as an expression of spiritual dissonance, eroticism, and thus anti-Biedermeier sentiments—a completely anomalous ballet in the Bournonville canon ("Danger," pp. 36, 48).

26. *Les Noces de Pélée et de Thétis* (1654), though danced by French courtiers, is an example of this trend.

Redeeming Giselle:
Making a Case for the Ballet We Love to Hate

JODY BRUNER

Of late, *Giselle* has become subject to unofficial censoring. This is due to the findings of certain ideologically based critiques that emphasize how the ballet represents the oppression and victimization of women and the working class. According to this criticism, victimization is present in the story line, is generally implicit in ballet aesthetics, and characterizes the conditions surrounding ballet production.[1] It is true that this ideological criticism reacts against a tradition that sees *Giselle* (and ballet in general) as a thing of beauty, a tradition that doesn't question or explore the political agenda it explicitly and implicitly supports. This leaves modern audiences with a dilemma: either they allow themselves to be transported by the power of the dancing in *Giselle*, or they adopt a critical distance and see the oppression this beauty demands. I know that for me, because I see *Giselle* both ways, watching it always involves a great deal of discomfort. Any pleasure I feel is tinged with guilt, and any judgment I make is weakened by the rapture I experience at the most powerful choreographic moments. This essay, then, is an attempt to accommodate the ballet's contradictions and to alleviate the discomfort I associate with it.

To achieve this reconciliation, I draw heavily on the writings of psychoanalyst, literary critic, and semiotician Julia Kristeva.[2] Kristeva's work is characterized by an attempt to accommodate conflicting, opposing, or—to use one of her favorite words—"heterogenous" forces. Her goal is to create greater tolerance of difference or otherness, and to achieve this she reveals the subtle ways in which the familiar harbors difference, or otherness, within itself. For example, in an important early work, *Revolution in Poetic Language*,[3] she demonstrates the heterogeneous nature of language, which can convey meaning both symbolically (or denotatively, as in ordinary forms of communication) and semiotically—through rhythm, tone, music, and dance—or what she likes to call "poetic language."

The following reading, by paying special attention to the dancing, semiotic body evoked by Kristeva, reveals the heterogeneity within *Giselle* and its surrounding world. In *Revolution in Poetic Language* Kristeva demonstrates how the semiotic reveals itself in places where it ruptures the symbolic or denotative surface of language. In *Giselle*, there are three such rupture points. The first is Albrecht, the ballet's narrative subject, who is both a hero and a villain; the second is the narrative structure, which mixes both dance and mime; the third is the shift in narrative modes between the two acts, which suggests a crisis in the larger social order. The heterogeneity that lies close to the ballet's surface acts then to defuse ideologically based criticism. For if the narrative subject is revealed to be fundamentally divided, how can he be a pure villain or victim? And if he is not seen as a purely aggressive villain, but as a victim who is also passive, how can we so readily reject him and his story?

Conceived by Théophile Gautier, *Giselle* premiered at the Paris Opéra in 1841. Act I takes place in a Rhineland village surrounded by vineyards. Giselle, a young peasant woman, is courted by Albrecht, Duke of Silesia, disguised as a peasant called Loys, and by Hilarion, a rough gamekeeper. The Duke of Courland and his daughter Bathilde, Albrecht's real fiancée, are out hunting and stop to refresh themselves at Giselle's cottage, where the new wine can be tasted. Peasants entertain them with dancing, and, after the hunting party leaves, Giselle and Albrecht join the harvest festivities at which Giselle is crowned queen of the vintage. Hilarion then exposes Albrecht's duplicity, which causes Giselle to lose her reason and die of a broken heart. Act II takes place at Giselle's grave in a forest clearing near a lake. Albrecht comes to mourn and is visited by the shade of Giselle, now numbered among the Wilis, the ghosts of dead girls jilted by their lovers and ruled by Myrtha. Men who wander into the Wilis' abode must either dance until dawn, when their power fades and they vanish, or be tossed into the lake. Protected by Giselle's love, Albrecht survives, but finds himself alone. In the original production, Albrecht was then reunited with Bathilde.

In its conception, *Giselle* reveals a kind of struggle between the poetic image of the Wili and conventional narrative. Gautier came upon an account of the Wilis, brides who died before being married, in Heinrich Heine's *De l'Allemagne*. Heine's book was conceived to explain Germany, and especially the world of German folklore, to the French. Germans, he explained, "are still deep in the Middle Ages," while the French have progressed beyond it:

> Ye French may admire and love chivalry. All that remains to you of it is charming chronicles and iron armor. You risk nothing by gratifying your imagination and satisfying your curiosity with it. But with us Germans the chronicle of the Middle Ages is not yet closed, the last leaves are still wet with the blood of our relations and friends, and the brilliant armor protects the still living bodies of our executioners.[4]

In Heine's account the Wilis are powerfully present and dangerous—not a picturesque decoration. It is this potential danger and power that provided the creative impetus for the ballet.

Gautier's problem was how to contain the Wilis within a narrative structure. Gautier tells us he considered adapting Victor Hugo's poem "Fantômes" for the first act. "I had thought," he later wrote,

> of making the first act consist of a mimed version of Victor Hugo's delightful poem. One would have seen a beautiful ballroom belonging to

some prince; the candles would have been lighted, but the guests would not have arrived; the Wilis, attracted by the joy of dancing in a room glittering with crystal and gliding, would have shown themselves for a moment in the hope of adding to their number. The Queen of the Wilis would have touched the floor with her magic wand to fill the dancers' feet with an insatiable desire for contredanses, waltzes, galops, and mazurkas. The advent of the lords and ladies would have made them fly away like so many vague shadows. Giselle, having danced all that evening, excited by the magic floor and the desire to keep her lover from inviting other women to dance, would have been surprised by the cold dawn like the young Spanish girl, and the pale Queen of the Wilis, invisible to all, would have laid her icy hand on her heart.[5]

There were certain obvious drawbacks to this scenario. As Cyril W. Beaumont pointed out in *The Ballet Called Giselle*, it was

little more than a succession of dances with a single dramatic note at the end; there is almost complete absence of action. In short, the theme is no more than an idea for a ballet, an idea which has still to be developed into an ordered drama, with its introduction, plot, and climax.[6]

With the help of librettist Vernoy de Saint-Georges, Gautier successfully imposed narrative order on the Wilis. In its original version, the libretto ended with Albrecht's union with Bathilde—a restoration of the ballet's social order. However, over time, the Wilis reasserted themselves, and the original ending changed. In all contemporary productions of the ballet, Albrecht is alone onstage when the curtain falls on Act II. Bathilde never reappears, and we leave the theater not knowing whether the social order will be restored or not.[7] We do know that Albrecht has been powerfully transformed and destabilized by his experience, and that this transformation is brought about by the Wilis. According to Kristeva, powerful emotion—or affect—destabilizes the identity, by returning the psyche to a state of primary narcissism.

According to the psychoanalytic model of development, the child initially experiences itself in union with the maternal—or semiotic—body. In this preverbal, autoerotic state the child does not distinguish between inside and outside or between pleasure and pain. The dawning perception of such differences coincides with the onset of primary narcissism. During this so-called mirror stage, the child begins to perceive the mother as a separate object, the source of its earlier, blissful state and thus an object of desire. This narcissistic object of desire is really a pre-object—not fully separate from the subject (who is a presubject). With the introduction of language, the child enters the Oedipal stage or symbolic order and identifies more completely with the paternal body. At this stage, the drives associated with the maternal body (especially the death drive) are repressed, as well as the pre-objects associated with them, in favor of the more discrete objects of desire associated with the paternal body. Kristeva's work on affect (abjection in *Powers of Horror*,[8] melancholia in *Black Sun*,[9] and love in *Tales of Love*[10]) explores its connection with the dynamics of narcissism. Kristeva explains in *Black Sun* that affects arise from the tension between the primary drive energies of the semiotic and the repressive forces of the symbolic. Affects are "[n]ot yet signs," she writes, but "inscriptions" of the struggles between the drive energies and the "threats, orders and injunctions of the superego."[11] Powerful affect, then, returns us to primary narcissism and presubjectivity. Abjection, love, and melancholy are the affects woven into *Giselle*.

Kristeva treats abjection in *Powers of Horror*. This is caused when the child begins to separate itself from the maternal body and identify with the paternal. However, because the symbolic function is still weak, separation is accompanied by the child's gradual abjection—or rejection—of the maternal body and its unruly drives. When the child is then confronted with modalities of these drives, which its internalized paternal "censor" has abjected, these repressed modalities give rise to revulsion, fear, and/or horror. For Kristeva, what causes abjection is that which "disturbs identity, system, order. What does not respect borders, positions, rules. The in-between, the ambiguous, the composite."[12] The most basic form of abject material is bodily waste, which must be expelled for life to continue. Its most perfect example, however, is a corpse. As Kristeva explains in *Powers of Horror*:

> If dung signifies the other side of the border, the place where I am not and which permits me to be, the corpse, the most sickening of wastes, is a border that has encroached upon everything. It is no longer I who expel, "I" is expelled.... The corpse, seen without God and outside of science, is the utmost of abjection. It is death infecting life. Abject. It is something rejected from which one does not part, from which one does not protect oneself as from an object. Imaginary uncanniness and real threat, it beckons to us and ends up engulfing us.[13]

Intimately connected with the abject is Kristeva's idea of *jouissance*—the experience of total joy and ecstasy. As Catherine Marchak explains in her article "The Joy of Transgression," *jouissance*

> is not the pleasure that one can experience in the prosaic world; in the homogenous world, joy and pleasure arise from attaining some object, something tangible or definable, while jouissance arises from seeking the abject, a non-object. The search for this pseudo-object, the abject, leads to excluded ground, the ground that has been excluded by the paternally-imposed prohibitions, taboos and law.[14]

For Kristeva, these prohibitions and taboos "cut short the temptation to return, with abjection and jouissance, to that passivity status within the symbolic function, where the subject, fluctuating between inside and outside, pleasure and pain, word and deed, would find death, along with nirvana."[15]

Act II of *Giselle* mobilizes all the elements of the abject psychological economy. The Wilis dominate this act. They are both seductive women and repulsive corpses. (As a Wili, and to the degree that she is subject to

Myrtha's power, Giselle herself is abject, but, as we will see shortly, she is also an object of love.) They promise pleasure but, at the same time, hold the threat of death. Albrecht finds himself caught in this dangerous web of abject desire when he is discovered by the vengeful Wilis. In order to protect him, Giselle draws him to the safety of the cross on her tombstone, where Myrtha's power has no influence. Although her magic cannot touch Albrecht, it can control Giselle. Cunningly, Myrtha commands Giselle to perform a dance of seduction, knowing Albrecht will find her irresistible. In a ballet about love and passion, this is actually the first time Giselle and Albrecht dance together. In the first act, they dance either in tandem with each other or for each other, while in the second act, she eludes all his efforts to dance with her. Only now, at the climax of the ballet, is their passion consummated in a pas de deux.

The dance begins with Giselle's adagio, a solo that is an extraordinary display of erotic power. She stands at center stage, alone and vulnerable. She is totally self-absorbed. Her gaze is downcast, always within her kinesphere or reach, and her movements seem drawn in on herself: even her jumps seem grounded. Drawn by the promise of intense pleasure, Albrecht cannot resist her. His capitulation is not voluntary, but instinctual. When he joins her at center stage, her body sensually claims the space around her. Her gaze is open; her movements fully extended; in her leaps, performed with his support, she soars. The space between their bodies is not a gap, but a connective.

Exquisitely erotic, this adagio is also profoundly disconcerting. The desire that Giselle elicits is neither conventional nor natural. Rather, it is akin to transgressive or "queer" desire for the unnatural. In "Tracking the Vampire," Sue Ellen Case explains that queer elements lie "not at the site of gender, but at the site of ontology,...thus challenging the Platonic parameters of Being—the borders of life and death. Queer desire is constituted as a transgression of these boundaries and of the organicism which defines the living as the good."[16] If heterosexual practice is considered "natural" because it is life-pro-

Kimberly Glasco in Giselle's adagio. National Ballet of Canada.

Albrecht answers the siren's call of Giselle's adagio. Veronica Tennant and Hazaros Surmeyan perform the Act II pas de deux. National Ballet of Canada.

ducing, queer sexual practice, because it is nonproductive, is viewed as taboo, monstrous, or immoral, a "[revelling] in the discourse of the loathsome, the outcast."[17] Queer desire typically animates vampire literature, and it also defines the quality of Albrecht's desire for Giselle in the adagio. Giselle's desire for Albrecht, however, is characterized by the affect "love." Love, in the sense that Kristeva uses the term, tends toward conventionality and symbolic—rather than semiotic—expression.

Kristeva examines love in *Tales of Love*. In this psychic scenario, the child identifies through the maternal body with "the father of individual prehistory," who represents the diverted desires of the mother for the father, or the 'Third Party.'"[18] When the mother says to the child, "I am proud of you," or "Isn't he beautiful?," this is "aimed at that Third Party."[19] The connection through the mother to the social, paternal function allows for the idealization characteristic of the amatory state. However, Kristeva reminds us, "without the maternal 'diversion' toward a Third Party, the bodily exchange is abjection or devouring."[20]

As a dangerously seductive Wili, Giselle represents the devouring abject mother. However, she also represents Kristeva's "Third Party," or imaginary father. In this capacity, Giselle struggles to divert Albrecht's deadly, abject passion away from herself and toward life. In *Powers of*

ABOVE: *Kimberly Glasco prays for Albrecht's safety.*
Photo by Cylla von Tiedemann. National Ballet of Canada.

RIGHT: *Margaret Illmann prays for Albrecht's safety.*
Photo by Cylla von Tiedemann. National Ballet of Canada.

Horror, Kristeva explains that "[t]he function of . . . religious rituals is to ward off the subject's fear of his very own identity sinking irretrievably into the mother."[21] The adagio and pas de deux contain a number of such rituals, beginning with Giselle's offering Albrecht the sanctuary of her tombstone. Time and again she presses her palms together in a gesture of Christian piety, praying Myrtha and her legion of Wilis for Albrecht's release. Giselle is thus associated not only with the vampire (because she is dead), but also (because of her goodness and self-sacrifice) with the idealized Christian saint. The struggle between abjection and love is the essential struggle in the ballet's narrative economy.

In Gautier's scenario and in early productions of the ballet, this struggle ended with the victory of love, restoration of the social order, and suppression of the abject power of the Wilis. In contemporary performances, the ending is more ambiguous. Albrecht is left alive (a victory for love, life, and symbolic idealism), but he is alone rather than in the arms of Bathilde and surrounded by retainers, and he is stunned and debilitated by his experience (a victory for death and the abject maternal body). What has changed is our faith in love as a foundation of the social order. In *Tales of Love*, Kristeva addresses the social and personal crisis of love resulting from the fact that "the guideposts that insured our ascent toward the good have been proven questionable."[22] This observation accords with what we have noted thus far in our discussion of the ballet—that Albrecht's personal crisis stems from a symbolic crisis and that the paternal, symbolic function is not sufficiently compelling to keep him safely within its borders. This weakness nourishes his desire for an abject Giselle over an object (Bathilde), and also keeps Giselle's love from reconciling Albrecht to the social order. This leads us to a consideration of melancholia, the affect that brings about a rupture in the narrative discourse.

In *Black Sun*, Kristeva considers the psychic workings of sadness. It is derived, she writes, from the "impossible mourning for the maternal object": "The child king becomes irredeemably sad before uttering his first words; this is because he has been irrevocably, desperately separated from the mother, a loss that causes him to find her again, along with other objects of love, first in the imagination, then in words."[23] When language cannot sufficiently compensate for this loss, the subject withdraws "to the point of inaction (pretending to be dead) or even suicide."[24] Kristeva's discussion focuses not on the mourning and melancholia that result from a real object-loss, but rather on narcissistic melancholia. She explains that for the narcissist, "sadness...[is] the most archaic expression of an unsymbolizable, unnameable narcissistic wound, so precocious that no outside agent...can be used as referent."[25] In fact, she continues, the depressed narcissist "mourns not an Object," but what she calls "Thing," defined as "the real that does not lead to signification, the center of attraction and repulsion, seat of sexuality from which the object of desire will become separated.[26] "Thing" can only be recovered through "melody," "rhythm," and "poetic form, which decomposes and recomposes signs."[27] Also, I would add, through the dancing body. Treatment for the melancholic involves becoming reconciled with the loss of Thing by love, or primary identification with the imaginary father. This identification would reconstitute "the bond of faith, which is just what disintegrates in the depressed person."[28]

For the depressive, surges of affect and the primary semiotic processes come into conflict with language (as well as with symbolic constructs such as ideologies and beliefs). This leads to the symptomatic distortion of language:

> Discourse allows itself to be changed by affective rhythm to the extent of fading into muteness....When the struggle between imaginary creation (art, literature) and depression is carried out precisely on that frontier of the symbolic and the biological we see indeed that the narrative or the argument is ruled by primary processes. Rhythms, alliterations, condensations shape the transmission of message and data.[29]

By the second act of *Giselle* the rhythm and music of the dancing determine the character of the transmitted data. In Act I, narrative and dancing are kept distinct. Dancing is used to describe, to demonstrate and declare love, and to celebrate, while mime is used to propel the story. In Act II, by contrast, dancing becomes the actual narrative. It is, first of all, what the Wilis do: they are vengeful dancing spirits. Dancing is how they lure their victims and the means by which they disarm them. Also, it is the means by which Giselle saves Albrecht. The blurring of narrative and dance is close to total in Giselle's adagio. Here she is compelled to seduce him (a narrative act) with ravishing poses (dance). Her seductive dancing is also a plea for his survival and, as such, includes a number of religious motifs, such as the prayerful attitude during the final plunge of the arabesque penchée. In short, melancholia displaces the narrative and forces it to give way to the dancing. Thus, the semiotic triumphs over the symbolic.

Because stories have a social as well as an artistic function, this breakdown has implications that transcend purely narrative concerns. In one of his essays, Roland Barthes explains how the elements of stories tend to fall into one of two categories.[30] They may be narrative, which is the part of a message that can be translated into other languages or media: in a ballet scenario this is analogous to mime. Alternatively, they may be "writing," or *écriture*, which is the part of a message that resists translation and requires its own technical language. Writing (or dancing) is descriptive, elaborating on situations set up by the narrative. In traditional story ballets the boundary between narrative and dancing is obvious: the first propels the story, creating appropriate occasions for the dancing. At the same time, to the extent that narrative is aligned with closure, discrete events, and the needs of the dominant social order, it also has an ideological dimension. Dancing (or writing) threatens to disrupt the social order represented by narrative closure.

The basic analytic model that Kristeva develops in *Revolution of Poetic Language* rests on the tension between narrative and dancing. The semiotic function is associated with the dancing body, pre-Oedipal drives, and the autoerotic mother/child dyad. The pre-Oedipal drives articulate what Kristeva calls the semiotic 'chora.' Neither model nor copy, "the *chora* precedes and underlies figuration and thus specularization, and is analogous only to vocal or kinetic rhythm."[31] The symbolic is associated with the Oedipal stage, when the child separates itself from the mother in exchange for language from the father. Toril Moi, in her introduction to *The Kristeva Reader*, explains that "once the subject has entered into the symbolic order, the chora will be more or less successfully repressed and can be perceived only as pulsational pressure on or within symbolic language: as contradictions, meaninglessness, disruption, silences and absences."[32] These gaps or ruptures in the symbolic are where the semiotic takes over.

Narratives generally unfold by introducing into a situation a disruptive or semiotic force that threatens the symbolic order. Narratives record the struggle between the semiotic and the symbolic, and end with some kind of resolution. In the case of *Giselle*, the heroine represents the unbridled semiotic force that animates and also endangers the social order, the reason she must be sacrificed. Although most evident in the second-act adagio, this aspect of Giselle is present from the beginning of the ballet. As an unmarried but marriageable young woman, she is associated with a socially disruptive (because nonprocreative) sexuality. The transgressiveness of her sexuality is reinforced by her excessive love for dancing, a form of self-absorption that recalls the a-sociality of autoeroticism. Early in the ballet Albrecht knocks on her door and hides. Giselle, unable to discover the mysterious caller, shrugs her shoulders and begins to dance. Her variation is full of exuberant jumps, which she performs with abandon and an appearance of self-enclosure that is emphasized by the body-circling arms and circular floor patterns. Her insular, yet generous sexuality threatens to disrupt the social order.

This threat as well as the pleasure that Giselle represents had a correlation in French society of the 1830s and 1840s. Like the dancers and cour-

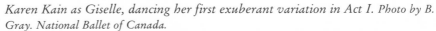

Karen Kain as Giselle, dancing her first exuberant variation in Act I. Photo by B. Gray. National Ballet of Canada.

tesans of the demi-monde who lived outside the pale of respectability,[33] Giselle disrupts the social and sexual order of the ballet's narrative. In theory, the threat she poses should be neutralized by Albrecht's willingness to sacrifice her for Bathilde, his socially acceptable fiancée who never dances. However, as Kristeva explains, "sacrifice can be viewed not only as an imposition of social coherence but also as its outer limit. On the other side of this boundary is the a-symbolic, the dissolution of order, the erasing of differences, and finally the disappearance of the human in animality."[34] Sacrifice is always accompanied by semiotic violence, which Kristeva calls "the laboratory for...theater, poetry, song, dance—art....By *reproducing signifiers*—vocal, gestural, verbal—the subject crosses the border of the symbolic and reaches the semiotic *chora*, which is on the other side of the social frontier."[35] If *Giselle* is supposed to deploy and then repress semiotic violence, it fails. Instead, the symbolic border is breached. Giselle's death marks this border: everything that comes before belongs to the realm of the symbolic, while everything that follows alludes to the realm of the a-symbolic.

Giselle's death marks a stylistic split between the first and second acts. Giselle is Yseult Lendvai; Vladimir Malakhov is Albrecht. Photo by Lydia Pawelak. National Ballet of Canada.

This accounts for the radical stylistic split between the ballet's two acts. The first act unfolds in the clear light of day, while the second takes place at night, in a misty clearing in the woods. Act I is set in a world of social hierarchy and procreative nature, while Act II is ruled by Myrtha, who founds her own order, which she uses to avenge the injustices visited upon her by the society to which she once belonged. The dancing in Act I is grounded and earthy, while in Act II it is dominated by the Wilis, light, airborne creatures in diaphanous tutus. The staging in the first act conveys an appearance of naturalness; that in the second emphasizes abstract, geometric elements. In Act I narrative dominates; in Act II, dancing. Act I describes the circumstances of Giselle's victimization and lends itself to moralizing. Act II, by contrast, muddies the moral issue: in the ambiguous realm of primary narcissism where the action takes place, the differences between victim and villain and even subject and object are obscured. Albrecht, who in the first act is the acting (villainous) subject to the passive (innocent) Giselle, regresses in the second to a state of presubjectivity and passivity, while she becomes his pre-object. The tension between the

Kimberly Glasco and Aleksandar Antonijevic in the ballet's final moments.
Photo by Vera Cammaer. National Ballet of Canada.

symbolic, which dominates Act I, and the semiotic, which dominates Act II, seems to reach a stalemate as the ballet draws to a close. Morning dawns (a victory for the social order), but Albrecht continues to yearn for Giselle and, through her, for the death and *jouissance* associated with the semiotic maternal body. The fact that closure fails to reassert the ascendancy of the social order points to a crisis in that order and suggests its inadequacy.

There are (at least) three ways to interpret this analysis. First, *Giselle* can be understood as depicting the social order in crisis and calling for laws to uphold it. Second, it can be understood as celebrating the triumph of the semiotic over the forces of repression. But laws can lead to tyranny, and unbridled transgression to delirium. Hence, the third alternative: constructing a new social order, one that embraces neither the tyranny of the law nor the delirium of *jouissance*, but accommodates both. To this end, Kristeva proposes an ethics that oscillates between law and transgression, that makes visible the processes underlying signification, questions the stability of identity, and reinforces instead its heterogeneity.

Kristeva's method reveals the unstable nature of key formal and ideological categories in *Giselle*. It also reveals their complexity and remarkably heterogeneous character. This heterogeneity remains unacknowledged in certain critical quarters, where the ballet is routinely dismissed as an instrument of class and gender oppression. But this cavalier treatment comes at a high price—the outlawing of pleasure. Rather than dismiss *Giselle* and other nineteenth-century works as politically regressive, why not embrace a critical practice that allows for *jouissance* as well as cultural and psychological difference?

Notes

1. In "Ballet and Ideology: *Giselle*, Act II," Evan Alderson argues that *Giselle*, like ballet generally, participates in the perpetuation of the ideological aims of the dominant social order, which it masks or veils with beauty. This experience of beauty is so powerful, especially in a ballet like *Giselle*, that we accept the naturalness of the ideology implicit in the work. He argues that *Giselle* embodies all that is wrong not only with classical ballet technique and aesthetics, but with bourgeois patriarchal values in general. His argument hinges on the fact that Giselle, by forgiving and rescuing the aristocratic lover who betrayed her, effectively condones his behavior. Alderson views this forgiveness as representing the acceptance of the dominant ideology and aesthetic that similarly victimizes ballet dancers, women, and the working class (*Dance Chronicle*, 10, no. 3 [1987], pp. 290–304). Susan Manning's feminist discussion of *Giselle* in *Ecstasy and the Demon* emphasizes how the ballet victimizes women by overdetermining the male gaze ([Berkeley: University of California Press, 1993], pp. 30–33). Christy Adair, in her rereading of *Giselle*, sees it as the tale of "the exploitation of a working-class woman by an aristocratic man" (*Women and Dance: Sylphs and Sirens* [New York: New York University Press, 1992], p. 102).

2. Ann Daly first used Kristeva in "Dance History and Feminist Theory: Reconsidering Isadora Duncan and the Male Gaze," in *Gender in Performance: The Presentation of Difference in the Performing Arts*, ed. Lawrence Senelick ([Hanover: University Press of New England, 1992], pp. 239–259). In Daly's article, Kristeva is called upon to account for how Duncan tipped the balance to effect change. In my article, I use Kristeva to account for an uncomfortable balancing act.

3. Julia Kristeva, *Revolution in Poetic Language*, trans. Margaret Waller, introd. Leon S. Roudiez (New York: Columbia University Press, 1984).

4. Heinrich Heine, *Germany*, trans. Charles Godfrey Leland (London: William Heinemann, 1892), pp. 204–205.

5. Quoted in Cyril W. Beaumont, *The Ballet Called Giselle* (London: C.W. Beaumont, 1944), p. 20.

6. *Ibid.*

7. For a detailed discussion of the original ending, see Marian Smith, "What Killed Giselle?" *Dance Chronicle*, 13, no. 1 (1990), pp. 68–81.

8. Julia Kristeva, *Powers of Horror: An Essay on Abjection*, trans. Leon S. Roudiez (New York: Columbia University Press, 1982).

9. Julia Kristeva, *Black Sun: Depression and Melancholia*, trans. Leon S. Roudiez (New York: Columbia University Press, 1989).

10. Julia Kristeva, *Tales of Love*, trans. Leon S. Roudiez (New York: Columbia University Press, 1983).
11. Kristeva, *Black Sun*, p. 22.
12. Kristeva, *Powers of Horror*, p. 4.
13. *Ibid.*, pp. 3–4.
14. Catherine Marchak, "The Joy of Transgression: Bataille and Kristeva," *Philosophy Today*, no. 34 (Summer 1992), p. 360.
15. Kristeva, *Powers of Horror*, pp. 63–64.
16. Sue-Ellen Case, "Tracking the Vampire," *Differences: A Journal of Feminist Cultural Studies*, 3, no. 2 (1991), p. 3.
17. *Ibid.*
18. Kristeva, *Tales of Love*, p. 34.
19. *Ibid.*
20. *Ibid.*
21. Kristeva, *Powers of Horror*, p. 64.
22. Kristeva, *Tales of Love*, p. 7.
23. Kristeva, *Black Sun*, p. 6.
24. *Ibid.*, p. 10.
25. *Ibid.*, p. 12.
26. *Ibid.*, p. 13.
27. *Ibid.*, p. 14.
28. *Ibid.*
29. *Ibid.*, p. 65.
30. Roland Barthes, "Introduction to the Structural Analysis of Narratives," *A Barthes Reader* (New York: Hill and Wang, 1966), pp. 251–295.
31. Kristeva, *Revolution in Poetic Language*, p. 26.
32. Toril Moi, "Introduction," *The Kristeva Reader*, ed. Toril Moi (New York: Columbia University Press, 1986), p. 13.
33. For the relationship between dancers and the demi-monde, see Susan Trites Free, "Dance of the Demi-monde: Paris Opéra Dance and Dancer in the Social Imagination of the Second Empire," M.A. Thesis, York University, 1986.
34. Kristeva, *Revolution in Poetic Language*, p. 76.
35. *Ibid.*, p. 79.

Women of Faint Heart and Steel Toes

JUDITH CHAZIN-BENNAHUM

Clothes, as despicable as we think them, are so unspeakably significant.[1]

Before the twentieth century changes in ballet costume often mirrored changes in fashion. This was especially true after the French Revolution, when a passion for the styles of ancient Greece and Rome—inspired in part by the paintings of Jacques-Louis David—swept the streets and ballrooms of Europe. The new fashion called for a high waist and long columnar line; breasts were prominent, and legs, sometimes revealed through transparent skirts, were elongated. Protective tights of white wool, silk, or cotton covered the legs, giving the body the appearance of a goddess sculpted in classical marble. Later in the century, Honoré de Balzac wrote of a character in his novel *Fausse Maîtresse*, "When I see her dressed in a gold-trimmed, white tunic

LEFT: *Isaac Cruikshank, "The Graces of 1794." "Feminine dress of the present fashion is perhaps the most indecent ever worn within this country. The breast is altogether displayed, the whole drapery is made to cling to the figure. Well may it be necessary to veil the face."* Print Collection, British Museum.

BELOW: *Adam Buck, "Two Sisters," 1796. Theatre Museum, London.*

"La Folie du Jour," 1792. In the ballroom, couple dancing and complicated partnering made dancing lessons more necessary than ever to those wishing to climb the social ladder. Napoleon himself took dancing lessons with Jean-Etienne Despréaux, the husband of ballerina Marie Guimard. Cabinet des Estampes, Bibliothèque Nationale.

Baron Gérard, "Madame Récamier," 1805. A great beauty and important salonnière of the 1790s, Jeanne Récamier was the queen of neoclassical fashion. Musée Carnavalet, Paris.

Jean-Simon Berthélémy, costume sketch, Proserpine, 1803. *Bibliothèque de l'Opéra.*

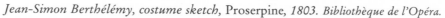

P.L. Débucourt, "La Dansomanie," 1809. The postrevolutionary dance craze led to the opening of many Paris dance halls and inspired Pierre Gardel's 1800 ballet La Dansomanie. *Gaston Vuillier,* History of Dancing *(London: Heineman, 1898), p. 189.*

and silk tights, she looks the image of a living Greek statue."[2]

The passion for white (or the palest of pastels) went along with the use of a newly stylish fabric: white muslin. A delicately woven cotton, it became the fabric par excellence of fashionable women. It was washable, pristine, and fell in a way that recalled the statues recently excavated in Pompeii. The cotton industry thrived. Cultivated in India and, especially, in the American South, cotton was brought to England where the new textile factories flourished. Thus, the French Revolution, the newly invented cotton gin, and slavery supported high fashion on the street and on the stage.[3]

Cotton allowed for clothes so light as to be almost weightless. This, along with shorter skirts and the flat, laced sandals that replaced heeled shoes in the 1790s, made possible the dramatic changes in ballet technique that took place in the following decades. Postrevolutionary costume allowed the legs, feet, and arms to move with unthinkable speed, amplitude, and freedom, as though the body had finally taken possession of the space it inhabited. Legs flew upward; in turns the number of rotations multiplied; leaps

"Costume de Bal," Costume Parisien, *1805. Cabinet des Estampes, Bibliothèque Nationale.*

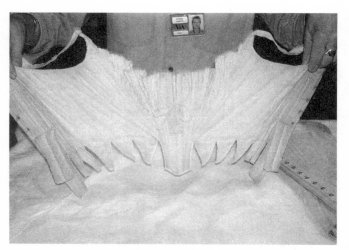

Early nineteenth-century corset. Dress Collection, Victoria and Albert Museum.

bounded further than ever before; the foot arched, stretched, and pointed. Partnering extended the conquest of vertical space, as did the use of pointe, which ballerinas such as Amalia Brugnoli were already exploring as an artistic device in the early 1820s. Nothing could be further from the eighteenth-century dancer in modified court dress than these lightly clad nymphs of Artemis.

Flesh-colored tights were integral to this revolution. Although their use was widespread among circus performers, they were almost never used by Opéra dancers prior to 1789. In 1791, however, Charles Didelot donned them (along with a tiger skin) in the Opéra's production of *Bacchus et Ariadne*. The following year, for the role of a sylph in the opera *Corisandre*, he wore them under a light gauzy tunic. His daring innovation caught on, and within a decade, when Maillot took charge of the Opéra's costume department, flesh-colored tights became commonplace. The combination of transparent fabrics, abbreviated skirts, and nude-looking tights created a new object for the male gaze—women's legs! The secret anodyne of neo-classical costume was the body suit (or *maillot*, as it was called in French after the costumer). Ballet dancers wore tights for the same reasons that other women did—for decency and for warmth.

Although styles inspired by antiquity were most popular, early nineteenth-century ballet costume also expressed a newfound interest in historical and geographical accuracy. In gothic works, where there was frequently an accent on the supernatural and the grotesque, the style was typically medieval; in works set in foreign or rural locales, authentic elements—Hungarian vests, Cossack spencers, Greek scarfs, Spanish mantles—might be juxtaposed with feathers and other wildly inauthentic frou-frou. Middle-class attire—jackets and trousers for men, day dresses and ball gowns for women—was another form of costuming that appeared in these decades, especially on the boulevard stage, where, by the 1820s, ballet had become an important attraction along with melodrama.

The waistline reached its highest level—just below the bust—in 1815–1817. Then, it gradually descended, reaching its natural level by the middle of the next decade. The high waist went along with an A-line skirt and a hemline bordered with ribbon pleats and flounces. In the early 1820s the skirt was still gored, with a back panel tightly gathered at the waist. As the waistline descended to its natural level, the gathering at the

RIGHT: *Early nineteenth-century dress shoe. Light, flexible, and narrow, the fashionable evening slipper had no heel and a sole that was slightly too small for the wearer's foot. The fabric wrapped closely around the foot, pressing the bones together, and creating a slender, elegant appearance. Dress Collection, Victoria and Albert Museum.*

LEFT: *Marie Taglioni's pointe shoe held by Dame Alicia Markova. Unlike today's shoes, Taglioni's slipper was unblocked and had no shank. The pointe and sides were strengthened by darning. Ribbons emphasized the close relationship with the early nineteenth-century dress shoe. Photo by Gordon Anthony. Theatre Museum, London.*

RIGHT: *Amalia Brugnoli and Paolo Samengo in* L'Anneau magique, *1832. Brugnoli began working on pointe in the early 1820s. An early admirer was Lady Blessington, who saw her dance in Italy in 1823: "She advances rapidly across the stage on the extreme point of her toes, without for a moment losing her* aplomb, *cuts into the air, and alights again on the point of her feet, as if she were no heavier than gossamer." Picture Library, Victoria and Albert Museum*

"Les Coulisses de l'Opéra," 1814. With the abdication of Napoleon in 1814, English and other foreign visitors flocked to Paris. This print is an Englishman's view of backstage at the Opéra. The devil on the extreme right is Louis Milon, the ballet master (1); to his left are Emilie Bigottini (2), Auguste Vestris (3), Mlle Virginie (4), and two "milords" (5 and 6). Print Collection, British Museum.

back was gradually extended to the sides of the skirt, while the individual panels became less tapered. By the late 1820s, skirts were fuller and supported by layers of petticoats—the prototype for the Romantic ballerina's costume. Meanwhile, the post-revolutionary sandal had given way to a close-fitting slipper based on the heelless, ribboned dress shoe.

In the early 1800s corsets had flattened the hips and raised the bust, while leaving the waist free. By the 1820s, however, tight-lacing had returned, with the new corset molding the torso into an hourglass figure. In his social history of the corset David Kunzle explains what was distinctive about the Romantic-era version:

> Bust and hips were padded, and tight-lacing was renewed in earnest with the aid of certain technical innovations: the metal eyelet, invented in 1828, and the split busk, fastened with catches.... Between 1828 and 1848 no less than sixty-six patents were registered in Paris, most of them affecting these two features. Tighter lacing was certainly good for business, since corsets thus treated gave an impetus to mass manufacture.[4]

The small waist was emphasized by huge balloon sleeves that reached their widest expanse around 1830. This sleeve, albeit in a less exaggerated form, became another important element of the period's ballerina costume, while the parted hair with plaits pinned up behind—a typical evening hairdo of the 1830s—became the Romantic coiffure par excellence. Corsets, of course, continued to be worn by women dancers until the early twentieth century.

LEFT: *Emilie Bigottini in* Clari, ou la Promesse de mariage, *1820. Choreographed by Louis Milon after a sentimental novel by Baculard d'Arnaud, the ballet featured characters from everyday life. Clari, a young peasant girl, is persuaded by the Duke of Mevilla to leave her parents' home on the strength of a promise of marriage that he has no intention of honoring. Although the Duke ultimately has a change of heart and agrees to marry her, the parallels with* Giselle *are obvious. Cabinet des Estampes, Bibliothèque Nationale.*

CENTER: *Bridal gown,* Costume Parisien, *1819. Cabinet des Estampes, Bibliothèque Nationale.*

TOP RIGHT: *Costume design by Auguste Garnerey for a female soloist in* Aladin, ou la Lampe merveilleuse, *1822. The jeweled embroidery gives the costume its "oriental" character, although the skirt closely follows the fashionable shape. Cyril W. Beaumont,* Ballet Design Past and Present *(London: Studio, 1946), p. 32.*

RIGHT: *Costume design by Hippolyte Lecomte for Marie Taglioni as Zoloe in* Le Dieu et la Bayadère, *1830. Note the freer handling of the skirt than in the* Aladin *design and the new emphasis on authenticity. Bibliothèque de l'Opéra.*

The revelation of the female body at the Paris Opéra did not go uncommented upon. "One never sleeps at the Opéra!" exclaimed an enthusiast in 1815, when Emilie Bigottini, a *premier sujet* or soloist, wore a light, white tunic in *Le Carnaval de Vénise.*[5] Her back, shoulders, and lower legs were completely bare, her breast nearly so. Mlle Brocard's sky blue, transparent costume in the opera *La Mort du Tasse* (1821), one of her greatest successes, had Castil-Blaze still dreaming about her thirty years later.[6] In *Aladin, ou la Lampe merveilleuse* (1822), Bigottini wore a tight, skin-colored bustier with a very short, transparent skirt and a white "oriental" scarf that floated down her legs. Another *Aladin* dancer, Mlle Caroline, wore an even more revealing outfit—a thigh-length white muslin tunic that was "the dancer's costume reduced to its simplest expression."[7] Lightly clad bayadères (the word is derived from the Portuguese *bailadera*, a female dancer) wore even less—a little half-skirt, all of it transparent, with a pearl-studded scarf over the shoulders and the hips. Finally, in *Olympie* (1826), the Young Ephesian Women were sheathed in tunics so short that they revealed the thighs and hips.

In 1837, Théophile Gautier speculated on the connection between the semi-clad dancers at the Opéra and the Greek ideal of female beauty:

> A woman who appears half-naked in a flimsy gauze skirt and tights to pose before your opera glasses in the glare of eighty footlights with no other purpose than to display her shoulders, bosom, arms and legs in a series of attitudes that show them off to best advantage, seems amazingly impudent if she is not as beautiful as Phaenna, Aglaïa or Pasithea. I am not very interested in seeing an ugly figure morosely jigging about in the corner of some ballet. The Opéra should be a sort of gallery of living statues in which all types of beauty are combined. Dancers, through the perfection of their figures and the grace of their attitudes, should serve to maintain and develop the sense of beauty that is vanishing day by day. They should be models, selected as carefully as possible, whose task is to appear before the public and instruct it in the ideas of elegance and good grace.[8]

Paris fashion plates, 1830: (BELOW) *"Petit Courrier des Dames" (from* Modes de Paris*);* (RIGHT) *"Les Trois Divinités du Jour" (from* Modes de 1830*). Cabinet des Estampes, Bibliothèque Nationale.*

These models were frequently at odds with historical veracity. As costume historian Carlos Fischer has observed, "Generally, the lead ballerina became accustomed to wearing the white, bell-shaped tutu while the corps or *figurantes* might, by accident, be clothed in costumes that reflected the historical period."[9] Or, as a disapproving critic of the period put it:

> Thus, they permit the dancers too much freedom in deciding the style of their dress, changing and disfiguring the designs so that they do not belong to any country, region or epoch. Isn't it ridiculous to see the corps de ballet of *La Servante justifiée* in a taffeta skirt and a thin gauze apron,...or to see the nymphs in *Flore et Zéphyre* laden with necklaces of *pastilles de sérail*?[10]

By the 1830s ballerina lithographs had become a thriving business. Appealing to a middle-class public, these images of sylphs, bayadères, naiads, wilis, and harem girls were the era's pinups. For the first time, the hungry public could savor in the privacy of their own homes the sight of beautiful legs and perfectly formed young bodies in semi-transparent dresses. The word tutu is derived from the street expression *cucu* or *petit cul* (the behind). It is said that Eugène

Marie Taglioni as Flore, lithograph by Alfred E. Chalon, 1831. Drawn in London in 1830, this celebrated lithograph shows Taglioni in a revival of Charles Didelot's Flore et Zéphire. *Although the premiere of* La Sylphide *lay two years in the future, Taglioni was already wearing the white, full-skirted costume that, with a few modifications, became the Romantic tutu. Dance Collection, New York Public Library for the Performing Arts, Astor, Lenox, and Tilden Foundations.*

Lami created the first tutu, but no one knows for sure because the design has disappeared from the portfolio containing the original costume designs for *La Sylphide*. More likely is the suggestion put forward by Fischer as well as by George Chaffée—that the tutu, as we know it, only came into existence in 1843, when Paul Lormier designed the ballerina costume for *La Péri*.[11] Whoever was responsible for it, the upshot was the same, an "abuse of white gauze, tulle, and tarlatan," as Gautier put it, with "the dancing shadows evaporate[ing] in a flurry of transparent skirts."[12]

The author gratefully acknowledges the assistance of Ivor Guest, Sarah Woodcock, Claude Fouillade, and Romain Feist in acquiring the illustrations.

Notes

1. Thomas Carlyle, *Sartor Resartus, the Life and Opinions of Herr Teufelsdrockh* (New York: AMS Press, 1969), p. 57. This volume was originally published in 1838.

2. Honoré de Balzac, *La Fausse Maîtresse*, in *La Comédie humaine, Etudes de moeurs*, 2, *Scènes de la vie privée* (Paris: Pléiade, 1951), p. 37.

3. For a fine discussion of the subject, see Elizabeth Ewing, *Everyday Dress, 1650–1900* (London: Batsford, 1984).

4. David Kunzle, *Fashion and Fetishism: A Social History of the Corset, Tight-Lacing and Other Forms of Body-Sculpture in the West* (Totowa, N.J.: Rowman and Littlefield, 1982), p. 121.

5. Quoted in Carlos Fischer, *Les Costumes de l'Opéra* (Paris: Librairie de France, 1931), p. 234.

6. Quoted *ibid*.

7. *Ibid*.

8. Théophile Gautier, "The Spanish Dancers," in *Gautier on Dance*, ed. and trans. Ivor Guest (London: Dance Books, 1986), pp. 6–7. This article was published in *La Charte de 1830* on 18 April 1837.

9. Fischer, p. 307.

10. Quoted *ibid*.

11. *Ibid*., p. 242; George Chaffée, "Three or Four Graces: A Centenary Salvo," *Dance Index*, 3, nos. 9–11 (Sept.–Nov. 1944), p. 153.

12. Théophile Gautier, *Histoire de l'art dramatique* (Paris: Hetzel, 1858–1859), 3, p. 225.

Blasis, the Italian Ballo, and the Male Sylph

GIANNANDREA POESIO

The aversion to the danseur, so emphatically stated in the writings of French Romantic critics such as Théophile Gautier, has often prompted the belief that "the male ballet dancer became an object of distaste in London, Paris and many other European cities during the first half of the nineteenth century."[1] Such an assumption, however, stems from a generalization that does not take into account the existence of European choreographic traditions other than the French one. A comparative analysis of these schools reveals that the allegedly secondary role of the male ballet dancer was not a characteristic feature of either the Danish or the Italian ballet cultures of that epoch. While the former has been thoroughly investigated, the latter has been frequently and hurriedly dismissed as a lesser example of theatrical dancing. Even the codification of ballet vocabulary ascribed to Carlo Blasis, the sole interesting aspect of Italian ballet for most dance scholars, has often been extrapolated from its context, thus allowing only a partial and superficial evaluation of Blasis's contribution to theatrical dancing and, more particularly, to male dancing. An investigation of the stylistic canons that distinguish Italian nineteenth-century theater dance from that of the rest of Europe is therefore essential to an understanding of a well-defined tradition of male dancers and to an in-depth appreciation of Blasis's work.

Portrait of Carlo Blasis. Carlo Blasis, Raccolta di vari articoli letterari *(Milan: E. Oliva, 1858).*

The peculiarity of nineteenth-century Italian ballet lies mainly in its failure to respond to foreign influence. Not unlike Italian opera, Italian theater dance remained linked to the modes of a national form of choreography that had its forerunner in the *"coreodramma"* of Salvatore Viganò. Formulated in the early nineteenth century, this genre marked the apex of the ballet d'action, concluding a process of development initiated more than sixty years before by Gasparo Angiolini and Jean-Georges

Noverre. The new Italian dance was structured on a well-balanced assimilation of mime into ballet and vice versa. Viganò rejected the principles of the danse d'école or pure dancing, also known in Italy as "dancing in the French style," favoring instead a type of expressive, rhythmic movement that corresponded more directly to psychological nuances of the plot. Although it originated from theories that had previously been expounded, *coreodramma* constituted a distinctive genre of choreographic composition. This uniqueness derived from the combination of several factors. Viganò's artistic skills found a fertile field of application in the dance activities of the La Scala theater in Milan, the most important stage for Italian ballet and opera. The plots of some tragic *coreodrammas* were prompted by the rediscovery and critical revaluation of Shakespeare's dramas that took place in Italy at the beginning of the nineteenth century. In addition, the massive proportions of Viganò's productions reflected the fashionable grandeur that marked both the Napoleonic era and the years immediately following the Congress of Vienna. Still, as a genre, *coreodramma* proved inseparable from the personality of its creator and could not be reproduced by the choreographer's successors.

Thus, after Viganò's death, the genre rapidly declined and disappeared. Yet, it had lasted long enough to imprint on Italian ballet those characteristics that denoted, for almost a century, the genre known as Italian "*ballo.*" *Coreodramma* also inaugurated a new performing style, soon to be defined as "dancing in the Italian style." A form of rhythmical mime, this style stood in contrast to "French dancing," which Viganò retained only for the sake of entertainment. An investigation of *coreodramma* and the Italian *ballo* reveals that both genres perpetuated eighteenth-century ideas and, more particularly, the principles of "*Classicismo,*" or classicism, an artistic movement derived from "*Illuminismo,*" the Italian variant of the Enlightenment. Central to *Classicismo* was the continuous quest for perfection and ideal beauty in every realm of art, along with the denial of human feeling and emotion as proper subject matter. The supporters of *Classicismo* thus rejected the presence of human passions within works of art, while longing for a "rational," exterior purity of forms. Although dancers, choreographers, and works in the Romantic style were generally welcomed and successful in every Italian city, the widespread appeal of French Romantic ballet did not alter the "classicist" nature of the Italian *ballo*, which retained its pre-Romantic identity throughout the century. Nor did the various imported French Romantic ballets diminish the popularity of the *ballo*, which, according to a wealth of sources, remained the favorite of audiences. This nationalist attitude toward theater dance, informed by the outbreak of Italian nationalist feeling characteristic of the period, was subtly underlined by the fact that most ballet scenarios or programs used the word "ballet" and its Italian equivalent *balletto* to designate productions imported from abroad, while the term *ballo* referred to creations in the Italian style.

Curiously, the "classicist" nature of the Italian *ballo* could also accommodate some characteristic elements of the Italian Romantic movement. Unlike its German and French counterparts, Italian romanticism—in reaction to the foreign regimes that governed various parts of the country—tended to focus on a patriotic rediscovery of a glorious, if often imaginary past rather than on phantasmagorical and supernatural themes. This obsession with historical events was reflected in the development of the historical novel and its theater equivalent, the "historical drama," exemplified by Victor Hugo's *Hernani* (1830) and operas such as Gaetano Donizetti's *Anna Bolena* (1830) and *Lucrezia Borgia* (1833) and Giuseppe Verdi's *Nabucco* (1842). Historical subjects were also ideal for theater dance works requiring a vast number of dancers, colossal settings, a wealth of mechanical effects, choral scenes, and

A couple in classical dress dances on the title page of the 1831 La Scala almanac. Teatro alla Scala: Almanacco 1831 *(Milan: Ubicini, [1831]).*

long mime sections interspersed with dancing, which generally took the form of folk or old social dances. The insertion of typical Romantic elements such as *couleur locale* and historical/geographical incongruity did not affect the solid structure of the *ballo*, which remained unaltered until the 1860s. On the contrary, what occurred was a gradual merger of Romantic and classicist elements, with the Romantic ones losing, to some extent, their distinctive features. Thus, one can say that Italian ballet never had a proper Romantic era of its own. By the time German Valkyries and other allegorical and supernatural beings invaded the Italian dance scene, the *ballo* had become an empty spectacle very similar to a music hall show and exploited those characters solely for ornamental purposes.

The cultural background concurrent with Blasis's early life was also imbued with classicist ideas. Among his mentors was Antonio Canova, whose sculptures and statuary groups, reproducing models from ancient Greece, are considered both the manifesto and the epitome of Italian *Classicismo*. The ballet masters with whom Blasis studied in his youth based their teaching on similar principles, for they instructed him in "French dancing," or the danse d'école, based on pure technique and on the geometrical harmony of lines. As an adult, Blasis preferred to uphold the old principles of his youth, rather than embrace the new ideas of the Romantic era in which he lived. According to his own writings and the few biographical accounts left by his contemporaries, he had a profound faith in the "classical" precepts of ballet technique; in his opinion the harmony of well-executed movements transcended the fashionable aesthetics of the period. According to the ballerina Claudina Cucchi, one of his pupils,

> Blasis's teaching was based on grace, vivacity, and the beauty of movement; Blasis was a cultured man, a celebrated intellectual, who wrote and published many works on dance, of which he knew the details and the nuances, in order to render this art an "art" and not just a display of gymnastics.... Monsieur Blasis wanted his pupils to have the highest degree of culture they could attain and to read as much as possible. He was not satisfied with the mere execution of *pirouettes* and *entrechats*; he wanted [his pupils] to perform their movements with grace and elegance, something that can be attained only by a refined training of the soul and of the mind.[2]

The ballerina's recollections indicate that in his teaching Blasis followed the rule, formulated by Gasparo Angiolini in 1765,[3] that dancers could attain the summit of their art only by adding the refinements of culture to the mechanics of mere technical training. Further evidence of the ballet master's attachment to *Classicismo* can be found in his *Studii sulle arti imitatrici* (1844), his third book published in Italian. In the second chapter Blasis formulated an idea of *"Bello Ideale,"* or "Ideal Beauty," that, in its emphasis on a classical purity of exterior forms, corresponded to the aesthetic canons of the late eighteenth-century visual arts. Expounded at the height of the Romantic era, this anachronistic notion occurs frequently in his writings, especially in the articles that Blasis published all over Europe in the following years. Finally, with the exception of the late ballets *A Diabrinha* (1857) and *Fiorina* (1858), billed as either "romantic" or "fantastic" ballets, all the remaining titles listed in his biographical sources, including *Notes upon Dancing* (1847) and *Il Genio e le Passioni* (1854), reveal an adhesion to the characteristic canons of late eighteenth-century theater dance and underscore his preferences in terms of subject matter.

Portrait of Claudina Cucchi by L.T. Neumann, 1858. Dance Collection, New York Public Library for the Performing Arts, Astor, Lenox, and Tilden Foundations.

It is not surprising, therefore, that in *The Code of Terpsichore* (1828) Blasis declared his distaste for Romantic ideas, affirming that a ballet composer should never take a literary work such as Goethe's *Faust* as the inspiration for a choreographic composition: the "Romantic" aspects of the story, he insisted, were not suitable for a ballet scenario.[4] Seven years after the publication of *The Code of Terpsichore*, however, Blasis

submitted to the impresario of La Scala the manuscript of a ballet scenario based on Goethe's poem.[5] In approaching *Faust*, however, Blasis virtually ignored its Romantic aspects. On the contrary, he approached the
project from a purely classicist point of view. As he explains on the first
page of the manuscript: "Apart from everything else, [the choice of this
subject] allows the staging of every sort of theater illusion."[6] The statement reveals that in choosing Goethe's story the young, ambitious choreographer was more interested in theatrical effects and spectacular
tableaux—two distinctive elements of *coreodramma*—than in the plot's
dramatic implications. Blasis believed that mythological dramas and
medieval tales, to which the public was becoming increasingly accustomed, could be the means for creating a series of plastic images and the
illusion comique that many eighteenth-century ballet masters, fond
admirers of the seventeenth-century French dramatist Pierre Corneille,[7]
had often praised in their theoretical works. For Blasis, the use of
medieval themes, a characteristic of the Romantic movement, did not necessarily translate into the creation of a Romantic ballet in the style of *La
Sylphide* (which Louis Henry had staged in Milan five years before Filippo Taglioni's Paris version). When considered from this perspective, the
contradiction between Blasis's statement in *The Code of Terpsichore*
about Goethe's work as being unsuitable for a ballet and the choreographer's written outline for a work based upon it ceases to be quite so glaring.[8]

The project itself, however, is difficult to assess. The manuscript reveals
that the choreographer conceived *Faust* as a "choral" work, indicating to
what extent Viganò's ideas had permeated Blasis's compositional methods. The witches' Sabbath, for instance, as revealed in one of the drawings
that complement the manuscript, was conceived in a spectacular manner
similar to a scene in Viganò's only "fantastic" work, *Il noce di Benevento*
(1802), as described by Carlo Ritorni.[9] Apart from these elements, the
manuscript is interesting because of the significant role played by the male
characters—another feature of Viganò's choreographic formulas.
Although the scenario does not specify the amount of dancing allotted to
each male role, one may assume that the work entailed a considerable
amount, both for the mime dancers and the "technical" or "French" ones.
It is worth recalling that, as a dancer, Blasis had belonged mostly to the
latter category and, therefore, might have drawn upon his own experience
in conceiving the parts of Faust and Mefistofele. Many secondary roles in
Faust are male ones, and the manuscript reveals the choreographer's intention of using several men from the corps de ballet for the choral scenes,
either as devils or angelic spirits.

The scenario thus reflects the hierarchical structure of the standard
Italian ballet company of the period, a structure originally devised by
Viganò and destined to remain unchanged until the demise of the Italian
ballo.[10] According to programs now in various public or private collec-
tions, each company included one or two *"primi ballerini di rango
francese"* (first male dancers of French rank), an equal number of *"primi*

ballerini di rango italiano" (first male dancers of Italian rank), and various *"secondi ballerini"* (or male soloists) of each rank for the secondary parts. The distinction between "dancers of French rank" and "dancers of Italian rank" did not refer to the birthplace of the performers or, as it as been suggested, to the training they had received. A "technical" or "French" dancer could become a "mime" or an "Italian" dancer at any point in his or her career. Blasis's artistry, for example, encompassed both genres. The *primi ballerini di rango francese* appeared mainly in the prototype of the pas de deux, the early nineteenth-century *"balladue alla francese,"* or French *"balladue"*—an untranslatable term—which provided an equal amount of technical dancing for both the man and the woman. In some instances, according to programs of works choreographed by Blasis, there were also solo dances for the principal "French" male dancer or ensemble numbers in which he performed with six or eight female members of the corps de ballet. Similarly, male mime dancers belonging to the "Italian rank" were given solos in which they could show their skills. Unfortunately, there are no sources providing a detailed technical description of these dances, although one can assume that it was in these sections that the interpreters showed the practical results of Blasis's teachings.

The ballet master's favorable attitude toward the male dancer is another interesting, if controversial aspect of his didactic writing. In Blasis's first publication on ballet technique, *Traité élémentaire. théorique et pratique de l'art de la danse* (1820), there are only sporadic references to the female dancer—two in the footnotes, one in the eighth chapter and one in the last chapter, about the different training for men and women. In addition, only two of the explanatory drawings—both showing group dances discussed in the book—include female figures. All the remaining thirteen plates, illustrating the execution of the steps analyzed by Blasis, show men with bare legs and torso. Finally, in describing the ideal dancer, the masculine ending is consistently used, as if the author's precepts were intended only for males. It could be objected that in French and in Italian, the two languages used in the treatise, the masculine ending is often employed in a general sense to embrace a category of people consisting of both females and males. Still, a comparison with other dance, mime, and acting manuals of the time, such as the 1820 Italian translation of Johann Jacob Engel's *Ideen zur einer Mimik* and Angelo Canova's *Lettere sopra l'arte d'imitazione* (1839),[11] shows that these publications commonly distinguished between genders. In the second chapter of the *Traité*, devoted to an analytical study of the legs, the terms *"un homme"* (a man) and *"un danseur"* are used throughout the footnotes.[12] The numerous Greek, Roman, and Italian Renaissance art works to which Blasis refers as examples of harmony and beauty are mostly well-known male icons, such as the "Mercury" by Jean Boulogne, which the ballet master discusses in connection with the attitude. Even the classification by role and physical appearance of the three types of dancer—"serious," "demi-caractère," and "comic"— seems to take only male bodies into account, the only exception being an ambiguous reference to Canova's sculpture "Hebe" as an example of the physical attributes of a female demi-caractère dancer.[13] Interestingly, in the subsequent *Code of Terpsichore*, which reproduced the *Traité* in its entirety with a revised ninth chapter, there is only one major amendment to the earlier text. While explaining how a good teacher should immediately identify the physical abilities of each pupil, Blasis acknowledges the existence of the two sexes. Where the 1820 treatise had read, "*Ceux qui possèdent une belle taille seront destinés, par le maître, au genre sérieux,*"[14] its 1828 successor stated, "All those of an elevated stature, of either sex, the master must set apart for the serious and more noble kind of dancing."[15]

It remains unclear, however, if this insertion should be ascribed to the author or to the chivalry of the English translator, Richard Barton. In a subsequent reprint of the 1820 manual, the *Manuel Complet de la danse, comprenant la Théorie, la pratique et l'histoire de cet art depuis les temps les plus reculés jusqu'à nos jours*, published in Paris in the collection of the popular Enciclopédie Roret, the sentence read, "*Hommes ou femmes, dès que la taille est élévée, le maître doit les consacrer à la danse la plus sérieuse et la plus noble,*"[16] thus indicating how the amended English version had prompted a revision of the original French text. An outstanding difference between the *Traité* and *The Code of Terpsichore* is to be found in the set of illustrations that complements the latter. Although the thirteen plates from the 1820 *Traité* have been retained, the drawings in *The Code of Terpsichore* show female dancers as well as male ones demonstrating the various steps and poses. Eighteen figures out of fifty-six have been modified, turning the bare-breasted, bare-legged men into classically clad women.[17] It is difficult to establish the exact reasons for these alterations, which could have been dictated either by the author's sudden awareness of the flaws in his previous publication or by a radical change of attitude toward the male body. The disappearance of the semi-naked men from the *Traité* is, in this sense, indicative of new aesthetic and moral canons. In *The Code of Terpsichore* the bodies of all the male figures are covered by many different kinds of attire, clothing that often spoils the clarity of the drawing. It is possible, however, that the modified and "censored" set of illustrations was simply an unavoidable concession Blasis had to make to pre-Victorian English prudishness. In *L'Uomo fisico, intellettuale e morale* (1857), a vast, ambitious dissertation on the human being and his mind, Blasis reverted to scantily clad male figures (plus two female ones) to illustrate the discussion of eye movements in relation to mood and his theory of the center of gravity. Incidentally, none of the numerous subsequent editions of both the 1820 manual and *The Code of Terpsichore*, generally reprinted and revised under Blasis's supervision, contains any reference to pointe technique, although pointework—the quintessence of female Romantic dancing—was taught at his academy in Milan.[18]

To accuse Blasis of male chauvinism would be erroneous, however. His writings as well as his own drawings bear the imprint of a son of *Classicis-*

mo, a man who positioned himself at the center of the universe and considered the opposite sex weak and inferior. In addition, the recurring use of the masculine ending in his treatises indicates that the author was constantly drawing from the vast practical knowledge of the subject he had acquired as a male dancer of great repute. It was this practical knowledge that allowed Blasis to perpetuate the eighteenth-century tradition of male dancing, while at the same time adding new blood to the celebrated line of Italian nineteenth-century male dancers. Yet, assessing his actual contribution is a problematic task.

The absence of source material has led many dance scholars to treat Blasis's publications as reliable sources documenting his career as a teacher. Indeed, most dance scholars have failed to distinguish between Blasis's activity as a pedagogue and his writings as a dance theorist. Although his written works deal with the principles he put into practice as a teacher, they do not provide any evidence of what he actually taught. In writing the *Traité*—his only real manual, the others being only expanded and revised versions of that "original"—Blasis did not intend to pass on to posterity a practical teaching "method": indeed, even though technical elements of dance practice are discussed, the 1820 treatise, like its subsequent reprints, is essentially a theoretical work, with only a general didactic purpose. In addition, one should remember that as director of the Imperial Ballet Academy attached to La Scala from 1838 to 1851, Blasis taught only the *"perfezionamento"* or *"refining"* class,[19] where, "after proper preparation, his pupils [were] allowed to attempt a *pas seul, pas de deux, pas de trois, pas d'ensemble*, and other steps, followed by every kind of dancing executed in the theater."[20]

As a "refining" teacher, Blasis did not deal with exercises meant to develop a dancer's basic technique. Rather, as Claudina Cucchi states in the passage quoted above, he concentrated on developing the artistic quality of his pupils' dancing. According to the regulations of the Academy, moreover, only six male students could be admitted each year, providing the male contingent throughout the eight-year course did not exceed thirteen.[21] As director, however, Blasis was granted permission to give private classes, from which some of the great Romantic ballerinas—Fanny Cerrito, Carlotta Grisi, Lucile Grahn, Augusta Maywood—benefited.[22] It is quite possible, therefore, that Blasis developed a group of male talents in spite of the limitations imposed by La Scala, by teaching privately. A survey of the La Scala records indicates, in fact, that Pasquale Borri (1820–1884), Ippolito Monplaisir (1821-1877), and Giovanni Lepri[23]—three celebrated dancers of the period—were not listed among the male pupils officially enrolled at the Academy.[24] Still, publications such as *Notes upon Dancing*, *Il Genio e le Passioni*, and Giovanni Berri's biography of Blasis,[25] as well as numerous articles in journals of the period, confirm that these dancers were the living proof of Blasis's "insuperable" teaching.

Although the existing source material does not allow us to analyze the

content of Blasis's private classes, his outstanding qualities as a teacher for male
dancers are clearly demonstrated in his
written works. The personal anatomical
knowledge of the male body that they
demonstrate, the balanced combination
of elegance and strength that they pre-
scribe, and all the other "pro-male" elements discussed above are evidence of his
genius in this regard. In addition, there is
the fact that most of his precepts are
regarded even today as fundamentals of
male technique. Interestingly, all these
principles were derived from the instruction that Blasis had received from teachers such as Jean Dauberval and Pierre
Gardel, exponents of the pre-Romantic
ballet d'action. Blasis may have revised
certain elements and updated others
according to the choreographic trends of
his era, but he "created" neither his own
system nor the celebrated "Italian
school" that came into existence only in
the second half of the nineteenth century,
that is, after he was forced to retire from
the academy at La Scala. Thus, it could be
said that, unlike female ballet technique—

Claudina Cucchi as Giselle. Raffaele Carrieri, La Danza
in Italia, 1500–1900 *(Milan: Domus, 1946), p. 67.*

which underwent radical changes during the Romantic period with the
introduction of pointework—the Italian male ballet technique taught by
Blasis perpetuated the late eighteenth-century French tradition with no
interruption of continuity.

Each of the three male dancers mentioned above preserved Blasis's
artistic legacy, albeit in different ways. Pasquale Borri, after an acclaimed
career as a dancer both in Italy and in Austria, became a choreographer of
international repute. His *La Giocoliera* (1856)—a *ballo* whose structure
scrupulously followed the choreographic precepts expounded by Blasis in
the fourth section of *The Code of Terpsichore*—was performed all over
Italy for more than ten years and was generally praised for its "refined,
spectacular, and operatic" qualities.[26] Five years later, moreover, Borri
won unanimous acclaim in Paris with *L'Etoile de Messine*, which premiered at the Opéra. Similarly, Ippolito Monplaisir, the applauded,
French-born partner of Marie Taglioni, Fanny Elssler, and Carolina
Rosati in Milan, gained a great deal of popularity as a choreographer.
Among his successful productions were *Brahma* (1869), an Indian fantasy
similar to Marius Petipa's *La Bayadère* (1877), but without the Romantic
implications, that was saluted as a masterwork of "choreographic clarity

and plastic beauty."[27] Giovanni Lepri, on the contrary, pursued a brilliant career as a *"primo ballerino di rango francese,"* often partnering the Italian ballerina Amalia Ferraris. He starred and created leading roles in successful works by Blasis such as *Le Galanterie Parigine* (1853), a comic *ballo*. According to an anonymous reviewer, Lepri's technique was "not mere physical exercise, like that of many other male dancers of today, but elegant, statuesque, yet brilliant, and precise. No one else can perform the most difficult steps in the same way."[28]

In 1864, while he was still performing, Lepri was appointed director and *perfezionamento* teacher of the newly opened Accademia della Danza in Florence, where one of his private pupils was Enrico Cecchetti, destined to become the most famous male dancer before Vaslav Nijinsky.[29] It is unfortunate, indeed, that Théophile Gautier was not aware of these dancers, for he would have discovered that Jules Perrot was not the only male "sylph" in Europe.[30]

Notes

1. Ramsay Burt, *The Male Dancer* (London: Routledge, 1995), p. 24.
2. Claudina Cucchi, *Venti anni di palcoscenico* (Rome: Enrico Voghera, 1906), p. 6.
3. Gasparo Angiolini, *Dissertation sur les Ballets pantomimes des anciens pour servir de programme au ballet pantomime de Semiramis* (Vienna, 1765; rpt. Rome: Delle Nogare e Armetti, 1965), p. 36.
4. Carlo Blasis, *The Code of Terpsichore* (London: Bulcock, 1828), p. 165.
5. This manuscript is housed at La Scala (Biblioteca teatrale della Scala, CR.Q.692). It is bound in brown cardboard with the words "Faust di C. Blasis" engraved in gold, although the first page, written by Blasis, bears the title *Mefistofele ossia il Genio del Male/Ballo Poetico Filosofico/in nove Quadri, di Carlo Blasis/Origine, Argomento e Allegoria del soggetto.*
6. *Ibid.,* p. 1.
7. Corneille's *L'Illusion comique*, a play within a play, was a theatergoers' favorite in both the seventeenth and the eighteenth centuries.
8. For more information about Blasis's *Faust* and its subsequent stagings see Elizabeth Souritz, "Blasis in Russia (1861–1864)," trans. Irene Huntoon, *Studies in Dance History,* 4, no. 2 (1993).
9. Carlo Ritorni, *Commentarii della vita e delle opere coreodrammatiche di Salvatore Viganò e della coreografia e dei corepei* (Milan: Guglielmini e Redaelli, 1838).
10. For a detailed description of the hierarchical structure of the nineteenth-century Italian ballet company, see U. Pesci, "Amor," *L'Illustrazione Italiana,* 14, no. 8 (Feb. 1886).
11. Johann Jacob Engel, *Lettere intorno alla mimica,* trans. Giovanni Rasori, (Milan: Batelli e Fanfani, 1820); Angelo Canova, *Lettere sopra l'arte d'imitazione* (Turin: Mussano, 1839).
12. Carlo Blasis, *Traité élémentaire, théorique et pratique de l'art de la danse* (Milan: Joseph Beati et Antoine Tenenti, 1820), pp. 46–49.
13. *Ibid.,* p. 91.

14. *Ibid.*, p. 102. "Those who possess a handsome appearance shall be assigned by the ballet master to the *genre sérieux*."

15. Blasis, *The Code of Terpsichore*, p. 95.

16. Carlo Blasis, *Manuel Complet de la danse. comprenant la théorie, la pratique et l'histoire de cet art depuis les temps les plus reculés jusqu'à nos jours* (Paris: Librairie Enciclopédique Roret, 1830), p. 83. "Men or women of an elevated stature shall be given over by the ballet master to the most serious or noble dance."

17. Blasis, *The Code of Terpsichore*, Pl. 1, figs. 4–5; Pl. 4, fig. 4; Pl. 5, figs. 1–4; Pl. 6, figs. 1–2, 4; Pl. 9, figs. 2–4; Pl. 11, fig. 1; Pl. 12, figs. 2, 4; Pl. 13, figs. 2–3.

18. Sofia Fuoco, one of Blasis's pupils and a famous ballerina of the Romantic era, was nicknamed "la pointue" by her Parisian admirers, because of her impeccable pointework.

19. Pompeo Cambiasi, *La Scala, 1778–1906* (Milan: G. Ricordi, [1906]), p. 377.

20. Carlo Blasis, *Notes Upon Dancing* (London: Delaporte, 1847), p. 61.

21. See *ibid.*, pp. 59–60, and Luigi Rossi, *Il ballo alla Scala, 1778–1970* (Milan: Edizioni della Scala, 1972), p. 71.

22. Rossi, *Il ballo alla Scala*, p. 76.

23. Lepri's biographical details are unknown.

24. See Cambiasi, *La Scala*, pp. 377–380.

25. Giovanni Berri, *Cenni biografici di Carlo de Blasis* (Milan: [G. Giovanni], 1871).

26. "La Giocoliera," *L'Italia Artistica*, 9, no. 8 (Feb. 1866).

27. "Brahma," *L'Italia Artistica*, 15, no. 9, (Mar. 1873).

28. "Il Carnevale del 1866–1867," *L'Italia Artistica*, 8, no. 8 (1867).

29. See Giannandrea Poesio, "Il Maestro Giovanni Lepri e la sua scuola fiorentina," *Chorégraphie*, 1, no. 1 (1993).

30. For Gautier's definition of Perrot ("Perrot the aerial, Perrot the Sylph, the male Taglioni"), see "Th. de la Renaissance: *Zingaro*," in *Gautier on Dance*, ed. and trans. Ivor Guest (London: Dance Books, 1986), p. 87.

Ballet Dancers at Warsaw's Wielki Theater

JANINA PUDEŁEK

In nineteenth-century Poland the ballet school attached to Warsaw's Wielki or Grand Theater was the only educational institution that did not charge tuition. This was a decisive factor in determining the social background of the pupils, who came, almost without exception, from poor families and were the children of small craftsmen, day laborers, and the like. Unable to pay for training in any other profession, parents sent their children "to the ballet." Sometimes several children in a family would be sent "to the ballet," and it was not uncommon for two or three siblings to be members of the company at the same time.

Apart from financial inducements, an additional attraction of a career on the ballet stage—especially for women—was the opportunity it opened for an advantageous marriage, which in those days meant, of course, the possibility of getting ahead in society and enjoying a comfortable life. Low social origins were carefully buried in silence, making it easier to discover a dancer's date of birth than anything about her parents. We know, for example, that the two greatest classical dancers in nineteenth-century Warsaw, Aleksander and Antoni Tarnowski, were the sons of a typesetter for the *Warsaw Gazette*. But the social origins of danseuses such as the Straus sisters, Karolina Wendt, Julia Trawna, and Maria Frejtag can only be inferred from the absolute lack of any mention of their parents or background in the available sources.

Another rather numerous group of pupils came from what were known as "theater children." The Krzesiński family of actors gave the Wielki troupe two well-known ballerinas, Matylda and Maria, and the pride of the company, Feliks.[1] Filipina Damse and Konstancja Turczynowicz were the daughters of a well-known Warsaw actor and composer, Józef Damse; Julia Mierzyńska, of the actor Andrzej Mierzyński. The father of the character dancer Ludwik Kuhne was the director of the orchestra at the Variety Theater. Similar examples could be multiplied at will: coming from a theatrical family was a mark of distinction for a dancer.

Only occasionally did ballet students come from somewhat higher social spheres. Hipolit Meunier was the son of a French teacher who had settled in Poland at the time of the Napoleonic wars and married a Polish wife; Mikołaj Grekowski was the son of a Russian officer; the Palczewski sisters came from a family of small landowners in the Płock region.

Differences in social origin lost their importance during the years of

Mathilde Kchessinska and her father Feliks Krzesiński—or Felix Kchessinsky, as he became in Russia—dancing a mazurka near the end of his career on the Imperial stage. Yearbook of the Imperial Theaters, *1897–1898, p. 273.*

study at the ballet school. A career depended on ability and progress; only rarely did other, incidental factors play a part in its development. Antonina, for instance, was the only one of the Palczewski sisters to become a prima ballerina, although Teresa excelled as a dramatic actress. The case of the Straus sisters was similar. Two of them, Anna and Karolina, became principal dancers, while the third, Paulina, remained a coryphée until the end of her stage career.

The financial situation of dancers in the Warsaw ballet was extremely modest. Until graduation, pupils of the ballet school, in exchange for free dance lessons, general education, and practice clothing, were obliged to appear in productions of ballets as needed. In the mid-1860s the starting salary for an artist entering the corps de ballet was five silver rubles a month, with a raise of two and one-half silver rubles every two or three years. At the same time coryphées earned twenty-five to seventy-five silver rubles a month, plus an additional one or two silver rubles as a bonus for each performance. The wages for soloists varied. In 1823, for example, Karolina Bizos and Maurice Pion were paid 324 złotys a month; Julia Mierzyńska received 270 złotys, plus a bonus of approximately five złotys for each performance. In the same year, Debray, a teacher at the school, was paid 400 złotys a month, and Thierry, the director of the ballet, received approximately 800 złotys. If a dancer who was active in the company also served as a teacher at the school, he was entitled to receive an additional salary, but a considerably lower one. During the 1832–1833 season, Maurice Pion, the director of the ballet, received a monthly salary of 558 złotys, Roman Turczynowicz 125, Eugenia Koss 216, the other soloists an average of 125 to 138, and the coryphées 60 to 70 złotys.

Thus, the wages were pitifully low, not even adequate to cover the living expenses of the dancers. Moreover, the artists were frequently obliged to buy various parts of their costumes with their own money, support families, and contribute small sums for birthday and jubilee gifts presented to colleagues.

Retirement posed a serious problem. General Józef Rautenstrauch, who was appointed chairman of the directorate of the Warsaw Theaters in 1832, won the right for ballet artists to retire with pensions, but only after thirty-five years of active service. Thus, if a dancer joined the corps de ballet at sixteen, she would be ineligible for a pension unless she remained on the payroll until the age of fifty-one! While soloists and principal dancers frequently remained on staff as administrators, assistants, or teachers in the school, for dancers in the corps de ballet the regulation was patently absurd. Not only did their meager wages rule out the possibility of accumulating any savings, but with the corps flooded year after year with youthful newcomers, there was little chance of dancers keeping their position until retirement age. There remained but two feasible solutions: an advantageous marriage or an outside source of income. And how could an attractive young girl who knew only how to dance and could scarcely sign her own name supplement her income? And when could she do so, given her numerous responsibilities in the theater? Unsurprisingly, moral standards among members of the corps de ballet were not especially high.

It was a situation that most people seemed to understand. "There are dancers earning five silver rubles or not much more than that," commented *Dziennik Powszechny* in 1861. "It goes without saying that no one is going to write anything derogatory about them. In fact, it is astonishing that given such scant salaries they haven't all quit the stage."[2] Still, there were moralists, such as novelist Józef Ignacy Kraszewski, who, without knowing the causes, condemned the effects. "The Grand Theater," he later wrote, "was famous for its selection of beautiful artists and for its ballet company, which was a seraglio for Moscow high society."[3]

The loose morals of a number of the Warsaw ballerinas was especially evident in the years after the abortive November Uprising of 1830.[4] As W. Zaleski later explained in his history of prostitution in Warsaw:

> Tsar Nicholas [I] considered the Warsaw Ballet and the St. Petersburg School of Ballet as government hothouses for prostitution. Unfortunate ballerinas did not dare to refuse an order to appear in the bedroom of the palace in Warsaw's Łazienki Park, where the Tsar stayed several times a year during his incessant tours of his Empire. The Tsar's chief purveyor of ballerinas was the Warsaw Chief of Police, General Abramowicz, a man of exceptional brutality and cruelty, who also held the position of chairman of the Directorate of State Theaters.
>
> Abramowicz would pick out the most attractive of the ballerinas of the Warsaw ballet company, have them bathe, provide them with silk lingerie, and send them to the Łazienki palace. When they reached their destination, servants would show them into the Tsar's bedroom located on the second floor just above the *salle de bain* to the left of the entrance. In total silence, buried in bed linen, the ballerina had to await the Tsar's amorous advances. For she would get a slap in the face if she spoke to the Tsar at the wrong moment, interrupting his train of thought as he habitually paced back and forth in the bedroom before climbing into bed.... Using all the powers at his command, Abramowicz attempted to plunge the entire company of artists into the very depths of prostitution, but his efforts proved to be fruitless except in the case of the ballet. Ballerinas who were especially trained as children had the idea of prostitution

slowly implanted in their minds from the age of fourteen. Abramowicz closely followed the methods used in St. Petersburg, where a ballerina who was a pupil of the State School of ballet upon reaching the age of sixteen would immediately become a plaything for the officers of the guard. But first she would undergo an appropriate "christening" at Court, and she had no choice but to accept her fate without a murmur.[5]

Abramowicz's "activities" were a typical of the policy adopted by the Tsarist authorities in the aftermath of the November Uprising. The atmosphere of the period is well described by Agaton Giller in one of his numerous works dealing with the later January Uprising and the causes that brought it about:

> People walked the streets with a measured step, furtively looking over their shoulders to see whether or not they were being followed. Any mildly outspoken opinion or raised tone of voice inspired fear and opened vistas of exile to Siberia. Poles resembled a frightened flock of animals. Dissension, dispersion, terror, and prison-like silence were interrupted by the screeching sounds of ball music coming from the Castle, which drove the sisters and widows of the fallen or absent warriors into a frenzied waltz. This ball music accompanied the decline of national dignity and lack of faith in a better future. The Field Marshall ordered merrymaking to take the place of the freedom that had been denied; laughter, dancing, and orgies would save one from persecution and cancel out feelings of hatred and revenge. Not tears but shameless flesh could appease the conquerors' relentlessness. Russian officers were advised to socialize with Poles, marry Polish girls, and by so doing contribute to the erosion of ancient customs and the destruction of Polish family ties. Thus joy under duress, dancing out of fear, and romance on command were part of the strategy of this policy. Overwhelmed by oppression and force, their instincts dulled by an incessant whirlwind of balls and orgies, Poles were rendered increasingly indifferent to the call of national aspirations and simple human duties; the conqueror had artfully infected them with a fatal disease of which entire peoples die.[6]

In such a propitious atmosphere and with encouragement from on high, inevitably there were people who took advantage of the situation. Historian Walery Przyborowski wrote about a particularly notorious and well-placed group:

> Ignacy Turkułł, already an old man, a cabinet minister and secretary of state of the Kingdom of Poland and a great womanizer, used to visit Warsaw frequently, and was surrounded by a flock of profligates who were as dissolute as he. This group included Teodor Paskiewicz, son of the Vice Regent; Prince Michał Radziwiłł; the Podczaski brothers; Edmund Chojecki, later to become a well-known French author, and others. They, so to speak, set the pace for debauchery in Warsaw. They squandered money recklessly, spent endless nights at the gambling tables, in fashionable restaurants, and in brothels. Not infrequently they would take the entire ballet company on out-of-town excursions and conduct flagrant orgies, much to the outrage of the public.[7]

Felicjan Faleński, a firsthand witness, recalled the atmosphere of the period in a memoir:

> Nowadays it is hard to conceive how in a Warsaw half its present size there could be so many dance halls, gardens, out-of-town excursions, and every sort of festive outing.... Golden youth, dissipated, loud-mouthed, drunken, and devoid of shame, ruined what was left of its health, having already dispensed with its conscience, and fell into the clutches of money-lenders, or even worse, lived on a secret subsidy from the government....
>
> The distinguished statesman, cabinet minister, and secretary of state of the Kingdom of Poland, Ignacy Turkułł, presided over these deplorable balls (known as spy-balls) himself. He was everywhere at once, as a matter of fact.... The more outrageously arrogant someone was, the more ready Turkułł was to adopt him, even to feel real emotion for him; such a one would be provided with food and drink, financially rewarded, and serve as an example for others to follow....
>
> Among the goddesses of this pandemonium three ballerinas clearly stood out above the others—Obuchowska, Bobrowska, and Jagielska—the most predatory harpies in the world, who would bring to ruin any young man, first reducing him to penury, and then throwing him down-stairs.... But it would be a mistake to assume that only the most notorious harlots ornamented those balls (which were called "friendly affairs" or "social gatherings"). Oh, no! The most distinguished and elegant ladies from high society would, it so happened, come directly from a ball given at the Royal Castle, wearing dominos so as not to be recognized.[8]

There was no shortage of those more than willing to frequent and make use of this "seraglio" outside the relatively narrow circle of "Moscow high society." Russian army units were always stationed in Warsaw, and lonely officers eagerly sought the company of beautiful dancers. Gilded youth, old men bored with family life, provincials on business trips to the capital constituted a wide circle of admirers, among whom it was easy to find a rich protector.

Without in any way questioning the credibility of these accounts, it should be said that there is a certain one-sidedness to them. Although insistent moral and financial pressure may have driven some ballet dancers to stray from the path of proper conduct, the great majority regarded the question of "additional income" as a necessary evil, and if there was no compulsion involved, knew quite well how to reject such advances. In fact, the sensationalism surrounding the likes of Bobrowska, Jagielska, and Obuchowska obscures the fact that most Warsaw ballet dancers chose a completely different way of securing their future—through marriage.

Most dancers found marriage prospects in the world of craftsmen, merchants, and civil servants. For example, Filipina Damse married one Mikulski, owner of a brick factory; Karolina Straus married a grocer named Hummel; the coryphée Józefa Wierzbicka married Adam Brandt, a municipal employee. Among the male dancers, Konstanty Budzyński, Franciszek Domagalski, Antoni Kwiatkowski, and Jan Popiel all married the daughters of local merchants and craftsmen.

Marrying into the landed gentry was considered very prestigious for a ballerina. Julia Trawna surpassed all hopes by marrying a titled landowner, Count Starzeński. All three Palczewski sisters married noblemen, as did Anna Straus and Józefa Karska (the mother of the celebrated playwright Gabriela Zapolska). Julia Mierzyńska's husband was a captain in the Polish army. Among the male dancers, only Hipolit Meunier could boast of marrying a noblewoman.

Marriage in all such cases inevitably meant the end of a stage career. Respectable husbands were not only unwilling to share their beautiful wives with the public but also tried to blot out everything connected with their theatrical "past." Moreover, at that time, normal family life could not be reconciled with an artistic career.

The numerous theatrical marriages constituted a separate group. In such cases there could be no question of any "career," especially if the marriage took place between two artists in the same company, as happened with Zuzanna Poliak and Mikołaj Woroniecki. Józef Cholewicki and his wife Maria (née Wojciechowska), parents of the great ballerina Helena Cholewicka, shared a life of poverty on their salaries as coryphés. In marriages of this sort, the husband usually supplemented the family's income by giving private lessons, while his wife tried for a position as an assistant in the school. If there were children, most often they were sent "to the ballet." In this fashion there arose entire dynasties of dancers and actors so characteristic of the Polish stage. Beside the Cholewickis, other Warsaw dance families included the Kwiatkowskis, Krzesińskis, Popiels, and Brandts. Some eventually abandoned ballet for drama, where the salaries were higher, the artistic fulfillment greater, the status more elevated, and finally, the chances of reaching retirement much more real.

Female dancers often married fellow artists from other branches of the theater. Thus, Katarzyna Frölich married the actor and playwright Stanisław Bogusławski; Honorata Laskowska, the renowned character actor Alojzy Stolpe; and Maria Frejtag, the composer and director of the ballet orchestra, Gabriel Rożniecki. Even such marriages often brought an active career to an end.

The only exception to this rule was the marriage of Konstancja and Roman Turczynowicz. He was the director of the ballet troupe, she a principal dancer. Roman Turczynowicz never took advantage of his position to promote the career of his wife at the expense of other talented women. Both were engagingly modest, simple, and unassuming, and their friendliness won them popularity and respect in the theatrical world. Their family life was a model of domesticity: indeed, it is hard not to admire this hardworking couple, who brought up five children and gave them a sound and thorough education. The atmosphere of the Turczynowicz home was so exceptional as to merit special comment in the memoirs of Jan Seweryn Jasiński, who as a rule was not inclined to gossip about nonartistic matters. However, the family was stalked by misfortune. Two of the sons, who took an active part in the January Uprising of 1863, were forced to emigrate and left Poland forever. The third son, Konstanty, a soloist with the Warsaw ballet and the pride of his parents, died prematurely of tuberculosis. The only daughter, Maria, who had trained to be an actress, also died at a very early age. The youngest son, Leon, an actor at the Variety Theater and later at the Mały Theater, lost in the course of a year, first, his mother, then his sister, and two years later, his father. With his passing, the Turczynowicz name disappeared from the Wielki's playbills, although not from its annals: Konstanty's second wife, Maria, worked for many years at the theater as a cashier.

Marriage caused a large number of talented dancers to quit the stage at a crucial moment in the artistic development of the ballet, resulting in severe setbacks to the Warsaw company. Poor working conditions also had negative effects. Ill-furnished and ill-equipped, the Wielki

Konstancja Turczynowicz as the Bridesmaid and Feliks Krzesiński as the Best Man in Cracow Wedding, *lithograph by Rignier, ca. 1842. Private collection, Warsaw.*

Theater was not a healthy environment. The dressing rooms were cramped, and there were drafts everywhere—in the gloomy auditorium, which was heated by only one stove, and the stage, which totally lacked ventilation. Colds were rampant, especially among the company's younger members. Coupled with inadequate nutrition and the low level of hygiene, these conditions created an ideal breeding ground for tuberculosis. The case of Konstanty Turczynowicz was not an isolated one; tuberculosis claimed the lives of Karolina Bizos, Ludwika Reppe, the coryphée Olga Charianov, and many others.

To this sad chronicle must be added the frequent accidents involving burns. The open gas lamps that lit the stage were a special source of danger for female dancers: their muslin dresses could catch fire at any moment. Most tragic was the accident that befell Józefa Oliwińska, who was burned in 1866; she suffered for two more years before dying at the age of thirty-one.

When a dancer (or other artist) of the Wielki Theater reached the age of retirement, a jubilee was organized to honor the artist. The ritual was the same for all theatrical departments. At an appointed time, usually around noon, representatives from the directorate and the administration, and artists from all the departments would gather on the Wielki stage. Speeches were given by officials, artists from other branches of the theater, and close associates; they were followed by applause and gifts of two kinds—a congratulatory scroll, painting, or photograph album signed by all the members of the theater community; and a present of some material value, usually a piece of jewelry for the women, and a ring, silver cigarette case, or snuffbox for the men—and, of course, the traditional bouquet of flowers. After an emotional speech of thanks by the jubilee artist, tears, kisses, and handshakes, the festivities ended, and everyone went about their usual business. The following day there would be a notice in the local press, the length of which depended on the artist's rank and popularity. The hero of the day now began the monotonous existence of a retired dancer or actor and at very best could count on only one more press notice: an obituary.

Only the most distinguished Wielki artists had a public jubilee joined to a benefit performance. Indeed, before 1866, only two ballet artists— Antoni Tarnowski and Roman Turczynowicz—were thus honored. A description of Turczynowicz's jubilee, which took place in 1865, was published in the *Daily Courier*:

Today at twelve noon local theater artists honored a fellow worker in a truly festive celebration. They paid homage to one of their colleagues, Roman Turczynowicz, the director of the Warsaw ballet, for his many years of service to the Polish stage. Thirty-five years have passed since he began his work, and he has earned the right to retire; accordingly, this date was chosen for the ceremonies dedicated to commemorating his unstinting service to the theater. For the occasion, the entire company from both theaters assembled on the stage of the Great Theater where they were joined by Mons. Hauke, chairman of the Directorate. One of the most distinguished actors, Alojzy Żółkowski, after first addressing the guest of honor in appropriate terms and presenting him with a painting as a gift from his colleagues, recited a poem especially written for the occasion by Mons. Jan Jasiński, the former director of the theaters.

Afterward, an equally distinguished artist, Mons. Jan Dobrski, presented Mons. Turczynowicz with a ring. The painting presented earlier has on one side Turczynowicz's portrait surrounded by scenes from ballets that he had arranged, each with its title inscribed beneath, and accompanied by a dedication and the poem. On the reverse side of the painting, there is a wreath composed of photographs of several hundred Warsaw artists, each of whom has signed his name under his likeness. The painting is the work of our well-known artist, Mons. Juliusz Kossak, who has executed a number of similar paintings for those celebrating jubilees or name days, which were commissioned by family or friends. In this manner the person so honored receives both a precious memento and a work of art. This sort of gift is becoming increasingly popular in Polish society, as we have mentioned elsewhere. The extremely beautiful and ornate frame for the painting also deserves mention; it was carved by Mons. Kowalski and was the subject of much admiration for its artistic qualities.

The festivity was adorned by an orchestra heard at the beginning and end of the celebration. The stage was splendidly lit throughout the ceremony, as it was during the performance that followed. To conclude this description of the memorable festivity so richly deserved by the guest of honor, we should like to furnish our readers with the following biographical information. Roman Turczynowicz was born on 14 March 1813, in Radom. In 1821 he enrolled in the School of Ballet, where he made such excellent progress that by 1825 he was employed by the ballet company. Talent, hard work, and love of his profession enabled Turczynowicz to become director of the ballet in 1853, after having first been a régisseur. In 1836 Turczynowicz married Konstancja Damse, daughter of the distinguished dramatic actor and composer, the late Józef Damse. Konstancja, herself a first-rate artist, shared with him the vicissitudes of married life and the triumphs of a professional career on the stage both at home and abroad. The only response that the guest of honor could make to the standing ovation of his colleagues and of the pupils from the ballet school, in whose name one of the youngest students, Mlle Adler, recited a poem, was the most beautiful answer of all: a tear of gratitude.[9]

RIGHT: *Portrait of Roman Turczynowicz, lithograph by M. Fajans. Private collection, Warsaw.*

BELOW: *Juliusz Kossak, design for a memorial tableau for Roman Turcynowicz's jubilee, 1865. Private collection, Warsaw.*

The ballet school produced far more graduates than the Wielki company could absorb. A rigorous process of selection thus had to be instituted, whereby future members of the corps de ballet were carefully chosen not only with regard to their artistic qualifications but also with regard to such matters as height, physical build, and appearance. The ever-present fact of competition had a stimulating effect on both the pupils in the school and the members of the company; for every opening there was a waiting list of candidates.

What happened to those who were rejected during the opening round of selections, and to those who for various reasons had to give up all ideas of working at the state theaters? The majority of those rejected after graduation simply looked for some other way to earn a living. Others joined various provincial companies and toured from town to town throughout Poland. Even the briefest connection with the Warsaw stage lent these wandering dancers a touch of reflected glory and warranted inclusion on the playbill of the significant phrase, "formerly with the Warsaw ballet." Maurice Pion heads the list of distinguished individuals who left Warsaw on such a permanent and pedestrian emigration, accompanied by his own touring company, which consisted of former pupils from the ballet school. His example was followed by the brother-and-sister team of Olimpia and Kornel Szczepański as well as Ludwika Springer, who also tried her hand at choreography.

Many others simply abandoned all thoughts of a career in the theater and devoted themselves professionally to teaching ballroom dancing. This calling was both better paid and offered more opportunities for a secure and comfortable life, since the study of ballroom dancing was at that time a requisite part of the upbringing of "respectable" children, whether in the city or in the country. And in this case as well, the label "formerly with the Warsaw ballet" was the best possible recommendation.

While young artists on the way up had difficulty staying with the Warsaw ballet and securing a more or less permanent position, popular, established dancers encountered enormous problems in obtaining permission from the management to appear in other cities and with other companies, not to mention abroad. Failure to obtain such permission could result in various penalties: a letter of reprimand, a fine, or even dismissal. For example, Olimpia Szczepańska, a promising young dancer, was dismissed for making several appearances in Cracow without obtaining the management's permission.

The management gave only its most grudging consent to guest appearances—especially abroad—by the company's most celebrated artists for fear of losing them, since the wages offered by the foreign companies were so much higher than those paid at home. Thus, the number of distinguished Polish artists appearing on foreign stages was reduced to a bare minimum, while the excellence of the Warsaw ballet and its soloists remained a local secret.

Yet the Polish ballet was hardly threatened by the danger of mass emigration for the simple reason that there were few places to go. Every outstanding company had its own school, as the Warsaw company did, and the ballet troupes attached to touring companies of Italian opera were neither numerous nor attractive enough to lure many Polish dancers from Warsaw. Besides, artistic peregrinations were largely the privilege of outstanding choreographers and soloists. The organization of a foreign tour entailed considerable financial expense and required proper social contacts, a knowledge of foreign languages, an ability to deal with people, or, quite simply, an impresario or a patron willing to cover the costs of an unpredictable venture.

No Polish dancer of the time, it goes without saying, had his own supply of money; generous patrons were not to be met with on the street every day of the week; and the private impresario was practically unknown in Poland at that time. At one point, Józef Zelt, a wealthy Warsaw mer-

Konstancja Tuczynowicz and Aleksander Tarnowski performing a cachucha in Le Diable à quatre, *lithograph by Hirszel. Private collection, Warsaw.*

chant, offered to organize and finance a grand European tour for the Tarnowski brothers. For reasons that are totally unknown today, the plan failed to materialize. It is possible that the Wielki management, fearing the loss of two of its stars, refused to grant the brothers a leave; it is also possible that the two, having little formal education or knowledge of the world, feared the machinations of a clever impresario. At any rate, the tour did not take place, and yet another chance for the Warsaw company to escape its isolation was lost.

From time to time the Wielki management would grant travel grants to promising individuals so that they could complete their studies and refine their art with famous Paris teachers. In the first half of the nineteenth century, however, only six dancers received such grants—Antonina Palczewska, Maurice Pion, and Mikołaj Grekowski during the 1825–1826 season; Konstancja and Roman Turczynowicz in 1842; and, finally, Maria Frejtag in 1857. Upon the completion of their studies, all these artists appeared at the Paris Opéra.

Very little material survives about the length of these stipends, the stage appearances of the recipients, and French reactions to their performances. Apart from occasional notices in the foreign press, the chief source of information is in the form of correspondence—letters written by Polish visitors or by the artists themselves to the editors of the era's most popular Polish dailies. Since these sources are far from reliable, it is extremely difficult to know how Polish dancers were received abroad. The task is rendered even more difficult because success or failure was not necessarily an accurate gauge of talent, but an indication, rather, that the dancer lacked the sponsorship needed to launch a successful career at the Opéra.

Of the three recipients of the 1825-1826 scholarships, only Palczewska's stay in Paris can be documented. Józef Elsner provided her with a letter of recommendation to Jean-François Lesueur, a composer and the director of the orchestra at the court of Napoleon I. She and her fellow dancers arrived in Paris in the middle of September, and she immediately contacted the well-known teacher Jean-François Coulon. Later, she attended the daily class that he conducted at the Paris Opéra. She appears to have spent a good deal of time at the theater, since she was given free passes by the French dancers whom she had met during their guest appearances in Warsaw. Taking advantage of the current ballroom fashion—Polish dances were at that time becoming the rage in French salons—she started giving mazurka lessons in the best houses of the capital.[10]

After eight months of study she earned the right to make a debut at the Paris Opéra on 19 April 1826. The program was modest enough, consisting of a solo mazurka to music by Józef Damse that was interpolated into the ballet *La Dansomanie*. The placement of the solo was highly disadvantageous to the debutante, as it directly followed the grand pas de trois with some of the Opéra's biggest names. The favorable notices that appeared the next day in the local newspapers are eloquent testimony to Palczewska's abilities as a dancer. However, the Polish community in Paris waited in vain for her debut in a more important role. In all likelihood Lesueur's sponsorship proved inadequate.[11]

Roman and Konstancja Turczynowicz, who studied in Paris in 1842, enjoyed genuine success and could have embarked on a European career had they so wished. Unlike their predecessors, they had an influential sponsor—Frédéric Chopin. "There was another reason why Chopin was seen more frequently than before at the theater," writes Ferdynand Hoesick in his study of the composer:

Appearing there at the time were the Turczynowiczes, ballet dancers from Warsaw, who had been warmly recommended to Chopin by [Józef] Elsner. In a letter of 2 June 1842, Elsner wrote Chopin on this matter in the following words:

"My dear Frédéric! The bearers of this letter, Konstancja and Roman Turczynowicz, dancers with the Warsaw ballet, are children of Mons. [Józef] Damse, the dramatic actor and most useful and even prolific composer of music for our theaters, whom you undoubtedly remember well. Mons. Damse has asked me for a letter of recommendation to you for his children, appealing to your heart and feelings, to help them during their stay in Paris. As it is, Mons. Damse is just now waiting in the next room while I am writing these words. I do this for him most willingly because they are worthy of your friendship and it gives me the opportunity to repeat once more in writing how much I love you and respect you more than anyone else in the world. Pray be assured of the sincerity of these words from one who has always been and who remains your loyal servant and friend. Józef Elsner. Enclosed is my composition *Ave Maria* as proof of these words."

Damse himself added a few words commending his children to Chopin:

Esteemed Mons. Frédéric! Despite the fame that all of Europe has showered upon you, I am certain that you still preserve in your heart the memory of your former friends, among whom I am happy to number myself. Our inestimable rector Elsner has been kind enough to write to you, Mons. Frédéric, at my request, while I waited in his room, and now I am setting down these few words, begging you to give help, protection, and guidance to my children, the Turczynowiczes, during their stay in Paris. Who knows, perhaps with your help, Mons. Frédéric, my children may have the chance to show their abilities in dance in Paris, and perhaps their dancing will remind you of our country dances and the tunes of the soil where you were born and where now you are a source of pride. Your loyal friend and servant, Józef Damse. P.S. My younger daughter gives me great pleasure by playing me your *Nocturnes*.

Upon receiving the letter, Chopin immediately extended to the Turczynowiczes his enthusiastic support, and what is most important, he made use of his numerous Paris connections—personal as well as professional—to arrange a series of appearances for them at the Théâtre des Italiens and to fill the hall with friends, led by George Sand. Thus, the Turczynowiczes had the chance to show Parisian audiences how the mazur and the cracovienne should be danced. The Warsaw dancers were warmly applauded, not only by the Polish émigrés, for whom these national dancers were deeply moving, but also by the French public. Continues Hoesick:

Satisfied with the outcome of their Paris appearances, and grateful to Chopin for furthering, in fact, for making possible their success, the Turczynowiczes left Paris in early November and returned to Warsaw. Before their departure, they paid a visit to Chopin, who gave them a note for Elsner, dated 8 November.

"My dear, ever dear Mons. Elsner! You cannot believe how much pleasure each word of your letter has given me. Many thanks too for the music which you sent me through the Turczynowiczes. They met with considerable success here, their appearances aroused a great deal of attention. They ought to be pleased with their accomplishments, and so should Mons. Damse, to whom I am not writing separately, but please be so kind as to tell him how his children (as he calls them) were greatly acclaimed here in Paris."[12]

The press notices that the Turczynowiczes received were also favorable. Long and appreciative reviews appeared in the *Revue et gazette musicale de Paris* and the *Messager*, with a comprehensive review by Jules

Janin appearing in *Le Journal des Débats*. Even before the Turczynow-iczes returned to Warsaw, extended excerpts had already appeared in translation in the Polish press.[13]

The last travel grant recipient in this period was Maria Frejtag, who in all likelihood embarked without a letter of recommendation. She left for Paris on 8 April 1857 in the company of Roman Turczynowicz and Jan Jasiński, the director of the Warsaw theaters.[14] According to a report filed by the Paris correspondent of the *Warsaw Courier*, Adolphe Royer, the director of the Paris Opéra, had invited her to dance at the prestigious house.[15] Subsequent reports noted that she was perfecting her skills in classical dance with the well-known teacher, Louis François Gosselin, while also taking lessons in the new and fashionable lancers dance, so that she could introduce this later on the Warsaw stage. She returned to Poland at the end of July, with a handful of laudatory reviews of her appearance at the Opéra. Wrote the *Warsaw Courier* a few days after her return:

> We have already told our readers about the trip to Paris undertaken by Mlle Frejtag, a dancer with our ballet company. Now we should like to say a few more words, making use of an article that appeared in *L'Europe artiste*, a French newspaper published in Paris, dated July 26 of this year: "A young dancer, Mlle Frejtag, a pupil of the outstanding teacher, Mons. Casselin [Gosselin] appeared in Act I of the ballet *Orfa*, dancing the pas de deux with Mons. [Alfred] Chapuy. We have already seen this same pas danced by Mlle Beretta in *Le Diable à quatre*, but Mlle Frejtag introduced several changes that were entirely of her own invention and used with great effectiveness. This dance proves that Mlle Frejtag is a dancer of the first class; she possesses remarkable grace, and her movements are digni-fied without a trace of vulgarity. She conquers all difficulties with extraor-dinary ease, enchanting and captivating the eye of the spectator. Her choreography has as its basis a poetic treatment of material aspects, and this is precisely where Mlle Frejtag excels." To sum up, Mlle Frejtag's appearance on the stage of the Paris Opéra turned out to be a personal success for the artist and likewise delighted Parisian ballet lovers who were pleased that their opera made such a happy choice in presenting Mlle Frejtag. In conclusion, at the end of the article the French journal adds that although Mlle Frejtag has already returned to Warsaw, the newspaper will follow her career so that the Parisian public will not forget her and perhaps will have an opportunity to see her again.[16]

However, as a follow-up article made clear, the paper had a bone to pick with the French critic it had quoted so euphorically:

> Although the article about Mlle Frejtag in *L'Europe artiste* was very flat-tering for us, all the more so in that it did justice to true merit, we still can-not pass over in silence the remark about the young dancer being "the pupil of the outstanding teacher, Mons. Gosselin," for even Mons. Gos-selin himself would not deny that three months would not suffice to train a pupil to obtain the sort of recognition on the stage of the Paris Opéra that the author of the article accords to Mlle Frejtag. Let us then state the

simple truth: Mlle Frejtag has been a pupil of the Warsaw School of Ballet since she was a child, and Mons. Gosselin can be credited only with showing the talented artist the changes and improvements that the art of choreography and the other fine arts have undergone.[17]

The European peregrinations of Mikołaj Grekowski and Kamila Stefańska deserve mention as well. Grekowski, who had studied in Paris in 1825–1826 on a Wielki stipend, returned to the city in 1830 with his friend, the young composer Antoni, or Antek, Orłowski. An article published nearly thirty years later described Grekowski's hopes at the time of their arrival in Paris:

> 1830. Orłowski was accompanied on the trip to Paris by Mikołaj Grekowski, who was later to become known in Warsaw as a first-class dancer, and who at the time still dreamed of achieving fame on the Parisian stage. The two artists not only shared the journey, but also an apartment in Paris, and Orłowski's first letters are signed by both Antoni and Mikołaj, although the latter didn't write anything himself, only adding a few words occasionally.[18]

> 1831. Grekowski, who for some time now has been studying with the ballet master Coulon, adds a few words to this letter [29 November 1831] and states that he has been engaged to dance at the Paris Opéra and that he continues to live with Antek.[19]

Additional information about Grekowski's activities comes from the *Warsaw Courier*. Thus, in early August 1832, it noted, "The Paris dailies report that the young dancer Grekowski, justly praised for his talent and handsome figure, will soon appear as a soloist at the Paris Opéra. Grekowski is a Pole who began his career at the Warsaw Theater."[20] On September 1 the paper published an even happier announcement: "The Paris dailies report that a few days ago the famous ballerina Mlle Taglioni, who has just returned to Paris, appeared in the ballet *La Fille Mal Gardée*, and the main role in this ballet, that of her lover, was for the first time presented by Grekowski, a dancer from the Warsaw School, who received richly deserved applause."[21] Despite this warm reception, Grekowski's plan of conquering Paris apparently failed. By July 1833, according to the *Warsaw Courier*, he had moved on to London.[22] However, London proved no more hospitable than Paris, and on 16 February 1834 Grekowski went back to Warsaw.[23] His return prompted only a short notice in the *Warsaw Courier*:

> After his return from another stay abroad, Mikołaj Grekowski appeared last evening on the Warsaw stage in a pas de deux, which he had executed on 9 August 1832, at the Paris Opéra, partnered by Mlle Leru [possibly Pauline Leroux]. A Paris daily commented on the event in the following words: "A young Polish dancer, Grekowski, was loudly and deservedly applauded; he has been praised quite justly for his force and plasticity. His performance indicates that he is a most promising acquisition for the stage."[24]

In 1837 wanderlust struck Grekowski again. Accompanied by his wife Helena Szlancowska, a Viennese dancer of Polish descent, he spent the next six years on the road. All that is known about his travels is that they took him to Naples, Vienna, and Moscow.

Kamila Stefańska's foreign career is equally sketchy. In his notes Jasiński mentions in passing that Stefańska had studied as a young girl with Gosselin and later traveled for several years throughout Europe. She made her debut at the Paris Opéra on 21 December 1857,[25] danced at the Teatro di San Carlo in Naples from September 1858 to February 1859,[26] and later that year appeared in Lisbon as prima ballerina of the local theater,[27] while also studying pantomime in Milan at the famous Academy of Dance.[28] In October 1859 she was dancing at the Royal Theatre in Manchester in an extravaganza entitled *O'Donoghue*. A review of the production in the *Manchester Examiner* mentions Stefańska as "a new addition to the company [with] every chance of becoming a favorite with audiences. She is a highly professional dancer endowed with a great deal of charm."[29]

Stefańska later appeared as a guest ballerina in Vienna and Berlin. She made her Viennese debut on 4 April 1866 in the role of Asmodée in *Le Diable amoureux*. At first received with reserve, she eventually won over the city's sophisticated balletomanes. She later appeared in the role of Haydée in the ballet *The Count of Monte Cristo*. The *Daily Courier* published an excerpt from a Viennese review of this performance, but without bothering to name either the periodical or the reviewer:

> Last night Frau Stefańska enjoyed a great success, made all the more triumphant since it was entirely due to her own talent. The fact that comparison of her dancing with that of Mlle Coqui [Cucchi] in no way diminished the audience's enthusiasm is proof that she occupies one of the highest positions in the hierarchy of choreographic talent. Astonishing lightness and extraordinarily animated expression in mime won her unanimous recognition.[30]

Stefańska went from Vienna to Berlin and on 9 May 1866 and made her debut at the Royal Opera as Mazourka in *Le Diable à quatre*. This time the *Warsaw Courier* quoted extensively from a review published in the Berlin *Kreuz-Zeitung*:

> Her execution of the mazur was forceful rather than soft. Frau Stefańska astounds the audience with her extraordinary elasticity and daring. Full of life in all her movements, she appears borne on wings of wind. Her *pas* are of lightning speed, . . . dart[ing] forward with a rapid rush, [although] even her most violent thrusts are executed with an assurance that is proof both of inborn talent and laboriously acquired skills. Her dancing of the mazurka put stress on the national traits of the dance, and in this respect her miming and her dancing had special charms. . . . At any rate, Frau Stefańska is a representative of the character school of dancing, no matter how greatly she differs from what has hitherto been regarded by ballet audiences as the model of character dancing. Future appearances by this

artist will show whether the Polish style, which in the *Le Diable à quatre* was totally appropriate, will be modified in roles of another kind to suit their specific character. If she does, in fact, display an adaptability to different styles, Frau Stefańska will indeed occupy a high place among the best *danseuses di bravoura*.[31]

The restrained tone and conditional praise of the review indicate that Stefańska's reception in Berlin was not as enthusiastic as her Warsaw admirers might have wished. Her next appearance, in the title role of Jules Perrot's *Esmeralda*, did not appeal to Berlin audiences. Stefańska, however, knew how to "manipulate" the Warsaw press in her favor. Thus, in commenting on her Esmeralda, the *Warsaw Courier* gave only a general summary of the German reviews.[32]

More successful with German audiences was Maria Frejtag, who charmed Hamburg in 1861 when she danced the role of Giselle. In fact, her reception was so enthusiastic that the editors of the *Warsaw Courier* decided to break the press boycott of local theatrical news (a response to events preceding the outbreak of the January Uprising) and publish two extensive reports about Frejtag's tour:

We have just received some interesting details about the appearance of the well-known Warsaw ballerina, Mlle Frejtag, on the Hamburg stage. Her appearance there was fraught with many difficulties. On one hand, the presence of Mlle [Katti] Lanner, a local dancer much admired by Hamburg audiences, could be felt; on the other hand, almost all the members of the local company were on tour, and it was next to impossible to mount a full production. Everything seemed to be working against the ballerina, however sure her talent might be. Despite these difficulties, thanks to the spirited efforts of the company's director and of the male dancer, Herr Knoll, the plan came to fruition. *Giselle* was presented, much to the chagrin of our ballerina, since, for lack of dancers, some roles in the ballet had to be assigned to dramatic actors. Finally, May 2 came, and posters announced Maria Frejtag's appearance in the role of Giselle. Spectators filled the house, but it was a very demanding audience, measuring beauty with a compass, as our great poet has put it. The reaction of the spectators grew quite enthusiastic as the ballet progressed, the climax of the evening being the pas de deux in which our ballerina incorporated Gabriel Rożniecki's variation from the final pas de cinq in the ballet *Carnevals Abenteuer in Paris*. The ice was broken, and the initial indifference and cool reception gave way to tumultuous applause. Our ballerina was repeatedly called back to the stage, and everywhere ladies were waving their handkerchiefs. From the moment that Giselle leaves the tomb until the end of Act III [sic], it was nothing but an uninterrupted triumph as the audience became totally carried away. Finally, . . . at a given sign the trumpets and drums began to play a triumphal fanfare in honor of the Warsaw dancer. At this moment other members of the cast took Mlle Frejtag by the hand and led her to the front of the stage, whereupon the audience gave her a tremendous ovation. In Hamburg such receptions are reserved for first-rate artists only, and since Fanny Elssler's time no artist had enjoyed the honor.[33]

The authenticity of this report is confirmed by a letter written to Frejtag by a Hamburg friend:

> I simply fail to understand how such a sublime artist as you are, Madame, can talk about unpleasantness on the part of the theater management toward you. They simply ought to be delighted to have you with them....On my word of honor, I have never heard such applause in Hamburg; everyone with whom I have talked is full of enthusiasm.[34]

As a result of her success in Hamburg, Frejtag was engaged by the Imperial Opera of Berlin, where she danced the roles of Giselle (May 21), Mazourka (May 27), and Esmeralda (May 30), all to great acclaim. Among the surviving memorabilia of the season is a sonnet in her honor by a German poet (in both a French version and a German one)[35] and a handwritten account by Daniel Nirstein. Although Nirstein's Polish is faulty, his observations are a penetrating appraisal of Frejtag's artistic qualities:

> Whereas last year the Russian capital sent us two agreeable and joyous theater guests, Mlles Bogdanoff [Bogdanova] and Friedberg, this spring we owe thanks to the Polish metropolis for sending us one of its most charming Sylphides, Mlle Frejtag, who was first seen on our stage last Tuesday.
>
> It was not accidental, we suppose, that our guest chose for her debut here the poetic ballet [*Giselle*] with its beautiful music by Adam. This shy and delicate creature of dance gives us the opportunity to admire choreographic art as well as her mastery of natural and expressive mime. In both of these, Mlle Frejtag has satisfied the highest demands made by our critical ballet gourmands. Her lovely, dexterous, and at the same time powerful body is filled with a fire found solely in Sarmatians. Despite her German-sounding name, Mlle Frejtag was born in Warsaw to a Polish mother. Each of her elevations is marked by graceful elasticity. Her attitudes in adagio parts are painterly masterpieces. Here she excels, since the ballerina pays great attention not only to the virtuosity of her legs, but also to the gracious bearing of the upper portion of her body. For example, the last scene when she slowly disappears into a sumptuous flowery tomb is one of the most beautiful of all mimed scenes presenting images in motion, precisely because the legs are no longer visible and the revelation or creation of gracefulness depends entirely upon the rest of the body: the head and the arms. In the tragic expression of a soul's ultimate suffering that ends in death as well as marking the end of a scene in the first act, we have totally forgotten the presence of the artist. Here is precisely what characterizes the highest achievement of this artist's work. The poetic quality of ballet flows naturally; the spiritual aspect of her art, in conjunction with an obviously elegant technique, creates a most pleasing harmony.
>
> Thus it is no wonder that she gave the audience great satisfaction and was recalled to the stage many times.
>
> Berlin / 24 May 1861 Daniel Nirstein of Warsaw[36]

Two weeks later the *Warsaw Courier* supplied additional details:

> We have already informed our readers about the successes that Mlle Maria Frejtag, an artist in our ballet company, has enjoyed in Hamburg. Now

we are happy to report that she has met with an enthusiastic reception on the Berlin stage. After her appearance in Act I, she was honored by personal thanks from His Majesty, the King of Prussia, who chatted with her in a most cordial fashion. The audience, although it was used to seeing first-rate European dancers, did not stint in showing its wholehearted approval. As word of Mlle Frejtag's talent spread, she received numerous invitations to appear in the best theaters of London, Amsterdam, Stockholm, Brussels, Vienna, Milan, and Turin, but the ballerina, faithful to her obligations, is soon expected in Warsaw.[37]

A note should be added to the account in the *Courier*. Frejtag returned to Warsaw not only out of loyalty to the theater, but also because her future husband Gabriel Rożniecki was waiting for her there.

The wanderings of Jan Żurkowski met with less fanfare. Ludwika Kowalska, Matylda Dylewska, and Helena and Jan Popiel all danced in St. Petersburg and Moscow at various times. A group of young dancers from the Warsaw company also appeared in St. Petersburg, to the great delight of audiences there, in a program of national dances, which were then the most sought-after item of export. And in 1853, Feliks Krzesiński—or

Cracow Wedding, *lithograph by Gavarni after the drawing of Antoni Zalewski, 1852. Private collection, Warsaw.*

Felix Kchessinsky, as he was called in Russia—became a member of the Imperial Ballet, St. Petersburg, where he danced for the next half-century.

Nevertheless, the number of Polish artists who appeared abroad is scant indeed when compared to the long list of foreign guests who danced on the Warsaw stage. Some of these guests were among the leading representatives of the European Romantic ballet, but the rest did not outshine the local Polish dancers and, in many cases, revealed a markedly lower artistic level. However difficult and unglamorous their everyday life, the Wielki dancers achieved genuinely astonishing things—a tribute to their training, discipline, and sense of artistic community.

—Translated by Jadwiga Kosicka.

Notes

1. Feliks Adam Walerian Krzesiński (1823–1905), better known by the Russian version of his name, Felix Kchessinsky, was a principal character dancer at the Wielki Theater from 1844 to 1852. In 1853, he was engaged by the Imperial Theaters, St. Petersburg, where he performed for more than fifty years. A brilliant character dancer and mime, he was the father of ballerina Mathilde Kchessinska.

2. *Dziennik Powszechny*, no. 91 (21 Apr. 1861).

3. Józef Ignacy Kraszewski, *Rachunki z roku 1856* (Poznań, 1867), p. 269. The various divisions of Poland in the eighteenth century had left the eastern and central provinces of the country under the control of Russia.

4. The Uprising of 1830, long prepared by Polish nationalists, was provoked by the Revolution of 1830 in France and the tsar's proposal to use the Polish army to suppress the new liberal governments in Belgium and France. The Russian garrison was expelled from Poland, and a revolutionary government proclaimed. In 1831, however, the Russian army defeated the Poles and finally took Warsaw. The revolution collapsed, and most of the Polish leaders escaped to the West, where they formed a powerful faction, especially in Paris. With its constitution now abrogated, Poland lost its political rights and retained only a small measure of administrative autonomy. This was the beginning of the policy of Russification (*An Encyclopedia of World History*, ed. William L. Langer, 5th ed. rev. [Boston: Houghton Mifflin, 1972], p. 750).

5. W. Zaleski, *Z dziejów prostytucji w Warszawie* (Warsaw, 1923), p. 23ff.

6. Agaton Giller, *Historia powstania narodu polskiego w 1861–1864 r.* (Paris, 1870), 3, pp. 4–5. The January Uprising took place in 1863.

7. Walery Przyborowski, *Historia dwóch lat 1861–1862* (Cracow, 1892), p. 51.

8. Felicjan Medard Faleński, "Wspomnienia z mojego życia," *Miscellannea z pogranicza XIX i XX wieku* (Wrocław, 1964), 8, p. 35ff.

7. *Kurier Codzienny*, no. 42 (19 Aug. 1865).

10. Józef Elsner, *Sumariusz moich utworów muzycznych* (Cracow, 1957), pp. 119–20; *Kurier Warszawski*, nos. 266, 272 (8, 15 Nov. 1825).

11. *Kurier Warszawski*, no. 110 (9 May 1826); *Gazeta Warszawska*, no. 75 (12 May 1826).

12. Ferdynand Hoesick, *Chopin, życie i twórczość* (Cracow, 1965), 2, pp. 394–96.

13. *Kurier Warszawski*, no. 285 (27 Oct. 1842); *Gazeta Warszawska*, no. 285 (27 Oct. 1842).

14. *Kurier Warszawski*, no. 95 (9 Apr. 1857).

15. *Kurier Warszawski*, no. 178 (12 July 1857).

16. *Kurier Warszawski*, no. 202 (5 Aug. 1857).

17. *Kurier Warszawski*, no. 203 (6 Aug. 1857).

18. *Pamiętnik Muzyczny i Teatralny*, no. 25 (25 June 1862), p. 390.

19. *Pamiętnik Muzyczny i Teatralny*, no. 27 (9 July 1862), p. 419.

20. *Kurier Warszawski*, no. 213 (9 Aug. 1832).

21. *Kurier Warszawski*, no. 235 (1 Sept. 1832).

22. *Kurier Warszawski*, no. 199 (27 July 1833).

23. *Kurier Warszawski*, no. 47 (18 Feb. 1834).

24. *Kurier Warszawski*, no. 76 (19 Mar. 1834).

25. *Kurier Warszawski*, no. 343 (30 Dec. 1857).

26. *Kurier Warszawski*, no. 158 (19 June 1858).

27. *Kurier Warszawski*, no. 48 (10 Feb. 1860).

28. *Ruch Muzyczny*, no. 23 (9 Mar. 1866).

29. *Manchester Examiner and Times*, no. 1772 (25 Oct. 1860); rpt. *Kurier Warszawski*, no. 302 (15 Nov. 1860).

30. *Kurier Codzienny*, no. 89 (20 Apr. 1866). See also *Kurier Warszawski*, no. 103 (7 May 1866).

31. *Kurier Warszawski*, no. 112 (19 May 1866).

32. *Kurier Warszawski*, no. 121 (1 June 1866).

33. *Kurier Warszawski*, no. 116 (13 May 1861).

34. The signature of the letter, which is unclear, appears to be "Josephine Jarael." The original reads: "Je ne comprends pas, comment une artiste fée comme vous, peut rencontrer des déboirs [sic] de la part d'une direction, qui devrait être heureuse de vous posséder.... Jamais, sur ma parole, j'en ai tout entendre applaudir à Hambourg; tous ceux à qui j'ai parlé sont dans l'enthousiasme."

35. *Commemorative Volume for Maria Frejtag*. Manuscript in the possession of Mme Eugenia Jurkiewicz, a granddaughter of Maria Frejtag. The entry and poem read as follows: "Le 30 Mai 1861 pour aujourd'hui l'Opéra Royale à/Berlin-Esmeralda/A Mlle Marie Frejtag/Première Danseuse du Théâtre Impériale de Varsovie pour les/débuts à Berlin, l'Opéra Royale le 21 et le 27 Mai–30 Mai/Gisela-Mazurka-Esmeralda/Sonnet":

> On vante avec raison Ton talent
> Tu charmes le public sans cesse
> Par Ton art unique, la grâce, la tendresse
> A Tes rôles Tu prêtes un savoir revissant [sic]!
> Ta belle et brillante carrière,
> Parsemée en Pologne des fleurs
> Tu rend célèbre sur la terre
> On Te comble partout d'honneurs!
> A Ta danse gracieuse, a Ta douce image,
> Sans tarder avec un vrai plaisir,
> On dédie enchanté un pûr hommage,
> C'est ici à Berlin pour Ta gloire en souvenir!

36. *Ibid*.

37. *Kurier Warszawski*, no. 130 (31 May 1861).

The Arrival of the Great Wonder of Ballet,
or Ballet in Rome from 1845 to 1855

CLAUDIA CELI

The period from 1845 to 1855 was rich in significant events both for the city of Rome and for the future kingdom of Italy. These events led to a process of radical renewal in Italian politics and society. In these same years the most celebrated Romantic dancers appeared on the stages of Rome—from Fanny Cerrito to Fanny Elssler, Lucile Grahn to Marie Taglioni and Carlotta Grisi, soon followed by the stars of La Scala. Through them, Romans came to know the era's most celebrated choreographers whose work reflected the dominant currents within ballet romanticism—the historical, which was especially popular in Italy and strongly tinged with patriotism, and the fantastic, of French derivation. By the end of the decade Giuseppe Rota's "dance-mime actions" had not only synthesized the stylistic solutions associated with these currents but also gone beyond them. Roughly speaking, the dance offerings of the Roman theater recapitulated styles set in other centers, most notably Milan and Venice. However, they also echoed the political events of the period, making a knowledge of the historical background essential.

In 1843 Vincenzo Gioberti, amid a climate of excited political debate, published his *Primato morale e civile degli italiani* (The Moral and Civil Primacy of the Italians) in which he supported the creation of an Italian confederation under the leadership of the Pope. Encouraged by the accession of Pius IX to the papacy, adherents to the neo-Guelph myth quickly appeared. Meanwhile, Pius IX (formerly Cardinal Giovanni Maria Mastai Ferretti), along with Charles Albert, King of Sardinia-Piedmont, and Leopold II of Tuscany, took an important step toward the creation of the first Italian customs league. Preceded by Ferdinand II, King of the Two Sicilies, all three promised to grant new constitutions within a year. Enthusiasm spread unrestrainedly. Its congenital apathy shaken, Rome sang the praises of the pope-king who embraced a liberal course, first with amnesty for political crimes and the concession of freedom of the press, then with the institution of the civil guard, and lastly by entrusting the consultative organs of government to laymen. In 1847, celebrations were permitted in honor of "Ciceruacchio," the commoner who had become a tribune, and a "motu proprio" abolished the act of subjection that Jews annually had to make to the Roman Senate. But despite the 1848 address in which the pope pronounced the famous words, "Great God, bless Italy," and the initial alignment of papal troops at Charles Albert's flank, the pontiff ended up keeping his distance from the insurrection, declaring that as head of the Church he could not bear arms against Catholics. The popular reaction against this change of course culminated in the assassination of Minister Pellegrino Rossi. As Pasquino bitterly commented: "Let us not delude ourselves.... To say `a patriotic priest' is to say a white raven; to be pope and to be liberal is a contradiction in terms."[1]

While the pope escaped to Gaeta, the triumvirs Giuseppe Mazzini, Carlo Armellini, and Aurelio Saffi proclaimed the Republic of Rome. But the dream of a "third Rome," the Rome of the people, collapsed despite the strenuous resistance put up by Giuseppe Garibaldi's forces against the French troops led by General Nicolas Oudinot. The failure of the revolutionary movements of 1848–1849 blocked the national unification process for the next two decades, when new upheavals led to the taking of Rome. In 1870, the city became the capital of the kingdom of Italy.

What was the character of this city that aroused such intense hatred and passionate love? Encircled by the Aurelian Walls, Rome lay concentrated around the Tiber River. The city's appearance was very different then from today. The river, undammed, had no banks, and everywhere there were gardens, even within the city walls. The watercolors of Franz Roesler convey some of the picturesque charm of the nineteenth-century Roman landscape. The fascination with Rome seemed to defy explanation, and foreigners sometimes considered the place a veritable enigma. They complained about the pollution and the dilapidated state of the city, the widespread panhandling, and the general ignorance of the common people, all the while flocking to the city and making it their home. On first arriving, many were shocked to see sheep grazing among the ruins, desecrating a landscape familiar to travelers from reproductions and written accounts. Then, almost unconsciously, a metamorphosis would take place in the attitude of the newcomers. "The foreigners who come to Rome," remarked E. About in mid-century, "begin by criticizing the lotto. After a time, the spirit of tolerance, so abundant in Roman air, slowly penetrates their minds, and they excuse a philanthropic game that allows poor people six days of hope for five *soldi*. Soon enough... these same foreigners... are swearing that it is unforgivable for a man not to leave a door open to fortune."[2] There was, in fact, a distinct contrast between the city's foreign population, which was largely bourgeois in mentality, and the natives of the "rural metropolis" (as Silvio Negro has called nineteenth-century Rome), where bourgeois influence was minimal. The local aristocracy was also relatively weak. Image, wealth, and pageantry more often than not masked a loss of effective power. Despite the strong presence of lay aristocrats in the papal administration, control of the *res publica* remained effectively in the hands of the clergy.

The Torlonia family, however, represented something of a case apart. Wealthy, recently ennobled bankers, Giovanni Torlonia and his son Alessandro were avid patrons of the arts. They sparkled in international high society, organizing lavish parties that helped create the Torlonia leg-

THE ARRIVAL OF THE GREAT WONDER OF BALLET / 167

end. By the mid-nineteenth century, Alessandro had brought the principal theaters in the city under his control. Now renamed the Teatro di Apollo, the Teatro di Tordinona became Rome's most prestigious theatrical venue—an ornament for the city and the Torlonia family alike.

Theater played an important role in mid-nineteenth-century Rome, as the Church itself recognized. Monsignor Luigi Ciacchi, who headed the Deputazione dei Pubblici Spettacoli during the 1830s, explained:

> To assure that a population is peaceful and content with the regime to which it is subject, centuries of experience have shown us that the theater is the most sensible and opportune means of keeping people conveniently distracted, decently entertained, and soberly amused. In these times, particularly, the distraction and amusement of the people is the most salutary medicine for those plagues that have emerged in almost every corner of the world.[3]

Mid-nineteenth-century Roman theater was a vital institution and meeting ground where novelty was at a premium and prized as much as success.[4] "Those who did not live in Italy before 1848 cannot appreciate what the theater was like at that time," recalled a contemporary. "The success of a new work was an event of capital importance, profoundly affecting the city fortunate enough to host it and spreading its renown throughout all of Italy."[5] Even Verdi, who was still idolized in Rome and for whom the impresarios Antonio Lanari and Vincenzo Jacovacci competed from the beginning of his career, described the theatergoing public of the city as "terrible and severe." Jacovacci himself experienced first-hand the snobbery of the Roman public when, in the 1840s, audiences ignored his production of Rossini's *William Tell* first at the Apollo and then at the Teatro Argentina.

The theatrical year began in the spring but reached its climax in the winter months of the carnival season, which opened at the Apollo on December 26 in the presence of the governor of Rome, the aristocracy, and the diplomatic corps. Because of its importance in renewing contracts, this season was crucial for impresarios. Artists had to be "of the highest rank and considerable renown." The impresario counted on the success of this season and therefore made great efforts to secure celebrated dancers. Such dancers would guarantee high attendance, increase receipts, and garner positive reviews in the press.

Among the impresario's worries was the ever-present threat of censorship, more keenly felt in Rome than elsewhere. Jacovacci, for instance, was fined for violating the order to cover the dancers' legs with *calzoncini alla napoletana*, or Neapolitan "drawers." The censors demanded changes in many works, sometimes asking for changes in titles or in names of characters that struck the public as grotesque and were greeted with loud disapproval.

Generally speaking, impresarios, and Jacovacci was typical in this regard, were a compromise between agent, producer, and artistic director.

Their existence was fraught with insecurity, and many worked at other jobs to pay the bills—Jacovacci, for instance, ran a fish market that he had inherited from his father—while building up a stock of theatrical properties. Despite the fish market, a warehouse full of scenery, and, by 1844, his virtual monopoly of Roman theatrical life, Jacovacci faced bankruptcy in the late 1840s. However, with support from Torlonia and the Pope, he continued more or less overtly to direct the destinies of Rome's principal theaters—the Apollo, Argentina, Valle, Fiano, and Corea.[6] These venues reflected the diversity of the city's theatergoing public, with the Apollo being the "aristocratic" theater par excellence, and the Corea a theater of decidedly popular character.

In Roman eyes, Jacovacci was most closely identified with the Apollo, where he died in 1881. People usually said that what killed him was sorrow over the announced demolition of "his" theater. Jacovacci had always curried favor with powerful Roman figures: at one point, for instance, he had used ballet to glorify papal policy; at another he had staged markedly patriotic works. Above all, he made a point of hiring local people, thus guaranteeing the theater's stable operation. This policy seems to have favored the creation of a local dance corps that, through its contact with artists of the highest caliber, improved its standard of professionalism. Some of these "local" dancers distinguished themselves in time as soloists and choreographers: this was the case, most notably, of Ludovico Pedoni.

In terms of numbers, most ballets produced in the 1845–1854 period were concentrated in the years 1845–1847. The political upheavals of the late 1840s caused a steep decline in production, which was partly reversed by the gradual increase in production in the early 1850s. The political and economic crisis of 1848–1849 marked a clear divide between the 1840s and 1850s.

1845–1849

Between 1845 and 1847 some of the most celebrated dancers of the Romantic era performed in Rome. The first was Fanny Cerrito, who danced at the Apollo with Arthur Saint-Léon during the 1844–1845 season. Already, in 1843, the couple had appeared together at the Teatro Alibert: on this occasion, the delirious public had unhitched Cerrito's horses from her carriage and carried her in triumph to the Piazza di Spagna where she was staying. A subscription to buy her a crown of gold was announced, and sonnets and odes were written in her honor. Not all the poetry was flattering. Giuseppe Gioachino Belli's sonnet "La Scerriti" was particularly mocking:

> Cert' è che sta Scerriti, sor Cammillo,
> tra ffiori a cceste e scartafacci a bbótte,
> da du'ora inzinent'a mmezza notte,
> sartò in zur gusto de' na purcia o un grillo.

Ma cc'a 'ggni zzompo meritassi un strillo
de sti guitti fijjacci de miggnotte,
saría faccenna de mannà a ffà fotte
loro e cchiunque s'azzardassi a ddillo.

Eh da cqui avanti appena pisscia un cane,
che ssiino bbuggiarati in zempiterno,
se sfogheranno a ffuria de campane.

A mmè cchi me fa sppesce è dder Governo
che invece, cazzo, de fa ccressce er pane,
averia da impedì ttutto st'inferno.[7]

Fanny Cerrito and Arthur Saint-Léon performing the Aldeana in La Fille de marbre. *Dance Collection, New York Public Library for the Performing Arts, Astor, Lenox, and Tilden Foundations.*

[About this "Scerriti" one thing is sure,
Amid flowers by the basket and notes by the ream,
From eight o'clock to midnight
She darted like a cricket or a flea.

At every jump the crowd roared,
What sons of bitches,
I felt like telling
All of them to go to hell.

From now on, as soon as a dog pisses,
May they rot forever after,
And ring the bells like mad.

What surprises me is this government.
Instead of upping the price of bread,
It should stop all this nonsense.]

"The Departure of the Ballerina," another sonnet inspired by Cerrito, adopted a mock heroic tone:

Ella è partita: o come afflitta e sola
questa città infelice oggi rimane!
Ahi, per le strade non s'incontra un cane,
o passa e non vi dice una parola!

Serrate le osterie, ferma ogni mola,
inariditi i pozzi e le fontane,
e appena, fra il tacer delle campane,
lieti i ragazzi che non vanno a scuola.

Paransi a lutto gli obelischi e i fori,
e si veggon per gli orti e pe' giardini
l'erbe ammalvate e intisichiti i fiori.

Oh genii de' teatri e teatrini,
o costei ridonate ai nostri cuori
o cangiateci almeno in burattini![8]

[She has left: oh, how afflicted and alone
This unhappy city today remains!
Alas, on the streets, not a dog is to be found,
And, in passing, no one says a word!

The taverns are closed, the millstones still,
Parched are the fountains and the wells.
The silent bells make only children happy
Because they're home from school.

The obelisks and forums seem to be in mourning,
And in orchards and little gardens,
The grass is diseased and the flowers withered.

Oh geniuses of the theater,
Either give this woman back to our hearts
Or else change us into puppets.]

Two satires also appeared in the Roman dialect—"The Arrival of the Great Wonder of Ballet" and "The Last Good-bye to the Great Wonder of Ballet."[9] However, in the following passage the anonymous author conveys quite a different impression:

I saw her one evening and, not content with that, saw her again on the second and then the third night. I regarded her proportions and her postures. I admired her *pas*, her movements, her flights, her finales, and her bows. Her grace delighted me. The creations of mythology raced through my soul....[Cerrito] reduced figurative art to dance, and this is the school of nature.[10]

Her admirer held Cerrito in no less regard than Giuditta Pasta, Maria Malibran, and Giulia Grisi, the "divine" singers of the epoch. (Belli, by contrast, treated the Tordinona ballerinas with a color that was far more in keeping with Roman sentiments.)[11] However, the highest recognition came from the Academy of Santa Cecilia, which elected Cerrito a member, an extremely rare honor for a dancer.

With Saint-Léon at her side, Cerrito performed the most famous ballets of her repertory, including *Alma, ou la Fille du feu*. This ballet exemplifies the difficulty in establishing the paternity of ballets. In his chronology of the Apollo, Alberto Cametti identifies André Deshayes as the author of *Alma* and at the same time notes that the principal choreographer for the 1844–1845 Apollo season was Filippo Izzo, leading one to believe that the latter had staged the ballet. The *Enciclopedia dello Spettacolo*, however, in the entry on Jules Perrot, asserts that Perrot worked with Deshayes and Cerrito (who played the role of the heroine) in choreographing the original production of the ballet, which premiered in 1842 at Her Majesty's Theatre, London. Since Cerrito's activity as a choreographer is well-known, this would suggest that the Roman edition of the ballet was hers. Unfortunately, the original libretto (at the Biblioteca Nazionale, Rome) fails to solve the matter. "*Alma, or The Daughter of Fire*," reads the frontispiece, "mythological fantasy composed by Sig. Deshayes in London in 1842, directed by Mademoiselle Cerrito, and staged by the choreographer Sig. Isso."

There are always problems in tracing a work back to its original authors, but the difficulties increase when the sources are scarce and contradictory. In the world of mid-nineteenth-century ballet, copyright did not exist, although it was in this period that the principle was first established under pressure from publishers and composers, who fought as well to preserve the integrity of their works. This, however, did not have much effect on choreographers of the time. In Rome the only ones to treat scenarios and musical scores as personal property were Giuseppe Rota and Antonio Cortesi. The latter, moreover, was one of the few choreographers to explain at length the literary sources of his libretti and also to discuss the production decisions he had made in translating works from other artistic media into choreographic form.

In fact, it is Cortesi who sheds interesting light on how French subjects were adapted to Italian tastes. His *La Silfide* (*La Sylphide*) (La Scala, 1841) and *Gisella ossia le Willi* (Gisella, or The Wilis) (La Scala, 1843) won greater success south of the Alps than the original productions of these ballets. In this regard, Kathleen Hansell cites an important passage from his libretto for *Gisella*: "If I return with a subject already used in France, I at least have the satisfaction of knowing that I have fashioned it to Italian tastes, broadening it"—the Italian version was in five acts—"trying to render the action more interesting, and furnishing it with dances of my own creation."[12] There are similar difficulties in identifying the protagonists during any one season. Indeed, some of the choreographers identified by us from holdings in various Roman libraries as being active between 1820 and 1860 do not appear in chronologies of the period, nor do their works.[13]

This was the case, for instance, of Filippo Termanini and his ballet *Ezzelino sotto le mura di Bassano* (Ezzelino Under the Walls of Bassano), given at the Apollo in 1845. Between 1849 and 1856, Termanini appeared as a soloist in at least twenty-three productions and was active as a

Domenico Ronzani as he appeared in Filippo Termanini's ballet Ezzelino sotto le mura de Bassano *at the Teatro di Apollo, 1845. A dancer of strong dramatic presence, Ronzani staged a number of Romantic ballets, including the first Roman production of* Giselle, *which premiered in 1845 at the Teatro Argentina. Bertarelli Collection, Milan.*

choreographer beginning in 1845. While it is undoubtedly premature to risk a critical assessment of his work, it is worth noting that his choice of subjects and even titles coincide with certain heroic-historical ballets by Giacomo Serafini and Luigi Astolfi.[14] It is unknown where some of Termanini's works were performed and if these ballets were actually staged. (The libretti in many instances were not printed by the usual typesetters, and staging information is incomplete.) We do know that some of his ballets were not produced for reasons of *force majeure*, as in 1849 when theaters closed because of the political situation.

Except for Cortesi and Rota, all the artists mentioned thus far worked at the Apollo in 1845. In that year, too, the Teatro Argentina presented works by Antonio Coppini and Domenico Ronzani with Cerrito's rival Fanny Elssler as their star. Elssler soon supplanted Cerrito in Roman affections, remaining for local dance fans the most resplendent of the Romantic ballerinas.[15] The appearances of Marie Taglioni and Carlotta Grisi made less of an impression, although they presented some of the most celebrated items from their repertory.

Elssler's success transcended her merits as an artist. The Roman public was dazzled by the woman who, at Metternich's request, was said to have seduced the unfortunate King of Rome, contributing to his premature death. Thus, when she appeared in Rome, audiences and critics alike, already anticipating her arrival with pleasure, welcomed her with wild, impetuous enthusiasm. "When she dances," wrote the critic for *La Rivista*,

> it is her neatness and the regularity of movements in her leaps and in her supremely difficult *pas* that delight and surprise. When she mimes, most would be forced to admit that she is inimitable. How she passes from simple to complex situations, from tender to brilliant ones, and comic to tragic ones—all without effort and apparent transition! With such rare gifts it is no wonder that fanaticism has followed this woman through all the capitals of Europe.[16]

"The most attractive part of the season," wrote the music historian Giuseppe Radiciotti,

> was the appearance of Elssler, new to the stages of Rome. This celebrated ballerina was justly appreciated by our public from her first evening— unlike her reception in Sinigallia, Bologna, and elsewhere—and she received thunderous applause despite the fact that the ballet she performed, *Gisella*, included dances in the worst taste and dreadfully dull music.[17]

So as not to rekindle the political tensions that almost certainly accounted for the Austrian ballerina's lukewarm reception outside Rome, Prince Doria opposed the offer of a crown of gold for Elssler. When asked to authorize the gift, Pius IX is said to have remarked with good-natured irony, "Crowns are for the head not the feet," although in the end he gave his assent.[18]

The staging of *Gisella o le Willi*, so deprecated by Radiciotti, was presented by Domenico Ronzani, who was also responsible for the ballets *La Esmeralda* and *Le illusioni di un pittore* (The Illusions of a Painter), which had been choreographed by Perrot with Elssler as the heroine. Ronzani's *Gisella* would thus seem at first to be a reproduction of the Coralli-Perrot

"Ronzani's Grand Ballet Troupe," lithograph by B.F. Smith, Jr., New York, 1857. In 1857, writes Lillian Moore, "the celebrated mime and choreographer Domenico Ronzani...brought to the United States the largest and perhaps the finest ballet company yet to arrive on these shores. Organized in Europe for the express purpose of the American tour, the Ronzani Ballet had been engaged to inaugurate the new Philadelphia Academy of Music....The leading dancers were Louise Lamoureux and Filippo Baratti, the principal mimes Cesare and Serafina Cecchetti. Their seven-year-old son Enrico, future great pedagogue, teacher of Pavlova and Nijinsky, was on hand to play the urchin in Il Birichino di Parigi. *It was Ronzani's production of Jules Perrot's* Faust *which was presented on the opening night, September 15, 1857. The Dance Collection's impressive lithograph may show a scene from this ballet. Probably used as a poster..., it conveys a graphic impression of the formal, decorative use of the ensemble and the airy brilliance of the stars. The American tour of the Ronzani company marked one of the last noteworthy manifestations of the romantic ballet in this country"* (Images of the Dance, pp. 82–83). *Dance Collection, New York Public Library for the Performing Arts, Astor, Lenox, and Tilden Foundations.*

original, but a glance at the libretto shows that the Roman version was quite different. For one thing, it had three acts. The rationale for the new act structure, Ronzani explained, was "the need for the costume changes that are indispensable to this ballet." The second act took place in the "hall of the prince's castle," where Bathilde's father asks his daughter why she remains so "sad and pensive" on the eve of her wedding. Albrecht (whose name was Italianized to Alberto) then appears with numerous wedding guests, including Giselle, Berthe, and Hilarion (Ilarione). When Alberto's true identity is revealed to Giselle in the castle, she quickly passes from desperation to madness and death. It is only in Act III, during the "Night with Moon," that the Wilis finally appear. Hilarion, after praying for Giselle, escapes unharmed from the Wilis' power. The scene ends with the following words: "With the dawn the Wilis must return to their graves, and Giselle must go with them. Myrthe, filled with compassion for Albrecht and Giselle's tender love for him, . . . unites her with the only object that could make her happy, even beyond the grave."

The differences between this and the French version of the ballet are obvious, as are the similarities with other Romantic-era plots. Such considerations suggest that in his choreographic solutions Ronzani was much closer to Antonio Cortesi than to Perrot. (Indeed, Ronzani, who was also a producer, specialized in revivals of Cortesi's works.) Moreover, as Hansell points out, Italian reproductions of the *ballet blanc* were seldom faithful to their originals.[19]

Another romantic ballerina who appeared in Rome in the second half of the 1840s was Lucile Grahn. She appeared at the Teatro Argentina in autumn 1848 in the title role of *Caterina degli Abruzzi* (Catherine of the Abruzzi), a version of Perrot's *Catarina, ou la Fille du bandit*, which had premiered two years before at Her Majesty's Theatre. In Rome she repeated her enchanting interpretation of the bandit maid. "She has "an agile figure, expressive features, an eloquent glance, [and] picturesque poses," wrote *La Rivista* on October 10 of her performance. Her masterful dancing was noted, and also the fact that she always remained true to the character she portrayed. Grahn appeared in other ballets from her usual repertory, but these works were performed without acknowledging the original choreographer.

This is not the place to expatiate on every production of the period or on the poetic choices and artistic achievements of every choreographer who mounted a ballet on the Roman stage. However, it is worth pausing for a moment over *Esmeralda* to consider the impact of censorship on the Roman version of the work. Although Ivor Guest has said that the ballet was never produced in Rome because of the local censorship,[20] Mario Rinaldi gives 1 December 1845 as its opening date.[21] The libretto, in the collection of dance materials at the Conservatory of Santa Cecilia, contains, as prescribed, two duly signed performance permits, one by the official censor appointed by the "Ecc.mo Vicario," that is the Cardinal in charge of the administration of the city of Rome, and the other by a member of the "Deputazione dei Pubblici Spetta-coli," the commission that supervised theatrical performances.

Although the ballet was not banned, the censor's impact was felt in the names of the characters. Frollo, the Canon, became Fazio, the alchemist (the same name given to Faust in Cortesi's 1851 ballet). Quasimodo became Thersites, the disfigured character from *The Iliad*. At one point, Esmeralda is referred to as `Genevrella,' probably an oversight due to a last-minute remake. Because of the censors, Cortesi changed the titles of *Giovanni da Procida* to *L'Isolano* (The Islander), and *Masaniello* to *Il Pescatore di Brindisi* (The Fisherman from Brindisi), both in 1847. The latter is particularly interesting because the subject is the same as Auber's *La Muette de Portici*, which enjoyed little success in Rome at almost the same time, while the choreographed version was performed twenty-one times during the carnival season. This relationship between "grand opera" and ballet was destined to change in the 1850s, which saw the rise of the former and the decline of the latter.[22] As for the relationship between opera and ballet, for most of the 1840s the number of productions was pretty much the same. However, beginning in 1848 the balance began to shift strongly in favor of opera. For example, in 1854 at the Teatro Argentina, nine operas were produced and not a single ballet. In 1855, there were thirteen operas but only three ballets.

Lucile Grahn in the title role of Catarina, ou La Fille du bandit, *London, 1846. The ballet was restaged in 1848 at the Teatro Argentina as* Catarina degli Abruzzi *with the ballerina repeating her role as the heroine. Bertarelli Collection, Milan.*

Three other Italian choreographers added flavor to the landscape of the middle and late 1840s—Giovanni Galzerani, Francesco Ramaccini, and Antonio Coppini. Of the three Coppini was the most highly esteemed. His *Adelaide di Francia* (Adelaide of France) and *Il figlio fuggitivo* (The Wayward Son), both staged in Rome in 1845, received good notices. However, he probably enjoyed his greatest success in 1848, when the Teatro Argentina was closed and he was engaged by the Apollo as its sole in-house choreographer. His ballets alternated with Verdi's operas and, like the latter, had patriotic overtones. His *Obizzo di Malaspina*, the work of "a Roman pen," even anticipated the success of Verdi's and Cammarano's *La battaglia di Legnano* (The Battle of Legnano), based on the same subject, when it premiered in 1849.

Giovanni Galzerani's *Il Corsaro*, inspired by Byron's "The Corsair," premiered in Rome in 1846 with Giovannina King in role of Medora. As a choreographer, Galzerani was not unknown in Rome, where he had

Giovannina King, "prima ballerina assoluta of the Teatro Valle, Rome, Autumn 1844." A principal dancer at the Teatro di Apollo and the Teatro Argentina, she played the role of Medora in Giovanni Galzerani's Il corsaro. *Bertarelli Collection, Milan.*

staged a number of productions in the 1830s revealing the influence of Gaetano Gioia and Salvatore Viganò.

Francesco Ramaccini, brother of the more famous Annunziata Ramaccini Blasis and a principal dancer at Turin's Teatro Regio in the late 1820s, appears to have enjoyed little success with the critics. His version of *Monsieur Chalumeaux* (a comedy in three acts inspired by a successful Galzerani production)[23] was bitterly attacked. Wrote the critic for *La Rivista* on 30 September 1847: "It is a pity that the adventures are so excessively drawn out—to see them come to an end takes at least an hour—which forces the spectator to remain at the theater until midnight or to leave the stupendous scene of symbolism of [Verdi's] *Macbeth.*"

1850–1855

During the late 1840s Italy was plunged in political and economic crisis. In Rome, the republic was proclaimed, and after a brief life, overturned. The chaos, which was not only political but also economic, had important repercussions for ballet. In the early part of the new decade, the resources available for production plummeted. The altered financial situation coincided with the arrival in Rome of the "Stars of La Scala," formed under the tutelage of Carlo Blasis. However proficient they may have been, the new "stars" failed to arouse the wild enthusiasm so typical of earlier years: an era had truly come to an end. In this period, too, Romans saw the "fantastic" ballets of the Lasina brothers, the choreographic frescoes of Emanuele Viotti, and the "dance-mime actions" of Giuseppe Rota.

The Lasina brothers, Giovanni and Giuseppe, had been active in Venice for some time.[24] *Il sogno* (The Dream), which they staged in Rome in 1853, exploited in the plot the same dramatic device as *La sventura in sogno, ovvero la bella fanciulla di Gand* (The Dreamed Mishap, or The Beautiful Maid of Ghent). In this ballet, however, it is the male hero, the poet Walters, who envisions the "fantastic dancer" played by Lorenzo Vienna. The presence of a male dancer in so important role is yet further evidence that in Italy—unlike France—he was never simply the ballerina's *porteur.*

Livio Morosini and Giovanni Casati were other choreographers whose ballets entertained Romans during the 1850s. In Morosini's *La figlia dell'aria* (The Daughter of the Air), the new romantic current could be felt: as Elena Ruffin has pointed out, this was gradually replacing the heroic-historical subjects of his earlier work.[25] According to the theater historian

Alberto Cametti, Morosini bid for contracts on various Roman theaters, thus joining the rather significant number of male dancers who were active both as performers and as impresarios.

Italian and French trends were also present in Casati's works. The leading male dancer of La Scala and the husband of ballerina Margherita Wuthier, Casati was well-versed in music and displayed in his choreography what one historian has called a rich "chromatic keyboard."[26]

Well-known dancers, Francesco Penco and David Mochi enjoyed only moderate success as choreographers. Mochi's *Adina* was considered a fiasco. However, in the case of *Il birichino di Parigi* (The Urchin of Paris), he was commended both as a performer and as a choreographer. "Every act and scene," commented one critic, "was vigorously applauded." The dancers appearing in his works also received high praise. Raffaella Santalicante Prisco, noted one reviewer, was "a mime of well-deserved fame.... It is difficult to say whether art or the expression of her heart deserve greater admiration."[27]

Egidio Priora, who had danced in Rome in the 1830s, now returned to the city with some of his own productions. His daughter Olympia, a "*ballerina di rango francese*," was his star. Like Cerrito, Priora *père* fell victim to Belli's poetic darts, in this case, a sonnet entitled "The Ballerino of Today":

Quer monzù a Ttordinone che ttiè ffora
Le zinne in ner ballà ccom'e mmadama,
Si vvolete sapé ccome se chiama,
Io j'ho inteso dì Rocca-priora.

Ttiè ccerti quarti tiè, per dina nora!,
Che 'ggni donna coll'occhi se lo sbrama:
Frulla le scianche poi com'una lama,
E ccrederessi che cce ggiuchi a mora.

Io so cche terminò er duetto
Che ffasceveno lui co le du' donne,
Pareva proprio che ccascassi er tetto.

E disse in piccionara er zor Marchionne
Cche cquanno mmanco ha inteso fà ttutto quer
    ghetto
Quanno upriveno l'occhi le Madonne.[28]

ABOVE: *Francesco Penco, "primo ballerino assoluto of the Teatro Valle, Autumn 1844." A principal dancer at the Teatro di Apollo and the Teatro Argentina, he partnered Marie Taglioni, Fanny Elssler, Lucile Grahn, Giovannina King, and Sofia Fuoco. Bertarelli Collection, Milan.*

BELOW: *Raffaella Santalicante Prisco, "prima mima assoluta," in* Renato d'Arles, *1848. Choreographed by Antonio Coppini, the ballet was presented at the Teatro di Apollo during Carnival season. Bertarelli Collection, Milan.*

Ottavio Memmi and Pia Cavalieri, eleven-year-old dancers in Francesco Marrochesi's Siena company. The troupe performed Gli amori campestri *at the Teatro Argentina in spring 1855. Bertarelli Collection, Milan.*

[This dancer at the Tordinona
Who struts like a dame,
If you want to know his name,
I've heard he's from Rocca Priora.

What hips he's got, my God!
And how the women's eyes devour him.
When he beats his legs like a razor,
You'd think he was playing *mora*.

I know that when his duet
with the two women ended,
The very roof seemed to fall.

And Marchionne said from the gods,
Such an uproar was never heard,
Even when the Virgins opened their eyes.]

In the 1854 and 1855 seasons at the Teatro di Apollo, only Emanuele Viotti's ballets were presented. The Teatro Argentina, which in 1854 produced no dance works, did present Giuseppe Rota's *Il trionfo dell'innocenza* (The Triumph of Innocence) and *Il giuocatore* (The Gambler) in 1855. For Marocchesi's *Gli amori campestri* (Rustic Loves), a company of twenty-four young dancers was imported from Siena. Both Viotti and Rota had Venetian backgrounds. Viotti was a popularizer, and his works, with their tragic-heroic treatment of historical and mythological subjects, touched the hearts of the public.[29] Rota, by contrast, combined the beauty of pure dance with a taste for mass movements, while deflating the technical aspects of the female dance. A decade before, in 1843, Viotti's tragic ballet *Dorliska* had impressed Roman critics with its "clever device of moving from one scene to the next with great clarity," the grandeur of its decors, the imposing number of dancers, and the "beautiful and expressive" music that accompanied the dancing.[30]

The productions of these author-choreographers, and Rota in particular, contributed to the formation of a distinctly Italian taste for spectacular dance. In the following decades, this taste would find its fullest expression in the "*balli grandi*" of Luigi Manzotti—symbols par excellence of the ruling class of the new, unified Kingdom of Italy.

—Translated by Michael Griffitts

Notes

This article, with the title "L'arivamento de la gran maravija der ballo ossia il ballo a Roma dal 1845 al 1855," was first published in *La Danza Italiana*, nos. 8–9 (Winter 1990).

1. Quoted in Fiorella Bartoccini, *Roma nell'Ottocento* (Bologna: Cappelli, 1988), 1, p. 32.
2. E. About, "Rome contemporaine (1860)," in Silvio Negro, *Seconda Roma 1850–1870* (Milan: Hoepli, 1943), p. 106.
3. Alberto Cametti, *Il Teatro di Tordinona poi di Apollo* (Tivoli: A. Chicca, 1938), 1, pp. 244–245.
4. For more on this, see John Rosselli, "Il sistema produttivo, 1780–1880," in *Storia dell'Opera Italiana*, eds. Lorenzo Bianconi and Giorgio Pestelli (Torino: EDT, 1987), 4, pp. 77–165.
5. Quoted *ibid.*, p. 156.
6. For a description of Roman theaters, see Marina Sennato, ed., *L'architettura dei teatri di Roma 1513–1981* (Rome: Kappa, 1987). For the structure of the Teatro Tordinona, see also Sergio Rotondi, *Il Teatro Tordinona* (Rome: Kappa, 1987). For the Teatro Argentina, see Giulio Tiricanti, *Il Teatro Argentina* (Rome: Palombi, 1971).
7. Giuseppe Gioachino Belli, *I Sonetti*, ed. Giorgio Vigolo (Milan: Mondadori, 1952), 3, no. 2002.
8. Quoted in Alberto De Angelis, *Il Teatro Alibert o delle Dame (1717–1863) nella Roma papale* (Tivoli: A. Chicca, 1951), p. 122.
9. De Angelis, p. 21.
10. Quoted *ibid.*, pp. 117–118.
11. See, for instance, "La ballarina di Tordinone" (dedicated to Clara Piglia) and "Le figurante," in Belli, nos. 412 and 794 respectively.
12. Kathleen Kuzmick Hansell, "Il ballo teatrale e l'opera italiana," trans. Lorenzo Bianconi and Angelo Bozzo, in *Storia dell'Opera Italiana*, ed. Lorenzo Bianconi and Giorgio Pestelli, vol. 5 (Turin: EDT, 1988), pp. 175–306. For the quotation, see p. 280.
13. This material was collected by Claudia Celi, Andrea Toschi, Gloria Giordano, and Giovanna Natalini; for the methodology, see Andrea Toschi, "Un esperimento di catalogazione elettronica dei balletti dell'ottocento," *La*

Danza Italiana, nos. 8–9 (Winter 1990), pp. 159–178.

14. See Maria Nevilla Massaro, "Il ballo pantomimo al Teatro Nuovo di Padova (1751–1830)," *Acta Musicologica*, 57, no. 2 (1985), pp. 215–275.

15. *La Rivista*, Nov. 1845. For quotations from the contemporary press, see Mario Rinaldi, *Due secoli di musica al Teatro Argentina* (Florence: Olschki, 1978), 1, pp. 785–903.

16. *La Rivista*, 1 Dec. 1842.

17. Quoted in Rinaldi, p. 804.

18. Ivor Guest, *Fanny Elssler* (London: Adam and Charles Black, 1970), pp. 217–218.

19. Hansell, p. 281.

20. Guest, p. 215.

21. Rinaldi, p. 803.

22. Hansell, p. 287.

23. *Ibid.*, p. 284.

24. See Elena Ruffin, "Il ballo teatrale a Venezia nel secolo XIX," *La Danza Italiana*, nos. 5–6 (1987), p. 159.

25. *Ibid.*, p. 175.

26. Luigi Rossi, *Il ballo alla Scala* (Milan: Edizioni della Scala, 1972), p. 77.

27. *Il Pirata*, 23 Sept. 1853.

28. Belli, no. 322.

29. Ruffin, p. 175.

30. *La Rivista*, 20 Nov. 1843.

Salvatore Taglioni, King of Naples

LAVINIA CAVALLETTI

Salvatore Taglioni's life spanned one of the most tumultuous periods in European history and a key era in the creation of modern Italy. He was born in 1789, the year the French Revolution broke out, in Sicily, which was then part of the Kingdom of Naples, one of the numerous states ruling Italy. He made his debut in Paris in 1806, at the height of Napoleon's First Empire, then, in 1808, moved to Naples, where Napoleon had just installed General Joachim Murat, an energetic modernizer, as king. After Murat's fall in 1815, the Neapolitan throne was restored to the legitimate Bourbon king, Ferdinand I, an elderly reactionary. Taglioni served under Ferdinand and under his descendants Francis I, who ruled from 1825–1830, Ferdinand II, who ruled from 1830 to 1859, and Francis II, who lost his throne in 1860 to the forces led by Giuseppe Garibaldi, the great Italian patriot, and the King of Piedmont, who sought to unite Italy under a constitutional monarchy on the English model. In November 1860, Victor Emmanuel, the first ruler of the new kingdom of Italy, arrived in Naples: he was the sixth monarch whom Taglioni served. Taglioni died in 1868. Two years later, Italian unification was complete.

"The finest living ballet composer in Italy," opined August Bournonville in the 1840s about Salvatore Taglioni.[1] However forgotten he may be today, Taglioni was the most eminent Italian choreographer of the Romantic period. In part, this was because of the exceptional longevity of his career, which began in 1806, when he made his debut as a sixteen-year-old dancer, and ended three years before his death in 1868.[2] In part, too, it reflected the prominence of the Teatro di San Carlo in Naples. The largest theater in Europe at the time and the one (according to Bournonville) with the best corps de ballet,[3] the San Carlo witnessed the creation of nearly all his ballets. Finally, it was a measure of the sheer number of works he produced there—more than 150.

Although Taglioni's career spanned the rise and fall of the Romantic movement in ballet, he himself remained somewhat on its margins. Unlike his older brother Filippo and Filippo's daughter, Marie, he never became an international celebrity. Indeed, Marie, the romantic ballerina par excellence, never once came to Naples to dance in her uncle's productions.[4] Moreover, although all the elements typical of Romanticism in general appear in Taglioni's works, they lack the characteristics specific to Romantic ballet. Thus, while he did not avoid fantastic themes, he did not

181

Salvatore Taglioni, lithograph by Luigi De Crescenzo, ca. 1850. The wreathed inscription reads, "Born in Palermo in 1791," and each laurel leaf bears the name and year of one of Taglioni's ballets. Dance Collection, New York Public Library for the Performing Arts, Astor, Lenox, and Tilden Foundations.

embrace the world of fairies, sylphs, and white tutus. Still, one can hardly deny that he was a Romantic choreographer: in their themes and settings, and taste for romance and atmosphere, his ballets reflected the era's fashions. Lasting five or six acts, his ballets were the movie epics of their time: the action was heroic, sentimental, and full of spectacular effects—fires, floods, volcanoes, and whatever other catastrophes the San Carlo's technical staff could manufacture. The pure dance sequences bore little or no connection to the events narrated in the ballet. The soloists inserted bravura variations at will,[5] and it was the mimes who carried forward the often highly complicated plot. To understand what was happening, the audience had the help of written libretti, but reading them today one wonders how the dancers could possibly have expressed certain concepts using only their hands and feet. Taglioni cultivated all the genres of the period—mythological heroic, Anacreonic (in which, according to certain critics, he excelled), historical and mythological historical, romantic, allegorical, and even comic. Various genres might appear in a single ballet. Overall, however, the historical genre predominated.

Taglioni was born into a family that gave eminent personalities to dance for a century. His father, Carlo, was a dancer; his sister Luisa and his brother Filippo were dancers, and his descendants were dancers, including his daughter Luigia, who danced at the Paris Opéra, and Filippo's children—Marie, the most famous member of the clan, and Paul, an acclaimed dancer and choreographer who was ballet master at the Berlin Court Opera from 1856 to 1883. But while Filippo's career was international in scope, Salvatore's—apart from some youthful ballets in France and occasional forays to Palermo, Milan, Turin, and Vienna[6]—was confined to Naples. His ballets remained unknown abroad and were not handed down in Italy. The only piece of his choreography that appears to have survived is the fantastic sea scene that is now part of Bournonville's *Napoli* and was probably lifted from Taglioni's ballet *Il Duca di Ravenna*, which the Danish choreographer saw in Naples.[7] Of course, in this period, the city was anything but a cultural backwater. During the 1830s, 1840s, and 1850s, more than 450 ballets by at least thirty-six choreographers were presented at the Teatro di San Carlo and the Teatro Fondo (which were under the same management). La Scala produced about 350 ballets during these years, while the Paris Opéra, for all its wealth and fame, managed to produce only about seventy.[8] The splendor of the San Carlo owed much to the impresario Domenico Barbaja, who ran the theater almost without interruption from 1809 to 1840.[9] Sparing no expense, he accustomed the public to a luxury that subsequently proved difficult to maintain.

In 1831, Ferdinand II conferred upon Taglioni the enviable title of "composer of ballets" at the San Carlo "for life."[10] This meant that the impresario charged with running the theater was obliged to engage Taglioni. Assured of this "fixed" or permanent post, Taglioni worked tirelessly for the next several decades. With a second composer of ballets on the permanent San Carlo roster and guest choreographers—who might be seasoned professionals or young tyros—invited on a seasonal basis, the atmosphere was stimulating as well as secure. The highly volatile Neapolitan public loved Taglioni. Colleagues and foreign travelers spoke well of him, and the King deemed his presence a matter of the highest importance.[11]

From this enviable position, Taglioni not only produced, but produced prolifically. The exact number of his ballets remains unclear. By 1841, according to Bournonville, the tally had reached 117. Francesco Regli, who tends to be reliable, put the total at 148, although a critic writing in 1861 about one of Taglioni's last works called it his 170th production. An anonymous list in the choreographer's file at the Paris Opéra library includes about two hundred titles, while Léandre Vaillat in his biography of Marie Taglioni speaks of 230 works. The present author has documented 154, excluding dances in operas, of which only nine titles can be identified. In the portrait by Luigi De Crescenzo, executed around 1850, there are ninety-six titles, but some works were not included.

Born in Palermo in 1789, Taglioni trained in Paris with Jean-François Coulon. In 1806, after a brilliant debut, he rejected an engagement that would have kept him in Paris because it fell short of his expectations. Instead, he accepted an engagement with the Denantes brothers, then the impresarios of the Teatro di San Carlo. He arrived in Naples in the summer of 1808 with his sister Luisa and his wife Adelaide Perrault, both first-rate dancers.

He made his Neapolitan debut in Louis Henry's ballet *Paolo e Virginia, o sia i due creoli* (Paul and Virginia, or The Two Creoles), dancing the "extremely well-known *pas* from Mons. Gardel's *Télémaque*" to accolades. A journalist of the era described him as an elegant dancer in the French style, in contrast to the more acrobatic mimes and *grotteschi* of the Italian school:

> Among the gifts that distinguish this young pupil from Mons. Coulon's school of grace is not strength, which the greatest of dancers can share with the least of the *grotteschi*, but uprightness, balance, and those simple, natural graces that produce so much pleasure when they appear effortless—sweetness and delicacy of expression, softness of pose, and a noble and animated air.[12]

Taglioni remained in Naples, partnering his wife and dancing principal roles in the ballets produced at the San Carlo in the next several years by Louis Henry, Pierre Hus, Francesco Clerico, Louis Duport, Salvatore Viganò, and Gaetano Gioia. His interest in choreography developed early,[13] although it was only during the 1814–1815 season that he staged his first ballets—*La Fille Mal Gardée* and *Il Barbiere di Siviglia* (The Barber of Seville). The results were apparently satisfying, seeing that in the following year he was asked to stage three works—*La casa disabitata* (The Deserted House), *Bacco in Erepoli* (Bacchus in Erepolis), and *Luca e Lauretta* (Luke and Lauretta). In 1816, the theater burned down, curtailing dance activity. However, the following year, he presented *Atalanta ed Ippomene* (Atalanta and Hippomenes), which won him popularity both with the public and the King. In 1818, feeling his position now considerably strengthened, Taglioni began pressing the management for an increase in his monthly stipend. (At the time, he and his wife were jointly earning 555 ducats; he wanted this raised to 600.) He even laid his case before the press. However, Barbaja proved a cunning adversary and won the day.[14] Taglioni's stipend remained the same, but his relationship with the impresario gradually improved. Barbaja was dynamic and flush with proceeds from the casino attached to the theater; later there would be government subsidies. Taglioni was a hard worker. Under the terms of his contract, he had to dance twenty performances a month in addition to rehearsing new programs and teaching at least five classes a week at the ballet school where he was the *maestro di perfezionamento*. Finally, he had to find time to read, think up plots, and write the libretti for his ballets. A veritable mountain of work!

Although happy for the most part, his collaboration with Barbaja was not exempt from difficulties arising from the complex operation of the administrative bureaucracy. This is evident from the correspondence between the impresario, the Superintendent of Theaters, the Deputation (which met weekly), and the Secretary of State for Internal Affairs. Sometimes the King himself personally intervened, or the Prefect of Police. The latter, for instance, on 25 June 1816, complained about the short black cloak worn by a patrolman in the front line of Taglioni's *Il Barbiere di Siviglia*: "This mode of attire," he wrote, "makes a caricature of public functionaries. I beg you to change it."[15]

In all likelihood, Taglioni's greatest problem was the limited time he had for production. Indecision on the part of the Superintendent and the Deputation kept him and Barbaja on continual pins and needles. On 31 August 1820 Barbaja wrote that Taglioni, "would commit himself to stage for October 4 his grand ballet *Otranto Liberata* (Otranto Liberated), already approved by Your Excellency, for which he has the music ready [and] the fashion-plates for the costumes.... Your Excellency will have the kindness to decide soon."[16] A few days later Barbaja wrote to the Duke di Noja, asking whether a decision had yet been made about Taglioni's ballet. Rehearsals were beginning, but no one knew whether to go forward or not. "Every moment is precious when time is so short," he wrote, almost as an apology. Composers were subject to similar time pressures. Late in April 1824, Count Gallenberg was only beginning to compose the music for Gioia's ballet *I seguaci di Bacco* (The Followers of Bacchus), which opened on May 31. Even as he was composing, the pages of the score were snatched by the choreographer, who had to begin rehearsals.[17]

Overall, however, the bureaucracy seems to have functioned fairly expeditiously, considering that fifteen to twenty-five different ballets were presented every year, at least during the 1820s. The bureaucratic procedure was more or less the following. The choreographer submitted a detailed proposal to the impresario; if the latter liked it, he passed it on to the Superintendent, who then submitted it to the Deputation (generally composed of four or five persons) and to the Minister of the Interior, who normally approved the project so long as it did not contain "anything

Portrait of Salvatore Taglioni. The inscription reads: "Signore Taglioni is most nimble, sparkling, and skilled in his art, a distinguished dancer such as may vie with anyone, and thus he has won praise and applause no less in France than in the principal theaters of Italy." Raffaele Carrieri, La Danza in Italia, 1500–1900 *(Milan: Domus, 1946), p. 44.*

contrary to decency or to the aims of the government." Production arrangements were left to the choreographer. Anticipating possible difficulties with a ballet scheduled to premiere in January 1825, Gioia wrote the Deputation that he "did not want to find himself...in the same unpleasant circumstances as with *Elizabetta*, that is, to be without scenery and important properties." The King followed these mishaps closely, especially when they concerned the opening of the spring season. In 1817, for instance, the Secretary of State for Internal Affairs wrote to the Superintendent that although the King was "now resigned to what you have related about the difficulties of giving [Taglioni's] grand ballet *Ippomene* for Easter, His Majesty has ordered said ballet to be given on May 30."[18] The opening of the season was politically important. Ferdinand had twice fled to exile when French troops invaded Naples. Now restored to the throne, he wanted to be forgiven, to show that everything was back to normal.

The presence of so many interests led to disagreements and complaints by the various parties. In connection with the staging of *Atalanta ed Ippomene*, for instance, Barbaja complained to the Duke di Noja that Taglioni had requested an excessive number of decorations: "Your Excellence would not want me to ruin myself by giving in to [his] whims and thus set a bad example for other choreographers." On 25 May 1815 Barbaja complained that the scenery and stage machinery for Taglioni's new ballet were still not ready, although the premiere was only five days away. He said that he was attending all the rehearsals and paying everyone, but would not be responsible for the ballet being ready on time. Even the Deputation remonstrated with Barbaja about the progress of the season.[19]

While the number of performances depended on the impresario's contract (in January 1825 the Deputation spoke of three performances a week "to maintain the schedule of 120 performances specified in Barbaja's contract"), Barbaja's obsession with continually updating the repertory seems to have had an economic basis. The habitués of the San Carlo public thirsted for novelty, and Barbaja was continually asking permission to withdraw a ballet from repertory "because the public has already seen it too many times" and to replace it with another. On 13 December 1815, for instance, Barbaja asked permission to withdraw *Cora*, "it being severely prejudicial to my best interests to maintain in repertory all the works presented at the San Carlo during the past two years." Barbaja's anxiety may have been excessive, or he may have detected a certain resistance on the part of the Deputation, since the reason he often gave for retiring a ballet was the burden it placed on scene painters and stage technicians preparing new ones. On 10 May 1815 Barbaja requested permission to give the ballet *Pandora* for the last time: he had received, he wrote, a written protest from the mechanic who wanted the stage free in order to arrange the complicated scene changes in Taglioni's ballet *Bacco in Erepoli*.

To these intrinsic difficulties were added personal rivalries, quarrels, the demands of certain dancers, and the insubordination of the "masses," as the theater staff as a whole was referred to. On 22 August 1816 the Prefect of Police reported to the Superintendent that Taglioni had been called to the prefecture and scolded for an altercation occurring during the ballet *Il Calzolaio* (The Shoemaker) with Professor Boffio, a violinist. Taglioni had reproved him for playing out of time, and Professor Festa, "believing the entire category offended, had recourse to the magistrate." The use of police was anything but sporadic. Disobedient dancers were routinely sent to prison for twenty-four hours: "Sig. Maglietta having capriciously refused to dance Sig. Taglioni's role...in the ballet *La casa disabitata*, the police have been summoned to place him under arrest and to use their discretion so long as he persists in his refusal. In the meantime, arrangements should be made for the...dancer Guerra to assume the aforesaid role this evening."[20] There was prison as well for "the offense committed by the ballerina Talamo in disturbing the evening concert by arguing with the dancer De Mattia; it has been resolved that after the 19th she shall be held under arrest for one day, together with her mother, who also took part in this affair."[21] The police were also used to keep the "masses" in line. In November 1823 the French choreographer Louis Henry wrote in desperation to Barbaja:

> [T]he rehearsals are going dreadfully. The day before yesterday the police officer-in-chief came, and things went very well; yesterday and today they realized that he was not here, and it took me more than an hour to get eight drums, eight cushions, and eight mandolins. When the opera took the theater from me, I had managed to compose only nineteen measures. If things continue in this fashion, I will be forced to throw myself at the feet of the King, because even if I work myself to death, things will not go any better. Act! You have the power; I can only execute orders.[22]

Taglioni also complained about making little progress during rehearsals—not because of insubordination, but because of the noise of work being done in the stalls.

Such episodes were minor, however. In the 1820s there was plenty of dancing at the Teatro di San Carlo. The ballets were sumptuous: if Barbaja's expenses in 1819 came to 93,000 ducats, in 1826 they amounted to 81,000. By and large, backstage relationships were amicable. If occasionally something got out of hand, the Deputation was always ready to take control: "in order to avoid the occurrence of any inconveniences, the Impresario is instructed not to make any changes in the ballets without the approval of the Duke di Noja for the Teatro di San Carlo and Marchese Cito for the Teatro Fondo. The composer must be notified of any changes."[23]

The year 1827 was a turning point. On April 13 a new Superintendent, Duke Carignano, was appointed. Taglioni had left for La Scala; the better dancers, not having been engaged in time, had gone abroad, and even the better pupils of the school had requested foreign leave.[24] The San Carlo languished. There was no dancing. A few performances were given in minor theaters. A search for new talent was on.

Taglioni was no stranger to La Scala. In 1820 he had staged his *Castore e Polluce* (Castor and Pollux) there and, in 1824, a number of ballets previously given in Naples, including *Sesostri* (Sesostris). During this stay, he started work on a new ballet. In 1826–1827, when he returned for a third visit, he staged two new ballets—*Pietro di Portogallo* (Pedro of Portugal) and *Il Paria* (The Pariah)—along with four works previously danced in Naples (with some minor changes in the titles). To judge from the number of performances they received, Taglioni's ballets were very popular. Indeed, when he remounted *Pietro di Portogallo* (as *Ines de Castro*) at the Teatro di San Carlo in 1831, he obtained the famous contract "for life." (He may also have used a stratagem, saying that the court in Berlin had made him a similar offer and that the terms being equal he preferred to stay in Naples.)[25] Financially, the contract seems to have favored management. In the years that followed, Taglioni's stipend (250 ducats) remained unchanged, while other, younger choreographers received the same amount or even more. (In 1843, when Taglioni was still earning 250 ducats, Antonio Guerra received 400, and Giovanni Briol 250.)

In Turin, Taglioni never presented new ballets, only restagings of existing ones, including some that were quite old. For instance, *La conquista di Malacca* (The Conquest of Malacca), which he mounted in Turin in 1830, was none other than *I Portoghesi nelle Indie* (The Portuguese in the Indies), created in Naples eleven years earlier. *Castore e Polluce*, which he produced at La Scala in 1820, was revived in Turin in 1832. The subject must have been very dear to him because he returned to it again, this time in Naples in 1842. The critics, who remembered the ballet very well, were not deceived.

Atalanta ed Ippomene, one of Taglioni's earliest ballets, belonged to the same heroic-mythological genre. Produced at the San Carlo in 1817, it offered plum roles for himself and his wife. Taglioni's libretto, now at the Angelica Library in Rome, merits a detailed examination, since it represented a vein that he successfully mined for decades. Believing herself to be invincible, Atalanta agrees to marry anyone who can beat her in a foot race. In Act I a centaur pursues several huntresses, including Atalanta, who is saved by Hippomenes. She falls in love with him and introduces him to her father, while maintaining a demeanor that "makes clear the inflexibility of her heart." In Act III Hippomenes's parents requests Atalanta's hand in marriage for their son. Her father replies that he will give her to whoever beats her in a foot race. Hippomenes asks Venus for help. The goddess appears on a cart driven by Cupid and drawn by doves. In Act IV Venus gathers three golden apples from the Garden of the Hesperides. She gives them to Hippomenes explaining that he must toss them at Atalanta's feet when she passes him. In Act V we see the race in the stadium. At the second turn she overtakes him; he throws the apples down, and amazed at their splendor, she stops and picks them up. Meanwhile,

Hippomenes reaches the finish line. Too late Atalanta realizes her error. Shuddering, and blushing at her greediness, she accuses Hippomenes of cunning and deceit. However, "disarmed by the constancy of virtuous love, she extends her right hand to her conqueror"—and agrees to marry him. A scene of general rejoicing follows, and the marriage of the protagonists is celebrated.

The ballet was a resounding success. Wrote the critic for the *Giornale del Regno delle Due Sicilie*:

> [T]he festivities, which could be introduced as episodes, naturally led to the dancing; the subject was appropriate for highlighting the talents of the scene designer and the stage mechanic with all the splendor of architecture, painting, and perspective. The choice of plot boded well for the entire composition; the execution confirmed these happy presages and has assured Mr. Taglioni of a definite place among the best choreographers that we have on the Italian scene today.... [T]his ballet was staged with the greatest care, with an extraordinary richness of costume and grandiose machinery. The entire corps de ballet could not have been better directed. Mme Taglioni enchants with the elegance of her movements, the special grace she imparts to her steps, the superior merit of her execution, and with that rare perfection that makes her dancing the living rule of her art.... As a choreographer and dancer, Taglioni is always worthy of theatrical crowns.... One can say that the greatest part of this glory is his own, which is even more striking because accompanied by rare modesty. At the opening performance His Majesty the King saw fit to encourage the young composer.[26]

To the sumptuousness of the scenery and costumes must be added the extraordinary number of people in the production—sixty dancers, some forty "little Cupids and pleasures" (who were probably children), and more than a hundred soldiers and extras.

Another genre that Taglioni favored was the historical-exotic, which included ballets such as *I Portoghesi nelle Indie* (1819) and *Tippoo-Saeb* (Tipu Sahib) (1823). Based on history, they were colorful, exotic, and full of excitement. *Tippoo-Saeb* was set in eighteenth-century India during the struggle against the British. There were legitimate and illegitimate sovereigns, kidnapped daughters who reappear as brides, and runaway princelings who are recognized. The scenery was equally picturesque— shadowy valleys and cliffs, flowering gardens with Hindu dancing girls, and palaces occupied by the British. The action called for masses of characters—Brahmins, grandees of the realm, officials of the Prince, bayadères, Salic's female slaves, in addition to pages, male slaves, British officers, cavalrymen, and soldiers, and Indian officials, soldiers, and musicians. As described in the libretto, the finale was packed with event: Tippoo, the hero wounded by the British, expires in the arms of the Sultana; the allies arrive on the scene, but so do the British, and

> through a gate flung open by the artillery, General Harris enters followed by the entire General Staff. The Misorani prisoners surrender to him. The

magnanimous general consoles the disconsolate family of the Sultan, who is dead, and calls for an immediate halt to the scenes of horror that the victorious soldiers are multiplying. In the meantime, preceded by Mulcar and a numerous entourage, Kajac Chisne arrives on the scene and is acknowledged by all as the lawful sovereign.[27]

The public followed breathlessly. The use of cavalry, soldiers, fireworks, and real cannon shot, however usual they may have been, created a splendid effect. But none of this hindered the creation in the preceding acts of grand *ballabili* and pas de deux in which the dancers showed off their bravura.

Beginning in the 1830s, the historical-romantic genre became more prominent in Taglioni's works. To be sure, the historical content of these ballets tended to be slight, although they aroused or reflected repressed feelings of patriotism. In fact, most of the ingredients were typical of Romanticism. In a program note for the ballet *Cristina di Svezia* (Christina of Sweden), which premiered in 1832, Taglioni spoke of a "dramatic plot in the current taste—romantic, plausible, and stirring." The libretto recounts the events as follows:

> Act I. A wild place on the coast. At a nearby hermitage, wedding dances are in progress. Fleeing Danish warriors arrive. Their wounded leader enters the hermitage seeking help.
>
> Act II. Harold arrives, envious of the victorious King who refuses to let him marry his daughter Christina. Harold invites the Danish general to attack Stockholm again, as the city prepares to welcome Edward of Scotland, Christina's intended husband. Unobserved, Arnulf has overheard the conversation.
>
> Act III. A great hall, with a broad staircase descending to a public square that borders on the harbor. Edward arrives and is presented to the court. The people applaud. Christina refuses him. Her father orders her to marry him. Gustav, who is already married to Christina, hesitates to confess. Harold understands, and explains the situation to the King.
>
> Act IV. Christina's apartment. Gustav asks Christina to see their secret son. The King and Harold arrive. Christina asks to postpone the marriage. Gustav and the baby are discovered. The King asks whose child it is. The maidservant says it is hers. The King wants it put to death. Christina swoons. With great effort, Harold succeeds in concealing his joy.
>
> Act V. Inside of a tower. Gustav is in prison. Christina arrives in disguise. She asks Gustav to flee in her cloak. He refuses, then agrees, when she tells him that she knows that the Danes are about to attack Stockholm and only he can save the city. The King arrives. Arnulf arrives with the news of Harold's treason.
>
> Act VI. The area of the city near the sea and the fishermen's quarter. A ruined tower to one side. Harold awaits the Danes. The attack is prepared. Harold is about to seize Christina. The King is about to be taken by the Danes. Gustav saves him. The King unites him with Christina. Mean-

while, the magazine of a Danish ship explodes. The actions ends with a "picture of terror."[28]

This final scene was so popular that it aroused "fanaticism and furor," as Barbaja put it.[29]

Taglioni choreographed a number of ballets based on popular novels, including *I Promessi Sposi* (The Betrothed) (1836), *Ettore Fieramosca* (Hector Fieramosca) (1837), *Marco Visconti* (1841). His *Faust* (1838), however, was quickly banned by the censor. Taglioni remained extremely productive throughout his later years. He produced seven ballets in 1838 and a similar number in 1839, four in 1850, five in 1855, and at least two every other year, even during 1848, which saw liberal revolutions all over Europe as well as in Naples. In this year of hope, national feeling ran high, but in Naples political repression was the answer to the voices crying for freedom and a united Italy.

Reviews of Taglioni's early work tended to be favorable and even enthusiastic. However, as tastes and critics changed, his ballets came in for a veritable drubbing. The sympathetic critic of the *Giornale del Regno delle Due Sicilie*—in the 1820s this was probably Abbé Taddei—was a romantic enamored of fairies and marvels who thought that mythological subjects were most suited to ballet. He adored pantomime and lamented the fondness of young people for virtuoso feats, fearing that the art of ballet was degenerating into leaps, cabrioles, and spins. He rejected terror and truculence in the theater although he recognized—with displeasure— that the public loved it. While reporting that *Tippoo-Saeb* was a great success, he noted that too many parts were lifted from the ballet *Sesostri*, which Taglioni had produced earlier in the year (1823).[30] Finally, the *Giornale* critic insisted that dances be introduced appropriately and have some connection with the action: too often, he felt, the opposite occurred.

In the 1830s *L'Omnibus* (The Omnibus), a weekly, went on the attack. Its critic, Vincenzo Torrelli, had no use for pantomime, which he considered suitable only for caricature or legend, and—this he also allowed— mythological subjects such as *Amore e Psiche* (Cupid and Psyche). But this happened to be the period when Taglioni was chiefly working the historical-romantic vein. One by one, his ballets were demolished by Torrelli. His criticism was often contradictory and less than fully convincing. When the ballet *Edwige o il sogno* (Hedwig, or The Dream) was given in 1839, he damned it; three years later, he spoke well of it and suggested that it be revived.[31] If a ballet was hissed, we have an account of all the particulars: in 1839, for *Amore alla prova* (Love to the Test), there was hissing and shouting, although when the two main dancers appeared, the boos turned to applause.[32] If *L'Omnibus* is to be believed, this is how things were until the end of Taglioni's career.

By the 1840s, however, the difficulties facing management were considerable. Newspapers lamented the decline in the theater, and reviews, even of works by other choreographers, were seldom flattering. The plots were uninteresting; the dances were too short or too long; the dancers were little known—so ran the litany of reproaches. However, the partiality displayed in the columns of *L'Omnibus* was notorious. If Antonio Guerra won praise as a choreographer, dancer, and even a music master, for Taglioni there was only venom. His ballet *Carlo di Ravenstein* (Charles of Ravenstein) had "some graceful dances recalling [his] great merit, but...runs into difficulty because of its little novelty."[33] *Don Quisciotte* (Don Quixote) "would be delightful if it were clearer."[34] *L'Assedio di Leyda* (The Siege of Leyden), which ended with an onstage flood, was "a dreadful subject."[35] *Il Vecchio della Foresta* (The Old Man of the Forest) was "old rubbish."[36] *Alfredo* had an "absurd" plot. Still, reading between the lines, one senses that the public did not, in fact, dislike these ballets. Spiteful critics probably did stir up discontent among subscribers, who saw the same show many times and were apt to feel cheated if ballerinas of international fame—as promised by the management—failed to materialize.[37]

For a balanced view of Taglioni's work, one would have to examine the response of the public in greater depth. However, it seems highly unlikely that Taglioni could have presented an uninterrupted succession of failures for so many decades. Rather, it seems, that on the whole his ballets continued to attract the public. With regard to *L'Omnibus*'s "avant-garde" taste, it is indeed odd that in 1849 when *Giselle* arrived in Naples, the paper mentioned it only briefly: "After the boredom of the opera, the ballet succeeded in being entertaining. Mlle Fitzjames and Mérante stood out and were applauded many times; the moonlight scene was also applauded."[38] In short, the *L'Omnibus* critic apparently failed to appreciate that with *Giselle* he had encountered one of the masterpieces of ballet history.

Taglioni's energy was apparently unflagging. When rioting broke out in Naples in 1848, he was mistakenly arrested as an insurgent and shot.[39] He was struck by fourteen bullets, and just as a soldier was about to cut off his finger to steal his ring, an officer recognized him and dragged him out from under a pile of corpses. Six months later, as he left his house for the first time, he fell down the steps and broke his clavicle. He did not give up, however, and at the end of the year staged a ballet entitled *Il Vampiro* (The Vampire), which had a strange and totally new plot for ballet at the time. A notice published in the libretto offered an explanation of the "superstitious" subject: vampirism was a punishment that people who had committed great crimes during their lifetime suffered after death. "It was believed that vampires sucked the blood of their victims....[V]ampires rose from their graves when the moon was full and returned there when it entered the first quarter." The notice, which was almost certainly dictated by the choreographer, ends: "Salvatore Taglioni, who had to compose this ballet during his convalescence from a grave and painful illness, begs the kind indulgence of the public for his composition."[40]

Undaunted by critics or health problems, Taglioni remained active for the next seventeen years. He kept abreast of the times, choreographing some of the ballets danced by his daughter abroad and calling upon his son-in-law, Alessandro Fuchs, for assistance. Meanwhile, the theatrical climate of Naples was changing dramatically. The San Carlo was in rapid decline, and criticism of the management was merciless. "Abominable execution, unworthy of a grand theater," wrote *L'Omnibus* in 1849. "Could we not have had a dress rehearsal instead of this unworthy first night?.... [T]he clamor going on backstage before the curtain went up for the first act—a half-hour late—was shameful!"[41]

Taglioni's final years must have been difficult. Political events came to the fore. With Italian unification under the House of Savoy a virtual certainty, funds for the San Carlo declined. Soldiers who had once performed walk-on parts were now fighting real wars; inside the theater the atmosphere was one of growing abandonment.[42] It was the end of the Bourbon monarchy, the end of an epoch. Taglioni remained on the sidelines. He would produce his last ballet, *Il Talismano* (The Talisman), in 1865.[43] Although it enjoyed a notable success, Taglioni's era was past. In 1861 in Davide Costa's ballet *Megilla*, Amina Boschetti had danced a solo in which the reflection of the moon was created by electric light. The dance that followed had Garibaldi motifs and produced a "standing ovation." In 1861, the Teatro di San Carlo was closed because of poor management, which roused the ire of the press. There was talk of scandal and squandering. "Favoritism is in progress," thundered *L'Omnibus* on 25 April 1861. "And the Nation pays!"

Taglioni passed quietly into oblivion. Commenting on one of his last ballets, *La pietra filosofale* (The Philosopher's Stone) (1860), *L'Omnibus* had written, "Taglioni's new ballet...was received with indulgence by the public, which did not disapprove of everything when the curtain went up only because he has the merit of being an old and respectable choreographer. This ballet was respected. But being poor in dances, it met with some disapproval toward the end. So it was that the audience was courteous but fair."[44]

Taglioni died several years later. His end came, as a French source relates, "on 4 October 1868 at eight in the morning." He was "perfectly lucid and bless[ed] his children, who surrounded him. It was a great loss for Italy, for he was its greatest artistic glory."[45]

—Translated by Susan I. Schiedel

Notes

This article was originally published in *La Danza Italiana* (nos. 8–9 [1990], pp. 109–126).

1. August Bournonville, *My Theater Life*, trans. Patricia N. McAndrew, foreword Erik Bruhn, introd. Svend Kragh-Jacobsen (Middletown, Conn.: Wesleyan University Press, 1979), p. 21.

2. According to the entry on Taglioni in *L'Enciclopedia dello Spettacolo*, the choreographer was born in Palermo in 1789, although Luigi De Crescenzo's

well-known portrait (executed around 1850 and published in Raffaele Ajello *et al.*, *Il Teatro di San Carlo* [Naples: Guida, 1987]) gives his date of birth as 1791. Other sources, such as Francesco Regli's *Dizionario Biografico 1800–1860* (Turin, 1860) and *La Moda*, a periodical published in Naples beginning in 1839, give July 1790 as the date. It seems likely that he was born in 1789, as this would make him seventy-nine, the age given at the time of his death in the *Giornale di Napoli*, which published the following announcement on 7 October 1868: "Deceased, buried on the 5th—Salvatore Taglioni of Palermo, aged seventy-nine." In 1830 Taglioni still held the title of "first dancer"; by 1831 the title had disappeared from his libretti.

3. John Rosselli, "Artisti e impresari," in *Il Teatro di San Carlo*, p. 28; Knud Arne Jürgensen, "Bournonville in Italia," *La Danza Italiana*, no. 7 (Spring 1989), p. 104.

4. According to Léandre Vaillat, the reason was probably her unwillingness to don the green trousers that women were required to wear under their tutus for reasons of decency (*La Taglioni, ou la Vie d'une danseuse* [Paris: A. Michel, 1942]).

5. A note from the impresario Domenico Barbaja to the ballerina Amalia Brugnoli on 13 August 1823 reads: "I have taken upon myself the duty of contacting you, inasmuch as you are engaged on next Friday, the 15th of the current month, for your debut, which you can make in a pas de deux with Mons. Hul[l]in in either the anacreonic ballet *Atide e Cloè* or the ballet *Gundberga*. Since the choice is entirely up to you, I beg you to do me the favor of indicating to me which ballet you choose, so that I may forward the appropriate orders to the costume department" (Fondo Teatri, fasc. 125, Archivio Storico Napoletano [henceforth cited as ASN]).

6. Milan, 1820, 1824, 1827–1828, 1836, 1838, 1839–1840; Palermo, 1823; Vienna, 1826–1827; Turin, 1831–1832, 1843–1844.

7. Knud Arne Jürgensen says that *Il Duca di Ravenna* was acclaimed as a great novelty and that the "swimming" choreography that found its way into *Napoli* made a great impression even in Copenhagen. See Jürgensen, "Bournonville in Italia," pp. 109–112. On the other hand, *L'Omnibus* (4 June 1840) described the ballet as a "complete and total fiasco."

8. For La Scala, see Giampiero Tintori, *Duecento anni di Teatro alla Scala. Cronologia opera-balletti-concerti 1788–1977* (Bergamo: Grafica Gutenberg, 1979); for the Paris Opéra, see Ivor Guest, *Le Ballet de l'Opéra de Paris* (Paris: Flammarion, 1976), pp. 304–310.

9. For more about Barbaja, see the second volume of *Il Teatro di San Carlo di Napoli*, eds. Bruno Cagli and Agostino Zino (Milan: Electa, 1987).

10. See Regli, *Dizionario Biografico*; see also "Deputazione," 28 Oct. 1831 and 10 Nov. 1831," Fondo Teatri, fasc. 2, ASN.

11. A royal degree fined the impresario Glossop's attorney 1,000 ducats when Taglioni failed to return to Naples at the designated time ("Deputazione," Nov. 1824, Fondo Teatri, fasc. 5, ASN).

12. *Corriere di Napoli*, 11 Nov. 1808.

13. Dossier d'artiste (Salvatore Taglioni), BN-Opéra. The Paris Opéra would not let him choreograph, and because of this he left.

14. See *Giornale del Regno delle Due Sicilie*, 17 and 18 Feb. 1818.

15. Fondo Teatri, fasc. 51, ASN.

16. *Ibid.*

17. *Ibid.*
18. *Ibid.*
19. *Ibid.*
20. Fondo Teatri, fasc. 5, ASN.
21. *Ibid.*
22. Fondo Teatri, fasc. 51, ASN.
23. Fondo Teatri, fasc. 5, ASN.
24. *Ibid.*
25. "Deputazione 28 Oct. 1831 and 10 Nov. 1831," Fondo Teatri, fasc. 2, ASN.
26. *Giornale del Regno delle Due Sicilie*, 22 June 1817.
27. Libretto, *Tippoo-Saeb*, Biblioteca Angelica.
28. Libretto, *Cristina di Svezia*, Biblioteca Angelica.
29. Fondo Teatri, fasc. 51, ASN.
30. For reviews of these productions, see *Giornale del Regno delle Due Sicilie*, 13 Jan. and 1 July 1823.
31. "The dances are rich and numerous, but neither happy nor new, and the scenes are mediocre," he wrote on 1 June 1839. In 1842, deploring the progress of the season and thoroughly rejecting the two ballets choreographed by Briol, he recommended the revival of Taglioni's *Edwige o il sogno*, "which seemed pleasing to us, not long or moral, and consisting of imagined events, well suited to the hybrid nature of ballet, which consists of things that are not human because people do not speak in them, yet are not entirely inhuman because they are represented by human beings. There are some mediocre dances, but others could be added, and it would be a good ballet for this season of hisses and failures" (*L'Omnibus*, 18 Aug. 1842).
32. "*L'Amore alla prova* by Taglioni is a strange, new, and unprecedented spectacle. The hissing, jeering, laughing, and all manner of shouting were such that it seemed as if the hall were filled with demons, but all displeasure with the ballet ceased and turned into great applause when [Amalia] Brugnoli and [Antonio] Guerra appeared. They could not have danced better: grace, precision, taste, supreme lightness—they had everything, so that at the end of their *pas* the clamorous applause redoubled. However, afterward, there was a return to the cacophony of whistles and shouts" (*L'Omnibus*, 23 Nov. 1839).
33. *L'Omnibus*, 20 Apr. 1839.
34. *L'Omnibus*, 15 Apr. 1841.
35. *L'Omnibus*, 1 Apr. 1843.
36. *Il Birichino*, 24 Apr. 1857.
37. On 22 November 1847, *L'Omnibus* attacked Taglioni's *Ifigenia in Aulide* (Iphigenia in Aulis): "The dances were so wretched that it's no use talking about them.... [L]oud hissing mingled with the laughter of the public." To save money, the cart that was used onstage at night to convey mythological figures was borrowed from the public market, where it served in the morning for all sorts of odd jobs and could be hired by anyone. Spectators would recognize it, call out its nickname, and crack jokes, thus setting the whole house a-giggle for the rest of the evening.

    Less than two weeks later the newspaper returned to the attack: "The audience never fails to hiss the pas de trois, *la* Graekoska, and the final scene of *Iphigenia*; actually, not many actually hiss, because after the opera two-thirds of the audience leaves and one-third watches the boxes, or rather the inhabitants of the boxes; only the subscribers in the front rows watch the ballet, but their attention does not extend beyond the feet and faces of the female dancers" (*L'Omnibus*, 1 Dec. 1847). More followed a few days later: "It would be a shame for this ballet to be withdrawn from the stage because we hope in the course of time to be able to divine the motives of the choreographer in serving it up to us. Perhaps it was to win the ongoing competition for the worst in which our choreographers have been engaged for some years now. The most fortunate will be the one who does the last ballet. The pas de trois born to hissing has died to hissing" (*L'Omnibus*, 6 Dec. 1847).

38. *L'Omnibus*, 11 Apr. 1849.
39. Biographical note, Fonds Taglioni, R/81, BN-Opéra.
40. Libretto, Biblioteca Nazionale, Rome.
41. *L'Omnibus*, 17 Oct. 1849.
42. Wrote *Il Nuovo Arlecchino* (The New Harlequin) on 14 Oct. 1860: "The ballet could not take place because the extras were not ready, the soldiers having left that morning.... Under the former paternal government, the management was accustomed to use the Neapolitan army as walk-on soldiers, and indeed they made a pretty sight, and it [the management] thought it could do the same with the current army as well; but when those gentlemen had the effrontery to depart for the defense of the fatherland without first taking care of Massimo's spectacles, what could the management do? You think perhaps that they would be obliged to *hire* people as extras? The management is poor, and the public indulgent."
43. In the absence of a libretto there remains some doubt as to whether the author was Taglioni, his son-in-law Alessandro Fuchs, or both. The review published in the *Giornale di Napoli* (28 Oct. 1865) mentions only Fuchs, but the ballet's fantastic sea setting is reminiscent of other works by Taglioni.
44. *L'Omnibus*, 11 Apr. 1860.
45. Biographical note, Fonds Taglioni, R/81, BN-Opéra.

Jules Janin: Romantic Critic

JOHN V. CHAPMAN

INTRODUCTION

Jules Janin (1804–1874) was a well-known literary figure during the July Monarchy and Second Empire, writing spirited, amusing, and sometimes perceptive literary and theatrical reviews for *Le Journal des Débats*. Known as the prince of critics, he was influential enough to merit a place in Danish ballet master August Bournonville's autobiography, *My Theatre Life*. "His original style of writing has secured him a position as aesthetic writer for the *Journal des Débats*, where each Monday he turns out a *feuilleton* which boils over with witty thoughts in a language so packed full of intensive adjectives and piquant syntax that his style is exclusively his own and would hardly dare to be used by anyone other than—Jules Janin!"[1]

Janin began writing dance reviews in 1832, shortly after the premiere of *La Sylphide*. This was a crucial moment in the history of ballet and the development of dance criticism. It was the beginning of the Romantic period, an era in which the neoclassical aesthetic that had dominated ballet since the publication in 1760 of Jean-Georges Noverre's *Letters on Dancing* was successfully challenged. In *Letters* Noverre described an approach to ballet that subordinated all its resources to the presentation of a dramatic action or story. Unlike the court dance prevalent at the time, the ballet d'action did not depend for significance on the symbolic, abstract nature of dance, but, rather, on the didactic, literal character of pantomime. Ballet, Noverre argued, should be a silent drama in which mute acting, or pantomime, conveyed a story that would teach the audience to admire the heroic and despise the ignoble. Only then, he believed, would ballet "finally receive the praise and applause that all Europe grants to Poetry and Painting, and the glorious recognition with which they are honored."[2] In the interests of dramatic coherence, everything—scenery, costumes, music, dancing—had to contribute to the telling of a story. Their value as simple entertainment was not enough to justify their presence in a ballet.

Ironically, the defining element of ballet—dancing—proved to be the most difficult component to bend to Noverre's approach. Dance is inherently nonliteral: pirouettes, entrechats, développés, and pas de bourrées possess no literal meaning. So how could they contribute to a dramatic action? It was a problem that ballet masters struggled with for more than half a century. Salvatore Viganò solved it by eliminating dancing almost entirely from his works and using a form of rhythmic pantomime to convey the narrative. Other ballet masters, such as Pierre Gardel, ignored Noverre's demand for absolute dramatic coherence and introduced dances as well as scenic spectacle into their ballets, regardless of whether these elements furthered the dramatic action.

Noverre's ideas were at the heart of ballet criticism in the early nineteenth century when Julien-Louis Geoffroy began taking a more analytical approach in his reviews for *Le Journal des Débats*. His application of serious aesthetic criteria to the appreciation of ballet was a milestone. In keeping with the aesthetics of the ballet d'action and the prevailing neoclassicism of the period, Geoffroy viewed ballet as a valid form of expression to the extent that it depicted significant human experience. "It is an art," he wrote in 1804, "only when it imitates the thoughts, characteristics, and feelings of men; this is how it becomes part of dramatic poetry. Jumps and pirouettes are not *the dance*."[3] Echoing Noverre, he claimed that "genius consists in the expression of the soul's sentiments through the silent eloquence of pantomime: here is what elevates dance to the dignity of an art."[4] Thus, Geoffroy found his greatest pleasure in watching expressive dancers such as Mme Gardel or Emilie Bigottini in action. "One proceeds continually from terror to hope, from despair to joy," he wrote of the former in *La Fête de Mars*.[5] At the other extreme, Geoffroy was an outspoken opponent of technical display for its own sake, especially the tours de force that were becoming increasingly important at the end of the eighteenth century. "Dance is surely dishonored and lost," he wrote in 1804, "when it comes to consist of the merits of tours de force."[6]

The mind-body dichotomy was prominent in Geoffroy's view of dance. He reasoned that dancing was executed by the lesser parts of the body, the legs and feet, whereas the nobler art of pantomime employed the arms, hands, and face. "Pantomime is the most beautiful and the most interesting part of dance because it uses only the noblest parts of the body. The legs and feet, which are so important in ordinary dance, are scarcely noticed in pantomime dance: here, it is the head, the face, and the arms that play the principal role."[7]

"C.," who took over Geoffroy's column after his death in 1815, continued to promote the neoclassical ballet d'action up to Marie Taglioni's debut in 1827. "C." admired Taglioni's dancing but qualified his praise with the observation that:

> Dance, properly called, that is to say, the talent of designing attitudes, agitating the legs with precision, rapidity, and finesse, of landing on balance *sur les pointes* of the feet, is only the mechanical part of the art, and even when one excels, the name of 'artist' is scarcely merited. It is pantomime, that is, expression, which alone can be the guarantee of the true connoisseur's esteem.[8]

Taglioni's true merits, he concluded, would only be known after she had performed a pantomime role, for "the distance from the head to the feet...is infinite since it is the interval that separates the material organs from the intellectual and thinking faculty."[9]

"C." was wrong, of course, for Taglioni's true achievement did not make itself evident in pantomime roles. The genius of her dancing was apparent only in the new type of ballet created by her father, Filippo. With her appearance in 1831 as the leader of the ghostly nuns in the opera *Robert le Diable* and then, more sensationally, the following year in the title role of *La Sylphide*, the stranglehold of the ballet d'action was broken. For perhaps the first time people witnessed a style of dancing that was fully expressive in and of itself. Taglioni's dancing did not convey prosaic dramatic actions: rather, it evoked the poetic sensibilities associated with romanticism. A new form of training developed by her father Filippo as well as by Auguste Vestris, Albert Descombe (Monsieur Albert), and others had given her the strength, stamina, agility, precision, and coordination to go beyond technique in the depiction of character and atmosphere. It imparted to her the total ease and naturalness that were necessary to evoke the illusion that she was a real sylph, not a dancer merely impersonating one. Her poetic style stood in sharp contrast to its neoclassical predecessor, just as her father's poetic visions had little in common with the edifying morals of existing ballet narratives. Traditional critics such as "C." were simply not equipped to appreciate the new ballet. To do this required critics with a radically new aesthetic.

Jules Janin, who succeeded "C." shortly after the premiere of *La Sylphide* in 1832, was one such critic. With all the bold rebelliousness of the Romantic age, Janin very quickly made clear his position on the ballet d'action, telling his readers that, as far as he was concerned, ballets were about dancing not dramatic actions. What mattered to him was the creation of beautiful images, seductive illusions, and poetic feelings.

Janin anticipated his better known colleague, Théophile Gautier, by three years in applying the aesthetic of *l'art pour l'art*—art for art's sake—to ballet. In the hands of Janin, *l'art pour l'art* became *la danse pour la danse*, a philosophy that he applied with the *épatisme* that would also characterize Gautier's dance writing. Both men were keenly aware of the radical nature of their ideas. Ridiculing the neoclassical obsession with narrative logic and coherent dramatic action, Janin taunted: "Logic is a fine thing, but too much logic is intolerable....Why deprive ballet of its most wonderful privileges: disorder, dream, and the absence of common sense?"[10] Turning Geoffroy's "head over feet" analogy upside down, he wrote that ballet was about dances and dancers. "[I]n the future we will occupy ourselves mostly with the dance," he wrote in one of his first articles. "Dance...has the great advantage of not being melodrama, tragedy, or comedy."[11]

Janin hated the ballet d'action with a passion. Its long tedious mime sections bored him. "Fie, therefore, on *ballets d'action*! Fie on the *danse noble*!" he wrote in a review of *Nina*, a sentimental story ballet first produced in 1813 by Louis Milon:

Abandon,...once and for all, the *danse noble*, the *ballet d'action*, the role of *grands danseurs*, the great desperate passions, the choreographic tragedies, the little Corneilles of the ballet, and, especially, we ask Mlle [Lise] Noblet's pardon for having been forced during two acts to subject her beautiful dark eyes and her pretty legs to the painful disorders and laborious strains that must have been as distasteful for her as they were in fact for us.[12]

Taking aim again at the didacticism of the ballet d'action (and neoclassicism generally), Janin wrote that "truth does not exist in the arts. On the contrary, truth stands in the way of art."[13] Here, he underscores a fundamental difference between eighteenth and nineteenth-century aesthetics. Rather than instructing the spectator about reality or being the great means of revealing universal truths, art existed to stimulate the imagination. Thus, ballet was a framework for the free-ranging expression of fantasy; it offered poetic images that could be turned by the viewer into whatever "little house in Spain" pleased him. After remarking that his predecessor had advised the reading of at least one relevant play before going to the ballet, Janin wrote that on the contrary:

[I]t is pleasurable for me to enter your Opéra auditorium to compose my own little drama at my leisure, to build my little house in Spain on plans that I improvise, to give a name to all the characters, a meaning to their gestures, to base my own little poem on the dances, gambols, and light steps in the kingdom of illusion, in the gardens of fantasy....I have come with nimble step to see, to hear, to dream, to applaud, in a word to amuse myself as my fancy takes me...I did not come here to read and do my homework. I come with sprightly steps to see, hear, dream, applaud.[14]

Janin's ballet writing was a dialogue between the spectator and the work. His goal was not to decipher the message of a ballet (the goal of the neoclassicist), but, rather, to involve the spectator fully in the appreciation of a ballet, an experience that depended more upon his own responses to the work than on the expressive aims of the choreographer. The successful ballet presented a rich array of poetic images to which the spectator could give any meaning he chose.

The similarities between Janin's attitudes and those of Théophile Gautier, who began writing criticism in *La Presse* in 1835, are striking. Like Janin, he regretted the public's weakness for narrative. The French, he wrote,

are not artistic enough in the rigorous sense of the word to be content with the plastic forms of poetry, painting, music and dance. They need a precise significance, an action, a logically formulated drama, a moral, a logical conclusion. Few of us look at a painting, read a book, listen to a song for the beauty of the colors, language, or sounds, in fact, for the true charm.[15]

Thus Gautier was no lover of dramatic ballets. Echoing Janin he wrote: "Nothing resembles a dream more than a ballet....One enjoys, while awake, the phenomenon that nocturnal fantasy traces on the canvas of sleep: an entire world of chimeras moves before you."[16]

Gautier did not confine himself to the appreciation of ballets; he wrote them as well. *Giselle* (1841) was his most successful, and Janin was extremely impressed by it. His review of the ballet went far beyond a mere description of what he had seen and heard. Speaking in the new poetic critical language that he and Gautier shared, he tried to recreate the images kindled by the work. In keeping with the vividness of the illusion, he wrote as if he were describing a real scene, not a ballet:

> Night has thrown her softest mists over the countryside. All is silent, even the nightingale in the woods. The shepherd's star rises in the sky; the silver lake murmurs its monotonous complaint, calm and splendid. Stirred by the wind, the reeds balance delicately. Oh, pity! Under this willow that weeps, under this mound of plants and wild flowers, what is this new grave? It is Giselle's. There she sleeps, or, rather, there she dreams, gently wrapped in her chaste shroud.... Let us begin! Sleepy Wilis, arise! It is your queen who commands you.[17]

In contrast to the Romantic critic's intimate engagement with a ballet and its dancers, the neoclassical critic remained aloof, distant, and prosaic. At best, Geoffroy could string together a list of adjectives to convey his impressions of a dancer. At worst, he simply observed that such and such a dancer's name was sufficient to evoke his or her attributes. Hippolyte Prévost, a neoclassical critic who wrote for *Le Moniteur* from 1829 until after 1850, was sorely aware of his deficiencies when faced with the wondrous talents of the Romantic ballerina:

> Marie Taglioni has never been younger, bolder, livelier, more surprising, more gracious, more ravishing, more reserved, more seductive, more overflowing with modesty and intoxications at the same time. These words, with which we seek vainly through accumulation to create a sense of life and substance, are so far from completely expressing our thoughts! In order to extol properly this exceptionally beautiful art, language lacks nuances: the praise of this admirable danseuse can be captured only by new expressions, unique like her talent.[18]

Although he remained loyal to his belief in the ballet d'action and the discursive writing style associated with it, Prévost possessed real insight into the nature of the new Romantic ballet. After another vain attempt to capture Taglioni's gifts, he lamented: "in order to paint and to praise the purity of her talent, is it not obligatory to speak, alas, as well as one can, the language of poetry?"[19] Alas, Prévost was no poet. Janin, on the other hand, though not the poet Gautier was, could paint word pictures when it suited him. He was never at a loss for words or poetic imagery to evoke his favorite ballerinas. Fanny Cerrito's debut in 1847 merited more words than Prévost, Geoffroy, or "C." would have devoted to ten such events:

> La Cerrito is an Italian; she is a woman; she understands all the difficulties and whims of dance, and she trembles!... Our daughter of Italy began

piano, piano, timidly. She scarcely dared breathe; she glided, skimmed the earth; she dared not rise too high, yet, little by little, as she saw the audience did not jeer her, she became bolder, took a leap, then two, three, and finally set off! She bounds like a gazelle and dances like the verdant hills; she is lively, alert, passionate, everything she could be. Imagine Mlle Taglioni transformed into a full-breasted woman, with beautiful well-connected limbs—legs, arms, hips—and no wings on her strong and proud shoulders. The song is the same; what is different is the tune. I know the words, but not the accompaniment. But what does it matter? Each danseuse makes her own song! La Cerrito has succeeded—and succeeded completely—in walking and dancing like a real, living person, not a sylphide. She is not the ideal, a daughter of clouds and mists or even a daughter of fire or marble.[20] This is altogether a good thing, quite substantial.... How can I put it? I have only one expression that serves: she is a good, lively darling who abandons herself to all the freedom of her attractions, all the truth of her feelings, to life, energy, gaiety, folly, and the bounding spirit that contains all her poetry. At the Venetian carnival she rises above the sound of the orchestra, defying the enflamed glances to dance for herself and the joy of dancing. Look at her, for all the good it will do you! Once started, she cares not if she is seen or applauded, if she dances well or is high or low on her pointes. She dances, which is enough for her. She is in her element, in her glory, at her ease.[21]

The combination of art for art's sake and the personalization of the ballerina led Gautier and Janin to offer increasingly detailed descriptions of dancers, descriptions that did not find their terms, as before, in the rigid concepts of the genre system but in individual human attributes. Janin's adoration of the ballerina was so extreme that she became the raison d'être of ballet itself. "The dance," he wrote in 1832, "is called Taglioni, Noblet, Julia [de Varennes], [Mme] Alexis Dupont, four great names!"[22] He went to the Opéra to see its ballerinas and only secondarily to experience the ballets that in his eyes were merely vehicles for the creation of images of beautiful women. Taglioni was his favorite:

> Of all the innocent joys in the world, the pleasures that cause neither fatigue nor regret, I know of no greater joy or more lively pleasure than seeing Mlle Taglioni dance, than hurrying after her (I will not say in her footprints, for she leaves none), than following her in spirit through the imaginary spaces where she is transported without even willing it.[23]

Janin was so taken by the depth of reality Taglioni brought to her roles that he wondered whether she was truly a mortal. "I have seen one who glides or, rather, walks almost on the ground, something of white and pink that has a form you would say is that of a daughter of man, but so light, so relaxed, so flowing, so delicate, so fine, so much a shadow, that one would have to be very bold to say for sure at a single glance: it is a daughter of man!"[24]

When the dance disappeared into the role a ballerina was performing, the illusion, the dream, became totally convincing. Of Fanny Elssler, he wrote that she "does not dance, she plays";[25] of Lucile Grahn, that she "dances as the bird sings";[26] of Carlotta Grisi, that she "dances like youth; she dances her thoughts and her feelings."[27] Janin and his fellow critics relished the feeling that the character portrayed on stage was someone they could love, esteem, and adore. Gautier dipped his pen deeply in the ink of sentiment to describe Taglioni's final Paris performance in 1844. "There is in these farewell evenings...an affecting and melancholy charm; it is like the perfume of the last rose that one wants to breathe fully....When the curtain falls at the end, one feels something of the sadness that is felt when a carriage bears a loved one away. The first turn of the wheel passes over the heart."[28]

Taglioni was Janin's most beloved ballerina. He felt so close to her that he experienced the jealousy and pain of an abandoned lover when she left to dance for admirers in distant places. After one such absence, he mused about her past desertions in the tone of a jilted lover:

> Certainly, if we had been able to anticipate all these miseries, if we had known that our creation would one fine day go up in smoke, that she would abandon us, we would not have done so much for her. We would have hidden our joy; we would have contained our transports; we would not have felt all these jealous passions, and all the better for us, alas!
>
> No, no, this time she will not have a single good word from me. I do not want to be near her. I will be as strong and courageous as necessary. You are coming, you are coming; if only I can maintain my resolution! She is here, I will not go to see her dance![29]

Thus, Janin resolved to pass up his idol's season: he was not going to add his applause to her praises. He stood firm until her final performance, when he found himself lurking near the Opéra. Ten minutes before the curtain went up his resolution broke down, and he entered the theater to see his unfaithful Marie weave her magic and grant her "un petit bravo." It is obvious that Janin is not entirely serious; his aim, as was frequently the case of his writing, was to entertain and amuse his readers. Nevertheless, there is a kernel of seriousness in his account stemming from a real sense of possessiveness.

The mixture of the aesthetic and the sensual, the sacred and the profane satisfied lovers of the Romantic ballet at many levels and in many parts of their beings. It was the consequence of an aesthetic of art for art's sake where the focus was on form and that form was the female body. Janin frequently expressed a subtle blend of formal satisfaction with an appreciation of feminine sensual charm. He wrote that "dance, for a woman who is nothing more than beautiful, who has no singing voice, no talent for drama or intelligence to understand great art, is a charming and assured means of showing that she is beautiful....Dance is therefore only the most charming and moral means that a woman has to demonstrate her beauty."[30] Thus, at one extreme, ballet was a wondrous stimulant to the imagination; at the other, it was a purveyor of sensual graces. Janin wrote that for *La Révolte au sérail*, "Mons. Taglioni required an abundance of danseuses, ribbons, lace, turbans, silk stockings, an abundance of naked shoulders, an abundance of arms draped like the shoulders; he has been given all the women he wanted; those chosen were young and pretty, comely, well made, bold, svelte. You want women? Here they are!"[31]

Gautier expressed similar views, writing that ballet was composed of "dance, poses, and rhythmic movement, and, why not admit it, the physical voluptuousness and beauty of woman."[32] With the unabashed confidence of a nineteenth-century male, neither Janin nor Gautier did anything to conceal their motives. Janin readily admitted that one of ballet's attractions was the dancers' revealing costumes. He was all in favor of ballet themes that "permit[ted] the nymphs to be lightly dressed."[33]

The identification of ballet with female beauty during the Romantic period left little room for male dancing, which underwent a rapid decline. To a critic such as Janin, the danseur was an unwelcome trespasser on the ballerina's territory. *"Under no circumstances do I recognize a man's right to dance in public,"* he wrote in 1832.[34] What is impressive about this statement, besides its being totally uncompromising, is that it was written at the beginning of the Romantic ballet. Janin's stance did not soften over the years. Just listen to him sneering in 1840:

> But a man, a frightful man, as ugly as you or me, with an empty, vacant gaze, who capers aimlessly, a creature made expressly to bear a rifle, saber, and uniform! That this being should dance like a woman, impossible! This bearded person, who is a community leader, an elector, a member of the municipal council, a man who makes and, more often, unmakes the laws to his own advantage.[35]

The danseur was physically unsuited to ballet simply because he was a man, like other men, and temperamentally unsuited, because he inhabited the real world, the antithesis of the dream world that was ballet's true realm.

Thus it was that, on the one hand, Jules Janin helped free ballet criticism from the restrictions of neoclassical aesthetics, make it responsive to the imagination, and involve the viewer actively in the interpretation of ballet meaning. On the other hand, it was in his writing—with its emphasis on the star at the expense of the work, the rejection of the male dancer, and the "feminization" of ballet ideology and personnel—that the seeds of ballet's decline as an art form were partly sown.

Notes

1. August Bournonville, *My Theatre Life*, trans. Patricia N. McAndrew, foreword Erik Bruhn, introd. Svend Kragh-Jacobsen (Middletown, Conn.: Wesleyan University Press, 1979), p. 489.

2. Jean-Georges Noverre, *Lettres sur la danse* (Lyon, 1760), p. 29.

3. Julien-Louis Geoffroy, "Début de madame Quériau dans *la Fille mal gardée*, ballet pantomime de Dauberval," *Le Journal des Débats*, 12 May 1804, p. 3.

4. Julien-Louis Geoffroy, "*La Mort d'Adonis*," *Le Journal des Débats*, 12 June 1809, p. 2.

5. Julien-Louis Geoffroy, "Première représentation de *la Fête de Mars*, diver-

tissement-pantomime en un acte," *Le Journal des Débats*, 29 Dec. 1809, p. 2.

6. Julien-Louis Geoffroy, "Rentrée de Duport," *Le Journal des Débats*, 20 May 1804, p. 2.

7. Julien-Louis Geoffroy, "Les Prétendus," *Le Journal des Débats*, 28 June 1807, p. 3.

8. "C.", "*La Vestale*. Mlle Taglioni. *Les Filets de Vulcain*," *Le Journal des Débats*, 3 Aug. 1827, p. 2.

9. *Ibid.*

10. Jules Janin, "*La Tentation*," *Le Journal des Débats*, 27 June 1832, p. 1. See below, pp. 206–212.

11. *Ibid.*, p. 3.

12. Jules Janin, "Le Ballet de *Nina*. Mlle Varin," *Le Journal des Débats*, 14 Dec. 1835, p. 2. See below, pp. 220–225.

13. Jules Janin, "Théâtre Nautique. *Le Nouveau Robinson*, ballet en un acte, par M. Blanche," *Le Journal des Débats*, 18 Aug. 1834, p. 2.

14. Jules Janin, "La Semaine dramatique," *Le Journal des Débats*, 13 July 1846, p. 1.

15. Théophile Gautier, "Opéra," *La Presse*, 23 Nov. 1849, p. 1.

16. Théophile Gautier, "Opéra. Rentrée de la Cerrito," *La Presse*, 9 Oct. 1848, p. 1.

17. Jules Janin, "*Giselle, ou les Wilis*," *Le Journal des Débats*, 30 June 1841, p. 1. See below, pp. 233–241.

18. Hippolyte Prévost, "Mlle Taglioni dans *la Sylphide*," *Le Moniteur*, 20 July 1840, p. 2.

19. Hippolyte Prévost, "Représentation au bénéfice de Mlle Taglioni," *Le Moniteur*, 1 July 1844, p. 2.

20. A reference to the title role of Arthur Saint-Léon's *La Fille de marbre* (1847).

21. Jules Janin, "*La Fille de marbre*, ballet-pantomime," *Le Journal des Débats*, 25 Oct. 1847, p. 1.

22. "*La Tentation*," p. 3.

23. Jules Janin, "Rentrée de Mlle Taglioni," *Le Journal des Débats*, 22 Aug. 1836, p. 1. See below, pp. 225–226.

24. Jules Janin, "Rentrée de Mlle Taglioni," *Le Journal des Débats*, 27 July 1835, p. 2.

25. Jules Janin, "*La Tempête*, ballet-féerie en deux actes," *Le Journal des Débats*, 22 Sept. 1834, p. 1.

26. Jules Janin, "Mlle Lucile Grahn. Mlle Noblet. Mme Dupont," *Le Journal des Débats*, 15 July 1839, p. 1.

27. Jules Janin, "*Giselle*. Mlle Grisi," *Le Journal des Débats*, 26 Aug. 1844, p. 1.

28. Jules Janin, "Théâtre de l'Opéra," *Le Journal des Débats*, 1 July 1844, p. 2.

29. Jules Janin, "Représentation au bénéfice de Mlle Taglioni," *Le Journal des Débats*, 27 July 1840, p. 1.

30. Jules Janin, "Débuts de Mlle Louise Ropiquet et de M. Carey. *Don Juan*," *Le Journal des Débats*, 10 Mar. 1834, p. 1.

31. Jules Janin, "*La Révolte au sérail*, ballet en trois actes," *Le Journal des Débats*, 6 Dec. 1833, p. 1.

32. Théophile Gautier, "*La Font*, ballet de M. Mazilier," *La Presse*, 10 Jan. 1855, p. 1.

33. Jules Janin, "Théâtre de la Gaîté. *La Bohémienne de Paris*," *Le Journal des Débats*, 26 Feb. 1844, p. 1.

34. "*La Tentation*," p. 3.

35. Jules Janin, "Théâtre de la Renaissance. *Zingaro*," *Le Journal des Débats*, 2 Mar. 1840, p. 2. See below, pp. 230–232.

SELECTED CRITICISM

"*La Tentation*,"[1] *Le Journal des Débats*, 27 June 1832.

Logic is a fine thing, but too much logic is intolerable. I am not interested in hearing about Condillac[2] in relation to an opera or ballet libretto. Once you have put a bridle on the imagination, allow me to lead the pretty thing at full gallop. Why deprive ballet of its most wonderful privileges: disorder, dream, and the absence of common sense?

The ballet *La Tentation* has greatly occupied the artists among us as well as the women who are all artists at heart, if they are the least bit happy or pretty, which is the same thing. The entire artistic public has contributed to this long story about heaven and hell, to the momentous clash of demons and angels, to the pell-mell of dance and song! After these public artists emerged from the volcanos, descended from the clouds, escaped from the harem, broken by the hair shirt worn by the hero, they were so dumbfounded that they did not know what to think. In fact, it was difficult to pass a judgment of any kind on this strange drama that proceeds wherever it can, whether on the stairway to hell, or in the brightness of flames, or before the setting sun in a French forest, or under a brilliant Oriental sky, or in the light of the moon in a Theban retreat;[3] this ballet that begins with the shouts of the damned and finishes with the sound of seraphic harps—what is the means of judging it all?

The means of properly judging it all is to abandon yourself to the impression of the moment, to be comfortable enough with your pleasure that you don't ask for an explanation; the means is willingly to follow the painter, the musician, the ballerina, wherever they want to lead you, in a word, to allow yourself to be happy. This is ballet's real secret, especially *La Tentation*, this strange ballet that is of no epoch, of no place, of no belief, of no culture, of no poetic school, or rather, is of all places, of all beliefs, of all schools! There is no critical approach that is appropriate.

The action begins as in a mystery play of yore. The principles of good and evil are there. The ascetic hero struggles with his passions. Woman pushes him toward evil as she has pushed so many desert saints. Lightning strikes at the final moment of venial sin, just before the sin is committed. The hermit falls dead, and his wavering soul departs, held between fires from below and glories from on high. You imagine you are reading a chapter of Saint Theresa or even the dissertation of Saint Paul on the first, second, and third heaven!

After the first act, ascetic in idea and substance, you pass to the second, which is a complete contrast. Just when you have formed an impression based on the lives of the saints of *La Légende*, suddenly you pass from *La Légende* to epic poetry, from Saint Catherine to Milton.[4] The poem that began with the cenobite proceeds to the Round Heads. Having seen the cave from *La Légende*, now you are going to climb the stairs described by old John. These flaming stairs lean on two monsters whose mouths gape. It is a very powerful set. The entire army of hell files in on it, drums, trumpets, infantry, hussars, artillery. Astaroth's forces pass in review, descending, climbing, clambering up. So much trouble and pain to make one poor man sin! It will happen in good time anyway. What does one soul more or less matter to the devil in this day and age?

See the illogic of this thing called ballet! The ballet's first act is based on *Lives of the Saints*; the first third of the second is based on Milton's stairway. This stairway, which is the basis of the most beautiful epic poem in the world outside of antiquity, scarcely sufficed for the first third of the second act of our ballet. When the devil has passed his army in review, the ballet suddenly leaves Milton. It passes from Milton to the beautiful pages of Buffon[5] where the author sets about recounting the first steps, the first feelings, the first thoughts of our first parents. The author is a little stiffer than nature, painting as he does in lace ruffles and silk clothes. A scene of earthly paradise passes beside the hellish stairway. You see woman born and growing up. She walks, she listens, she sniffs; she tastes a fruit that has been thrown to her. She gathers a rose and is pricked by a thorn. Here Dorat[6] replaces Buffon. Dorat, the hidden god of ballet, the great unknown of the ballet; Dorat, without whom there would be no ballet in this world. It is he who has sketched the scene in which Miranda appears. It is he who has designed her poses. Miranda walks; it is Dorat who sets her on the path of evil. Miranda would rather kiss than eat an apple; it is Dorat who makes Miranda kiss the apple. Miranda wants to fish sounds from the air; it is Dorat who throws her rounded arms into the air. At the end of the scene, Miranda leans on the devil for support; it is Dorat who throws her to the devil, who pricks her pretty finger with a rose; and this sentence that you read, perfumed, trimmed, embroidered, dazzling like Louisa, it is again Dorat who wrote it.

The first performance included a section that is absolutely necessary to the scene in which the demons create this woman. Before making the pretty woman, Miranda, it transpires that the devils create a hideous little creature, all green, the color of monsters, a capering abomination that seems to have escaped from the witches' cauldron in *Macbeth*. The ugly creature prepared us admirably for the perfect creation. If the pure young girl is to produce the greatest effect, it is vital to have the green woman.

After the woman is formed, the devils rejoice like mortals. They dance a gallop just as we do at the end of a ball when the candles go out, the pale morning appears through the curtains, and the weariness of the dancers resembles madness. This hellish gallop, the melody of which is very well contrived, has a strange effect. Simon[7] and Mme Elie[8] perform it like the truly damned. This Simon, valet de chambre of the devil, is a wanton, frightful and full of energy. He is very ugly, all hoary, with white teeth, and hands that gnash like his teeth. He brings to mind very clearly Frederick's dance in *Faust* when Mephistopheles intoxicates a poor girl with a look and amuses himself by turning her round and round!

The act finishes with gun shots aimed from hell to heaven; then the volcano explodes; the army leaves as it entered, by the stairs. In the second act, you have already exhausted all the material from legend, poetry, and light verse; you have exhausted the Fathers of the Church, Dorat, and Milton; you have exhausted heaven and earth—this is ballet!

We leave heaven and hell, and arrive on the earth. At last the drama begins! The drama is the temptation. At last the hero appears! He is the tempted man. What drama is worthy of an introduction that begins with a clap of thunder, a combat of angels and devils? What hero is worth the trouble taken by the infernal legion? This is the problem with the subject; this is the obstacle. You have to create an inexorable, inflexible saint, a man of iron, living alone, without any other companion than the impure animal that I dare not name, whose hidden graces he knows all too well, the worthy fellow! If, in fact, Saint Anthony was the true hero of the ballet, he would have been too great a saint. The unshakable austerity, the heart of stone, the hair shirt that one always sees, all that would obstruct our bayadères. Therefore nothing can be made of a great saint; it would be impossible to tempt him. No artist has tempted Saint Anthony. Callot[9] and especially Teniers,[10] who have made good "Temptations"—God have mercy!—have not dreamed in the least of tempting the saint, they had such a high opinion of his virtue. What is the "Temptation" of Teniers other than the vengeance of a disappointed devil? The hideous forms, the continual and ever fatiguing mockery, the piercing and satanic will, all that would make the saint die of fear, but tempt him! To be sure, neither Callot nor Teniers claimed to have induced Anthony to sin, yet in the Opéra ballet, the sin is the goal of every effort. It is therefore necessary to put Saint Anthony forcefully aside.

And it is this that happens. So instead of an anchorite with a thick beard, we have a handsome young man, hot-blooded and tenderhearted. A hermit has been fabricated just as a woman was fabricated. Yet it is all wrecked on another rock. The old Anthony was too tough, the young Anthony a little too tender. We have already seen him, prior to his death, becoming intimate with a young woman to whom he gave aid. Brought back to life, Anthony is the same as before his death. He runs after danger like a student in the fourth grade. I am only astonished by one thing: that our young man succumbs but twice.

In the third act his active role begins. He arrives, weakened by hunger and thirst, carrying an empty purse. He has neither drunk nor eaten since his death, how unfortunate! He descends into the valley with small steps. It is a romantic valley that might have been painted by Watteau. Snow has been falling all day. An iron cross is seen downstage across from the lodge of a grand château. The lodge was to be topped with a pointed roof that would have given it more character. This roof has been left out. Such as it is, the decor is charming. In the distance the noise of the hunt is heard, the sound of the horn, the gallop of horses. The hunters pass on ten horses. At the first performance four spurred riders stopped on stage and sound-

ed the halali! It was very effective. The horses have been cut, which is too
bad. The fanfare is sung backstage, and these gentlemen sound quite good.

As for the costumes of the third act, they are truly the costumes of
Charles IX, all trimmed in gold. The lodge is also of the time of Charles
IX. Those who want logic must be most disappointed when they see the
drama suddenly pass from the beginnings of the militant Church to the
epoch of Saint Bartholomew. That is how it is. Since I am speaking of costumes, I regret also that Mlle Duvernay[11] has not kept her white costume
from the first act during the whole ballet. It is her appropriate dress, made
as it was in hell. Sometimes it is a little difficult to recognize Miranda in
her second costume. There are moments of confusion, especially at the
end of the third act when Miranda falls to her knees with the pilgrims.
Give her back her white costume!

Whatever, the hunters return home at the sound of a horn. The lodge
is lit up, the tables laid. On the ground floor can be seen the white hats of
chefs who are working in the red light of the oven. Pages take food and
wine to the guests using a stairway that is outside the hall. There is singing
above, laughter below, and drunkenness high and low. The poor hermit, at
the foot of the cross, shivers, dying of hunger. The entire scene is well laid
out and presented. A couplet, sung without accompaniment by the guests,
is ineffectual. On the other hand, the drinking song has a charming effect.
It has rhythm. And you know the power of rhythm! When the night cur-
few strikes, you see a Paris urchin beating time with the drum almost to
the barracks, except when he is trounced by his father. It is rhythm that
makes the drum so dear to the Paris urchin.

Our pilgrim is therefore tempted by hunger, by cold, by fatigue, by all
the contrasts between winter and a good fire. Recall the verse of Tibullus:[12]

> Quam juvat immites ventos audire cubantem,
> Et Dominam tenero detinuisse sinu![13]

Thus we go from Buffon to Tibullus. The damned send Miranda to the
pilgrim. Miranda calls to him and draws him near. He is on the point of
giving in; he follows her; he is going to enter! Suddenly more pilgrims
arrive. The temptation that began so well is without effect. Our fellow is
saved this time! I imagine, though, that there has been some interference
by the angels. The young Anthony should be left completely to himself so
that the weapons are equal. But what do you expect? He is such an unsophisticated young man!

The act finishes with an ingenious and touching idea that could not
have come from a hard-hearted ballet master. This woman, Miranda, this
fallen angel, seeing the pilgrims praying on their knees, hands joined,
throws herself at the foot of the cross, kneeling, hands joined. The idea is
charming. It is a mistake, here as elsewhere, that Miranda has not kept her
original costume, insuring there is no doubt it is her. It is also a mistake to
have the scene take place on the second stairway in the back depths of the
stage. It loses its effect.

Originally, says the libretto, the lodge fell piece by piece under the blade of the angel like the walls of Jericho. This explains why only a simple lodge was made in place of an immense gallery that would have given a better idea of a fete! If someone could manage the impossible, it would be the machinist[14] of the Opéra.

The decor of the fourth act is one of the most beautiful things that can be seen. It is a true harem like those described by women who have entered them, Milady Montagu,[15] for example, who did not, however, describe all its beauties. The vast hall is garnished with divans. A fountain flows in the background. The hot sun of the Orient burns yonder through the lattice. A gallery with a golden balustrade decorates the hall. In this gallery are the rooms of the odalisques. There are women on divans, women in the gallery, women on the front of the stage—scattered in profusion. We were just in the snows of a French forest, and now we are in the perfumed court of His Highness. What would logic say?

The anchorite is introduced into this harem. It is hell's second test, and it must be confessed it is daunting. All these women dance in front of our hermit. It is a charming dance. Just imagine, there are only women, not the blemish of a man. After a well-sung vaudeville, I know nothing more abominable in the world than a danseur. Remember this, though I may eventually have to pay for saying so. Under no circumstances do I recognize a man's right to dance in public.

And if you please, we will concentrate on the dance from now on. Dance is the most serious of lighthearted things. It has the great advantage of not being melodrama, tragedy, or comedy, which means it is something. It is silent, and this is an important point. The dance is called Taglioni, Noblet, Julia, Alexis Dupont, four great names!

At the premiere Mme Alexis Dupont[16] sprained her foot when her cavalier allowed her to fall from such a height that she was injured. Mlle Noblet[17] was much admired in her bayadère costume, correct, decent, pure, perhaps a little too much so. Mlle Julia,[18] the beautiful dark-eyed one, pale with the first admirable paleness of youth, comes and dances as a bird sings in its cage, without sadness and without joy, simply doing what it does. When I was young, I admired before all else the energetic dance of Mme Montessu;[19] I liked the vigorous leg that struck the floor with sureness. Now I find Mme Montessu complacent, less light, and too plump. It is as if I had become quite fat and heavy since then.

This elegant dance, these charming costumes, these Turks and bayadères who are so realistic that they resemble neither Turks nor bayadères, this busy, lively place, all this creates a very well managed contrast with the fires of hell, the pale sun of France, and the blue clarity of the sky. This time, as usual, the anchorite wants nothing more than to give in. He is going to stab the sultan, a powerful sin that has another name: it is called a crime. Luckily, Miranda saves him in the fourth act, as the angel saved him in the third. Truly, the anchorite has missed his vocation. He was born for fighting duels, seducing women, collecting money, and eat-ing every morning at the Café Tortoni.

Guess what happens in the fifth act. Something again that is not logical but quite natural. After having subjected the worthy fellow to all possible temptations, cold near a fire, thirst beside a full cup, love in the midst of a chaste harem of gauze pantaloons, ambition for the throne of an Oriental despot, the only desirable throne in this world of charters, the demons, who do not really care about one soul more or less, give up, and renounce this difficult conquest. All they can do is dream of doing their best to torment the escaped victim. This is why there is no story to the fifth act. It is no longer a question in the fifth act of the devils conquering a poor soul, but of how to amuse themselves after losing him. Thus the fete begins. The noise, the tumult, the skulls, the skeletons, the swinging children, the demons who pull their own tails, this ghastly joy, these loud shouts. The opera, no longer thinking of its hero, of its plan, of its drama, of the temptation, of the tempted man, has reproduced the "Temptation" of Callot. The drama ends weakly, it is true, but as recompense we have a beautiful tumult, a sublime bacchanal, a hellish tableau, an admirable cacophony of figures, sounds, masks, and dances. Then,

Lise Noblet in a zapateado, lithograph by Louis Lassalle, 1838. Dance Collection, New York Public Library for the Performing Arts, Astor, Lenox, and Tilden Foundations.

when the time comes, the sky opens, a sky like that of Martin's[20] London etchings, all white on a background of black, with myriads of people and angels who swim in waves of light. The hermit's cell disappears beneath a sky painted by Delaroche.[21] And there is one more soul in heaven—and one more grand ballet at the Opéra!

1. A work that mixed opera and ballet, *La Tentation* was produced by Eugène Coralli (1779–1854), who created many of the romantic period's most successful ballets, including *Le Diable boiteux* (1836), *Giselle* (with Jules Perrot, 1841), and *La Péri* (1843).
2. Etienne de Condillac (1715–1780) was an influential philosophe who believed that logical reasoning could be applied in metaphysics and morals with the same precision as in geometry.

3. An allusion to *La Thébaïde* (1664), Racine's first tragedy. The theme is the conflict of Eteocles and Polynices for the throne of Thebes.
4. The references are to John Milton's *Paradise Lost* (1667).
5. Georges-Louis Leclerc Buffon (1707–1788) was a scientist who wrote on the various epochs of the world.
6. Claude-Joseph Dorat (1734–1780) was a poet and the author of tragedies and comedies, the themes of which were borrowed for ballets.
7. François Simon (1800–1877) danced at the Opéra from 1822 to 1824.
8. Madame Elie, née Louise Launer, danced at the Opéra from 1810 to 1835.
9. Jacques Callot (1592–1635) was an eminent engraver known for his fanciful drawings.
10. David Teniers (1610–1690), a Flemish genre and religious painter, did several versions of "The Temptation of Saint Anthony."
11. Pauline Duvernay (1813–1894), who performed Miranda, was a popular dancer at the Opéra in the 1830s, although overshadowed by Marie Taglioni and Fanny Elssler. Miranda was her only leading role.
12. Albius Tibullus (*ca.* 60–19 B.C.) was a Roman poet famous for his elegies and his love poems.
13. "How pleasing it is for a man in bed to hear the ungentle winds."
14. During the Romantic period the complicated and sophisticated machinery of theaters such as the Opéra produced truly spectacular effects—erupting volcanos, falling castles, shipwrecks, flying dancers, etc. The position of machinist was one requiring great skill and experience.
15. Lady Mary Wortley Montagu (1689–1762) was a traveler and writer whose *Turkish Letters* (published in 1763 after her death) piqued the romantic imagination.
16. Alexis Dupont (stage name of Félicité Noblet, 1807–1877) danced at the Opéra from 1826 to 1841. She was the sister of the dancer Lise Noblet.
17. Lise Noblet (1801–1852) danced at the Opéra from 1818 to 1841. She was one of the most popular French dancers of the Romantic period.
18. Julia de Varennes (1805–1849) danced at the Opéra from 1823 to 1838. She was considered pretty, technically precise, and correct.
19. Pauline Montessu (née Paul, 1805–1877) danced at the Opéra from 1820 to 1836. She was sister of the famous demi-caractère dancer (Antoine) Paul. In the late 1820s and early 1830s she performed lead roles in ballets such as *Manon Lescaut* (1830) and *La Somnambule* (1827).
20. John Martin (1789–1854) was a painter of Romantic epics depicting the grandeur of nature.
21. Paul Delaroche (1797–1856) was a salon painter of sentimental religious and historical subjects of a style between the classical and romantic.

"Mlle Taglioni," *Le Journal des Débats*, 24 Aug. 1832.

At last she has returned to us and with what lightness! She has been given back to us by the Prussian king—Taglioni applauded alongside Meyerbeer.[22] She has returned from England as she has returned from suppers with the king of Prussia. *Le National* has made political news on the subject of these suppers. For heaven's sake, don't speak of politics and Taglioni in the same breath.

She has returned as she departed, lively, light, fresh, reserved in her grandest passions, never leaving the earth, not even when she is in the sky. Taglioni is the dance of antiquity, modest and gentle, a dance that causes all other poetry to be forgotten and eliminates the need for all other poetry. Seeing her, we cannot understand the fanaticism for the dance of times past.

But it is also true that before her no one danced in France. Dance in France was a continual torture, an unending assault on never-ending difficulties, a perpetual tournament of the leg and the face. The dance in grand style was the most painful exercise in the world after that of the lifter. Look again at Mons. Albert,[23] that perfectly stilted leftover of the *danse noble*! He appears, he poses. One, two, three! The jump is made, and nothing else happens. Then it starts all over again. One, two, three! Like a puppet that leaps well! And what admirable strings! Who holds the string to the machine? One, two, three! But it is not a string; it is better than a string; it is a spring, by heavens! And the machine goes on. One, two, three! Is it a string? Is it a spring? The spectator throws his opera glasses and eyes to the dogs.

No, it is not a spring or a string. It is something less—a *danseur noble*.

The *danseur noble*, when he is about to dance, usually rushes from the wing. He is hidden there, under a flowering apple tree, when it is a country scene; behind Nero's column, as in *Britannicus*,[24] if it is a heroic scene. He progresses to the front of the stage. As soon as he arrives, he stiffens his leg and thigh, and his calf, when he has one, and his two little arms, to puff up his veins; he sucks in his chest beyond limits, and pants; his face is very red; then he aimlessly beats his legs; he goes to the right, and to the left; to the front with one leg; to the front with the other. He jumps! He jumps! He turns! He turns! Then, at the end of several minutes, he returns to the back of the stage, lifts his arms to the right, and poses with his legs to the left; or, by a refinement of good taste, he lifts his arms to the left and poses with his legs to the right. The aim of all this is to say to the audience "applaud me." The audience does not disappoint him. It applauds with enthusiasm. This is the full secret of the *danse noble*!

People say, "He is so noble! He is so noble! What deportment! What looks! What deportment!" It is truer to say, "He is so stiff!"

I abhor the *danse noble* just as I detest the noble style of declamation and all the routines, reflections, and genuflections of the Conservatory. When one considers how skillfully these fine fellows would have charged into battle in four-four time, one regrets that His Majesty King Louis XV was deprived, out of sheer wantonness, of similar soldiers.

After the *danseur noble* comes the *danseuse noble*. Instead of hurling herself like the danseur, she appears with little steps. She poses as if on a brass wire. She begins with jetés-battus, bends almost to the ground, then rises and bends again. She turns the foot from one side to the other, a large foot usually squashed and flattened by exercise. But little by little she comes alive. She hops; she does more than hop; suddenly she jumps—

arms stiff, body immobile, face smiling! After the smile of a *danseur noble*, I know of nothing more hideous than the smile of a *danseuse noble*!

Come forward, therefore, *danseur noble* and *danseuse noble*, come forward! Tic, tac, toc; the floor cries out. Their hips groan; their hearts leap in their breasts and bounce like their jowls; it is a punishment. He does Amour, she does Venus; he carries a quiver, she a rose. The gracious mythology of Ovid is represented by Graces or demigods of this type. This is what used to be called dance.

The pleasure was always the same, more or less. Happily, from time to time, these dancers descended to earth and performed a pantomime. They became more human, made gestures, pursued feelings, went through the motions of a dialogue. The public, which could not follow these expressions, liked pantomime without knowing why. It was just because in pantomime the women were less like *danseuses nobles*, and the men danseurs. There was no other secret.

In pantomime, the dance lets up. Sometimes the dancer simply walked; the poses were clearer, the women more natural, and the men sometimes wore a tie that concealed, after a fashion, the ignoble Adam's apple that you always find on Mons. Albert's neck in particular, and on all the danseurs, noble or otherwise, in general.

At that time, when it was said of a man that he was is a zephyr, nothing more could be said: Nicolas-Zéphyre, Paul-Zéphyre, Grégoire-Zéphyre.[25] Hyperbole could go no further.

I imagine that the predecessors of Mme Saqui, who capered on the tightrope and saw the public flock to other tumblers, found the sovereign public unjust. These women reasoned well and the public poorly.

The public, licentious as an old bachelor (nothing is more bachelorlike than the public), says: What does it matter to me as long as the women are pretty and as long as they do their *bouffantes*!

For those of you in the provinces sleeping in your orchards and watching the peaches ripen on a sunny trellis, let me explain what a *bouffante* is.

The *bouffante* is an old dance trick that is used more often in our day and will be used in times to come for the edification of our last descendants.

After a *danseuse noble* has displayed her noble airs and revealed herself nobly from all angles (most often with an inclination of the head), she finishes her assault with a pirouette *sur la pointe* of the foot. This pirouette begins in a lively manner and then slackens, while the gauze dress of the goddess inflates like a balloon. The attention of the orchestra and parterre is immense. It is this billowing that I call a *bouffante*. The *bouffante* never fails to achieve its effect. It is usually followed by a murmur of approval. It rescues mediocrity, protects genius, eliminates years and wrinkles, and is the goal of the *danse noble*. The *bouffante*, for the danseuse, is the great flourish at the end of MM. Dumilâtre and Saint-Aubaire's[26] tragic tirade. This is what a *bouffante* is; I am much relieved that you know now, if you did not know before.

Honoré Daumier, "The danseur who prides himself on having preserved the noble traditions of Vestris," lithograph, ca. 1847. Golden Legend, Inc., Los Angeles.

As long as dance has existed, the *bouffante* has existed. Was the dance invented for the *bouffante* or the *bouffante* for the dance? This is an important question. I am willingly of the former opinion.

Who does not perform *bouffantes*? The most beautiful execute the *bouffante* very well. Mlle Julia executes it very well without appearing to do so. Mlle Noblet herself does not disdain it, and the public appreciates her good will.

The *bouffante* is the drinking song of the *danse noble*.

The mother of the danseuse says to her daughter when she is making a debut, "Be careful of your *bouffante*!" And when the dear little thing has danced, "You have performed ravishing *bouffantes*." Dear mother!

The great disadvantage of the danseurs is not the Adam's apple of which we have already spoken, but the total absence of the *bouffante*. Danseurs used to have satin skirts that permitted a *bouffante* of the second order. Now, they no longer have *bouffantes* of any order.

Imagine, then, the joy we all felt when one night, without warning, as if by chance discovering a pearl by the wayside, we saw something arrive that was not the *danse noble*!

Something, say, like Taglioni: natural, flowing, graceful without trying to be, with unparalleled elegance of form, with two arms like supple serpents, and legs like the arms, and the foot of an ordinary woman. This is a danseuse! We need know nothing else when we see her so relaxed, so happy to dance, dancing like the bird sings. "Where is the *danse noble?*" cry the old people. The *danse noble* is as foreign to Taglioni as natural dancing is to her rivals. Look! She uses her hands when she dances! Look at her bending torso! Such novelty! Look at her two legs, they walk! Look at how she always remains on the ground! Look! There is not a pirouette, entrechat, or difficulty in sight—nothing but dance! This woman walks, performs dramas and idylls—as a woman! Oh, this ravishing girl! She has given us a new art and taught us one more pleasure.[27] She has corrected the ballet of her day. All these *danseuses nobles*, seeing her applauded, have dispensed with some of their nobility just as they have already disposed of their panniers. They have made use of their arms and legs like simple mortals, and dared to crack their satin corsets. Their corsets have bent much more and their arms much less since Taglioni. Taglioni's great revolution has been carried out especially in the arms. There is an appreciable improvement in balletic heads and shoulders, an improvement that began in the legs. This is progress. While the revolution is being accomplished, Taglioni pursues her triumphs. She studies every day to become more of a woman and less the danseuse. Thank heavens!

Marie Taglioni as the Sylphide, lithograph after a drawing by Achille Devéria based on the statue by Jean-Auguste Barre, 1837. Dance Collection, New York Public Library for the Performing Arts, Astor, Lenox, and Tilden Foundations.

What astonished these women the most was that this newcomer who, with all her naive passion, charming shyness, and elegant caprices, could do whatever she pleases, does not do the *bouffante*. Not a single little *bouffante* for this poor public that adores her! She is so hard and unyielding! Thank heavens!

Alas, in the corps de ballet there are so many pretty women who would give half their lives—the half, to be sure, over twenty years—for the right to dance a solo or a single *première entrée*. For this solo, this *entrée*, would give them the right to do a *bouffante*, and their talent would be saved.

Whoever says *première danseuse* is really saying *première bouffante*, nothing more and nothing less.

When Taglioni returned last Monday, she returned as she departed, in a single bound...gliding across the English Channel, returning to Paris where she is loved. This Paris, always happy to discover enthusiasm for something, was moved to applaud passionately. Enthusiasm is so good!

At present, Taglioni is realizing in dance the revolution that Rossini carried out in singing and Victor Hugo in drama. Rossini, Hugo, and Taglioni—join hands: you are reformers or, I should say, revolutionaries.

For three or four hundred years before the new school, our ancestors worked in what they thought was Greek and Roman style. In the family of Agamemnon, king of kings, they created an enormous number of vulgar French bastards. Four centuries passed, and some poets believed that something better—or worse—could be achieved, by working differently. This is already an advance, whether for better or worse.

If our Mlle Taglioni had been there when *La Tentation* was performed, the Temptation would have remained in heaven. She would have thrown into this drama, which is twice as long as it should be, the great variety and irresistible charm that follows her everywhere. Seeing her emerge from the cauldron, one could have believed in demonic powers. The role of Miranda should have been given to Mlle Taglioni long ago, if she would have taken it, for we need to be rescued from the pretty little wax girl who is put there—why I do not know—and who is saved only by the power of her *bouffantes*. If Mlle Taglioni wants to take over the part, *La Tentation* will truly become a ballet.

This is provided we are not given any more surprises like yesterday's, when, in the fourth act, the sultan was found gravely seated in the dazzling harem, his eyes following the multicolored garland of women. The scene is ravishing! The dance is designed with great care, and Mlle Noblet is very pretty in her white and gold costume. Suddenly Astaroth the devil approaches the ear of the sultan and appears to say something. I imagine that he speaks to him like this: "Three dancers pass in the street and ask to dance before Your Highness." To which the sultan seems to respond: "I'll see them, but it does not make that much difference to me!" Astaroth leaves and returns followed by the three dancers, my faith! The danseuses, in white Paris gowns, created a rather poor effect among the oriental furs and pretty Greek caps trimmed in gold, but what does it matter! Here are three dancers who dance their hearts out. Two are named Taglioni: they were watched avidly. One is the brother[28] of the true Taglioni. He is a tall young man with a very noble dance style who has worked very hard to achieve his gracelessness; moreover, he kicked the face of a houri squatting on the floor who had the goodness to watch his dancing too attentively. The danseuse[29] is the sister-in-law of Mlle Taglioni. She is young and pretty—very good height in the leg, body a little stiff—and does not much imitate her sister, for which I am grateful. She dances as well as everyone else, and was a success.

But why abuse her family name? As an artist, she does not belong to this family. She has her own name. It is not necessary for her to take a name that overwhelms her. Mme Taglioni arranged to appear with her sister at her first debut; the juxtaposition was fatal. At her second debut she was much wiser and much more successful. Her success would have been even greater if she had borne another name. Mlle Taglioni dances like no one else. Why use her name when you dance like everyone else?

22. Giacomo Meyerbeer (1791–1864), a German-Jewish composer who worked chiefly in Paris during the late 1820s and 1830s, composed the opera *Robert le Diable* (1831), in which Taglioni first revealed the expressive potential of her new style.

23. Monsieur Albert (François Descombe, 1787–1865) danced at the Opéra from 1808 to 1831. He was the most celebrated *danseur noble* of his era.

24. *Britannicus* was an opera based on the Racine tragedy of that name.

25. Nicolas, Paul, and Grégoire were male dancers associated with the Opéra and various popular theaters.

26. Actors of the Comédie Française.

27. In Gautier's preface to *Mademoiselle de Maupin* (1835), one of the first manifestoes of art for art sake, he says that he would sacrifice everything just to be taught one new form of pleasure.

28. Paul Taglioni (1808–1884), a fine dancer and ballet master in his own right, worked largely in Berlin. He partnered his sister during her first appearances at the Opéra in 1827 and was the first James in *La Sylphide*.

29. Amalia Taglioni (née Galster, 1801–1881) married Paul Taglioni in 1829. She was the first Effie in *La Sylphide*.

Jules Perrot in Zingaro. *Dance Collection, New York Public Library for the Performing Arts, Astor, Lenox, and Tilden Foundations.*

"Return of Mons. Perrot,"[30] *Le Journal des Débats*, 29 Apr. 1833.

A very minor event has occurred at the Opéra—the return of Mons. Perrot. I went to see him dance once and for all. I wanted to see him dance all alone, without Mlle Taglioni, without Mlle Dupont, and without Mlle Noblet. Thus I saw him, and truly, for though I am a regular at the Opéra, this is the first time I have seen him dance, since it is the first time that I have paid any attention to him. Alas, despite all my good will, all I saw was a danseur! Mons. Perrot is a man of great lightness, it is true; but that is all. He leaps into the air, then lands, less heavily than any other man, but that is all. What he does signifies neither more nor less than what other danseurs do. His dancing is vague; it says nothing, teaches nothing, proves nothing, does not please, is tiresome and boring. A man has no right to dance, no right to round a leg or an arm, or smile while doing an entrechat. The male animal is too levelheaded, too ugly. His habits are too disgusting, his neck too thick, skin too tough, hands too red, legs too lanky, and feet too flat to practice the same trade as the likes of Mlle Taglioni, Mlle Dupont, Mlle Noblet, Mlle Julia, and so many others who have a pretty face, a charming neck, flawless white hands, a very fine leg, a bosom that thrills, an eye that shines, a warm pink mouth, and a white dress that floats in the breeze. This must be said again and again to all the gentlemen who dance, light or not.

Moving on, the Opéra is at last reassured and tranquil, for it is keeping its director.[31] The new arrangements have satisfied all sides. The minister of public works gains a little money for his other theaters, which have great need of it. The director of the Opéra gains a little more freedom. The public loses absolutely nothing. The crowds abound, Mlle Taglioni returns, the danseurs depart. Everything has worked out for the best in the realm of opera.

30. Jules Perrot (1810–1892) was the male equivalent to Marie Taglioni, possessing unprecedented ease and effortless grace. It is said that Taglioni was uncomfortable dancing with him due to the applause he garnered. Because male dancing was not popular, he was relegated to a place considerably lower than he deserved. Fortunately, he was a brilliant ballet master whose genius was recognized across Europe.

31. Dr. Louis Véron directed the Opéra from 1831 to 1835, during which time he amassed a profit to himself of roughly 900,000 francs from an institution that before his arrival and after was never a sous in the black. His cagey manipulation of the press, his promotion of rivalries between star ballerinas, and his production innovations stirred enthusiasm for the Romantic ballet.

"Debut of Mlle Thérèse Elssler,"[32]
Le Journal des Débats, 6 Oct. 1834.

Mlle Thérèse Elssler is Fanny Elssler's[33] sister, elder brother, and ballet master all in one. Mlle Thérèse is a tall and handsome person with admirable legs; she will become the best danseur at the Opéra, Perrot not excepted. Our danseur Thérèse has the advantage over him of a very fine figure and a pretty face. As a danseuse, Mlle Thérèse is a little too tall, especially beside her delicate sister. The pas de deux they danced in the admirable ball from *Gustave* was made by Thérèse especially for Fanny. The generous Thérèse, without thinking of herself, gave Fanny the most beautiful poses, the most lively melodies. She did her best to exhibit Fanny, dancing only to allow her sister time to rest and catch her breath, as if an Elssler has need of catching her breath. The parterre, which understands generous sentiments, has perfectly understood the taller Elssler's efforts on behalf of her younger sister and, in consequence, has

American sheet music cover depicting Fanny Elssler as Lauretta in La Tarentule. *American Antiquarian Society*

applauded them both excessively. In particular, the ending of the above mentioned dance, which finishes with an admirable back-to-back inter-lacing, is of an entirely new and very piquant effect.

Thus, as things go, Fanny becomes the first to establish the Elssler name with three pirouettes. Thérèse, for her part, has come to protect Fanny in her second test. And the Opéra sails forth under the power of three women—Taglioni, Fanny Elssler, and Thérèse Elssler!

32. Thérèse Elssler (1808–1878) danced at the Opéra from 1834 to 1840. A frequent partner of her sister Fanny, she was also a choreographer and arranged many of the dances they performed together. Her ballet *La Volière* premiered at the Opéra in 1838.

33. Fanny Elssler (1810–1884), the Viennese ballerina who was the second great star of the Romantic period, danced at the Opéra from 1834 to 1840. Among her greatest successes were *Le Diable boiteux* (1836), in which she performed her famous cachucha, *La Gipsy* (1839), and *La Tarentule* (1839).

"The Ballet *Nina*.[34] Mlle Varin," *Le Journal des Débats*, 14 Dec. 1835.

The ballet *Nina* is, without a doubt, one of the most mediocre choreographic inventions that has ever been successful at the Opéra. And in truth, it took Mlle Bigottini's[35] two large and very beautiful eyes (judging by the brilliance they still possess!) to make this lusterless masterpiece succeed. It appears that in the year of our Lord 1803 mad lovers were singularly in fashion. All the theaters and concerts had their mad lovers. It was a time when Elleviou's[36] eyes and smile sent more than one poor girl whose reason was lost in the bowers of the Opéra-Comique to the Salpetrière.[37] The Opéra, in turn, wanted its own mad lovers, so, with a goose quill trimmed with Graces holding the knife of Cupid in the left hand, it drew up a story; this quill has passed from hand to hand, choreographer to choreographer, from Mons. Milon to Mons. Taglioni.[38]

Thus, the curtain opens revealing villagers dispersed here and there. These villagers are the count's vassals, and Nina shows them considerable charity. In the meantime, Germeuil arrives and presses Nina's hand amorously to his breast: the two lovers swear fidelity. Nina accepts and kisses a ring that becomes a sacred pledge.

During this scene, the count leaves his château and feigns surprise at seeing the two lovers together. A musket volley announces the arrival of the governor. Naturally enough, the music and the governor's guard duly arrive on the terrace. The governor announces the honors the sovereign is bestowing upon the count and invests him with the distinctive badges of a Grand Officer; thus, he gives him a warrant and the ceremonial embrace. I should tell you that this Grand Officer made the parterre roar with laughter, in spite of his ceremonial embrace, his warrant, and his badges of distinction.

Scene V. The count remains with the gentlemen of Blinval. One of these gentlemen describes with energy the passion that he feels for Nina and asks for her hand in marriage. This proposition stirs profound thought in the count. He consents to everything. However, he induces the governor to keep this marriage temporarily a secret.

Nina invites the gentlemen of Blinval to the fete. However, during the fete, the young Blinval, burning with the desire to reveal his sentiments, throws himself at Nina's feet. Blinval's indiscretion throws everyone into great confusion. Nina, as if struck by thunder, is dumbfounded; she would like to give voice to her feelings but cannot. For their part, the gentlemen of Blinval are banished from this scene. The young Blinval assumes that he has a rival; this rival is Germeuil, who is cruelly sent packing by the count, Nina's father. Germeuil, who assumes, for his part, that he has a rival, provokes one of the gentlemen of Blinval. Germeuil fights in despair and is defeated. Giving up hope, he throws himself into the sea.

This deed throws the spectators into heartfelt trepidation. Nina falls as if dead. She is carried to a grassy bank; there she reopens her eyes and haggardly contemplates her father, who weeps over the body of his daughter. In other words, Nina is mad. She smiles, dances mechanically, recovers her bouquet, and smiles again; she sees Georgette's father and exclaims: "If I had a father like this, would I be as miserable as I am?" However, Germeuil is not dead. He has been rescued from the sea. Returning, he is told that Nina is alive but that she has lost her reason. When Nina sees Germeuil, she thinks that her overwrought imagination is deceiving her senses. Finally, Germeuil proposes to Nina that he recount for her the incidents of their love, something only he could do. Nina consents with great satisfaction.

Germeuil duly conducts Nina to a grassy bank and picks up a bouquet that he finds there. He gives his hand to Nina, who recalls that in fact she usually placed her hand on his breast. But, wonder of wonders, it is a kiss that contributes the most to restoring her reason. When this is recovered, Nina falls on her knees among her father, her spouse, and the gentlemen of Blinval.

Do you think that *La Laitière suisse* or *Brézila*[39] or any other masterpiece by Mons. Taglioni is much better? And how can you be entertained for an hour by the ballet *Nina*? Everyone says, "But it is a *ballet d'action*! It is the *danse noble*!" In that case, Mlle Taglioni, save us from the *danse noble* and the *ballet d'action*! What is the meaning of these women in ball gowns and these men, large and small, dressed as officers? Do you go to the Opéra to watch the dancing of society women who are not society women? Are we expected to accept these theatrical dandies as genuine dandies? I wouldn't say that a fashionable ball is a very entertaining thing, but I would say that it is a thousand times more entertaining to see and experience and follow with the eyes than all the *ballets d'action*. At least, at a dance in a fine salon, you have surprises; you find slender figures, supple as reeds; you find flawlessly gorgeous shoulders, animated glances, happy smiles, delicate feet, decent nudity; you find flowers, gauzes, ribbons, floating hair, and a thousand invisible perfumes from all those cool springtimes and brilliant summers, and even those leafy autumns that dance to the animated sounds of a lively orchestra. There are men who are attracted to such things, men who lose their lives and souls in them. But at the Opéra these danseuses imitate women of fashion, with satin dresses that fall below the knee and a demeanor that has become too proper, with decently adorned shoulders, and everything modest, counterfeit, and miserable: I find it a ridiculous and boring concoction. Of all the tales from this land of tales, the saddest without a doubt is that which makes countesses and duchesses of these women and governors and Grand Officers of these men. Yes, let us have *ballet d'action*, but the action of a danseuse is to display all that constitutes a danseuse, to be light and passionate, and to display all the caprice and brilliance of her profession. A danseuse who imitates the great lady, performs drama, or falls as if dead is not behaving naturally, just as the gentlemen of Blinval—the governor, the count, the Grand Officer decorated with top boots and orders, and fighting a duel with Mons. Germeuil—are not danseurs in their natural sphere. A danseur in his natural sphere is a man who dances in the background of the theater and serves to mark the rhythm onstage like the bass drum in the orchestra. Fie, therefore, on *ballets d'action*! Fie on the *danse noble*! Fie on the satin dresses and the velvet lovers who carry a sword! Once and for all, this ballet, *Nina*, is boredom dancing beside stupidity. It is boredom that amuses itself by grimacing in rose arbors; tragedy with danseuses in the place of beautiful verses. Abandon, therefore, once and for all, the *danse noble*, the *ballet d'action*, the role of *grands danseurs*, the great desperate passions, the choreographic tragedies, the little Corneilles[40] of the ballet, and, especially, we ask Mlle Noblet's pardon for having been forced during two acts to subject her beautiful dark eyes and her pretty legs to the painful disorders and laborious strains that must have been as distasteful for her as they were in fact for us.

Nina, this unlucky ballet, is not the only unfortunate trial that dance has been subjected to at the Opéra. I know too well that Mlle Taglioni's wing is again wounded; I know that the two Elsslers are absent; I know for a fact that the Opéra is thus reduced to its third level, and that we have fallen all the way down to Vagon[41] and Augusta;[42] but why, I pray you, fall still lower to Mlle Varin,[43] the English Taglioni, as she has been called. And what's more, if it is necessary that Mlle Varin have her turn, why permit her the incredible boldness of performing one of Mlle Taglioni's most charming roles? A profanity indeed. A big woman with graceless brilliance, who is at one and the same time bony and flabby, with great, thick, unfeeling legs—this is what we have been given in place of the bayadère's delicate, graceful, and chaste lightness, in place of these things that rival Mme Damoreau's[44] voice! Mlle Varin! As if she had not seen Mlle Taglioni! Mlle Varin! As if certain roles created by Mlle Taglioni should not be kept for her alone! As if it were easy to borrow her inspirations and attributes from on high in the third celestial realm! Mlle Varin in the dances of Mlle Taglioni! Mlle Varin! And why not give her Mlle Taglioni's

"Dances of the haute école,*" after a lithograph by Honoré Daumier. Gaston Vuillier,* La Danse *(Paris: Hachette, 1898), p. 257.*

wings next week? Does it follow that if Nourrit[45] has a cold, a tenor can be taken from the chorus to sing *Robert le Diable*? And does it follow that one has the right to replace Nourrit as one can fill in for Talma?[46] *Robert le Diable* and *Britannicus* are works that live their own separate lives and sustain the singer and the actor, when it is not the singer or the actor who sustain them. But *La Sylphide*! *La Bayadère*![47] These aerial creations are poetic caprices of an art that is, itself, only a caprice. The young woman whose gesture has given them form, who has given them substance with a glance, who has caused all these trifles to blossom forth with the power of her foot, is vital if they are to stay at the heights to which she has taken them. Suspecting nothing, she comes and goes, leaps and turns and moves within the invisible Taglioni airs, as if in fact she were moving and dancing in the smoke of a London where she was nicknamed Taglioni. Mlle Varin! Surely not! She is the English Taglioni to be sure, but she remains in a fog. Is there not also in England an English Bonaparte and an English Voltaire? Mlle Varin in place of Mlle Taglioni!

You have not wings and you want to fly? Dance!

In this regard, we ask in the interests of the Opéra if it is at all beneficial, in the absence of Mlle Taglioni and the two Elsslers, to confide their roles to inferior legs, graces, and smiles? Might it not ruin Opéra ballets to give them wantonly to danseuses of the third rank? Do you expect that Fanny Elssler will not find her role somewhat disfigured by Mlle Augusta? And would Mlle Taglioni want the Sylphide's wings back on her own shoulders after they had been placed upside down on those of Mlle Varin? In general, changes and substitutions rarely succeed, even in less elevated circumstances. It is thus that we saw Mlle Pauline Leroux,[48] who is a hundred times prettier, lighter, and better as a dancer than Mlle Varin, fail in playing Mme Montessu's pretty role in *La Somnambule*.[49] On that night everyone agreed that Mlle Leroux lacked facility and grace, and that she would have been better to leave Mme Montessu's role to the one who had created it with such spirit, grace, and happiness.

Haven't we talked a long time about dance? But dance is one of our national glories. It is one of our least demanding pleasures, a form of relaxation at the service of idle and tired minds. Describe something to me that is sillier and at the same time more entertaining to see than a ballet! Ballet is the pleasure of minds that have toiled all day: one does not judge, hear, see, feel, sleep, or dream. But it is a pleasure that pertains to dream and slumber; it is the pleasure of fools and men of intelligence, the joy of the old, and the hope of the young. As such, it is necessary to guard against spoiling this pleasure by putting danseuses of the second rank into the first. Leave each of these danseuses where she is valuable—Mlle Taglioni in the highest place, the two Elsslers a little below her, the two Noblets a little lower, and after them the entire army of pretty girls without names but not without charms—Mlle Fitzjames,[50] Mlle Vagon, Mlle Varin, Mlle Augusta, butterflies less light and less brilliant, who must dread above all else burning their little diaphanous wings in the sun of Mlle Taglioni.

And in one month Fanny Elssler! And, to be sure, when Fanny Elssler is here, Mlle Taglioni will not be far off.

34. *Nina, ou la Folle par amour*, a sentimental story ballet produced by Louis Milon in 1813, delighted Napoleonic audiences with its melodramatic scenes of despair, madness, passion, and joy.
35. Emilie Bigottini (1784–1858) danced at the Opéra from 1801 to 1823. She was the greatest dancer-actress of her day and Louis Milon's greatest interpreter.
36. Baptiste François Elleviou (1769–1842) was an Opéra-Comique tenor.
37. A Parisian prison for the insane. It was used extensively during the Revolution for political prisoners and is still today a mental hospital.
38. Filippo Taglioni (1777–1871) was a brilliant teacher and ballet master who trained his daughter in the new Romantic dance technique as well as creating ballets that utilized the potential of the new dance style for Romantic expression. His *La Sylphide* (1832) inaugurated the Romantic age. His ballets emphasized the beauty and expressive potential of dance over serious, dramatic stories.
39. *Nathalie, ou la Laitière suisse* (1832) and *Brézila, ou la Tribu des femmes* (1835) were two of the less successful of Filippo Taglioni's ballets.
40. Pierre Corneille (1606–1684), the greatest of classical dramatists, is remarkable for his great tragic personages, the grandeur of his style, and the high ethical quality of his drama. It was the aim of the ballet d'action, as outlined by Noverre, to reproduce many of the features of French classical drama.
41. Mlle Vagon was a soloist largely ignored by critics.
42. Mlle Augusta (stage name of Caroline Fuchs, 1806–1901) danced at the Opéra in 1835, then went to New York, where she was the first to dance the title role in *Giselle*.
43. Elise Varin danced at the King's Theatre in London in 1832, 1835, and 1836, where she made little impact though she did perform the title role in *La Sylphide*.
44. Madame Laure-Cinthe Montrelant Damoreau (1801–1863) was an Opéra and Opéra-Comique singer who played the role of Isabelle in *Robert le Diable*.
45. Adolphe Nouritt (1802–1839), a tenor at the Opéra, was the first Robert in

Robert le Diable. He subsequently wrote the scenario for *La Sylphide*.

46. François-Joseph Talma (1763–1826), celebrated tragic actor of the Comédie-Française.

47. *Les Bayadères*, an opera by Catel, contained dances that adapted themselves well to the Romantic taste for Oriental exoticism.

48. Pauline Leroux (1809–1891) danced at the Opéra from 1826 to 1837 and from 1840 to 1844.

49. *La Somnambule* (1827) was a sentimental, somewhat melodramatic ballet d'action by Jean Aumer.

50. The Fitzjames sisters, Louise and Nathalie, were popular soloists. Louise, who is referred to here, danced at the Opéra from 1832 to 1846 and was considered to be of the Taglioni school.

"Return of Mlle Taglioni," *Le Journal des Débats*, 22 Aug. 1836.

When the Opéra saw its great passion once again—the returning Taglioni—it applauded her with the usual admirable fury. Then all of a sudden the most profound silence fell. Everyone wanted to see what had become of her in the heavens where she had hid for so long. It was therefore in the midst of an uneasy and restless silence that this amiable woman first danced. You all know very well what she is like—calm, sincere, modest. She begins on the ground; then, without thinking, without trying, she rises; and, at last in her customary realm, she abandons herself once more to her chaste and simple passions. The public recognizes her and cries out, "It is her!" And the parterre applauds with hands and hearts. Not a feather is missing from the brilliant wing; not a petal has fallen from the crown of flowers. Finding its masterpiece complete and whole, the audience abandons itself wholeheartedly to the proffered happiness, a happiness of which it has been so long deprived. Of all the innocent joys in the world, the pleasures that cause neither fatigue nor regret, I know of no greater joy or more lively pleasure than seeing Mlle Taglioni dance, than hurrying after her (I will not say in her footprints, for she leaves none), than following her in spirit through the imaginary spaces where she is transported without even willing it. When the spell has ended, we return with her as calmly as we left, wanting nothing more than this dance which is not a dance, guarding only pure, peaceful memories and tranquil sleep, regretting nothing that was left, only saying: "I will see her again in three days!" Here, surely, is a very simple emotion, one unknown in the intoxicating realm of the vulgar dance, an emotion above the senses, because it is not of the earth. This, in fact, is the great triumph, the great superiority of Mlle Taglioni.

On the day of her return Mlle Taglioni found her faithful supporters, and they found her, ever light, ever pleasing, ever given up to the beautiful art that is her life. You must have heard the applause and the clamor. You know that on that day there were no flowers to be had in Paris. Many a young lady, arriving with a fresh bouquet that was precious to her, that she had promised to give up or to keep, could not resist the pleasure of throwing it at the feet of Mlle Taglioni, the danseuse of virtuous young women. What untold sacrifices were thus thrown by hands trembling with emotion at the feet of this child of a Sylphide! Still more happened in the first tier of Opéra boxes that day. A handsome young man was so swept away that he forgot even to applaud. He followed the rain of flowers with heart and eyes. He would have given his life, even his mistress, to have had a bouquet to throw. Suddenly, a young lady leans from a neighboring box to look; she holds a bouquet in her hand but hesitates; she wants to throw it to Mlle Taglioni, but she would also like to keep it. What does our young man do? He snatches the bouquet from the stranger's little hand and throws it to the stage. The young lady applauds and withdraws her pretty head into the box. On this head, where I still see beautiful black hair, dark eyes, and a flush of intelligence and feeling, was delicately posed a little crown of white roses, the twenty-year-old's legitimate diadem. The lady's movement caused the light crown to come loose, just as so many flimsier golden crowns have done elsewhere. What does our young man do? He removes the pretty flowers from the pretty head, and the crown goes to join the bouquet, while the young lady applauds even harder. Only this time the rose was in her cheeks, for everyone was looking at her, except the young enthusiast who only watched Mlle Taglioni.

Long live enthusiasm! It is, after love, the most beautiful and the most charming passion in the world.

"Mme Paradol's Benefit Performance. Perrot. Mlle Carlotta Grisi," *Le Journal des Débats*, 5 Sept. 1836.

I have only one word to say about this performance, it was extraordinary in every sense of the word. Though the hall was full and everyone was entertained, there was little to like in the ill-considered mixture[51] of good and bad, foolish and serious, Racine and Mons. Gavaux,[52] comic opera and tragedy, Mons. Henry[53] and Mme Paradol, the gracious and light Mlle Duvernay and Mlle Fitzjames senselessly plunked down in the middle of the third act of *Moïse*.[54] All these haphazardly collected amusements are more fatiguing than diverting. The human mind is not so nimble that it can simply pass without transition from Italian tarantellas to the death of Britannicus, things with little to nothing in common. Rome enslaved by the emperors, and Italy, with Austria's permission, dancing the tarantella.

Nevertheless, it is necessary to offer justice to those who have earned it. Perrot, who appeared with his pupil, Mlle Carlotta Grisi,[55] performed with great lightness a rather badly composed dance of his own making. This dance resembled nothing and everything. One comes, one goes, one does some pointe work, one shows off, then shows off the other. Perrot displays even worse judgment than this, since, in view of his figure, which is far from attractive, he should avoid such anacreontic poses and occupy himself more with displaying his danseuse. For her part Mlle Carlotta Grisi, who is light and young, was rather badly costumed: cheap satin, ugly ribbons, a sad pale dress having something of that unfavorable Italian neglect that not even the most talented Italian knows how to rectify. Happily, Mlle Grisi saw Mlle Duvernay and Mlle Fitzjames with her own eyes last evening, both spotless, starlike, all in white, and sparkling like two pale suns in the midst of the rags, tatters, beards, helmets, and shields of Moses.

The Italian tarantella displayed Perrot and Mlle Grisi in a different light. When Perrot puts a hat on his head and a jacket over his shoulders, he becomes quite decent. He danced the tarantella with incredible lightness. Mlle Grisi, for her part, dances with considerable national enthusiasm. She circles, stops, and turns, pretending marvelously to be lame. In fact, there is something Italian about the way she performs this Italian dance. But Mlle Grisi was as badly costumed as ever. There is carelessness in her dress as in her performance, but this carelessness is not an effect of art, because there is no effect without a cause.

After they danced their best, Perrot and Mlle Grisi set off to foreign lands where they will be much admired. It is what they do best for them and for us.

51. Star performers were allowed a benefit performance each year from which they received all or part of the box office receipts. Such "extraordinary" performances usually consisted of a potpourri of dance, drama, and opera performed by artists from various theaters.
52. Pierre Gaveaux (b. 1761) was a singer and composer who went mad. He composed over thirty stage works, including many comic operas and the opera-ballet *L'Amour à Cythère* (1805).
53. Louis Henry (1784–1836) was a ballet master trained at the Opéra, where he produced *L'Ile des pirates* (1835).
54. *Moïse*, better known by its Italian title *Mosè in Egitto* (1818), was an opera by Gioachino Rossini.
55. Carlotta Grisi (1819–1899) appeared briefly and not very successfully at the Opéra in 1836. She was much improved on her return in 1841 and continued to dance there until 1849. The third great romantic ballerina to appear there, she made her mark as the first Giselle.

"*Les Mohicans*,[56] Pantomime Ballet in Two Acts," *Le Journal des Débats*, 10 July 1837.

Rome is no longer in Rome, while Paris is in the Pyrenees, in Plombières, and in the baths of Boulogne and Dieppe. The old town of Dieppe is all decorated; the seashore rejoices; the theater rises from its ruins; the waves are filled with harmony and with bathers. The great artists whom Paris applauds during its winter evenings have fortified their voices and their talents in the salutary waters.

In the midst of this general migration, what is the use of performing masterpieces? If Mlle Taglioni, that charming daughter of the air, were at the Opéra again, the Opéra would do well to keep her in reserve, hidden in a transparent cloud. For these reasons one might say that the new ballet *Les Mohicans* is entirely a summer ballet.

Do not expect a long summary of this spectacle. It is a comedy ballet, and we are among those who do not recognize ballet's right to be funny. A pretty girl, very light, a beautiful person who is naturally beautiful, whose beauty is emphasized by the dance, is anything but comical. If you want me to laugh at a great booby who flops about like a fish, who plays a role that will break his arms and legs twenty times, I reply that there is no man alive who can make me laugh at such shoddiness. Therefore, allow the dance to be what it is, an intoxicating spectacle filled with sweet feelings. Do not allow it to descend to the level of a boulevard harlequinade.

In the first act, English soldiers under the command of Major Arwed, give themselves up to various sports, as do the nuns in *Robert le Diable*. An old Mohican, Eye of the Falcon, Jonathas, the dance master, and Mlle Alice, the daughter of the major, dance separately, then all together. Their pleasure is disturbed by savages who arrive on stage. In the general melee, Alice is led away by the Mohicans, and Jonathas is carried off by an old savage, etc.

In the second act, Jonathas is going to be eaten by the Mohicans; not only eaten but cooked, cooked and eaten. "The unfortunate Jonathas, trembling in all his limbs, cries, begs...shows the savages his arms, meager and thin, his long legs, his skinny body." Perhaps Jonathas has good reason to show the savages all these pretty things, but civilized men do not come to the Opéra to see meager, thin arms, skinny bodies, pink clothes and flesh. In the end, however, the savages understand that Jonathas would be too tough to cook. They will not eat Jonathas, and Jonathas performs a comic dance with an old savage. Old savages, male and female, abound in this ballet.

Suddenly a great noise is heard—the triumphal march of the warriors leading a prisoner who has just been captured. This prisoner is Major Arwed! "The chief of the Mohicans, filled with rage and jealousy, orders that the major be immediately tied to a post and delivered to the flames."

Jonathas adopts the same method to save Major Arwed that was successful for himself. He dances and makes everyone else dance. Seizing the opportunity offered by this dance, Major Arwed fires a pistol into the air. Arwed is saved. Jonathas is named drum major. "Jonathas takes the staff and orders roll call." The ballet finishes as it began—with a general divertissement.

This choreographic composition appeared rather simple and entirely worthy of ballet's younger days when it was still an infant among garlands of flowers. Rather drab decorations, some untoward rifle shots, grotesque costumes, the absence of the two Elsslers, Mlle Fitzjames, and Mlle Noblet, such are the insurmountable obstacles that have rendered Mons.

Adam's[57] music almost useless. A rather pretty little girl made her debut in the ballet. She is pale, lean, thin, light, but with the sort of lightness that lacks vigor, that can be compared to the lightness of a soap bubble. This young danseuse's name is Mlle Nathalie Fitzjames.[58] In summary, the ballet is a trifle entirely unworthy of a theater such as the Opéra, and we would very much hope that this will be *The Last of the Mohicans*.[59]

56. *Les Mohicans* was the only ballet produced by Antonio Guerra (1810–1846) at the Opéra. Guerra spent time as ballet master at Her Majesty's Theatre in London and at the Vienna Court Opera.

57. Adolphe Adam (1803–56), the composer of *Giselle*.

58. Nathalie Fitzjames (b. 1819) danced at the Opéra from 1837 to 1842.

59. The ballet, to Janin's satisfaction, was only performed twice.

"Mlle Lucile Grahn.[60] Mlle Noblet. Mme Dupont," *Le Journal des Débats*, 15 July 1839.

Mlle Lucile Grahn arrives straight from the world of Mlle Taglioni. Imagine a svelte and delicate young lady, very pale, very pretty, very composed, very timid, who dances sweetly without noise, without effort, without smiling and with such a look of repose! There is nothing more charming than a danseuse who is above the gestures, efforts, agitations, and grins of dance. Mlle Grahn brings something that is new and unexpected, a naturally supple body, legs that have not been subjected to the tortures of the classroom, a foot that no ballet master has deformed, a pretty person who dances as the bird sings, who is born expressly to be light! Her ease puts to rest the wild boundings, furious leg kicks, and endless pirouettes! Such was the achievement of the new Swede. To let her dance for an instant, Mozart's music abruptly stopped, and we saw her in pale costume calming the turmoil of Don Juan's ball, holding in suspension the furious passions, imposing silence on the ravings. I imagine old Mozart lending an attentive ear to his masterpiece and curtly demanding why his story has stopped? Do not vex yourself, my dear Mozart, it is nothing—a pretty daughter of the North who, seeing Don Juan's palace illuminated for a lively fete, has sought permission to join the party. She wanted to dance just this one time in the midst of your formidable music. During this moment she is studied, admired, and given full attention. In order to see the foreign dancer better, Donna Anna has postponed her vengeance. Let her, this daughter of Norway, dance in the middle of your drama, divine Mozart. She is so

Lucile Grahn, lithograph by Henri Grevedon, ca. 1842. Dance Collection, New York Public Library for the Performing Arts, Astor, Lenox, and Tilden Foundations.

happy, and you know that no human power can prevent your story from being completed!

At this performance, the two Noblets, in their turn, performed the terrible incendiary dance that agitates so many petticoats and hearts. Mlle Elssler, with her usual grace and good taste, tempered the Aragonaise fling a little, but Mme [sic] Noblet and Mme Dupont have restored all its frenzies. They have certainly acted wisely. They are so quick that the ground spins around them! The parterre enthusiastically applauded Mlle Lucile Grahn and the two Noblets, the former because she is quite artless, very reserved, as you would expect a child of Mlle Taglioni to be, the latter, to the contrary, because they are as frolicsome and bold as any Parisian who wants to have the last word as the Opéra's prettiest legs. Due to the heat and languors of the evening it is appropriate that dance be honored. Dance is an amusement without fatigue. You go with distracted attention, eyes wandering, yet you are sufficiently aware of all that happens. In contrast, it takes effort to pay proper attention, as one must, to masterpieces such as *Robert le Diable* or *Les Huguenots*.[61] Therefore, let them dance, these dancers, as they want to dance!

60. Lucile Grahn (1819–1907) danced at the Opéra in 1839 and 1840. Trained by August Bournonville in Copenhagen, she was much admired in Paris for her lightness, which recalled Taglioni's. She approached, without quite attaining, the stature of Taglioni, Elssler, and Grisi.

61. *Les Huguenots* (1836) was an opera by Giacomo Meyerbeer.

"Théâtre de la Renaissance. *Zingaro*, Ballet-Opera in Three Acts. Perrot. Mme Perrot-Grisi," *Le Journal des Débats*, 2 Mar. 1840.

The Théâtre de la Renaissance was wise to count on its gypsies to defend against outside attack. These *Zingari* are in fact droll foxes, gallant, well armed, and formidable even when they sing. It really is too bad that this fine theater was brought to the point of writs and forced expropriation. For the record here is the assistance it well receive:

First Act. In a Bohemian forest, an old gypsy rascal, named Haryddin, has hidden a treasure chest he stole ten years before. For ten years our man has led the life of a vagabond beggar, as if he did not have a farthing to his name. Now Haryddin is going to arrange his affairs by retrieving his treasure from the large cave where he buried it. Unfortunately, an honest young man, called Zingaro in the playbills (but elsewhere Bohemian), has slipped by chance into the band of thieves. Bohemian, in spite of his name, reared himself all alone with the best of morals. He is in love, a state that spoils nothing, not even honesty. Thus, while his leader dreams of ways of retrieving his treasure chest, Bohemian dreams only of ways of seeing his dear mistress, Gianina, again. This pretty girl's tutor is a good doctor named Collmann. Bohemian has, as a rival, a rich German baron who does not beat about the bush, but out and out kidnaps the child.

Happily, Bohemian is there watching over his dear love. He wrests her from the ravisher's arms and as a reward is shot in the chest. In consequence, Collmann and Gianina remove Bohemian to their house.

Second Act. But, strange thing, the good doctor Collmann is also in love with his pupil and wants to marry her. Thus, the situation is complicated for us and our little Gianina, there being a total of three lovers—Collmann, Bohemian, and the baron. But this baron is incorrigible. First, he tried to steal the little one away; now he wants to make her destitute. To achieve this he asks the gentlemen gypsies to rob the doctor's house, thus reducing him to the depths of misery. The gypsies, good devils, do not need to be asked twice. The doctor's house is robbed. Collmann is completely ruined, and in an instant you see the bailiff's men arrive to throw him into prison. Bohemian is extremely disturbed; he disappears, but not without indicating by a gesture that he knows a sure way of preventing Gianina from loosing her tutor.

Third act. In fact, our little dear Gianina is moved to tears for her tutor. True, the brave man wanted to marry her, but he was a decent devil, not troublesome or jealous, and he liked Bohemian. But Gianina is not the only woman who sheds tears in this play. You also have Mme Dorothée, who heaves a first-rate sigh. I think the lady, Dorothée, has been, though I wouldn't not swear to it, the mistress of the frightful baron, who burned down her house because another lover serenaded her. Abandoned by the villain, Mme Dorothée says very softly to herself that she will always love him. These two women, Dorothée and Gianina, are in the process of doing their best to console themselves when Bohemian unexpectedly arrives bent under the weight of a heavy chest. The honest thief has stolen the treasure of his legitimate leader, a treasure he delivers to his mistress. Brave man, come see your luck! This treasure, stolen ten years ago, belongs to Gianina! The chest comes from her father's château! And where, one might ask, was her father's château? The château was in the chest! For it is here that the deeds are rediscovered. It follows that 1) we have gold, and 2) we have property. Liquid assets, fixed assets, what more could we want? In consequence, the gypsy leader will be hung. The baron, who was in possession of our château (I forgot to inform you of this), returns it, and Bohemian marries Gianina for his troubles. Come, do not be so sad, those of you who shed a tear for the château-less baron! Rest assured there are châteaux enough to go around. The fine lady Dorothée owns one, not as beautiful as Gianina's, it is true, but quite presentable nonetheless. And Mme Dorothée would be all too happy to marry the baron and give him her heart, her hand, and her château.

You know, perhaps, that we are hardly partisans of what are called les *grands danseurs*. The *grand danseur* appears so sad, so heavy! He is at once so unhappy and so pleased with himself! He reacts to nothing, he represents nothing; he is nothing. Speak to me of a pretty dancing girl, who willingly offers her graceful airs and elegant figure, who shows us in such subtle ways all the treasures of her beauty. God have mercy, how

Carlotta Grisi in Le Diable à quatre, *lithograph by Alexandre Lacauchie, ca. 1845. Dance Collection, New York Public Library for the Performing Arts, Astor, Lenox, and Tilden Foundations.*

wonderfully I understand that. I know exactly what to expect from this pretty person and am quite willing to follow wherever she leads in the sweet lands of love. But a man, a frightful man, as ugly as you or me, with an empty, vacant gaze, who capers aimlessly, a creature made expressly to bear a rifle, saber, and uniform! That this being should dance like a woman, impossible! This bearded person, who is a community leader, an elector, a member of the municipal council, a man who makes and, more often, unmakes the laws to his own advantage, appears before us in a sky blue satin tunic, a cap with a floating plume that amorously strokes his cheek—a frightful danseuse of the masculine sex who pirouettes center stage, while the pretty ballet girls respectfully keep their distance. Most certainly these *grands danseurs* are something impossible, intolerable, something made expressly to deny all our pleasures. Now, because of the revolution that has been set in motion, woman is the queen of ballet. She lives in ballet; she dances so naturally there. She is no longer forced to cut away half her petticoat to dress her partner. Today, the dancing man is tolerated only as an useful accessory. He is the shading in a painting, the green hedge that surrounds the flowers of the parterre, the obligatory foil. So then, the more I am convinced of this truth, the more you can believe me when I say that Perrot is the most admirable danseur that can be seen! He seems incredibly light, even to those who have seen Taglioni's exceptional lightness up close. Though Perrot was already the master of the Opéra when he left, we did not regret allowing him to leave. We even said bon voyage with some pleasure, for danseurs truly frighten us. But this danseur has made marvelous progress. He has returned as an ingenious ballet master and as an excellent mime with a tolerable face. We are unable to describe the extent of his success. His young wife and pupil, Grisi by name, has profited from her master's lessons. Not only does she dance in a charming manner, but she also sings like a slightly hoarse nightingale that has fallen a little too soon from the harmonious Grisi nest.[62] Pleasing choruses, duos, romances, and nocturnes were distributed throughout the ballet. We truly hope that Paris will be pleased this time and will adequately repay with attendance all the expenses and efforts made to supply a little amusement to this jaded old sultan, who needs to be powerfully persuaded if he is going occasionally to dole out even a scrap of his handkerchief.

62. There were several famous opera singers in the Grisi family: Giuditta, a mezzo-soprano, and Giulia, a soprano, were the most famous.

"*Giselle, ou les Wilis*, Supernatural Ballet in Two Acts, by MM. de Saint-Georges,[63] Théophile Gautier, and Coralli; music by M. Adolphe Adam; decors by Mons. Ciceri,"[64] *Le Journal des Débats*, 30 June 1841.

It is Heinrich Heine[65] who speaks, and if the skeptic believes him, it is absolutely necessary that everyone believe him. The story takes place in one of the quietest and quaintest corners of Germany. Young girls who loved to dance even a little when they were alive and died before having said I do in the presence of a priest and all fiancées carried to the tomb without a dowry become Wilis after death. Pale and diaphanous phantoms, they abandon themselves every night to ghostly dances. This dance of the dead in no way resembles that of earth. It is tranquil, grave, and silent, [...] illuminated by the pale light of the moon. As soon as night appears on earth and in the sky, an immortal round traces its path through the woods and mountains and along the shores of lakes blue as the sky. At the end of a hard day's journey, when you have wandered far from the road and your work-wearied horse searches in vain for the beaten track, have you ever encountered isolated glowings here and there among the rushes of the fen? Unlucky traveler, take heed! The Wilis dance, and their infernal ball has a powerful fascination. Take heed, do not go further, or you are lost. Thus tells us Heinrich Heine, a German poet possessed of the irony and spirit of Voltaire. Poet, German, irony, Voltaire, what con-

"Come Away to the Glen," English sheet music cover for a cavatina by F. Lancelott, early 1840s. The Giselle is Carlotta Grisi; her Albrecht is Jules Perrot. Dance Collection, New York Public Library for the Performing Arts, Astor, Lenox, and Tilden Foundations.

trasts! As is Heine's story of the Wilis, who dance their mortal partners to complete destruction.

It happens, then, that the imprudent man, wandering while the mournful ball is in progress, sees, at the instant a Wili takes flight, a little hand reach for him, inviting him to dance. That hand, how it burns with passion! But do not all the hands of eighteen or twenty-year-olds burn with passion? With the hand comes a sweet smile, a smile that dances even before the ritornello of the orchestra is heard. Once again, travelers, way-laid travelers, take heed! Close your eyes! Not only is the hand burning, and the smile, but even the glance is limpid and full of fire; the figure is slender and svelte, and the shoulder...rendered whiter and more striking under the pale mantle of the moon—fragile lace cut from tree leaves and the profiles of flowers. How is one to resist a Wili made like this when she says to you, "Enter into the dance and what you desire will be granted." You know the melody and the refrain of this children's round, "Join in the dance." And then what? Oh, seventeen-year-old Wilis! Oh, pale girls from our poetic rounds who sing while dancing, "Join in the dance!" Miserable as I am, I have forgotten the remaining verses, but they would have said, "Embrace whoever comes to you!" Blushing, you join in. The round begins—joyous, animated, rosy—a brunette here, a blond there—long hair, flawless bust, innocent airs, naive glances—she turns and turns, and you, you remain motionless, lending an ear to the beautiful refrain, "Embrace whoever will love you!" "Which one?" you ask yourself. "Which?" "Which?" The malicious Wilis quicken the dance; each cheek teases your desires....Too bad if you catch nothing. This is, as Heinrich Heine tells us, the true Wili, the true dance of innocent youth, of fifteen-year-old martyrs.

But be still! Can you hear the prelude to this beautiful story of German fairies? In a peaceful valley, behold the day, and with it, the dew. Everything awakens, love first of all, then the festival of the grape harvest. The hills rise from night's breast and appear radiant in robes of green vines yellowing around the edges. Who is this young shepherd leaving his cottage as if besotted? He is the lover of the story. But he is not a herdsman; he is a prince, Prince Albert of Silesia, of all Alberts the one most in love. To avoid recognition our prince is called Loys, a pretty name that compromises no one. "Giselle! It is I! It is I!" Soon Giselle, scarcely awake, is leaping around Albert. What! Already so light? Wait until you are dead, dear girl. Wait until your soul leaves you before you stir. What will you do when, in your turn, you, too, become a Wili? But what does it matter to her? She is a young girl who dances like a sprite, and so active a sprite that her mother, Berthe, softly accompanied by sad music, tells of all the dangers of dancing. You can die from it! You can die from it! And what's more it's not only death...for the tomb is no repose for a young girl who dies from dancing. Each night, a ball must take place, a ball without lovers, an empty ball, without smiles, without hope, without feeling—you become, alas! only a frail beauty that none can hold, that the wind carries away the moment dawn appears. Think about that, Giselle! But it has been said much better than old Berthe and I could have said:

> She loves dancing too much, it is this that kills her,
> The dance fantastic, the delightful dance!

How much happiness there would be if the wisdom of grandmothers influenced their little girls! Giselle hears no one—scarcely even the lover who speaks to her. So, allow the dancing girl her poetic intoxication. Alas! The poor child will not die from dancing, but of love. Already, it is over for this delicate beauty. She has just learned that Loys, her dear love, is a young prince. He, a prince! And, what's worse, a prince betrothed to a princess! Giselle immediately goes mad with grief. In her madness she dances, but it is a soulless dance, of love that has fled to the mists—a dance of the body, not the heart. We must say in passing that the breakdown was performed marvelously. And finally, when she can no longer dance, Giselle falls dead. There she is, drained by grief of life. Everyone cries over the pretty

Portrait of Lucien Petipa, the first Albrecht, lithograph by C. Valette, 1840s. Dance Collection, New York Public Library for the Performing Arts, Astor, Lenox, and Tilden Foundations.

child, the prince as much as anyone else, and also the prince's fiancée, H.R.H. Bathilde, the Duke of Courland's own daughter. It is all over, hopeless according to the program, the inflexible program that tells you in the style of Saluste,[66] for every ballet writer is from the school that produced *La Guerre de Jugurtha*, the eyes of Giselle are closed forever.

Second act. Night has thrown her softest mists over the countryside. All is silent, even the nightingale in the woods. The shepherd's star rises in the sky; the silver lake murmurs its monotonous complaint, calm and splendid. Stirred by the wind, the reeds balance delicately. Oh, pity! Under this willow that weeps, under this mound of plants and wild flowers, what is this new grave? It is Giselle's. There she sleeps, or, rather, there she dreams, gently wrapped in her chaste shroud. Silence! Do you see the mists parting and the pale vapors lifting little by little? As in Sir Walter Scott's poem about the White Lady? The vapor is Myrtha, the Queen of the Wilis. The first rays of the September moon have given Myrtha the fine contours of her beautiful form. A strange light accompanies her mysterious majesty. She has wings because it is her whim, a white tunic because it is the fashion at balls given under old oaks to the song of crickets, beating bat wings, and the thousand unexpected laments murmured in the forest's gloomy depths. Let us begin! Sleepy Wilis, arise! It is your queen who commands you. Gather together, all of you. It is a night for a fete. Flutter your vaporous wings. Nothing will be missing tonight—not dew, flowers, cool earth, limpid waters, or the imprudent traveler. And then, one after the other, sometimes in groups, from everywhere they come—from the river banks, where they sleep on beds of reeds like plain-

Adèle Dumilâtre, the first Myrtha, lithograph by J. Bouvier, 1843. Dance Collection, New York Public Library for the Performing Arts, Astor, Lenox, and Tilden Foundations.

tive spirits from the depths of springs; from the edges of mists that serve as funeral shrouds; from the hearts of oaks they have stirred; from rocks carpeted in moss; from cups of roses and lilies; from where comes the butterfly, the nightingale's song, the flower's scent, and the sound of love when it enters a young heart. At once the fete begins. At first it stirs softly; then it grows, expands, and takes over the forest. What began as a dance becomes madness, a cold madness. The furious whirlwind comes to a halt before the mound of Giselle's tomb. See for yourself the sad epitaph, a pale crown of oak.

Giselle! "She is ours," says the queen. She lacks nothing, not even wings. Yet, poor child, you are pale and cold under the veil that covers you. It has been at least a month since you danced, an entire month! How restless your feet must be, how tired your legs! Now you must ready your ear to hear if the old fiddler is about to tune his rustic violin! Come! The moon is favorable, the night air still; everything is ready. Rouse yourself, Giselle! Slowly, like a plume of white smoke over a cottage roof, the sweet phantom rises. What an awakening! What a dream! "I was so uncomfortable in this shroud!" Thus she speaks, and little by little returns to something better than life: she returns to dance. Look! She has her two wings, and how well they serve her! They are at once lively and delicate, animated and serene. Giselle, or if you prefer, Carlotta Grisi, was ravishing in her use of all the gracious magic that a pretty person, who is master of each muscle in her body and commands them like a sovereign, can possess. There was no hesitation, no discomfort, and her poses were marvelous, unexpected and charming. Woman or phantom, she is as happy in the mists as in the winding sheet. She glides as she walks; she flies as she dances. Her flight resembles nothing more than what we know of fluttering wings. But, you might say, she is the Sylphide! No, I would reply, she is not the Sylphide; this is not the realm of Mlle Taglioni. Without doubt, Mlle Taglioni has passed nearby, but she folds her wings. In contrast to Carlotta Grisi, she dwells in a cloud, living, breathing, perched like a bird on a branch, unaware of peril. But wait, what fools we are, everyone of us. True, we grant stardom to the first person who pleases public caprice. Stars are made by us, and we worship them passionately. But scarcely does one become the object of our worship than she asks us for millions. Finally, because we are not so rich as the former absolute princes, she takes off, saying that we are beggarly. Still, we weep all our tears. See how sad we are, unhappy, distracted beyond measure. How shall we live? Remain active? What will happen? Oh, by God, my good friend, leave your tears behind! Why run after the unfaithful one? You ruined yourself for her, and she laughs at you. Behave more wisely. Let the faithless one go, and find a newcomer willing to console us. When one has the honor of being part of that great overlord called the French public, one is sure of bringing forth great artists with the power of a small, friendly glance of interest. Thus has come, to replace Mlle Taglioni in her seventh heaven, a person just as charming and considerably younger, the light, pretty danseuse named Carlotta Grisi.

Who could have foretold that Grisi, worthy child of her family, born on the knee of Rossini, raised by and for song, would one day be the most charming of dancers? One fine day her husband[67] said to her, "You must dance." She did as she was told. She danced, and so well that today the Opéra ignores the buoyant Perrot to applaud his pupil. This, it must be said in passing, appears to us inordinately cruel and foolish.

Hilarion meets his end. Les Beautés de l'Opéra *(Paris: Soulié, 1845).*

Thus, Giselle, the completely new Wili, abandons herself to the passion of her life. She dances. She regrets nothing: she is dead, so what does she care if she dances alone? Then, all of a sudden, the ugly Hilarion stumbles among the gay dances and extravagant joys. This Hilarion was the rustic lover of the living Giselle. It was he who spied upon and denounced Loys, who brought death. Scarcely has he appeared in the fantastic whirl than, behold, our cruel beings fling themselves at the clumsy danseur. They take him, push him, throw him, each in her turn. Pass the man to me! To me! He is taken, pushed, turned, made weary, unfortunate man! He can do no more. He begs for mercy. No, no, no mercy, no pity. He must dance. Alas! What an activity for virtuous newlyweds on their honeymoon!

In brief, our man—broken, tired, exhausted, lost, crippled—is flung by the Wilis into the depths of the abyss. From the shore the dancers watch with charming smiles as the victim is pulled into the deep.

Such refined pleasures! But after all, what good is a man who can no longer dance except to be thrown into the water? The implacable Wilis reason just as would a young Wili of our own world.

Giselle triumphs through Hilarion's destruction. She is happy. What pleasure vengeance is for a Wili! Yes, but after the crude Hilarion, whom does she see by the empty tomb? Loys himself. Yes, it is truly him! A little changed, perhaps, pale, sad, worn out. But how beautiful is the beloved man who weeps for you! Beautiful, too, is the silent lament that comes from the depths of the grave! In the presence of her lover, behold, our Wili once again becomes a simple mortal. She moves her hand to the place where her heart used to be and finds it again. Here is my heart. I would like to describe how this young woman appeared to her lover, but it is impossible. Imagine her in a dream when you were very much in love—an ideal form in an unearthly light, noble and pretty, with thick dark hair, tranquil, blue eyes, proud, and delicate. The sky opens; she disappears, leaving you to recall the dream. If you are lucky, the dear apparition disappears only to return.

But, what bad luck! Suddenly, guided by their queen, the troop of Wilis arrive. She leaps toward the handsome Loys. He must perform for us! He is an accomplished dancer; the disagreeable Hilarion was only a formless lump. Now begins a desperate and charming drama. "Flee, Loys," cries Giselle, "Flee. Beware of these rosy phantoms! Do not look into their sparkling eyes! They do evil with their deceptive smiles. Beware of delicate figures that the wind itself cannot hold. Poor Loys, stay, close to the one who loves you. Cling to the cross on my tomb. Put my half open tomb between yourself and these cruel women, these cold deserted brides, these loveless girls!" Thus she speaks, but I swear to you that her speech is finer than that. Her gesture is an idea, her dance a speech; her little head, pale and fine, sparkles with pity and love. At first, Loys obeys; he keeps his foot on the grave and holds fast. Then the Wilis advance in pitched battle against the poor young man. What stops them? Only the cross on the tomb, and the love of Giselle. But what violence cannot be accomplished with a smile? You do not want us to come to you, Loys? Then, you must come to us. Look how beautiful we are! Look! We scarcely touch the earth, scarcely bend the flowers. Look! Are we so frightening? As for me, faithful historian of this tale, the Gedesiah Cleisbotham of this pleasing phantasmagoria, I must add that in this struggle the young Loys is all the more meritorious because the temptress in question is called Adèle Dumilâtre.[68] She is young and beautiful, well made, sweetly blooming, and pretty beyond the usual Opéra prettiness. Bitten by the most innocent of tarantulas, she obeys with joy. Giselle had to be very powerful, indeed, for her lover to resist this elegant Wili of eighteen years.

Thus outdone, the Queen of the Wilis, by an infernal ruse, or if you prefer, by a totally feminine ruse, summarily orders Giselle herself to tempt Loys. Now, you cannot be a Wili and have free will. You are part of a Wili army, body and soul. You dance for your companions, not for your-

Carlotta Grisi as Giselle, lithograph by Pierre Joseph Challamel. Dance Collection, New York Public Library for the Performing Arts, Astor, Lenox, and Tilden Foundations.

self. You possess a handsome danseur, which is fine, but only on condition that he belongs to everyone. It is only fair. We have given you what is ours; now you must give us what is yours. You have played your part with our Hilarion; now we want to play our part with your handsome Loys. "But that is infamous!" responds the sweet phantom. "For Loys is mine, my well-being, my life. What is a single Loys to all of you? What do you want with him? What good will it do if he dances with each of you? And what is the use of flinging him into the bottomless waters? Why kill him? What is the use?" "Dance! Dance!" replies the Queen of the Wilis. "Dance. We need Loys. All power to him if he has the courage to remain in this holy place. If not, he is ours." Alas! It is necessary to obey. Giselle begins to dance, at first, like a poor soul troubled with the fear of losing its last ideal, but, soon, with the lightness of a phantom who no longer thinks of anything except dancing. It is both charming and touching—a marvelous creation. Let me tell you, these men of talent and intelligence can invent anything, even a ballet. Where did Mons. Théophile Gautier learn that a ballet can be made quite simply with poetry? Who told him that, in certain arts, the most impossible things are the truest? Where has he learned to present such audacious elegiac dreams in the theater? True, he is a poet, an artist, and a critic who brings honor to us all. He creates, and he judges. He also speaks the language of painters. Color obeys him like the word. He held the brush before holding the pen, and from the happy mixture of such beautiful and fine things comes an excellent artist in several of the fine arts. As for the critic, his skills are evident in the choice of a collaborator versed in these mysteries. It is Mons. de Saint-Georges, who has spun out the thread that keeps Mons. Théophile Gautier from losing his way in the labyrinth, enchanted as it is with greenery, mist, smiles, gambols, flowers, naked shoulders, awakening dawn, blazing twilight, wit, poetry, dreams, passions, music, and love.

Where did we leave Giselle? High above, in the clouds! It is over: Loys can no longer fight. He needs Giselle, and, then, what is death? Thus, he abandons the protective grave, the holy asylum of the cross. Scarcely awake, he dances and dances and dances as if eternity were before him. Now the bacchantes awake, as the German poet says. The round is truly infernal. Never has dance stirred young girls so violently. The abyss is there awaiting its victim. He is pushed; he is pulled. It is over, poor Giselle: Loys is dead! But, I pray you, listen to the sweetly strident viol of Urban,[69] that great and serious artist beloved by Baillot[70] and Mons. Ingres.[71]

Be reassured, my reader, Loys will not die. He will be saved by the rising sun. Worn out with fatigue, he staggers. Then, suddenly, it is day, the joyous morning that returns the dead to their tombs and chases the lark from its nest. It is day! The air is less heated; the flowers, tired of these gambols, beckon the sweet dew. The forest rejoices at the return of the ancient stag and the young gazelles. Yes, Loys is saved. Look down at the cloud sinking at your feet: it is the troop of Wilis returning to the earth's breast, melting in the sun like manna in the desert. How welcome the sun is! Kiss the rosy fingers of dawn, even at the risk of being pricked by a thorn. "Adieu, Loys!" says Giselle, "Adieu, love of my heart! Adieu, my dancer of earth and the infernal countryside! Adieu! Never return to this deadly fete. Never come again to this ball of pale, husbandless fiancées. Remain in the land of the sun. Fear the moonlight where all things vacillate, even the head and the heart!" Thus she spoke. Then, little by little she faded, folding in on herself like a shadow. Fold by fold, leaf by leaf, the day chased her away. First, the foot went; after an instant, the waist. Only the smile remained—to fade in its turn. All is over: nothing remains of the beloved shadow, nothing, not even the shadow of a shadow. The sun has fully risen.

In order to complete this beautiful dream, this feast for the eyes, this aerial composition, this danced drama that so little resembles the faded compositions that we have described for ten years, in order to describe this new Sylphide, you need to slip, if you can, into the midst of these sweet landscapes, overflowing with pastoral poetry that Ciceri has brought back from the shores of the Rhine. Abandon yourself to the ingenious and brilliant melodies of Mons. Adolphe Adam. Nothing is missing from this charming work: there is invention, poetry, music, newly arranged dances, lots of pretty danseuses, lively harmony, grace, energy, Adèle Dumilâtre, and, especially, *la* Carlotta Grisi. This, for sure, is what a ballet should be!

63. Jules-Henri Vernoy de Saint-Georges (1801–1875), popular dramatist who supplied scenarios for *La Gipsy* (1839), *Le Diable amoureux* (1840), *La Jolie Fille de Gand* (1842), and *Lady Henriette* (1844). He collaborated with Gautier on *Giselle* (1841).

64. Pierre-Luc Charles Ciceri (1782–1868) designed many notable Opéra ballets during the first half of the nineteenth century, including Didelot's *Flore et Zéphyre* (1815), Aumer's *La Somnambule* (1827), and Taglioni's *La Sylphide* (1832).

65. Heinrich Heine (1797–1856), German lyric poet and man of letters, wrote the tale upon which Gautier based the *Giselle* libretto.

66. Guillaume de Saluste, Seigneur du Bartas (1544–1599), wrote several religious epics, the most famous of which was *La Semaine*.

67. Jules Perrot.

68. Adèle Dumilâtre (1821–1909) danced at the Opéra from 1840 to 1848.

69. Chrétien Urban (1790–1845), composer and instrumentalist who joined the Opéra orchestra in 1816.

70. Pierre-Marie-François de Salles Baillot (1771–1842), composer and virtuoso, was first violin at the Opéra.

71. Jean-Auguste-Dominique Ingres (1780–1867), the painter.

APPENDIXES

National Dance in the Romantic Ballet

LISA C. ARKIN AND MARIAN SMITH

Examples of National Dance in Operas

La Muette de Portici
Premiere: 29 February 1828, Paris Opéra
Music: Daniel-François-Esprit Auber
Choreography: Jean Aumer
National dance(s): Spanish and Neapolitan dances, including the bolero and saltarello
NOTE: The libretto lists four Spanish, eight Neapolitan, six bolero, and six saltarello dancers.[1]

Guillaume Tell
Premiere: 3 August 1829, Paris Opéra
Music: Gioacchino Rossini
Choreography: Jean Aumer
National dance(s): Tyrolean dance
Dancer(s): Marie Taglioni
NOTE: The corps included ten "Tyroleans" and fifty-seven "peasants," of whom fourteen were children.[2]

Gustave III
Premiere: 27 February 1833, Paris Opéra
Music: Daniel-François-Esprit Auber
Choreography: Filippo Taglioni
National dance(s): Styrian dance, allemande[3]

Don Giovanni
Premiere: 10 March 1834, Paris Opéra
Music: Wolfgang Amadeus Mozart
Choreography: Jean Coralli
National dance(s): Spanish dances
NOTE: These dances, variously identified as "seguidillas de Andalucía," "boleras de Cádiz," and the "Ollia,"[4] were sometimes arranged by dancers or choreographers other than Jean Coralli. On at least one occasion, a Hungarian dance was performed in the ball scene.[5]

Les Huguenots
Premiere: 29 February 1836, Paris Opéra
Music: Giacomo Meyerbeer
Choreography: Filippo Taglioni
National dance(s): gypsy dances[6]

Stradella
Premiere: 3 March 1837, Paris Opéra
Music: Louis Niedermeyer
Choreography: Jean Coralli
National dance(s): saltarello
NOTE: This was performed by dancers portraying characters from the environs of Rome and the towns of "Albane, Tivoli, and Frascati."[7]

Zingaro
Premiere: 29 February 1840, Théâtre de la Renaissance, Paris
Music: Uranio Fortuna
Choreography: Jules Perrot
National dance(s): bohemischka, Saxon waltz (or Styrian rondo), forlana, ziguerrerina
Dancer(s): Carlotta Grisi, Jules Perrot
NOTE: This comic opera was written expressly for Grisi and Perrot. The ballerina sang as well as danced.[8]

La Favorite
Premiere: 2 December 1840, Paris Opéra
Music: Gaetano Donizetti
Choreography: Albert (François Descombe)
National dance(s): Spanish dancing[9]

La Fiancée
Premiere: 30 April 1842, Her Majesty's Theatre
Music: Daniel-François-Esprit Auber, J.B. Nadaud
National dance(s): boleras de Cádiz
Dancer(s): Marie Guy-Stéphan, Jules Perrot[10]

La Prophète
Premiere: 16 April 1849, Paris Opéra
Music: Giacomo Meyerbeer
Choreography: Auguste Mabille
National dance(s): redowa[11]

L'Enfant prodigue
Premiere: 6 December 1850, Paris Opéra
Music: Daniel-François-Esprit Auber
Choreography: Arthur Saint-Léon
National dance(s): Egyptian dance

NOTE: The libretto calls for twenty-four "Egyptian" dancers, eighteen almées, four "Nègres," eight "Ethipians," and twelve sword dancers.[12]

Notes

1. *La Muette de Portici*, libretto (Paris, 1828).
2. Ivor Guest, *The Romantic Ballet in Paris* 2nd rev. ed. (London: Dance Books, 1980), p. 94.
3. *Gustave III*, libretto (Paris, 1933), and *Galerie dramatique ou Recueil de différents costumes* (Paris: Jules Rigo, n.d.).
4. Lola Montez performed the latter two dances in *Don Giovanni* on 27 March 1844 (Guest, *The Romantic Ballet in Paris*, p. 229). In 1839, the seguidillas and boleras arranged by Manuela Dubinon for the production were danced by six Opéra danseuses (*La Presse*, 28 July 1839, cited by Ivor Guest in "Théophile Gautier on Spanish Dance," *Dance Chronicle*, 10, no. 1 [1987], pp. 34-35).
5. Jules Janin, *Le Journal des Débats*, 17 Mar. 1834.
6. *Les Huguenots*, libretto (Paris, 1836).
7. *Stradella*, libretto (Paris, 1837).
8. Ivor Guest, *Jules Perrot* (New York: Dance Horizons, 1984), pp. 51-59. Anténor Joly, the manager of the Théâtre de la Renaissance, commissioned the opera.
9. *La Favorite*, score (Paris: Schlesinger, 1842).
10. Guest, *Perrot*, p. 83. See also Ivor Guest, *The Romantic Ballet in England: Its Development, Fulfilment and Decline* (London: Phoenix House, 1954), p. 158.
11. *Le Prophète*, libretto (Paris, 1849).
12. *L'Enfant prodigue*, libretto (Paris, 1850).

Examples of National Dance in Divertissements, Benefit Performances, and Entr'actes

Divertissement
7 July 1836, King's Theatre
National dance(s): tarantella
Dancer(s): Jules Perrot, Carlotta Grisi
NOTE: Billed as the "original Tarantella, as imported from Naples," this may have been performed at the Teatro di San Carlo, Naples, the previous winter.[13]

Divertissement
1838
National dance(s): Scottish dance
Dancer(s): Fanny and Thérèse Elssler[14]

Die neapolitanischen Fischer
(also known as *Le Pêcheur napolitain*)
Premiere: 10 January 1838, Hofoper, Vienna
Choreography: Jules Perrot
National dance(s): tarantella
Dancer(s): Jules Perrot, Carlotta Grisi
NOTE: This ballet has been described by Ivor Guest as "a scene of summer jollity by the Mediterranean seashore, culminating in [a] rousing tarantella."[15] The work was revived at Her Majesty's Theatre on 28 April 1842 and 24 April 1845, on this occasion with Lucile Grahn as Perrot's partner.

Le Carnaval de Venise (divertissement)
22 February 1838, Paris Opéra
Choreography: Louis Milon
National dance(s): bolero
Dancer(s): Mme Alexis Dupont
NOTE: This was a benefit performance for the soprano Laure Cinti-Damoreau.

Benefit performance for Fanny and Thérèse Elssler
5 May 1838, Paris Opéra
National dance(s): bolero
Dancer(s): Lise Noblet, Mme Alexis Dupont[16]

Benefit performance for Fanny Elssler
30 January 1840, Paris Opéra
National dance(s): smolenska
Dancer(s): Fanny Elssler[17]

Benefit performance for Fanny Elssler
9 April 1840, Her Majesty's Theatre
National dance(s): tarantella (from *La Tarantule*), cachucha, cracovienne
Dancer(s): Fanny Elssler[18]

Une Nuit de bal (divertissement)
2 May 1840, Her Majesty's Theatre
Choreography: Antonio Guerra
National dance(s): lituana

Dancer(s): Fanny Cerrito
NOTE: This was an arrangement of a *pas seul* Cerrito had danced in the ballet *Romanow* in Milan.[19]

5 August 1841, Her Majesty's Theatre
National dance(s): Spanish dance (from *La Gitana*)
Dancer(s): Fanny Cerrito[20]

Entr'acte
14 August 1841, Her Majesty's Theatre
National dance(s): Spanish dance (from *La Gitana*), Styrian dance
Dancer(s): Fanny Cerrito, Auguste Albert
NOTE: This was performed between the acts of an opera.[21]

Une Soirée de carnaval (divertissement)
14 July 1842, Her Majesty's Theatre
Choreography: Jules Perrot and others
National dance(s): double cachucha, cracovienne
Dancer(s): Jules Perrot, Fanny Cerrito, Marie Guy-Stéphan
NOTE: This was a benefit performance for Perrot. A forlana and tarantella were also planned, but eliminated at the last minute to shorten the program.[22]

Benefit performance for Fanny Cerrito
21 July 1842, Her Majesty's Theatre
Choreography: Fanny Cerrito(?)
National dance(s): varsovienne
Dancer(s): Fanny Cerrito[23]

Benefit performance for Arthur Saint-Léon
May 1843, Her Majesty's Theatre
National dance(s): Styrian dance
Dancer(s): Arthur Saint-Léon, Fanny Cerrito[24]

Le Délire d'un peintre (divertissement)
3 August 1843, Her Majesty's Theatre
Choreography: Jules Perrot
National dance(s): bolero
Dancer(s): Jules Perrot, Fanny Elssler[25]

Bonne Bouche[26]
11 April 1844, Her Majesty's Theatre
Choreography: Jules Perrot
National dance(s): polka
Dancer(s): Jules Perrot, Carlotta Grisi
NOTE: This was also performed as an entr'acte at Her Majesty's Theatre on 13 April 1844.[27] Souvenirs of the dance include sheet music (by Cesare Pugni) called the "Opera House Polka" and the well-known lithograph by Joseph Bouvier.[28]

Benefit performance for the Viennese Dancers
15 February 1845, Paris Opéra
National dance(s): hornpipe, Swiss dance, tarantella, Tyrolian dance, cracovienne, linzer tanz, Polish dance, polka, Hungarian dance, jaleo de Jérez[29]
Dancer(s): Viennese Dancers
NOTE: The Viennese Dancers were a children's ballet company managed by Josephine Weiss, the ballet mistress of the Josephstadt Theater, Vienna. The troupe danced in Paris, London, the United States, and Canada, appearing to great acclaim at the Opéra in January-March 1845.

Notes

13. Guest, *Perrot*, p. 352.
14. Eugène Desmares, quoted in Léandre Vaillat, *La Taglioni, ou la Vie d'une danseuse* (Paris: Albin Michel, 1942), p. 412.
15. Guest, *Perrot*, p. 147.
16. Guest, *The Romantic Ballet in Paris*, p. 167.
17. Ivor Guest, *Fanny Elssler* (Middletown, Conn.: Wesleyan University Press, 1970), pp. 116-117.
18. *Ibid.*, p. 124.
19. Ivor Guest, *The Life of a Romantic Ballerina: Fanny Cerrito* (London: Dance Books, 1974), p. 24.
20. *Ibid.*, p. 35.
21. *Ibid.*, p. 36.
22. Guest, *Perrot*, p. 87; see also Guest, *Cerrito*, p. 44.
23. *Ibid.*, p. 45.
24. *Ibid.*, p. 57.
25. Guest, *Perrot*, p. 110.
26. This term means "ending tidbit."
27. Guest, *Perrot*, p. 117. This was performed on the same night as *Esmeralda*.
28. *Spectator*, 13 Apr. 1844, quoted in Guest, *Perrot*, p. 127.
29. Guest, *The Romantic Ballet in Paris*, p. 240.

Examples of Ballets with National Dancing

Although, today, the minuet and waltz have largely lost their national connotations, in the first half of the nineteenth century the minuet was strongly associated with France and the waltz with the German-speaking countries.

An asterisk connotes a ballet-pantomime in which at least one of the principal characters performed national dance.

Les Pages du Duc de Vendôme
Premiere: 18 October 1820, Paris Opéra
Choreography: Jean Aumer
Music: Adalbert Gyrowetz
National dance(s): Spanish dance

La Fête hongroise (divertissement)
Premiere: 15 June 1821, Paris Opéra
Choreography: Jean Aumer
Music: Adalbert Gyrowetz
National dance(s): Hungarian, Cossack, and others

Le Page inconstant
Premiere: 18 December 1823, Paris Opéra
Choreography: Jean Aumer (after Jean Dauberval)
Music: François Antoine Habeneck (after Adalbert Gyrowetz)
National dance(s): farandole[30]

Le Sicilien
Premiere: 11 June 1827, Paris Opéra
Choreography: Anatole Petit
Music: Fernando Sor, Jean-Madeleine Schneitzhoeffer
National dance(s): allemande, tarantella, Spanish dance[31]

Masaniello
Premiere: 24 March 1829, Her Majesty's Theatre
Choreography: André Deshayes
Music: Daniel-François-Esprit Auber
National dance(s): Spanish dances[32]

L'Orgie
Premiere: 8 July 1831, Paris Opéra
Choreography: Jean Coralli
Music: Michele Carafa
National dance(s): bolero, fandangos, sarabande[33]

La Sylphide
Premiere: 12 March 1832, Paris Opéra
Choreography: Filippo Taglioni
Music: Jean-Madeleine Schneitzhoeffer
National dance(s): Scottish jig, anglais[34]

Beniowsky
Premiere: 5 May 1836, Her Majesty's Theatre
Choreography: André Deshayes

Music: Nicholas Charles Bochsa
National dance(s): cachucha, mazurka
NOTE: The cachucha may have been added at the time of the ballet's revival (16 March 1837).[35]

*Le Diable boiteux
Premiere: 1 June 1836, Paris Opéra
Choreography: Jean Coralli
Music: Casimir Gide
National dance(s): cachucha
Dancer(s): Fanny Elssler[36]

*La Fille du Danube
Premiere: 21 September 1836, Paris Opéra
Choreography: Filippo Taglioni
Music: Adolphe Adam
National dance(s): mazurka
Dancer(s): Marie Taglioni[37]

*La Gitana
Premiere: 23 November/5 December 1838, Bolshoi Theater, St. Petersburg
Choreography: Filippo Taglioni
National dance(s): mazurka, cachucha, Spanish, gypsy, and Styrian dances
Dancer(s): Marie Taglioni[38]

*La Tarentule
Premiere: 24 June 1839, Paris Opéra
Choreography: Jean Coralli
Music: Casimir Gide
National dance(s): tarantella
Dancer(s): Fanny Elssler
NOTE: In this dance Elssler also played the castanets.[39]

*La Gipsy
Premiere: 28 January 1839, Paris Opéra
Choreography: Joseph Mazilier
Music: François Benoist, Ambroise Thomas, Marco Aurelio Marliani
National dance(s): gypsy dance, cracovienne, allemande[40]
Dancer(s): Fanny Elssler (gypsy dance, cracovienne)[41]

*Le Diable amoureux
Premiere: 23 September 1840, Paris Opéra

Choreography: Joseph Mazilier
Music: François Benoist, Henri Reber
National dance(s): cachucha, mazurka, bayadère
   dance
Dancer(s): Nathalie Fitzjames, Auguste Mabille
   (mazurka)
NOTE: The *pas de bayadère* was said to resemble a
saltarello.[42] The mazurka, which was memorialized
in a statuette, was danced as a pas de deux.[43] The
libretto called for eight "Nègres," eight bayadères,
and twenty odalisques.

*Ondine, ou la Naïade
Premiere: 22 June 1843, Her Majesty's Theatre
Choreography: Jules Perrot, Fanny Cerrito
Music: Cesare Pugni
National dance(s): tarantella
NOTE: This was performed both as a pas de deux and
by the ensemble.[44]

*Giselle
Premiere: 28 June 1841, Paris Opéra
Choreography: Jean Coralli, Jules Perrot
Music: Adolphe Adam
National dance(s): waltz
NOTE: There may have been additional character
dancing by the Wilis (Spanish, odalisque, bayadère,
German, French).[45]

*La Jolie Fille de Gand
Premiere: 22 June 1842, Paris Opéra
Choreography: Albert (François Descombe)
Music: Adolphe Adam
National dance(s): cracovienne, gypsy dance,
   "Quadrille of the Four Parts of the World"[46]
NOTE: The "Quadrille of the Four Parts of the
World" included dances from Europe, Asia, Africa,
and America. An allemande and a Hungarian dance,
both performed by the Viennese Dancers, were
interpolated into the Kermess scene and the ball
scene, respectively, on 15 January 1845.[47]

*La Péri
Premiere: 17 July 1843, Paris Opéra
Choreography: Jean Coralli
Music: Friedrich Bergmüller
National dance(s): *pas de l'abeille*, bolero, waltz,
   minuet, jig
NOTE: The *pas de l'abeille*, or bee dance, was an
Egyptian-style dance. The other dances were per-
formed respectively by the Spanish, German,
French, and Scottish members of Achmet's harem.[48]
Both Adeline Plunkett and Carlotta Grisi substitut-
ed a manola for the *pas de l'abeille*.[49]

*La Esmeralda
Premiere: 9 March 1844, Her Majesty's Theatre

Choreography: Jules Perrot
Music: Cesare Pugni
National dance(s): truandaise
NOTE: A dance "of the bolero class," the truandaise
was intended to show Esmeralda's artlessness.[50]

*La Vivandière
Premiere: 23 May 1844, Her Majesty's Theatre
Choreography: Arthur Saint-Léon
Music: Cesare Pugni
National dance(s): mazurka, redowa, polka
NOTE: Reviewing a performance of the ballet in
1848, Théophile Gautier wrote: "The [wedding]...is
celebrated with that assortment of *pas—cabrioles,
mazurkas* and *redowas*—that are to the climax of a
ballet what Bengal fire [fireworks] is to the climax
of a pantomime."[51]

*Eoline
Premiere: 8 March 1845, Her Majesty's Theatre
Choreography: Jules Perrot
Music: Cesare Pugni
National dance(s): Silesian waltz, *mazurka d'extase*

*Kaya ou l'Amour voyageur
Premiere: 17 April 1845, Her Majesty's Theatre
Choreography: Jules Perrot, Lucile Grahn
Music: Cesare Pugni
National dance(s): Norwegian dance
NOTE: Pugni incorporated Norwegian folk melodies
into the score.

*Le Diable à quatre
Premiere: 11 August 1845, Paris Opéra
Choreography: Joseph Mazilier
Music: Adolphe Adam
National dance(s): mazurka, polka

*Caterina, ou la Fille du Bandit
Premiere: 3 March 1846, Her Majesty's Theatre
Choreography: Jules Perrot
Music: Cesare Pugni
National dance(s): romanesque, saltarello[52]

*Paquita
Premiere: 1 April 1846, Paris Opéra
Choreography: Joseph Mazilier
Music: Ernest Deldevez
National dance(s): gypsy and Spanish dances,
   tambourine dance, cloak dance, fan dance, hussar
   dance
NOTE: The cloak dance was a sort of cachucha
danced by couples with half the women in male
attire brandishing red cloaks. In the fan dance the
women played castanets with one hand while holding a fan in the other.[53]

Lalla Rookh
Premiere: 11 June 1846, Her Majesty's Theatre
Choreography: Jules Perrot
Music: Cesare Pugni
National dance(s): chibouk
NOTE: "There was in this dance," wrote the reviewer for *The Morning Post*, "the characteristic movement, as well as measure, of the dances of the East— of the Eastern world, which through the Moors conveyed the premature form of the bolero, cachucha, guaracha, etc. to Spain."[54]

Ozaï
Premiere: 26 April 1847, Paris Opéra
Choreography: Jean Coralli
Music: Casimir Gide
National dance(s): South Seas "native dances" with "artificial wings" and "bamboos,"[55] "Quadrille of the Four Parts of the World," "Quadrille of Europeans," American, Tahitian, and Provençal dances,[56] dances for almées
NOTE: During the "Four Parts of the World," national airs of each country were played.[57]

La Fille de marbre
Premiere: 20 October 1847, Paris Opéra
Choreography: Arthur Saint-Léon
Music: Cesare Pugni
National dance(s): aldeana, bolero, cachucha, "Quadrille of the Four Parts of the World"
Dancer(s): Fanny Cerrito (aldeana, bolero, cachucha)[58]
NOTE: The "Four Parts of the World" was performed by an ensemble of sixteen.

Pâquerette
Premiere: 15 January 1851, Paris Opéra
Choreography: Arthur Saint-Léon
Music: François Benoist

Vert-Vert
Premiere: 24 November 1851, Paris Opéra
Choreography: Joseph Mazilier
Music: Ernest Deldevez, Jean-Baptiste Tolbecque
National dance(s): Spanish dance, Chinese dance, Hungarian waltz

War of the Women
Premiere: 23 November 1852, Bolshoi Theater, St. Petersburg
Choreography: Jules Perrot
Music: Cesare Pugni
National dance(s): Slavonian dance, mazurka

Gazelda
Premiere: 24 February 1853, Bolshoi Theater, St. Petersburg

Choreography: Jules Perrot
Music: Cesare Pugni
National dance(s): gypsy dance, bolero, zinganka, "Cosmopolitana"
NOTE: In the zinganka, commented a Russian reviewer, Perrot "skilfully introduced steps from Russian folk dances."[59] The "Cosmopolitana" was a suite of dances "intended to convey the nomadic nature of gypsy life by introducing a succession of national dances—Moorish, Tyrolese, Spanish and English."[60]

Jovita, ou les Boucaniers
Premiere: 11 November 1853, Paris Opéra
Choreography: Joseph Mazilier
Music: Théodore Labarre
National dance(s): gypsy dance, dances from Europe and the Americas[61]
NOTE: Creole, Mexican, or black slaves as well as Europeans performed their native dances.

Le Corsaire
Premiere: 23 January 1856, Paris Opéra
Choreography: Joseph Mazilier
Music: Adolphe Adam
National dance(s): character dances
NOTE: These dances may have been performed by the slaves—Moldavian, Italian, French, English, and Spanish—listed in the libretto.

Notes

30. The farandole is an old folk dance from Provence. Today, it is danced as a simple serpentine line dance; however, in the early nineteenth century, it may have had a more distinct Provençal step vocabulary.
31. *Le Sicilien*, libretto (Paris, 1827).
32. Guest, *The Romantic Ballet in England*, p. 50.
33. *L'Orgie*, libretto (Paris, 1831); *Le Journal des Débats*, 20 July 1831.
34. *La Sylphide*, score, A.501, BN-Opéra. Gautier refers to the "slipshod execution" of the Scottish jig in a performance of *La Sylphide* on 1 June 1844 (*La Presse*, 3 June 1844, in *Gautier on Dance*, ed. and trans. Ivor Guest [London: Dance Books, 1986], p. 132.
35. See Cyril W. Beaumont, *Complete Book of Ballet* (London: Putnam, 1937), p. 148.
36. For a description, see Guest, *The Romantic Ballet in Paris*, pp. 152-153.
37. Mat 19[294-22], BN-Opéra. This score indicates that the mazurka was danced by Taglioni.
38. Edwin Binney III, *Longing for the Ideal: Images of Marie Taglioni in the Romantic Ballet*

(Cambridge, Mass.: Harvard Theatre Collection, 1984), pp. 29-32; Beaumont, *Complete Book*, pp. 129-136; Vaillat, *La Taglioni*, pp. 404-405.

39. *La Tarentule*, libretto (Paris, 1839).

40. *La Gipsy*, score, A.522, BN-Opéra.

41. Guest, *The Romantic Ballet in Paris*, p. 174. Mazilier's first dance was called "a saltarella after the Scottish fashion."

42. *La Sylphide*, 26 Sept. 1840, quoted *ibid.*, pp. 193-194.

43. *Ibid.*, p. 194.

44. Guest, *Perrot*, p. 102.

45. *Giselle*, libretto (Paris, 1842); *Giselle*, autograph score, Rés MS 2639, BN-Opéra.

46. Beaumont, *Complete Book*, p. 191; *La Jolie Fille de Gand*, libretto (Paris, 1842).

47. Guest, *The Romantic Ballet in Paris*, p. 239.

48. Gautier, who wrote the libretto for *La Péri*, also included Georgian, Greek, Arab, and Jewish women in Achmet's harem. See his article in *La Presse*, 25 July 1843, in *Gautier on Dance*, p. 114.

49. See Gautier's review in *La Presse*, 31 Mar. 1845, in *Gautier on Dance*, pp. 161-162.

50. *Court Journal*, 16 Mar. 1844, quoted in Guest, *Perrot*, p. 118.

51. *La Presse*, 23 Oct. 1848, in *Gautier on Dance*, p. 205.

52. Pugni called this dance a saltarella or a tarantella (Guest, *Perrot*, p. 162). Guest notes that Pugni's waltz in 5/4 was arranged for amateur performance as "La Perrotiana" and dedicated to the ballroom teacher Henri Cellarius.

53. Beaumont, *Complete Book*, pp. 229-230; Guest, *The Romantic Ballet in Paris*, p. 253; *Paquita*, libretto (Paris, 1846).

54. *The Morning Post*, 11 June 1846, quoted in Guest, *Perrot*, p. 171.

55. Beaumont, *Complete Book*, pp. 175-176. The bamboo dance may have been related to the Tinikling, a Philippine folk dance in which the performers move over bamboo sticks held close to the ground and clapped together rhythmically.

56. *Ozaï*, libretto (Paris, 1847).

57. *Ibid.*

58. Gautier, *La Presse*, 25 Oct. 1847, in *Gautier on Dance*, pp. 185-188.

59. *Sankpeterburgskie vedomosti*, 26 Feb./10 Mar. 1853, quoted in Guest, *Perrot*, p. 271.

60. *Ibid.*

61. Beaumont, *Complete Book*, pp. 249-252.

Ballets Performed in Rome from 1845 to 1855 at the Teatro di Apollo and Teatro Argentina

CLAUDIA CELI

The following chronology derives from several sources. Since the theatrical season began the day after Christmas, ballets given during the last week of the "old" year are listed together with those produced during the new calendar year.

1845

TEATRO DI APOLLO

Ezzelino sotto le mura di Bassano (Ezzelino Under the Walls of Bassano)
Choreography: Filippo Termanini
Principal dancers: Filippo Termanini, Orsolina Catte

La vendetta d'amore (Love's Revenge)
Choreography: Filippo Izzo(?)

La vincita al lotto (Win at the Lottery)
Choreography: Arthur Saint-Léon
Principal dancers: Fanny Cerrito, Arthur Saint-Léon

La festa in maschera ossia l'ospedale dei pazzi (The Masquerade, or The Hospital for Madmen)
Choreography: Filippo Izzo(?)
Principal dancers: Fanny Cerrito, Arthur Saint-Léon

Alma ossia la figlia del fuoco (Alma, or The Daughter of Fire)
Choreography: Fanny Cerrito and Filippo Izzo (after André Deshayes)
Music: Enrico Rolland(?)
Principal dancers: Fanny Cerrito, Arthur Saint-Léon, Filippo Termanini, Domenico Segarelli

La Manola (pas de deux)
Choreography: Fanny Cerrito and Arthur Saint-Léon
Principal dancers: Fanny Cerrito, Arthur Saint-Léon

1845

TEATRO ARGENTINA

Adelaide di Francia (Adelaide of France)
Choreography: Antonio Coppini (after Louis Henry[?])
Music: Cesare Pugni(?)
Principal dancers: Adelaide Cherrier, Domenico Matis, Raffaella Santalicante Prisco, Alessandro Bustini, Antonio Coppini

Gisella o le Villi (Giselle, or The Wilis)
Choreography: Domenico Ronzani (after Antonio Cortesi[?])
Music: Adolphe Adam(?), Giovanni Bajetti(?)
Principal dancers: Domenico Matis, Fanny Elssler, Raffaella Santalicante Prisco, Adelaide Cherrier, Domenico Ronzani

Esmeralda
Choreography: Domenico Ronzani (after Jules Perrot)
Music: Cesare Pugni(?)
Principal dancers: Fanny Elssler, Alessandro Bustini, Domenico Ronzani, Domenico Matis, Antonio Coppini

Il figlio fuggitivo (The Runaway Son)
Choreography: Antonio Coppini
Principal dancers: Antonio Coppini, Raffaella Santalicante Prisco, Gaetano Prisco

Le illusioni di un pittore (The Illusions of a Painter)
Choreography: Domenico Ronzani(?) (after Jules Perrot)
Principal dancer: Fanny Elssler

1846

TEATRO DI APOLLO

La sventura in un sogno (The Dreamed Mishap)
Choreography: Domenico Ronzani (after Antonio
  Cortesi[?])
Music: Filippo Moncada
Principal dancers: Fanny Elssler, Francesco Penco,
  Gaspare Pratesi, Concetta Liuzzi

La Silfide (La Sylphide)
Choreography: Giovanni Galzerani (after Filippo
  Taglioni)
Principal dancers: Marie Taglioni, Francesco Penco

Il corsaro (The Corsair)
Choreography: Giovanni Galzerani
Principal dancers: Giovannina King, Francesco
  Penco

Virginia
Choreography: Giovanni Galzerani
Principal dancers: Giovannina King, Francesco
  Penco

1846

TEATRO ARGENTINA

Il folletto a quattro o la capricciosa punita
  (The Devil to Pay, or The Capricious Woman
  Punished)
Choreography: Lucile Grahn (after Joseph
  Mazilier[?])
Principal dancers: Francesco Penco, Lucile Grahn,
  David Venturi, Amalia Fasciotti

Il conte della Gherardesca (Count della Gher-
  ardesca)
Choreography: Domenico Ronzani
Principal dancers: Domenico Ronzani, Amalia
  Fasciotti

Arianna e Bacco (Ariadne and Bacchus)
Choreography: Lucile Grahn
Principal dancers: Lucile Grahn, Francesco Penco

La tarantola (The Tarantula)
Choreography: Domenico Ronzani (after Jean
  Coralli[?])
Music: Casimir Gide(?)
Principal dancers: Fanny Elssler, Francesco Penco

Il sogno della vita ossia la bella fanciulla di Gand
  (The Dream of Life, or The Beautiful Maid of
  Ghent)

Choreography: Domenico Ronzani (after Antonio
  Cortesi[?])
Principal dancer: Fanny Elssler

Caterina degli Abruzzi (Catarina of the Abruzzi)
Choreography: Lucile Grahn (after Jules Perrot)
Principal dancers: Lucile Grahn, Francesco Penco,
  Vincenzo Schiano

1847

TEATRO DI APOLLO

La peri (La Péri)
Choreography: Eugenio Coralli (after Jean Coralli)
Principal dancers: Vincenzo Schiano, Carlotta Grisi

Il pescatore di Brindisi (The Fisherman of Brindisi)
Choreography: Antonio Cortesi
Principal dancers: Antonio Ramaccini, Amalia
  Fasciotti, Vincenzo Schiano, Concetta Liuzzi

L'isolano (The Islander)
Choreography: Antonio Cortesi
Music: Egisto Napoleone Pontecchi, Luigi Maria
  Viviani
Principal dancers: Antonio Ramaccini, Amalia
  Fasciotti, Vincenzo Schiano

1847

TEATRO ARGENTINA

I due forzati (The Two Prisoners)
Choreography: Francesco Ramaccini (after
  Ferdinando Rugali[?])
Principal dancers: Rosina Ravaglia, David Mochi

Scherzo di gioventù di Enrico V re d'Inghilterra
  (The Youth of Henry V, King of England)
Choreography: Francesco Ramaccini
Principal dancers: Antonio Ramaccini, Ludovico
  Pedoni, Concetta Liuzzi

Monsieur Chalumeaux
Choreography: Francesco Ramaccini (after
  Giovanni Galzerani)
Principal dancers: Rosina Ravaglia, David Mochi

La festa campestre (The Rustic Festival)
Choreography: Livio Morosini
Principal dancers: Rosina Ravaglia, David Mochi

Eco e Narciso (Echo and Narcissus)
Choreography: Francesco Ramaccini

1848

TEATRO DI APOLLO

Il conte Pini (Count Pini)
Choreography: Antonio Coppini (after Paolo Samengo)
Principal dancers: Rosina Gusman, Francesco Penco, Raffaella Santalicante Prisco, Concetta Liuzzi

Obizzo di Malaspina (Obizzo of Malaspina)
Choreography: Antonio Coppini
Music: Giovanni Campi, Filippo Moncada
Principal dancers: Rosina Gusman, Francesco Penco, Carolina Coppini, Concetta Liuzzi

Renato d'Arles (Renato of Arles)
Choreographer: Antonio Coppini
Music: Luigi Maria Viviani, Egisto Napoleone Pontecchi, Filippo Moncada
Principal dancers: Rosina Gusman, Francesco Penco, Carolina Coppini, Gaetano Prisco, Raffaella Santalicante Prisco

1849

TEATRO DI APOLLO*

Le sette reclute (The Seven Recruits)
Choreography: Filippo Termanini

La famiglia svizzera (The Swiss Family)
Choreography: Filippo Termanini

*NOTE: Because the theater closed, these ballets were scheduled, but not performed.

1849

TEATRO ARGENTINA

Mazeppa
Choreography: Antonio Cortesi
Music: Luigi Maria Viviani
Principal dancers: Assunta Razzanelli, Annunziata Ramaccini

Ebuzio e Facenia ossia i baccanali (Ebuzio and Facenia, or The Bacchanalia)
Choreography: Antonio Cortesi
Music: Filippo Moncada
Principal dancers: Antonio Ramaccini, Assunta Razzanelli

1850*

TEATRO DI APOLLO

Dianora de' Bardi (Dianora of the Bardi)
Choreography: Egidio Priora
Music: Cesare Ferrarini
Principal dancers: Olimpia Priora, Edoardo Carey, Rosina Clerici, Costanza Segarelli, Antonio Pallerini

Gli afghani (The Afghans)
Choreography: Egidio Priora
Principal dancers: Olimpia Priora, Edoardo Carey, Costanza Segarelli, Rosina Clerici, Antonio Pallerini

*NOTE: It is unclear whether Filippo Termanini's ballet *Un matrimonio in un festino*, which was scheduled for production during this season, was actually performed. Because the libretto gives the names of Cesare Cecchetti and Serafina Casagli Cecchetti, who, according to legend, gave birth that year to the future pedagogue Enrico Cecchetti in an Apollo dressing room, it is likely that the ballet was intended for production at this theater. The libretto listed as principal dancers Margherita Gottier (Wuthier) Casati, Francesco Penco, and Costanza Segarelli.

1850

TEATRO ARGENTINA

La Rosiera (The Crown of Roses)
Principal dancers: Giovannina King, Francesco Penco

1851

TEATRO DI APOLLO

Ali Pascià di Delvino (Ali Pasha of Delvine)
Choreography: Antonio Cortesi
Music: Luigi Maria Viviani
Principal dancers: Assunto Razzanelli, Domenico Segarelli

Mereguita
Choreography: Antonio Cortesi
Music: Luigi Maria Viviani, Filippo Moncada
Principal dancers: Melina Marmet, Assunta Razzanelli, Domenico Segarelli

Fazio (Faust)
Choreography: Antonio Cortesi
Principal dancers: Domenico Segarelli, Filippo Termanini, Assunta Razzanelli

1851

TEATRO ARGENTINA

La fanciulla dell'aria (The Maid of the Air)
Choreography: Livio Morosini
Principal dancer: Maria Luigia Bussola, Lorenzo
    Vienna, Filippo Termanini

1852

TEATRO DI APOLLO

Boemondo
Choreography: Luigi Astolfi
Principal dancers: Fanny Mazzarelli Astolfi, Filippo
    Termanini

La dea Flora (The Goddess Flora)
Choreography: Francesco Penco

Stella
Choreography: Francesco Penco
Music: G.A. Scaramelli
Principal dancers: Carolina Pochini, Francesco
    Penco, Maria Luigia Bussola, Ettore Poggiolesi

1852

TEATRO ARGENTINA

La ballerina in viaggio (The Traveling Dancer)
Choreography: Filippo Termanini
Principal dancers: Adelaide Zabò, Ludovico Pedoni,
    Ettore Poggiolesi, Tomassina Lavaggi, Filippo
    Termanini

Zuleika
Choreography: Antonio Coppini
Principal dancers: Sofia Fuoco, David Mochi,
    Filippo Termanini

Isaura o la bellezza fatale (Isaura, or The Fatal
    Beauty)
Choreography: Antonio Coppini
Principal dancers: Carolina Pochini, Sofia Fuoco,
    Antonio Coppini

Il saltimbanco (The Juggler)
Choreography: Antonio Coppini
Principal dancers: Angiolina Negri, David Mochi,
    Antonio Coppini

1853

TEATRO DI APOLLO

Il sogno (The Dream)
Choreography: Giovanni Battista Lasina and
    Giuseppe Lasina

Principal dancers: Filippo Termanini, Augusta
    Maywood, Lorenzo Vienna

Lucilla ossia la figlia del torrente (Lucille, or The
    Daughter of the Torrent)
Choreography: Giovanni Battista Lasina and
    Giuseppe Lasina
Principal dancers: Augusta Maywood, Lorenzo
    Vienna, Carolina Calabi, Giuseppe Lasina

1853

TEATRO ARGENTINA

Adina
Choreography: David Mochi
Principal dancer: Raffaella Santalicante Prisco,
    Filippo Termanini, Gaetano Prisco

Il birichino di Parigi (The Urchin of Paris)
Choreography: David Mochi
Principal dancers: Raffaella Santalicante Prisco,
    Gaetano Prisco, Filippo Termanini

Il Furioso (The Madman)
Choreography: David Mochi
Principal dancers: David Mochi, Carolina(?)
    Granzini

1854

TEATRO DI APOLLO

Margherita di Scozia (Margaret of Scotland)
Choreography: Emanuele Viotti
Principal dancers: Giovanni Lepri, Amalia Ferraris

Ileria
Choreography: Emanuele Viotti
Principal dancers: Amalia Ferraris, Giovanni Lepri,
    Raffaella Santalicante Prisco, Ludovico Pedoni

Emma
Choreography: Emanuele Viotti
Principal dancers: Raffaella Santalicante Prisco,
    Gaetano Prisco

1855

TEATRO DI APOLLO

Clotilde di Pomerania (Clothilde of Pomerania)
Choreography: Emanuele Viotti
Music: Giacomo Meyerbeer, Eugenio Terziani
Principal dancers: Sofia Fuoco, Francesco Penco,
    Raffaella Santalicante Prisco, Raffaele Rossi

Le due sorelle (The Two Sisters)
Choreography: Emanuele Viotti

Principal dancers: Sofia Fuoco, Francesco Penco, Raffaella Santalicante Prisco

Paquita
Choreography: Emanuele Viotti (after Joseph Mazilier[?])

1855

TEATRO ARGENTINA

Il trionfo dell'innocenza (The Triumph of Innocence)
Choreography: Giuseppe Rota
Music: Antonio Mussi, Paolo Giorza
Principal dancers: Augusta Maywood, Ferdinando Croci,* Raffaele Rossi, Adelaide Rossi, Ludovico Pedoni

Il Giuocatore (The Gambler)
Choreography: Giuseppe Rota
Music: Luigi Madoglio
Principal dancers: Augusta Maywood, Ferdinando Croci,* Raffaele Rossi, Adelaide Rossi, Ludovico Pedoni

*NOTE: Ferdinando Croci choreographed the pas de deux that he performed with Maywood.

Gli amori campestri (Rustic Loves)
Choreographer: Francesco Marocchesi
Principal dancers: Ottavio Memmi, Pia Cavalieri**

**NOTE: *Gli amori campestri* was performed by a company of twenty-four boys and girls from Siena. Cavalieri herself was only eleven years old.

Ballets by Salvatore Taglioni

LAVINIA CAVALLETTI

MONTPELLIER, NIMES, GRENOBLE

1807 *Una mezz'ora di capriccio* (A Half-Hour of Whim)
L'amante Statua (The Loving Statue)
Il volubile fissato (The Taming of the Rake)
I giochi di Paride (The Games of Paris)
Annetta e Lubino (Annette and Lubin)

TEATRO DI SAN CARLO AND TEATRO FONDO, NAPLES

1814 *La figlia mal custodia* (La Fille Mal Gardée)
1815 *Il Barbiere di Siviglia* (The Barber of Seville)
Bacco in Erepoli (Bacchus in Erepolis)
Luca e Lauretta (Luke and Lauretta)
1816 *L'Aurora* (The Dawn)
La casa disabitata (The Deserted House)
1817 *Errore e perdono* (Error and Forgiveness)
Atalanta e Hippomene (Atalanta and Hippomenes)
1818 *Il Flauto magico, ossia le convulsioni musicali* (The Magic Flute, or Musical Fits)
1819 *I Portoghesi nelle Indie* (The Portuguese in the Indies)
La nascita di Flora (The Birth of Flora)
La prigione di Cnido ossia Pelia e Mileto (The Prison of Cnidus, or Pelias and Miletus)

LA SCALA, MILAN

1820 *La conquista di Malacca* (The Conquest of Malacca)
Castore e Polluce (Castor and Pollux)
I due Figaro (The Two Figaros) (dance in opera)
La Gazza Ladra (The Magpie Thief) (dance in opera)

TEATRO DI SAN CARLO AND TEATRO FONDO, NAPLES

1820 *Otranto liberata* (Otranto Liberated)
Narciso corretto (Narcissus Chastened)
1821 *Gustavo Vasa* (Gustavo Vasa)
Castore e Polluce (Castor and Pollux)
1822 *La festa di Terpsicore* (The Festival of Terpsichore)
Il Natale di Venere (The Birth of Venus)
La promessa mantenuta (The Promise Fulfilled)

ROYAL PALACE, NAPLES

1822 Allegorical entertainment (30 November)

TEATRO SAN CARLINO, PALERMO

1823 *Zeffiro* (Zephyrus)
Luca e Lauretta (Luke and Lauretta)

TEATRO DI SAN CARLO AND TEATRO FONDO, NAPLES

1823 *Sesostri* (Sesostris)
L'oracolo in cantina (The Rotten Oracle)
Cerere fuggitiva (Ceres in Flight)
Atide e Cloe (Attis and Chloe)
Tippoo-Saeb (Tipu Sahib)
1824 *Zeffiro* (Zephyrus)

NAPLES

1824 Entertainment for the Duchess of Parma

LA SCALA, MILAN

1824 *Sesostri* (Sesostris)
Tippoo-Saeb (Tipu Sahib)
Bianca di Messina (Bianca of Messina)
Nozze di Flora e Zeffiro (The Marriage of Flora and Zephyrus)
La donna del Lago (The Lady of the Lake) (dance in opera)
Il sonnambulo (The Somnambulist) (dance in opera)
Temistocle (Themistocles) (dance in opera)
Torvaldo e Dorliska (Thorvald and Dorliska) (dance in opera)
Allegorical entertainment for the Emperor of Austria

TEATRO DI SAN CARLO AND TEATRO FONDO, NAPLES

1825 Anacreontic divertissement
Tirsi e Fillide (Thyrsi and Phylius)
I paggi del Duca di Vendôme (The Pages of the Duke of Vendôme)
1826 *Alcibiade* (Alcibiades)

259

L'ira d'Achille (The Wrath of Achilles)
Le due zie (The Two Aunts)
Acbar gran Mogol (Akbar, the Great Mogol)

TEATRO SAN CARLINO, PALERMO

1826 *Atide e Cloe* (Attis and Chloe)
Sidney e Damio (Sydney and Damius)

KÜRNTNERTOR THEATER, VIENNA

1826 *I Portoghesi nelle Indie* (The Portuguese in the Indies)
Il Flauto magico (The Magic Flute)
1827 *Castore e Polluce* (Castor and Pollux)

LA SCALA, MILAN

1827 *Pietro di Portogallo ossia Ines di Castro* (Pedro of Portugal, or Inez de Castro)
Pelia e Mileto (Pelias and Miletus)
Euticchio della Castagna ossia la casa disabitata (Euticchio della Castagna, or The Deserted House)
Il Paria (The Pariah)
Il Flauto Incantato (The Enchanted Flute)

TEATRO DI SAN CARLO AND TEATRO FONDO, NAPLES

1828 *Amore Filosofo* (Philosopher Love)
La corona d'alloro (The Laurel Wreath)
La fata Urgella (The Fairy Urgella)
1829 *Le montagne russe* (The Roller Coaster)
1830 *Il Paria* (The Pariah)
I collegiali in vacanza (Schoolboys on Holiday)
Apollo Pastore (Apollo the Shepherd)
La prigione di Cnido ossia Pelia e Mileto (The Prison of Cnidus, or Pelias and Miletus)

TEATRO REGIO, TURIN

1830 *La conquista di Malacca* (The Conquest of Malacca)
Il Flauto magico (The Magic Flute)
1831 *Euticchio della Castagna ossia la casa disabitata* (Euticchio della Castagna, or The Deserted House)
Sesostri (Sesostris)
I collegiali in vacanza (Schoolboys on Holiday)

TEATRO DI SAN CARLO AND TEATRO FONDO, NAPLES

1831 *Amore e bizzaria* (Love and Folly)
Ines de Castro (Inez de Castro)

TEATRO REGIO, TURIN

1831 *Sesostri* (Sesostris)
I collegiali in vacanza (Schoolboys on Holiday)
1832 *Castore e Polluce* (Castor and Pollux)
Masked ball

TEATRO DI SAN CARLO AND TEATRO FONDO, NAPLES

1832 *Romanow* (Romanov)
Carlo il Temerario (Charles the Reckless)
Cristina di Svezia (Christina of Sweden)
Il felice Imeneo (The Happy Hymenaeus) (dance in opera)
1833 *Bianca di Messina* (Bianca of Messina)
L'ombra di Tsi-Ven o la costanza premiata (The Ghost of Tsi-Ven, or Constancy Rewarded)
La porta murata (The Walled Gate)
1834 *La saracena in Sicilia* (The Saracen Woman in Sicily)
L'eredità (The Inheritance)
Tolomeo Evergete (Ptolemy Evergete)
1835 *I prigionieri* (The Prisoners)
Amore e Psiche (Cupid and Psyche)
Le nozze di Figaro (The Marriage of Figaro)
1836 *Il ritorno di Ulisse* (The Return of Ulysses)
L'assedio di Calais (The Siege of Calais)
Rosina e Tonino (Rosie and Tony)
I Promessi Sposi (The Betrothed)

LA SCALA, MILAN

1836 *I Promessi Sposi* (The Betrothed)
Amore e Psiche (Cupid and Psyche)
1837 *Romanow* (Romanov)
Le nozze campestri (The Country Wedding)

TEATRO DI SAN CARLO AND TEATRO FONDO, NAPLES

1837 *Ettore Fieramosca* (Hector Fieramosca)
1838 *Alfredo* (Alfred)
La notte di un proscritto o l'ospitalità scozzese (The Night of an Exile, or Scottish Hospitality)
Isabella di Lorena (Isabelle of Lorraine)
Furio Camillo (Furius Camillus)
Le nozze di Flora (The Marriage of Flora)
La gratitudine (Gratefulness)
1839 *Il Rajah di Benares* (The Rajah of Benares)
Edwige o il sogno (Hedwig, or The Dream)
Il perdono (Forgiveness)
La scommessa (The Bet)
Nadam d'orgoglio punito (Nadam Punished in His Pride)
Amore alla prova (Love on Trial)

LA SCALA, MILAN

1839   *L'ombra di Tsi-Ven* (The Ghost of Tsi-Ven)
1840   *Romanow* (Romanov)
        L'assedio di Sciraz ossia l'amor materno (The Siege of Shiraz, or Mother Love)
        La Zingara andalusa (The Andalusian Gypsy Girl)

TEATRO DI SAN CARLO AND TEATRO FONDO, NAPLES

1840   *Il Duca di Ravenna* (The Duke of Ravenna)
        La caccia di Enrico IV (The Hunt of Henry IV)
        Basilio III Demetriovitz (Vassily Dimitrievich III)
        Un episodio della campagna di Costantina (An Episode from the Campaign of Constantine)
1841   *Don Chisciotte* (Don Quixote)
        Marco Visconti
        La foresta di Armanstadt (The Forest of Armanstadt)
        La falsa sposa (The False Bride)
1842   *La zingara* (The Gypsy Girl)
        Le reclute (The Recruits)
        Castore e Polluce (Castor and Pollux)
1843   *Carlo di Ravenstein* (Charles of Ravenstein)
        L'assedio di Leyda (The Siege of Leyden)
        Il sarto di Sondrio (The Tailor of Sondrio)

TEATRO REGIO, TURIN

1843   *L'assedio di Leyda* (The Siege of Leyden)
        Amore e Psiche (Cupid and Psyche)
        Le avventure di Don Chisciotte (The Adventures of Don Quixote)

TEATRO DI SAN CARLO AND TEATRO FONDO, NAPLES

1844   *La nascita di Flora* (The Birth of Flora)
        La protetta del Danubio (The Protégée of the Danube)
        La coppa de' Fidanzati (The Goblet of the Fiancés)
        Claudina
1845   *Il Cid* (El Cid)
        L'assedio di Corinto (The Siege of Corinth)
        Erissena (Erissena)
        Il biglietto d'alloggio (The Billet)
1846   *Merope* (Merope)
        L'Eroe cinese ossia Fedeltà e Clemenza (The Chinese Hero, or Faithfulness and Mercy)
        Guglielmo di Provenza (William of Provence)
        Margherita Pusterla
        Tirsi e Fillide (Thyrsi and Phylius)

1847   *La straniera* (The Foreign Woman)
        Ifigenia in Aulide (Iphigenia in Aulis)
1848   *Il vampiro* (The Vampire)
        Paquita
1849   *Bradamante e Ruggiero* (Bradamante and Ruggiero)
        Il Candiano (The Cretan)
1850   *Mocanna*
        Il ritorno di Alfonso d'Aragona dalla guerra di Otranto (The Return of Alphonse of Aragon from the War of Otranto)
        La figlia di Alfeo (The Daughter of Alfeo)
        Divertissement
        Il sogno di un emiro (An Emir's Dream)
        La fedeltà premiata (Faithfulness Rewarded)
1851   *La stella del marinaio* (The Mariner's Star)
        La protetta di Venere (The Protégée of Venus)
1852   *La vedova scaltra* (The Cunning Widow)
        Bassora ossia il fantasma di Arafat (Basra, or The Ghost of Arafat)
1853   *Anacreonte* (Anacreon)
        Olfa
1854   *L'araba* (The Arab Girl)
        Hulda leggenda islandese (Hulda, An Icelandic Legend)
        La scelta di una sposa (The Choice of a Wife)
1855   *Shakespeare ovvero il sogno di una notte d'estate* (Shakespeare, or A Midsummer Night's Dream)
        Raimondo o il vecchio soldato (Raimondo, or The Old Soldier)
        Zilmé o la dea delle dovizie (Zilmé, or The Goddess of Abundance)
        Groa (Groa)
        Naama regina delle api (Naama, Queen of the Bees)
1856   *Isaura ossia la protetta della fata* (Isaura, or The Fairy's Favorite)
        Lady Enrichette o la fantesca di Greenwich (Lady Henrietta, or The Maid of Greenwich)
        I Bucanieri (The Buccaneers)
1857   *Il vecchio della foresta* (The Old Man of the Forest)
1858   *La corte d'Amor* (Cupid's Court)
        L'equivoco (The Misunderstanding)
1859   *Il venturiero* (The Free Lance)
1860   *Rita*
        La pietra filosofale (The Philosopher's Stone)
        Il figlio dello Shah (The Son of the Shah)
1865   *Il talismano* (The Talisman)

GENERAL

JOELLEN A. MEGLIN
with contributions by Claudia Celi and Lynn Garafola

Archives

In addition to the major repositories listed below, dozens of archives with material pertinent to the study of the romantic ballet exist all over Europe. Many opera houses have excellent archives, and there are also important government archives, such as the Staatsbibliothek in Berlin. Their rich holdings remain largely untapped by dance scholars.

Archives Nationales (Paris)

> For a description of the Paris Opéra material in the National Archives collection, see *Archives du Théâtre National de l'Opéra (AJ¹³ 1 à 1466): Inventaire*, preface by Jean Favier (Paris: Archives Nationales, 1977).

Biblioteca teatrale della Scala (Milan)

Biblithèque de l'Opéra (Paris)

> For a description of the special archives and collections held by the Bibliothèque de l'Opéra, see "The Library and the Archives of the Paris Opéra: The Opéra Preserved" by Ivor Guest in *Dance Research,* 2 (Summer 1984), pp. 68–76; "The Library and Archives of the Paris Opéra: Part 2" by Martine Kahane, translated by Margaret M. McGowan, in *Dance Research,* 3 (Autumn 1984), pp. 67–71; Théodore Lajarte, "Bibliothèque musicale du Théâtre de l'Opéra" (Paris: Librairie de Bibliophile, 1878); and Nicole Wild's catalogue *Les Arts du spectacle en France: Affiches illustrées (1850–1950)* (Paris: Bibliothèque Nationale, 1976), *Archives de l'Opéra de Paris—Inventaire Sommaire* (Paris: Bibliothèque Nationale, 1988), *Décors et costumes du XIXe siècle à l'Opéra de Paris,* vol. 1 (Paris: Bibliothèque Nationale, 1987), and *Dictionnaire des théâtres parisiens au XIXe siècle* (Paris: Aux Amateurs de Livres, 1989). See also Peter Brinson's *Background to European Ballet: A Notebook from Its Archives* (Leyden, Netherlands: Sijthoff, 1966), which includes an appendix of the various archives in Europe containing ballet material, including the Bibliothèque de l'Opéra, the Archives Nationales, and various divisions of the Bibliothèque Nationale, including the Département des Arts du Spectacle (Bibliothèque de l'Arsenal).

Bibliothèque Nationale, Cabinet des Estampes (Paris)

Bibliothèque Nationale, Département de la Musique (Paris)

> For a partial listing of the letters in the Music Division collection, see Antoine Bloch-Michel's *Lettres autographes conservées au département de la Musique: Catalogue sommaire* (Paris: Bibliothèque Nationale, 1984).

British Library (London)

> Cyril W. Beaumont's *A Bibliography of Dancing* (New York: Benjamin Blom, 1963) catalogues the collection at the British Museum Library.

Carvalhaes Collection, Biblioteca del Conservatorio di Santa Cecilia (Rome)

Dance Collection, New York Public Library for the Performing Arts

Fondo Ferrajoli, Biblioteca Apostolica Vaticana (Rome)
For a description of the music libretti in the Vatican Library's Ferrajoli collection, see G. Gialdroni and T.M. Gialdroni, *Libretti per musica del Fondo Ferrajoli della Biblioteca Apostolica Vaticana* (Luca: LIM, 1993). For current projects to catalogue nineteenth-century Italian dance libretti, see Andrea Toschi, "Verso una catalogazione unica dei libretti di danza italiani dell'Ottocento," in *Le fonti musicali in Italia* (no. 7 [1993]).

Harvard Theatre Collection
For a description of the holdings of the Harvard Theatre Collection see Jeanne T. Newlin, "Preserving Our Heritage," and Edwin Binney, 3rd, "Prints and Drawings in the Dance Division," *Dance Magazine*, Dec. 1981, pp. 47–51.

Rolandi Collection, Fondazione Cini (Venice)
For the music holdings of the Fondazione Querini-Stampalia, also in Venice, see Franco Rossi, *Le opere musicali della Fondazione Querini-Stampalia di Venezia* (Turin: EDT, 1984).

Royal Library (Copenhagen)

Royal Theatre (Copenhagen)

Teatro di San Carlo (Naples)
For the collection of opera libretti at the Teatro di San Carlo, see Marta Columbro, *La Raccolta di libretti d'opera del Teatro San Carlo di Napoli* (Lucca: LIM, 1992).

Theatre Museum (Copenhagen)

Theatre Museum (London)

Secondary Sources

Adice, G. Léopold. *Théorie de la gymnastique de la danse théâtrale*. Paris, 1859.
Alderson, Evan. "Ballet as Ideology: Giselle, Act II." *Dance Chronicle*, 10, no. 3 (1987), pp. 290–304.
Arkin, Lisa C. "The Context of Exoticism in Fanny Elssler's Cachucha." *Dance Chronicle*, 17, no. 2 (1994), pp. 303–325.
Aschengreen, Erik. "The Beautiful Danger: Facets of the Romantic Ballet." Trans. Patricia N. McAndrew. *Dance Perspectives*, no. 58 (1974), pp. 1–52.
Au, Susan. "The Bandit Ballerina: Some Sources of Jules Perrot's *Catarina*." *Dance Research Journal*, 10, no. 2(1979), pp 2–5.
———. "Prints of a Parisian Péri." *Dance Perspectives*, no. 61 (Spring 1975), pp. 30–49.
———. "The Shadow of Herself: Some Sources of Jules Perrot's *Ondine*." *Dance Chronicle*, 2, no. 3 (1978), pp. 159–171.
Balli teatrali a Venezia (1746–1859). Introd. José Sasportes. Chronology by Elena Ruffin and Giovanna Trentin. 2 vols. Milan: Ricordi, 1989.
Beaumont, Cyril W. *The Ballet Called Giselle*. London: Dance Books, 1969; 1988.
———. *Complete Book of Ballets: A Guide to the Principal Ballets of the Nineteenth and Twentieth Centuries*. London: Putnam, 1937.
———, trans. *The Romantic Ballet as Seen by Théophile Gautier*. London, 1932; rpt. New York: Dance Horizons, 1973.
———, and Sacheverell Sitwell. *The Romantic Ballet in Lithographs of the Time*. London: Faber and Faber, 1938.

Bersaucourt, A. de. "La Danse en 1830." *L'Art Vivant*, 15 July 1926, pp. 540–544.

Binney, Edwin, 3rd. *Les Ballets de Théophile Gautier*. Paris: Nizet, 1965.

———. "A Century of Austro-German Dance Prints 1790–1890." *Dance Perspectives*, no. 47 (Autumn 1971).

———. *Glories of the Romantic Ballet*. London: Dance Books, 1985.

———. *Longing for the Ideal: Images of Marie Taglioni in the Romantic Ballet*. Cambridge, Mass.: Harvard Theatre Collection, 1984.

———. "Sixty Years of Italian Dance Prints 1815–1875." *Dance Perspectives*, no. 53 (Spring 1973).

Blasis, Carlo. *The Code of Terpsichore: A Practical and Historical Treatise, on the Ballet, Dancing, and Pantomime; With a Complete Theory of the Art of Dancing: Intended as Well for the Instruction of Amateurs as the Use of Professional Persons*. Trans. R. Barton. London: James Bulcock, 1828; New York: Dance Horizons, [1976].

———. *Notes Upon Dancing*. London, 1847.

——— (as Karl Blazis). *Tantsy voobshche, balletnye znamenitosti i natsional'nye tantsy* (Dances in General, Ballet Celebrities, and National Dances). Moscow: Lazarevsk, 1864.

———. *L'uomo fisico, intellettuale e morale*. Milan: Guglielmini e Redaelli, 1857.

Boigne, Charles de. *Petits Mémoires de l'Opéra*. Paris: Librairie Nouvelle, 1857.

Bournonville, August. "The Ballet Poems by August Bournonville: The Complete Scenarios." Trans. Patricia N. McAndrew. *Dance Chronicle*, 3, no. 2–6, no. 1 (1979–1983).

———. *My Theatre Life*. Trans. Patricia N. McAndrew. Middletown, Conn.: Wesleyan University Press, 1979.

Burt, Ramsay. *The Male Dancer*. London: Routledge, 1995.

Castil-Blaze [François-Henri-Joseph Blaze]. *L'Académie Impériale de Musique de 1645 à 1855*. Paris: Castil-Blaze, 1855.

———. *La Danse et les Ballets depuis Bacchus jusqu'à Mademoiselle Taglioni*. Paris: Paulin, 1832.

Celi, Claudia. "Il balletto in Italia." In *Musica in Scene: Storia dello Spettacolo musicale*. Ed. Alberto Basso. Vol. 5. Turin: UTET, 1995, pp. 89–138.

———. "Roma, il Risorgimento in ballo." In *Incontri con la Danza 1993*. Ed. Elena Grillo. Rome: Opera dell'Accademia Nazionale di Danza, 1994.

———, and Andrea Toschi. "Alla ricerca dell'anello mancante: 'Flik e Flok' e l'Unità d'Italia." *Chorégraphie*, 1, no. 2 (Autumn 1993), pp. 58–72.

———. "Lo spartito animato, o delle fortune ballettistiche dell'*Adelaide di Francia*." In *"Di sì felice innesto": Rossini, la danza e il ballo teatrale in Italia*. Ed. Paolo Fabbri. Pesaro: Fondazione Rossini, 1996.

Chapman, John. "Auguste Vestris and the Expansion of Technique." *Dance Research Journal*, 19, no. 1 (1987), pp. 11–18.

———. "The Paris Opera Ballet School, 1798–1827." *Dance Chronicle*, 12, no. 2 (1989), pp. 196–220.

———. "An Unromantic View of Nineteenth-Century Romanticism." *York Dance Review*, 7 (1978), pp. 28–40.

Chaffee, George. "The Romantic Ballet in London, 1821–1858." *Dance Index*, 2, nos. 9–12 (Sept.–Dec. 1944).

———. "Three or Four Graces, A Centenary Salvo." *Dance Index*, 3, nos. 9–11 (Sept.–Nov. 1944).

Cohen, Selma Jeanne. *Dance as a Theatre Art: Source Readings in Dance History from 1581 to the Present*. 2nd ed. New York: Dodd, Mead and Company, 1992.

———. "Freme di Gelosia! Italian Ballet Librettos, 1766–1865." *Bulletin of the New York Public Library*, 67, no. 9 (Nov. 1963), pp. 555–564.

———. "Virtue (Almost) Triumphant." *The Dancing Times*, Mar. 1964, pp. 297–301.

Costonis, Maureen Needham. "Fanny Elssler in Havana." *Choreography and Dance*, 3, pt. 4 (1994), pp. 37–46.

———. "The Personification of Desire: Fanny Elssler and American Audiences." *Dance Chronicle*, 13, no. 1 (1990), pp. 47–67.

———. "'The Wild Doe': Augusta Maywood in Philadelphia and Paris, 1837–1840." *Dance Chronicle*, 17, no. 2 (1984), pp. 123–148.

Cucchi, Claudina. *Venti anni di palcoscenico*. Rome: Enrico Voghera, 1906.

Daly, Ann. "Classical Ballet: A Discourse of Difference." *Women and Performance: A Journal of Feminist Theory*, 3, no. 2 (1987–1988), pp. 57–66.

Delarue, Allison, ed. and introd. *Fanny Elssler in America*. New York: Dance Horizons, 1976.

Deldevez, Edouard. *Mes Mémoires*. Le Puy: Marchessou Fils, 1890.

Deshayes, André. *Idées générales sur l'Académie Royale de Musique*. Paris: Mongie, 1822.

Escudier, Léon. *Mes souvenirs*. Paris: E. Dentu, 1863.

Fabbri, Paolo, and Roberto Verti. *Due secoli di teatro per musica a Reggio Emilia. Repertorio cronologico delle opere e dei balli 1645–1857*. Reggio Emilia: Teatro Municipale Valli, 1987.

Falcone, Francesca. "The Arabesque: A Compositional Design." Trans. Irene Minafra and Brett Shapiro. *Dance Chronicle*, 19, no. 3 (1996), pp. 231–254.

Fischer, Carlos. *Les Costumes de l'Opéra*. Paris: Librairie de France, 1931.

Foster, Susan Leigh. "The Ballerina's Phallic Pointe." In *Corporealities*. Ed. Susan Leigh Foster. London: Routledge, 1996, pp. 1–24.

———. *Choreography and Narrative: Ballet's Staging of Story and Desire*. Bloomington, Ind.: Indiana University Press, 1996.

Gallini, Giovanni-Andrea. *A Treatise on the Art of Dancing*. London, 1772.

Garafola, Lynn. "A las márgenes del occidente: el destino transpirenaico de la danza española desde la época del romanticismo." *Cairón*, 1 (1995), pp. 9–22.

———. "The Travesty Dancer in Nineteenth-Century Ballet." *Dance Research Journal*, 17, no. 2 (1985–1986), pp. 35–40.

Gatti, Carlo. *Il Teatro alla Scala nella storia e nell'arte, 1778–1963*. 2 vols. 2nd ed. Milan: Ricordi, 1964,

Gautier, Théophile. *A Romantic in Spain*. Trans. Catherine Alison Phillips. New York: Knopf, 1926.

———. *Histoire de l'art dramatique en France*. 6 vols. Paris: Magnin, Blanchard, 1858–1859.

———. *Souvenirs de Théâtre, d'Art et de Critique*. Paris: Charpentier, 1883.

———. *Théâtre, mystères, comédies et ballets*. Paris: Charpentier, 1872.

Gautier on Dance. Ed. and trans. Ivor Guest. London: Dance Books, 1986.

"Théophile Gautier on Spanish Dancing." Ed. and trans. Ivor Guest. *Dance Chronicle*, 10, no. 1 (1987), pp. 1–104.

Gautier, Théophile, Jules Janin, and Philarète Chasles. *Les Beautés de l'Opéra*. Paris: Soulié, 1845. As *Beauties of the Opera and Ballet*. Trans. Charles Heath. London: D. Bogue, 1845; rpt. New York: Da Capo, 1977.

Girardi, Michele, and Franco Rossi. *Il Teatro La Fenice: Cronologia degli spettacoli 1792–1936*. Venice: Albrizzi, 1989.

Giselle. L'Avant-scène Ballet/Danse, 1 (1980). Special volume devoted to Giselle.

Gourret, Jean. *Histoire des Salles de l'Opéra de Paris*. Preface by Jean-Pierre Samoyault. Paris: Guy Trédaniel, 1985.

Guérard, Eugène. *Les Annales de la danse et du théâtre*. Paris: Goupil et Vibert, [1845].

Guest, Ivor. "Dandies and Dancers." *Dance Perspectives*, no. 37 (Spring 1969).

———. *Fanny Cerrito: The Life of a Romantic Ballerina*. London: Dance Books, 1974.

———. *Fanny Elssler*. Middletown, Conn.: Wesleyan University Press, 1970.

———. *Jules Perrot: Master of the Romantic Ballet*. 2nd ed. rev. New York: Dance Horizons, 1984.

———. "Parodies of Giselle on the English Stage (1841–1871)." *Theatre Notebook*, 9, no. 2 (Jan.–Mar. 1955), pp. 38–46.

———. *The Romantic Ballet in England: Its Development, Fulfilment and Decline*. London: Phoenix House, 1954.

———. *The Romantic Ballet in Paris*. Middletown, Conn.: Wesleyan University Press, 1966.

———. *Victorian Ballet Girl: The Tragic Story of Clara Webster*. London: Adam and Charles Black, 1957.

Hammond, Sandra Noll. "Ballet's Technical Heritage: The Grammaire of Léopold Adice." *Dance Research*, 13, no. 1 (Summer 1995), pp. 33–58.

———. "Clues to Ballet's Technical History from the Early Nineteenth-Century Ballet Lesson." *Dance Research*, 3, no. 1 (Autumn 1984), pp. 53–66.

———. "A Nineteenth-Century Dancing Master at the Court of Wurttemberg: The Dance Notebooks of Michel St. Leon." *Dance Chronicle*, 15, no. 3 (1992), pp. 291–315.

———. "Searching for the Sylph: Documentation of Early Developments in Pointe Technique." *Dance Research Journal*, 19, no. 2 (1987/1988), pp. 27–31.

Hansell, Kathleen Kuzmick. "Il ballo teatrale e l'opera italiana." Trans. Lorenzo Bianconi and Angelo Bozzo. In *Storia dell'Opera Italiana*. Vol. 5. Ed. Lorenzo Bianconi and Giorgio Pestelli. Turin: EDT, 1987, pp. 175–306.

Heiberg, Johanne Luise. "Memories of Taglioni and Elssler." Trans. by Patricia McAndrew from *A Life Relived in Memory* (1891). *Dance Chronicle*, 4, no. 1 (1981), pp. 14–18.

Huckenpahler, Victoria, trans. and ed. "Confessions of an Opera Director: Chapters from the Mémoires of Dr. Louis Veron." *Dance Chronicle*, 7, nos. 1–3 (1984–85), pp. 50–106, 198–228, 345–370.

Hutchinson, Ann. *Fanny Elssler's Cachucha*. Introd. Ivor Guest. New York: Theatre Arts Books, 1981.

Join-Diéterle, Catherine. *Les Décors de Scène de l'Opéra de Paris à l'époque romantique*. Paris: Picard, 1988.

Jowitt, Deborah. *Time and the Dancing Image*. Berkeley: University of California Press, 1988.

Jürgensen, Knud Arne. *The Bournonville Ballets: A Photographic Record 1844–1933*. London: Dance Books, 1987.

———. "Bournonville in Italia." *La Danza Italiana*, no. 7 (Spring 1989), pp. 99–120.

———. "Sulle tracce della Silfide italiana." *Rivista Illustrata del Museo Teatrale alla Scala*, 1, no. 4 (Autumn 1989), pp. 18–39.

Kirstein, Lincoln. *Movement and Metaphor: Four Centuries of Ballet*. New York: Praeger, 1970. Rev. ed. *Four Centuries of Ballet: Fifty Masterworks*. New York: Dover, 1984.

Lecomte, Nathalie. "Maria Taglioni alla Scala." *La Danza Italiana*, nos. 8–9 (Winter 1990), pp. 47–73.

Levinson, André. "The Anatomy of a Sylph: Concerning the Beauty of Marie Taglioni." In *André Levinson on Dance: Writings from Paris in the Twenties*. Ed. with introd. Joan Acocella and Lynn Garafola. Hanover, N.H.: Wesleyan University Press, 1991.

———. *Marie Taglioni (1804–1884)*. Paris: Librairie Félix Alcan, 1929.

———. *Marie Taglioni*. Trans. Cyril W. Beaumont. London, 1930; rpt. London: Dance Books, 1977.

———. *Meister des Balletts*. Trans. Reinhold von Walter. Potsdam: Müller, 1923.

———. "Théophile Gautier et le Ballet Romantique." *La Revue musicale*, Dec. 1921, pp. 53–66. Rpt. in *L'Art du Ballet des origines à nos jours.* Preface by R[oger] W[ild]. Paris: Editions du Tambourinaire, 1952.

Lifar, Serge. *Giselle: Apothéose du ballet romantique.* Paris: Albin Michel, [1942].

———. *Carlotta Grisi.* Paris: Albin Michel, 1941.

Magri, Gennaro. *Theoretical and Practical Treatise on Dancing,* trans. Mary Skeaping. London: Dance Books, 1988.

Massaro, Maria Nevilla. "Balli e ballerini fra Padova e Venezia." *La Danza Italiana,* nos. 5–6 (Autumn 1987), pp. 77–88.

Maurice, Charles. *Histoire anecdotique du théâtre.* Paris, 1856.

McCarren, Felicia M. "The Female Form: Gautier, Mallarmé and Céline Writing Dance." Ph.D. diss., Stanford University, 1992.

Meglin, Joellen A. "Le Diable Boiteux: French Society Behind a Spanish Facade." *Dance Chronicle,* 17, no. 3 (1994), pp. 263–302.

———. "Fanny Elssler's Cachucha and Women's Lives: Domesticity and Sexuality in France in the 1830s." In *Dance Reconstructed: Conference Proceedings,* ed. Barbara Palfy, pp. 73–96. New Brunswick, N.J: Mason Gross School of the Arts, Rutgers, State University of New Jersey, 1993.

———. "Representations and Realities: Analyzing Gender Symbols in the Romantic Ballet." Ed.D. diss., Temple University, 1995.

Mellor, Anne K., ed. *Romanticism and Feminism.* Bloomington: Indiana University Press, 1988.

Migel, Parmenia. *The Ballerinas: From the Court of Louis XIV to Pavlova.* New York: Macmillan, 1972.

———. *Great Ballet Prints of the Romantic Era.* New York: Dover, 1981.

Monaldi, Gino. *Le regine della danza nel secolo XIX.* Turin: Bocca, 1910.

Moore, Lillian. *Artists of the Dance.* New York: Crowell, 1938.

———. "Elssler and the *Cachucha.*" *The Dancing Times,* Aug. 1936, pp. 495–497.

———. "George Washington Smith." In *Chronicles of the American Dance: From the Shakers to Martha Graham.* Ed. Paul Magriel. 2nd ed. New York: Da Capo, 1978, pp. 138–188.

———. *Images of the Dance: Historical Treasures of the Dance Collection 1581–1861.* New York: New York Public Library, 1965.

———. "Mary Ann Lee: First American Giselle." In *Chronicles of the American Dance: From the Shakers to Martha Graham.* Ed. Paul Magriel. 2nd ed. New York: Da Capo, 1978, pp. 102–117.

———. "The Petipa Family in Europe and America." *Dance Index,* 1, no. 5 (May 1942, pp. 72–84.

Mueller, John. "Is Giselle a Virgin?" *Dance Chronicle,* 4, no. 1 (1981), pp. 151–154.

Murphy, Anne. "Age of Enchantment." *Ballet News,* Mar. 1982, pp. 11–14, 42–43.

Neidish, Juliet. "Whose Habitation is the Air." *Dance Perspectives,* no. 61 (Spring 1975), pp. 4–17.

Olson, Nancy. *Gavarni: The Carnival Lithographs.* New Haven: Yale University Art Gallery, 1979.

Pearce, Charles E. *Madame Vestris and Her Times.* London, [1923]; rpt. New York: Benjamin Blom, 1969.

Petipa, Marius. "The Diaries of Marius Petipa." Ed., trans., and introd. Lynn Garafola. *Studies in Dance History,* 3, no. 1 (Spring 1992).

———. *Russian Ballet Master: The Memoirs of Marius Petipa.* Trans. Helen Whittaker. Ed. Lillian Moore. London, 1958; rpt. London: Dance Books, n.d.

Pistone, Danièle. "L'Opéra de Paris au siècle romantique." *Revue Internationale de la Musique Français,* 1 (1981), pp. 7–56.

Poesio, Giannandrea. "Giselle." 3 pts. *The Dancing Times,* Feb. 1994, pp. 454–461; Mar. 1994, pp. 563–573; Apr. 1994, pp. 688–697.

———. "Maestro's Early Years." *The Dancing Times,* Sept. 1992, pp. 1125–1127.

———. "Il maestro Giovanni Lepri e la sua scuola fiorentina." *Chorégraphie*, 1, no. 1 (Spring 1993), pp. 68–75.

Prudhommeau, Germaine. "Naissance des pointes: deux petits chaussons. *Danser*, no. 18 (Dec. 1984), pp. 48–50.

Pudełek, Janina. "The Warsaw Ballet under the Directorships of Maurice Pion and Felippo Taglioni, 1832–1853." Trans. and introd. Jadwiga Kosicka. *Dance Chronicle*, 11, no. 2 (1988), pp. 219–273.

———. *Warszawski balet romantyczny (1802–1866)*. Krakow: Polskie Wydawn. Muzyczne, 1968.

———, with Joanna Sibilska. "The Polish Dancers Visit St. Petersburg, 1851: A Detective Story." *Dance Chronicle*, 19, no. 2 (1996), pp. 171–189.

Raimondi, Ezio, ed. *Il sogno del coreodramma: Salvatore Viganò, poeta muto*. [Bologna]: Il Mulino, 1982.

Regli, Francesco. *Dizionario biografico dei più celebri poeti ed artisti melodrammatici, tragici e comici, maestri, concertisti, coreografi, mimi, ballerini, scenografi, giornalisti, impresarii, ec. ec. che fiorirono in Italia dal 1800 al 1860*. Turin, 1860; rpt. Bologna: Forni, 1990.

Ries, Frank W.D. "In Search of Giselle: 'Travels with a Chameleon Romantic.'" *Dance Magazine*, Aug. 1979, pp. 59–74.

Robin-Challan, Louise. "Danse et Danseuses à l'Opéra de Paris, 1830–1850." Thèse de 3ème Cycle, Université de Paris VII, 1983.

———. "Social Conditions of Ballet Dancers at the Paris Opera in the 19th Century." *Choreography and Dance*, 2, no. 1 (1992), pp. 17–28.

Roqueplan, Nestor. *Les Coulisses de l'Opéra*. Paris: Librairie Nouvelle, 1855.

Rossi, Luigi. *Il ballo alla Scala, 1778–1970*. Milan: Edizioni della Scala, 1972.

Rowell, George. *Queen Victoria Goes to the Theatre*. London: Paul Elek, 1978.

Ruffin, Elena. *Il ballo teatrale a Venezia nel secolo XIX*. La Danza Italiana, nos. 5–6 (Autumn 1987), pp. 151–179.

———. "Il ruolo del ballo nelle vicende del romanticismo a Venezia." *La Danza Italiana*, nos. 8–9 (Winter 1990), pp. 27–46.

Saint-Léon, Arthur. *De l'Etat actuel de la danse*. Lisbon, 1856.

———. *Letters from a Ballet Master. The Correspondence of Arthur Saint-Léon*. Ed. and trans. Ivor Guest. New York: Dance Horizons, 1981.

———. *La Sténochorégraphie*. Paris, 1852.

Sasportes, José. "La Danza (1737–1900)." In Raffaele Ajello et al., *Il Teatro di San Carlo*. Naples: Guida, 1987, pp. 367–396.

———, ed. *Balli teatrali a Venezia (1746–1859)*. With a chronology by Elena Ruffin and Giovanna Trentin. Milan: Ricordi, 1994.

———, ed. *La Danza Italiana*, nos. 8–9 (Winter 1990). Special issue on the romantic ballet in Italy.

Scafidi, Nadia. "La danza nelle istituzioni scolastiche governative nell'Italia dell'Ottocento." Pt. 1. *Chorégraphie*, no. 3 (Spring 1994), pp. 75–90. Pt. 2 ("Il Maestro"). Chorégraphie, no. 4 (Autumn 1994), pp. 27–48.

———. "La Scuola di ballo del Teatro alla Scala: l'ordinamento legislativo e didattico nel XIX secolo." Pt. 1. *Chorégraphie*, no. 7 (Spring 1996), pp. 51–72. Pt. 2 ("L'Allievo"). *Chorégraphie,* no. 8 (Autumn 1996), pp. 27–48.

Second, Albéric. *Les Petits Mystères de l'Opéra*. Paris: Kugelman, 1844.

Slonimsky, Yury. "Jules Perrot." Trans. Anatole Chujoy. *Dance Index*, 4, no. 12 (Dec. 1945), pp. 208–225.

Smith, Albert. *The Natural History of the Ballet Girl*. London, 1847; . London: Dance Books, 1996.

Smith, Marian. "What Killed Giselle?" *Dance Chronicle*, 13, no. 1 (1990), pp. 68–81.

Solomon-Godeau, Abigail. "The Legs of the Countess." *October,* 39 (Winter 1986), pp. 65–108.

Sorell, Walter. *Dance in Its Time: The Emergence of an Art Form*. Garden City, N.Y.: Anchor Press/Doubleday, 1981.

Souritz, Elizabeth. "Carlo Blasis in Russia (1861–1864)." *Studies in Dance History*, 4, no. 2 (Fall 1993).

Sowell, Debra H. "Virtue (almost) Triumphant" Revisited: Of Sylphs and Silfidi." *Dance Chronicle*, 18, no. 2 (1995), pp. 293–301.

Sticklor, Susan Reimer. "Angel with a Past." *Dance Perspectives*, no. 61 (Spring 1975), pp. 18–29.

Testa, Alberto. *Due secoli di ballo alla Scala 1778–1975*. Milan: G. Ferrari, 1975.

———. "Cronologia dei balli, 1740–1936." In *Storia del Teatro Regio di Torino*. Vol. 5. Ed. Alberto Basso. Turin: CRT, 1988, pp. 313–453.

———. *I grandi balletti*. Rome: Gremese, 1991.

Théleur, E.A. *Letters on Dancing*. London, 1831; rpt., with introd. by Sandra N. Hammond, *Studies in Dance History*, 2, no. 1 (Fall/Winter, 1990).

Tintori, Giampiero. *Duecento anni di Teatro alla Scala. Cronologia opere-balletti-concerti 1778–1977*. Bergamo: Grafica Gutenberg, 1979.

Vaillat, Léandre. *La Taglioni, ou la Vie d'une danseuse*. Paris: Albin Michel, 1942.

Véron, Louis-Désiré (Dr.). *Mémoires d'un Bourgeois de Paris*. Paris: Guy le Prat, 1945.

Wiley, Roland John, ed. and trans. *A Century of Russian Ballet: Documents and Eye-witness Accounts, 1810–1910*. Oxford: Oxford University Press, 1990.

———, ed. and trans. "Images of *La Sylphide*: Two Accounts by a Contemporary Witness of Marie Taglioni's Appearances in St. Petersburg." *Dance Research*, 13, no. 1 (Summer 1995), pp. 21–32.

Winter, Marian Hannah. "Augusta Maywood." In *Chronicles of the American Dance: From the Shakers to Martha Graham*. Ed. Paul Magriel. 2nd ed. New York: Da Capo, 1978, pp. 118–137.

———. *The Pre-Romantic Ballet*. London: Pitman, 1974.

Zambon, Rita. "Alla riscoperta di Giovanni Galzerani." Pt. 1 ("L'interprete"). *Chorégraphie*, no. 5 (Spring 1995), pp. 35–45. Pt. 2 ("Il coreografo"). *Chorégraphie*, no. 6 (Autumn 1995), pp. 67–90.

———."Quando il ballo anticipa l'opera: 'Il Corsaro' di Giovanni Galzerani." In *Creature di Prometeo. Il ballo teatrale dal divertimento al dramma. Studi offerti a Aurel M. Milloss*. Ed. Giovanni Morelli. Florence, 1996.

———. "'Sulle traccie dell'immortale Astigiano': influenze alfieriane nei libretti di danza della prima metà dell'Ottocento." *Chorégraphie*, no. 2 (Autumn 1993), pp. 73–84.

MUSIC

MARIAN SMITH

Adam, Adolphe. *Derniers souvenirs d'un musicien*. Paris: Michel Lévy, 1859.

———. *Souvenirs d'un musicien, précédés de notes biographiques écrites par lui-même*. Paris: Michel Lévy, 1857.

———. "Lettres d'Adolphe Adam." *La Revue de Paris*, 10, no. 15 (Aug. 1903).

Arvey, Verna. *Choreographic Music: Music for the Dance*. New York: Dutton, 1941.

Baron, A. *Lettres et entretiens sur la danse*. Paris: Dondey-Dupré, 1824.

Castil-Blaze [François-Henri-Joseph Blaze]. *Dictionnaire de musique moderne*. 2 vols. Paris: Magasin de Musique de la Lyre Moderne, 1821.

———. *L'Académie impériale de musique: histoire littéraire, musicale…politique et galant de ce théâtre, de 1645 à 1855*. 2 vols. Paris: Castil-Blaze, 1855.

Chouquet, Gustave. *Histoire de la musique dramatique en France*. Paris: Librairie Firmin Didot, 1873.

Clark, Maribeth. "Understanding French Grand Opera Through Dance." Ph.D. diss., University of Pennsylvania, forthcoming.

Cohen, H. Robert, and Marie-Odile Gigou. *Cent ans de mise en scène lyrique en France (env. 1830–1930).* New York: Pendragon, 1986.

Conati, Marcello. "Ballabili nei 'Vespri.' Con alcune osservazioni su Verdi e la musica popolare." *Studi verdiani*, 1 (1982), pp. 21–46.

Day, David A. "Early Romantic Ballet in Brussels, 1816–1830." Ph.D. diss., New York University, forthcoming.

Escudier, Léon and Marie. *Dictionnaire de musique théorique et historique.* 5th ed. Paris, 1872.

Evans, Edwin. *Music and the Dance for Lovers of the Ballet.* London: H. Jenkins, 1948.

Fétis, François-Joseph. *Biographie universelle des musiciens.* 8 vols. 1835–1844; rpt. Brussels: Culture et Civilisation, 1963.

Fiske, Roger. *Ballet Music.* London: George G. Harrap, 1958.

Guest, Ivor. "Cesare Pugni: A Plea for Justice." *Dance Research*, 1, no. 1 (Spring 1983), pp. 30–38.

―――, and John Lanchbery. "The Scores of 'La Fille Mal Gardée.'" Pt. 1: "The Original Music." Pt. 2: "Hérold's Score." Pt. 3: "The Royal Ballet's Score." *Theatre Research/Recherches Théâtrales*, 3, no. 1 (1961), pp. 32–42; 3, no. 2 (1961), pp. 121–134; 3, no. 3 (1961), pp. 191–204.

Hansell, Kathleen Kuzmick. "Opera and Ballet at the Regio Teatro of Milan, 1771–1776: A Musical and Social History." Ph.D. diss., University of California at Berkeley, 1980.

―――. Il ballo teatrale e l'opera italiana." Trans. Lorenzo Bianconi and Angelo Bozzo. In S*toria dell'opera italiana.* Ed. Lorenzo Bianconi and Giorgio Pestelli. Vol. 5. Turin: EDT, 1988, pp. 175–306.

Jordan, Stephanie. "The Role of the Ballet Composer at the Paris Opéra: 1820–1850." *Dance Chronicle*, 4, no. 4 (1982), pp. 374–388.

Jouvin, Benoît. *Hérold: sa vie et ses oeuvres.* Paris: Heugel, 1868.

Jürgensen, Knud Arne. *The Verdi Ballets.* Parma: Istituto Nazionale di Studi Verdiani, 1995.

―――. *The Bournonville Heritage.* London: Dance Books, 1990.

―――. "Reconstructing La Cracovienne." *Dance Chronicle*, 6, no. 3 (1983), pp. 228–266.

Kahane, Martine. "La danza nelle versioni parigine delle opere di Verdi." *La Danza Italiana*, 1 (Autumn 1984), pp. 43–60.

Lichtenthal, Peter. *Dictionnaire de Musique.* Trans. Dominique Mondo. 2 vols. Paris: Troupenas, 1839.

Lifar, Serge. *La Musique par la danse de Lulli à Prokofiev.* Paris: R. Laffont, 1955.

Nettl, Paul. *The Dance in Classical Music.* New York: Philosophical Library, 1963.

―――. *The Story of Dance Music.* New York: Philosophical Library, 1947.

Pendle, Karin. *Eugène Scribe and the French Opera of the Nineteenth Century.* Ann Arbor, Mich.: UMI Research Press, 1979.

Pougin, Arthur. *Adolphe Adam: sa vie, sa carrière, ses mémoires artistiques.* Paris: Charpentier, 1877.

―――. *Hérold: biographie, critique.* Paris: Librairie Renourd, n.d.

Porter, Andrew. "Verdi's Ballet Music and 'La Pérégrina.'" In *Atti del II Congresso Internazionale di Studi Verdiani*, pp. 355–367. Parma: Instituto di Studi Verdiani, 1971.

Searle, Humphrey. *Ballet Music: An Introduction.* Rev. ed. New York: Dover, 1973.

Smith, Marian. "Music for the Ballet-Pantomime at the Paris Opéra, 1825–1850." Ph.D. diss., Yale University, 1988.

―――. "Borrowings and Original Music: A Dilemma for the Ballet-Pantomime Composer." *Dance Research*, 6, no. 2 (Autumn 1988), pp. 3–29.

———. "'Poésie lyrique' and 'Chorégraphie' at the Opéra in the July Monarchy." *Cambridge Opera Journal*, 4, no. 1 (March 1992), pp. 1–19.

———. "Staging Practices at the Paris Opéra: The Operatic Livrets de mise en scène and the Ballet Pantomime." In *La Realizzazione Scenica dello Spettacolo Verdiano*, ed. Pierluigi Petroballi. Parma: Verdi Institute, in press.

Studwell, William E. "The Choreographic Chain: Seventy Years of Ballet Music." *Dance Scope*, 10, no. 2 (Spring/Summer 1976), pp. 51–55.

Recommended Reading on Related Topics

Allanbrook, Wye. *Rhythmic Gesture in Mozart: Le Nozze di Figaro and Don Giovanni.* Chicago: University of Chicago Press, 1984.

Bartlet, M. Elizabeth C. "Etienne Nicolas Méhul and Opera During the French Revolution, Consulate, and Empire." Ph.D. diss., University of Chicago, 1982.

Becker, Heinz. "Opern-Pasticcio und Parodie-Oper." In *Musicae scientae collectanea: Festschrift Gustav Fellerer zum siebigsten Geburstag*, pp. 40–46. Cologne: Arna Volk Verlag, 1973.

Bloom, Peter. "François-Joseph Fétis and the *Revue Musicale* (1827–1835)." Ph.D. diss., University of Pennsylvnia, 1972.

———, ed. *Music in Paris in the Eighteen-Thirties.* Vol. 4, *Musical Life in Nineteenth-Century France.* Stuyvesant, N.Y.: Pendragon, 1987.

Brown, Bruce Alan. *Gluck and the French Theatre in Vienna.* New York: Oxford University Press, 1991.

Abbate, Carolyn, and Roger Parker. *Analyzing Opera: Wagner and Verdi.* Berkeley: University of California Press, 1989.

Cagli, Bruno, and Agostino Zino, eds. *Il Teatro di San Carlo di Napoli (1737–1987).* Vol. 2. Naples: Electa, 1987.

Carlson, Marvin. "*Hernani*'s Revolt from the Tradition of French Stage Composition." *Theatre Survey*, 13, no. 1 (1972), pp. 1–27.

Cohen, Robert H. "Berlioz on the Opera, 1829–1849: A Study of Music Criticism." Ph.D. diss., New York University, 1973.

Comettant, Oscar. *Musique et Musiciens.* Paris: Pagnerre, 1862.

Crosten, William. *French Grand Opera: An Art and a Business.* New York: King's Crown Press, 1948.

Dahlhaus, Carl. *Nineteenth-Century Music.* Trans. J. Bradford Robinson. Berkeley: University of California Press, 1989.

———, ed. *Studien zur Trivialmusik des 19.Jahrhunderts.* Vol. 8, *Studien zur Musikgeschichte des 19.Jahrhunderts.* Regensburg: Gustav Bosse Verlag, 1967.

Della Seta, Fabrizio. "Il librettista." In *Storia dell'Opera Italiana.* Vol. 4. Ed. Lorenzo Bianconi and Giorgio Pestelli. Turin: EDT, 1987, pp. 231–291.

Dent, Edward J. *The Rise of Romantic Opera.* Ed. Winton Dean. Cambridge/New York: Cambridge University Press, 1976.

Dorris, George. "Once More to the Lake." *Ballet Review*, 6, no. 4 (1977–1978), pp. 99–108.

Dunn, Thomas D. "Delibes and 'La Source': Some Manuscripts and Documents." *Dance Chronicle*, 4, no. 1 (1981), pp. 1–13.

Evns, Edwin. "Choreography and Polyphony." *The Dancing Times*, Nov. 1942, pp. 53–54.

Fulcher, Jane F. *The Nation's Image: French Grand Opera as Politics and Politicized Art.* Cambridge/New York: Cambridge University Press, 1987.

Gerhard, Anselm. *Die Verstüdterung der Oper: Paris und das Musiktheater des 19.Janrhunderts.* Stuttgart: J.B. Metzler, 1992.

Gossett, Philip. "Verdi, Ghislanzoni, and Aida: The Uses of Convention." *Critical Inquiry*, 1 (1974), pp. 291–334.

Jordan, Stephanie. "Dance and Music: Partners in Reconstruction." *The Choreologist*, 45 (1993–1994), pp. 25–29.

———. "Ballet Imperial." *Dance Now*, 2, no. 4 (1993–1994), pp. 28–37.

———. "Music Puts a Time Corset on the Dance." *Dance Chronicle*, 16, no. 3 (1993), pp. 295–321.

Leo, Sophie. "Music Life in Paris (1817–1848): A Chapter from the Memoirs of Sophie Augustine Leo." *The Musical Quarterly*, 17, no. 2 (1931), pp. 259–271; 17, no. 3 (1931), pp. 389–403.

Locke, Ralph. "Constructing the Oriental 'Other': Saint-Saens's Samson et Dalila." *Cambridge Opera Journal*, 3, no. 3 (1991), pp. 261–302.

Petrobelli, Pierluigi. *Music in the Theater*. Princeton, N.J.: Princeton University Press, 1994.

Powers, Harold. "'La solita forma' and 'The Uses of Convention.'" *Acta Musicologica*, 59 (1987), pp. 65–90.

Rosselli, John. *L'impresario d'opera*. Turin: EDT, 1985.

———. "Il sistema produttivo, 1780–1880." In *Storia dell'opera italiana*. Vol. 4. Ed. Lorenzo Bianconi and Giorgio Pestelli. Turin: EDT, 1987, pp. 77–165.

Sala, Emilio. *L'Opera senza canto. Il melo romantico e l'invenzione della colonna sonora*. Venice: Marsilio, 1995.

Studwell, William E. *Adolphe Adam and Léo Delibes: A Guide to Research*. Garland Composer Resource Manuals. Vol. 5. New York: Garland, 1987.

Wiley, Roland John. *Tchaikovsky's Ballets*. Oxford: Oxford University Press, 1985.

———. "Jean-Georges Noverre: The Music of 'Iphigénie en Aulide.'" *Harvard Library Bulletin—Bits and Pieces: Music for the Theatre*, 4 (Winter 1991), pp. 31–53.

LISA C. ARKIN has directed three dance companies, including the Khadra International Folk Ballet in San Francisco, and created commissioned works in the character idiom for companies in Seattle, Minneapolis, Portland, Tucson, and New Orleans. Her research in nineteenth and early twentieth-century dance history has been published in *Dance Research Journal* and *Dance Chronicle*.

SALLY BANES is the Marian Hannah Winter Professor of Theatre and Dance History at the Unviersity of Wisconsin-Madison. The author of several books, including *Terpsichore in Sneakers: Post-Modern Dance* and *Writing Dancing in the Age of Postmodernism*, she is currently writing *Dancing Women: Female Bodies Onstage*, to be published by Routledge.

JODY BRUNER completed her M.F.A. in Dance at Toronto's York University in 1993 with a Major Research Paper entitled "Narrative Theory: An Annotated Bibliography for Dance Researchers." At present she is pursuing graduate study at York in the English Department, with an emphasis on the links between literary theory, criticism, and dance.

NOËL CARROLL is the Monroe C. Beardsley Professor of the Philosophy of Art at the University of Wisconsin-Madison. His most recent book, *Prolegomena to the Philosophy of Mass Art*, is forthcoming from Oxford University Press.

LAVINIA CAVALLETTI studied dance with Attilia Radice at the Rome Opera. A former journalist with a degree in political science and a contributor to *La Danza Italiana*, she is completing an M.A. in Portuguese Medieval History at the Universidade Nova, Lisbon.

CLAUDIA CELI teaches dance history at the Accademia Nazionale di Danza in Rome and is a member of the Renaissance Dance Group directed by Barbara Sparti. A contributor to the *International Encyclopedia of Dance*, *La Danza Italiana*, *Chorégraphie*, and *Cairón* and author of the chapters on nineteenth-century Italian ballet in *Musica in Scena: Storia dello Spettacolo Musicale*, she is at work on a catalogue of nineteenth-century Italian ballet libretti.

JOHN V. CHAPMAN dances, reviews dance, and writes on ballet history in Santa Barbara where he is an Associate Professor at the University of California. A former editor of *Studies in Dance History*, he has published in *Dance Chronicle* and other journals. He has served as an education officer of the Royal Ballet and a panel member of the Arts Council of Great Britain.

JUDITH CHAZIN-BENNAHUM, Professor of Theatre and Dance at the University of New Mexico, is a former member of the Metropolitan Opera Ballet Company. She is the author of *Dance in the Shadow of the Guillotine* and *The Ballets of Antony Tudor: Studies in Psyche and Satire*.

LYNN GARAFOLA has edited the series "Studies in Dance History" since 1991. She is the author of *Diaghilev's Ballets Russes*, editor and translator of *Petipa's Diaries*, and coeditor of *André Levinson on Dance: Writings from Paris in the Twenties*. A senior editor of *Dance Magazine*, she has published criticism, book reviews, and historical essays in numerous periodicals, including *The Nation*, *Ballet Review* and *Experiment*. She holds a Ph.D. in Comparative Literature.

JOELLEN A. MEGLIN is Associate Professor at Temple University and reviews editor of *Dance Research Journal*. She has published in *Dance Chronicle* and *Kinesiology and Medicine for Dance*, and presented her research on gender representations in eighteenth and nineteenth-century French ballet at numerous conferences and seminars throughout the United States and in Japan.

GIANNANDREA POESIO, a Lecturer in the Department of Dance Studies, Roehampton Institute, London, holds a Ph.D. in Dance History from the University of Surrey. A regular contributor to *The Dancing Times* and the dance critic for *The Spectator*, he is working on a book about Enrico Cecchetti.

JANINA PUDELEK received her doctorate from Warsaw University in 1968 with a thesis on the romantic ballet in Warsaw. In 1981, she published *A Short History of Ballet* and a history of the Warsaw ballet from 1865–1915 and, with Pawel Chynowski, wrote *An Almanach of 200 Years of the Warsaw Ballet, 1785–1985*. Translations of her articles have appeared in *Dance Chronicle*.

MARIAN SMITH is Associate Professor and Chair of Musicology at the University of Oregon. Here research on nineteenth-century ballet and opera has appeared in dance history and musicology journals, including *Dance Chronicle* and *The Cambridge Opera Journal*.

Abbate, Carolyn, 68
abjection, 110, 113
About, E., 166, 179
Abramowicz, General, 145–46
abstract ballet, 52–53
Accademia della Danza
  (Florence), 140
Academy of Dance (Milan), 158
Acocella, Joan, 67
action scenes, 20–22, 53
Adair, Christy, 119
Adam, Adolphe, 24–25, 46, 49,
  66, 229, 233, 249, 250, 253
Adami, Heinrich, 16
Adelaide di Francia (Adelaide of
  France), 175, 253
Adina, 177, 256
Adler, Mlle., 151
aesthetics, 128, 198, 200, 204
Afghani, Gli (The Afghans), 255
Agulhon, Maurice, 70, 71, 86
Aida, 8, 63
Ajeilo, Raffaele, 194
Aladin, ou la Lampe merveilleuse,
  127, 128
Albert, Mons. (stage name of
  François Descombe), 59, 199,
  218, 245, 250
aldeana (dance) 169, 251
Alderson, Evan, 119
Alfredo, 192
Ali Pascià di Delvino (Ali Pasha
  of Delvine), 255
allemande, 245, 249, 250
Allen, James Smith, 57
Alma, 45, 65, 94
Alma, ou la Fille de feu (also
  known as *Alma ossia la figlia
  del fuoco* [Alma, or The
  Daughter of Fire]), 170–71, 253
Amore alla prova (Love to the
  Test), 191, 195
Amore e Psiche (Cupid and
  Psyche), 191

Amori campestri, Gli (Rustic
  Loves), 177, 178, 257
Amour à Cythère, L', 227
Angiolini, Gasparo, 131, 134, 140
anglaise (dance) 17, 249
Anna Bolena, 133
Anneau magique, L', 125
Antonijevic, Aleksandar, 118
Apollo Theater (Rome), 167, 168,
  170, 172, 176, 177, 178
Applewhite, Harriet Branson, 88
Arab, 3
Arianna e Bacco (Ariadne and
  Bacchus), 254
Arkin, Lisa C., 3, 11–68, 245–52,
  275
Arnaud, Baculard d', 127
art for art's sake (*l'art pour l'art*),
  199, 202, 203, 218
Aschengreen, Erik, 86, 100, 102,
  103, 104, 105
Assedio di Leyda, L' (The Siege of
  Leyden), 192
Astolfi, Fanny Mazzarelli, 256
Astolfi, Luigi, 172, 256
Atalanta ed Ippomene (Atalanta
  and Hippomenes), 184, 186,
  188–89
Atide e Cloé (Attis and Chloe),
  194
Au, Susan, 88, 103
Auber, Daniel-François-Esprit,
  175, 245, 249
audiences, 6, 8, 13, 16, 17, 20–22,
  26, 39, 48, 53, 56, 68, 91, 107,
  159, 200, 206, 213, 221, 225–26;
  French, 6, 70; Italian, 5, 167,
  182, 186, 192–93, 195–96
August, Mons., 34
Augusta, Mlle (stage name of
  Caroline Fuchs), 222–24
Aumer, Jean, 87, 225, 241, 245, 249
authenticity, 3, 6, 13, 23, 26–28,
  30–44, 124, 127

autoeroticism, 116

Bacchus et Ariadne, 124
Bacco in Erepoli (Bacchus in
  Erepolis), 184, 186
bailadera. See bayadères
Baillot, Pierre-Marie-François de
  Salles, 240, 241
Bajetti, Giovanni, 253
Balanchine, George, 3, 55
balladeiras, 37. *See also*
  bayadères, *devadasis*
balladue alla francese, 136.
ballerina, 2–3, 4, 5, 8, 202–03, 206
Ballerina in viaggio, La (The
  Traveling Dancer), 256
ballerino, 31
ballet, feminization of, 7; and
  politics, 176; and opera, 179
ballet blanc, 4, 12, 13, 52, 53, 174;
  and national dance, 45–51
ballet d'action, 131, 139, 197,
  198–201, 221, 222. *See also*
  action scenes
ballet dancers (Warsaw), 143–50
ballet-pantomimes. *See* narrative
  ballet
Ballets Russes, 8, 9
ballet school (Warsaw), 143–52
ballo, 5, 131–41
ballroom dancing, 152
Bal sous Louis XIV, Un, 42
Balzac, Honoré de, 121–22, 130
bamboo dance, 251, 252
Bancroft, George, 33
Banes, Sally, 7, 91–105, 275
Baratti, Filippo, 173
Barbaja, Domenico, 183,
  184–187, 190, 194
Barbier, Auguste, 87
Barbiere di Seviglia, Il (The
  Barber of Seville), 184, 185
Barker, Barbara, 10

Barnard, Frederick M., 57
Barre, Jean-Auguste, 216
Bartered Bride, The, 11
Barthes, Roland, 115, 120
Bartlet, M. Elizabeth C., 61
Bartoccini, Fiorella, 179
Barton, Richard, 137
Baryshnikov, Mikhail, 55, 56
Barzel, Ann, 10
Battaglia di Legnano, La (The Battle of Legnano), 175
Bayadère, La, 56, 139, 223
Bayadères, Les, 225
bayadères, 24, 35, 48, 61, 129, 210, 222, 250
Beaucé, V., 94–98
Beaumont, Cyril W., 58, 86, 109, 119
Beautés de l'Opéra, Les, 237
Beecher, Jonathan, 89
bee dance (*pas d'abeille*), 27, 62, 250
Bell, Susan Groag, 90
Belli, Giuseppe Giachino, 168, 170, 177–78, 179
Beniowsky, 249
Benoit, François, 249, 251
Beretta, Caterina, 156
Berri, Giovanni, 141
Berthélémy, Jean-Simon, 122
Betty, 6
Bianca de Nevers, 6, 9
Bianconi, Lorenzo, 179
Bigottini, Emilie, 126, 127, 128, 198, 220, 224
Binney, Edward, III, 59, 251
Birichino di Parigi, Il (The Urchin of Paris), 173, 177, 256
Bizos, Karolina, 144, 149
Blanche, M., 205
Bland, Alexander, 67
Blasis, Annunziata Ramaccini, 176
Blasis, Carlo, 5, 31–37, 41, 59, 63, 64, 131–41, 176
bled, Victor de, 60
Blessington, Lady, 125
Bobrowska, 147
Bocharov, Alexander, 67
Bochsa, Nicholas Charles, 249
Boemondo, 256
Boffo, Professor, 187
Bogdanova, Nadezhda, 160
Bogdonovich, Elena, 63
Bogusławski, Stanisław, 148

Bohémienne de Paris, La, 205
Boigne, Charles de, 40, 64
bolero (Andalusian dance), 6, 15, 17, 20, 31, 35, 47, 245, 247, 249, 250, 251
Bolshoi Theater (St. Petersburg), 251
Bonfanti, Maria, 10
Bonne Bouche, 247
Borri, Pasquale, 138, 139
Boschetti, Amina, 193
bouffante, 214, 215, 217
Boulogne, Jean, 136
Bournonville, August, 5, 9, 29, 34–44, 54, 60, 63, 92–93, 103–05, 181, 183, 193–94, 197, 204, 230
Bouvier, Joseph, 236, 247
Brahma, 139, 141
Brandes, Edvard, 105
Brandt, Adam, 148
Brennan, Mary A., 102
Brézilia, ou la Tribu des femmes, 26, 70, 86, 221, 224
Bridenthal, Renate, 88
Briol, Giovanni, 188, 195
Britannicus, 213, 218, 223
Brocard, Caroline, 127
Brown, Marilyn R., 74, 87
Brugnoli, Amalia, 123, 125, 194, 195
Bruhn, Erik, 63, 193, 204
Bruner, Jody, 7, 107–20, 275
Buck, Adam, 122
Budzyński, Konstanty, 147
Buffon, Georges-Louis Leclerc, 209, 212
burlesque, 83–84
Burt, Ramsay, 140
Bussola, Maria Luigia, 256
Bustini, Alessandro, 253
Byron, Lord, 175

C. (critic), 198–99, 201, 205
cachucha, 6, 12, 13, 14, 16–17, 20, 30, 40, 59, 65, 67, 153, 220, 247, 249, 250, 251; double, 40–41, 46, 50
Calabi, Carolina, 256
Callot, Jacques, 211, 212
Calzolaio, Il (The Shoemaker), 187
Camargo Society, 9
Cambiasi, Pompeo, 141

Cametti, Alberto, 170, 177, 199
Camille, Mme., 38–39
Campi, Giovanni, 255
Camprubí, Mariano, 19, 30, 34
cancan, 59
Canova, Angelo, 136, 137, 140
Canova, Antonio, 134
Carafa, Michele, 249
Carey, Edouard (Edoardo), 205, 255
Carignano, Duke, 187
Carlo di Ravenstein (Charles of Ravenstein), 192
Carlson, Marvin, 62
Carlyle, Thomas, 130
Carmen, 35
Carnaval de Venise, Le, 127, 247
Carnevals Abenteuer in Paris, 159
Caroline, Angelique and Sophie, 90, 129
Carrieri, Raffaele, 139, 185
Carroll, Noel, 7, 91–105, 275
Casa disabitata, La (The Deserted House), 184, 187
Casati, Giovanni, 176, 177
Case, Sue Ellen, 111, 120
Castil-Blaze (François-Henri-Joseph Blaze), 21, 128
Castore e Polluce (Castor and Pollux), 188
Caterina, ou la Fille du Bandit, 5, 6, 65, 68, 88, 174, 175, 250
Caterina degli Abruzzi (Catherine of the Abruzzi), 5, 174, 175, 254
Catte, Orsolina, 253
Cavaggi, Tommassina, 256
Cavalieri, Pia, 178, 257
Cavalletti, Lavinia, 5, 181–96, 259–61, 275
Cecchetti, Cesare, 173
Cecchetti, Enrico, 7, 140, 173, 255
Cecchetti, Serafina (*née* Casagli), 173
Cellarius, Henri, 19, 38, 58, 59, 252
Celi, Claudia, 5, 9, 165–80, 253–57, 275
censorship, 107, 110, 191; in Rome, 167, 174–75
Cerrito, Fanny, 37–42, 46, 61, 65, 68, 138, 165, 168–71, 201–02, 205, 247, 250, 251, 253
Chaffee, George, 1, 9, 129, 130

Challamel, Pierre Joseph, 239
Chalon, Alfred E., 93
Chapman, John, 5, 57, 67, 88, 89, 197–241, 275
Chapuy, Alfred, 156
character dance, 11–68, 158; definition, 57. *See also* national dance
Charianov, Olga, 149
Chazin-Bennahum, Judith, 3, 86, 102, 121–30, 275
Cherrier, Adelaide, 253
chibouk (dance), 250. *See also* pas de Chibouque
Chinese dance, 251
Chojecki, Edmund, 146
Cholewicka, Helena, 148
Cholewicki, Józef, 148
Cholewicki, Maria (*née* Wojciechowska), 148
Chopin, Frédéric, 154–55, 162
choreographers, 8, 29, 165, 170, 175–77, 179
choreography, 22, 92, 132, 134–35, 139; character, 26, 55, 131; in *La Sylphide*, 95–102; swimming, 194
Chorley, Henry, 42, 65
Christianity, 70, 72
Christine-Sophie, 89
Ciacchi, Monsignor Luigi, 167
Ciceri, Pierre-Luc Charles, 23, 61, 233, 241
Cieplinski, Jan, 60
Circonstances embarrassantes, Les, 75
Cito, Marchese, 187
Clari, ou la Promesse de mariage, 127
Clark, Robert T., Jr., 63
class struggle, 80, 84
classical dance, 30, 37, 42, 46
classicism, 11, 28, 132–34, 137–38
Clerici, Rosina, 255
Clerico, Francesco, 184
Clotilde di Pomerania (Clothilde of Pomerania), 256
Cohen, Marshall, 67
Cohen, Selma Jeanne, 103
Collignon, Jules, 94–98
colonialism, 3, 54, 189–90
La Colonie, 75
comic roles, 31
composers, 24–26
Condillac, Etienne de, 206, 211

Conquista di Malacca. See I Portoghese nelle Indie
Conte della Gherardesca, Il, 254
Conte Pini, Il (Count Pini), 255
contredanse, 17, 18
Cook, Susan, 102
Copeland, Roger, 67
Coppini, Antonio, 172, 175, 177, 253, 256
Coppini, Carolina, 255
copyright, 45, 171
Cora, 186
Coralli, Eugenio, 58, 211, 254
Coralli, Jean, 9, 233, 245, 249, 250, 251, 254
Corea Theater (Rome), 168
coreodramma, 131, 132, 135, 140
Corisandre, 124
Corneille, Pierre, 135, 140, 200, 222, 224
corps de ballet, 14, 82, 181, 216
Corsaro, Il (Le Corsaire), 175, 176, 251, 254
Cortesi, Antonio, 5, 171, 172, 174, 254, 255
coryphées, 15, 18, 144, 145, 148. *See also* corps de ballet
Cossack dance, 17, 31
Costa, Davide, 193
costumes, 2, 15, 74, 78, 123–24, 129, 167, 185, 203–04, 209; and fashions, 121–29; androgynous, 76, 77; national or character, 15–17, 34, 46, 50–51, 59, 73, 127–28, 133. *See also* authenticity
Coulon, Jean-François, 154, 157, 184
Count of Monte Cristo, The, 158
courtesans, 77, 83, 116–17. *See also* harem
cracovienne, 17, 38, 47, 65, 155, 247–50
Cracow Wedding, 6, 149, 161
Cristina di Svezia (Christina of Sweden), 190, 195
critics, 15, 22, 34, 38–44, 47–48, 58, 61, 94, 155–56, 158, 172, 176, 197–241. *See also* Gautier, Théophile, and Janin, Jules
Croci, Ferdinando, 257
cross-dressing, 4–5, 76, 83
Crosten, William, 61
Cruikshank, Isaac, 121

Cucchi, Claudina, 134, 138, 139, 140, 158
czardas, 4, 34

Daguerre, Louis-Jacques-Mandé, 61
Dahlhaus, Carl, 61
Daly, Ann, 119
Damoreau, Laure-Cinthe Montrelant, 222, 224
Damse, Filipina, 143, 147
Damse, Józef, 143, 154, 155
Damse, Konstancja, 151
dance halls (Paris) 123
dancers, female, 137, 139; social origins of, 143, 144. *See also* specific dancers
Danilova, Alexandra, 55
danse d'école, 4, 15, 16, 20, 29, 52, 54–55, 132, 133, 135, 184. *See also* classical dance, classicism
danse noble, 213, 215, 216, 221, 222
danseur noble, 4–5, 7, 30, 213, 214, 216. *See also* male dancer
danseuse noble, 213–14
danseuse en travesti (travesty dancer), 6. *See also* cross-dressing
Dansomanie, La, 123, 154
Danza Italiana, La, 179, 193
Dauberval, Jean, 139
Daumier, Honoré, 215, 223
David, Jacques-Louis, 121
Day, David, 60
La dea Flora (The Goddess Flora), 256
DeAngelis, Alberto de, 179
Debray, (?), 144
Débucourt, P.L., 123
De Crescenzo, Luigi, 182, 184, 193–94
Degotti, Ignazio, 61
Delacroix, Eugène, 71
De l'Allemagne (known in English as *On Germany*), 46, 66, 108
Delaroche, Paul, 211, 212
Deldevez, Ernest, 250, 251
Delire d'un peinture, Le, 247
Demar, Claire, 90
De Mattia, (?), 187
demi-monde, 120. *See also* courtesans

Denantes (brothers), 184

Deroin, Jeanne (Jeanne-Victoire), 86

Descombes, François. *See* Albert, Mons.

Deshayes, André, 170–71, 249

Despréux, Jean-Etienne, 122

devadasis, 35, 41, 64. *See also* bayadères

Devéria, Achille, 216

Diable amoureux, Le, 13, 14, 22, 158, 241, 249

Diable à quatre, Le, 24–25, 27, 53, 153, 156, 158–59, 232, 250

Diable boiteux, Le, 20, 25, 40, 53, 54, 65, 67, 211, 220, 249

Diabrinha, A , 134

Diaghilev, Serge, 2, 8

Dianora de' Bardi (Dianora of the Bardi), 255

Didelot, Charles, 124, 241

Dieu et la Bayadère, Le, 127

divertissements, 4, 13, 15, 39, 60; character, 57, 62, 247–48; at public ball, 18–20

Dobrski, Jan, 150

Domagalski, Franciszek, 147

Don Giovanni, 13, 20, 27, 245, 246

Donizetti, Gaetano, 133, 245

Don Quisciotte (Don Quixote), 68, 192

Dorat, Claude-Joseph, 208, 212

Dorliska, 179

Doubrovska, Felia, 55

dress. *See* costumes

Dubinon, Manuela, 19, 246

Duca di Ravenna, Il (The Duke of Ravenna), 183, 194

Due forzati, Il (The Two Prisoners), 254

Due sorelle, Le (The Two Sisters), 256

Dumilâtre, Adèle, 214, 236, 238, 241

Duncan, Isadora, 119

Dupont, Mme. Alexis (*née* Félicité Noblet), 35, 202, 210, 212, 218, 229–30, 247

Duport, Louis, 60, 184

Duvernay, Pauline, 21, 77–78, 209, 212, 226–27

Dylewska, Matylda, 161

Dziennik Powszechny, 145

Ebuzio e Facenia ossia i baccanali (Ebuzio and Facenia, or The, Bacchanalia), 255

Eco e Narciso (Echo and Narcissus), 254

Edwige o il sogno (Hedwig, or The Dream), 191, 195

Egyptian dance, 37, 41–42, 245, 250

Eléments, Les, 44

Elie, Mme. (*née* Louise Launer), 73, 207, 212

Elizabetta (Elizabeth), 186

Elleviou, Baptiste François, 220, 224

Elsner, Józef, 154, 155, 162

Elssler, Fanny, 5–6, 15–16, 20–21, 26–28, 34–35, 38, 40, 42, 45–47, 54, 59, 61, 65, 67, 88, 139, 159, 165, 172–73, 180, 202, 212, 219–20, 223–24, 247–49, 253–54

Elssler, Thérèse, 219–20, 223–24, 247

Emma, 256

Enfant prodigue, L', 245, 246

Enfantin, Prosper, 69

Engel, Johann Jacob, 136, 140

Engels, Friedrich, 84, 90

Englund, Sorella, 104

Eoline, 3, 44–45, 60, 65, 250

eroticism, 74, 105, 111

Esmeralda, 6, 53, 65, 159, 163, 173–74, 250, 253

ethnic dances. *See* character dance, folk dances

Etoile de Messine, L', 139

Ettore Fieramosca (Hector Fieramosca), 191

Ewing, Elizabeth, 130

exoticism, 3–6, 67, 74, 189–90, 225. *See also* orientalism

Ezzelino sotto le mura di Bassano (Ezzelino Under the Walls of Bassano), 171, 253

Fajans, M., 151

Faleński, Felicjan, 147, 162

Famiglia svizzera, La (The Swiss Family), 255

fan dance, 250

Fanciulla dell'aria, La (The Maid of the Air) (also known as *La*

figlia dell'aria [The Daughter of the Air]), 256

fandango (Andalusia), 17–18, 20, 35, 249

farandole, 249, 251

Fasciotti, Amalia, 254

Faust, 65, 134–35, 173, 191, 207

Favorite, La, 13, 14, 245, 246

Fazio (Faust), 255

Feist, Ramon, 129

female, body, 75, 77, 127–28, 203–04; dancers, 137, 139; imagery, 6, 70–72, 204

feminism, 7, 69, 72, 77, 84–86, 119

Femme libra, La. See Tribune des Femmes

Ferdinand I (King of Naples), 181, 186

Ferdinand II (King of Naples), 181, 183

Ferrarini, Cesare, 255

Ferraris, Amalia, 140, 256

Festa campestre, La (The Rustic Festival), 254

Festa in maschera ossia l'ospedale dei pazzi, La (The Masquerade, or The Hospital for Madmen), 253

Fête de Mars, La, 204

Fête hongroise, La, 249

Fêtes ou les Jalousies du sérail, Les, 75

fetishism, 69, 77–78, 130

Fiancée, La , 245

Figlia dell'aria, La, 176

Figlio fuggitivo, Il (The Runaway Son), 175, 253

Filets de Vulcain, Les, 205

Fille du Danube, La, 22, 61, 65, 249

Fille du marbre, La, 22, 41, 61, 169, 205, 251

Fille Mal Gardée, La, 1, 9, 94, 157, 184, 204

Fiorina, 134

Fischer, Carlos, 129, 130

Fitzjames, Louise, 224, 225

Fitzjames, Nathalie, 192, 224–27, 229, 250

Flik e Flok, 9

Flore et Zéphyre, 129, 241

Fokine, Michel, 9, 54, 57

folk, 35, 92, 95; culture, 11; dances, 3, 13–15, 30–44, 57,

96–98, 101, 133; music, 15–16, 25. *See also* particular dances
folklore, 46, 51, 91, 108
Folletto a quattro o la capricciosa punita, Il (The Devil to Pay, or The Capricious Woman Punished), 254
Font, Francisco, 19
Font, La, 205
forlana, 245
Fortuna, Uranio, 245
Foster, Susan Leigh, 8, 10
"Four Seasons," "The," 18–19
Fouillade, Claude, 129
Fourrier, Charles, 79, 89
Foyer de la Danse, 82–83, 92
Francis I (King of Naples), 181
Francis II (King of Naples), 181
Free, Susan Trites, 120
Freischütz, Der, 46
Frejtag, Maria, 143, 148, 153, 156–57, 159–60, 163
Friedberg, (?), 160
Frölich, Katarzyna, 148
French style. *See* danse d'école
Fuchs, Alessandro, 193, 196
Fuchs, Caroline. *See* Augusta, Mlle.
Fuoco, Sofia, 41, 141, 256, 257
Furioso, Il (The Madman), 256

Galanterie parigine, Le, 140
Gallenberg, Count Robert von, 26, 185
Gallet, Sébastien, 75
Gallini, Giovanni-Andrea, 30, 63
galop delle barsagliere, 9
Galzerani, Giovanni, 175–76, 254
Garafola, Lynn, 1–10, 54, 57, 67, 87, 102, 275–76
Gardel, Pierre, 14, 30, 58, 123, 139, 184, 198
Garibaldi, Giuseppe, 181
Garnerey, Auguste, 127
Gautier, Théophile, 6, 9, 14–15, 21, 23, 26–27, 30, 35, 37, 39–40, 43–46, 48–49, 51, 60–63, 88, 91, 102–04, 108, 113, 128–31, 140–41, 199–202, 204–05, 218, 233, 240–41, 246, 250–52
Gavarni (pseud. of Sulpice-Guillaume Chevalier), 161
Gaveaux, Pierre, 226–27

Gazelda, 45, 251
gender, 4–6, 8, 76–79, 88, 92, 135–36. *See also danseur noble, danseuse noble*, female body, male dancer
genre (of ballet), allegorical, 183; anacreonic, 183, 194; comic, 183; heroic, 183; heroic-mythological, 188; historical, 5, 165, 183; historical-exotic, 189–90; historical-romantic, 190–91; mythological, 183, 191; mythological-historical, 183; romantic, 183
Geoffroy, Julien-Louis, 198–99, 201, 204–05
Gérard, Baron, 122
Gerdt, Pavel, 7
Germanic dances, 31, 39, 43, 46–47
Germeuil, Mons., 222
Gide, Casimir, 25, 249, 251, 254
Gide, Charles, 89
Gilbert Abbot à Beckett, 83, 89
Giller, Agaton, 146, 162
Gioberti, Vincenzo, 165
Giocoliera, La, 139, 141
Gioia, Gaetano, 176, 184–86
Giordano, Gloria, 179
Giorza, Paolo, 257
Giovanni da Procida (also known as *L'Isolano* [The Islander]), 175
Gipsy, La, 21–22, 28, 38, 42, 47, 60, 220, 241, 249, 252
Gisella o le Villi (Giselle, or The Wilis), 171, 173–74, 253
Giselle, 1, 3, 5–9, 11, 15, 21–22, 46–49, 51–53, 60–61, 66, 94, 107–20, 127, 139, 159–60, 172, 192, 201, 205, 211, 224, 233–41, 250, 252
Gitana, La, 12, 16, 28, 34, 44, 47, 50, 53, 59, 247, 249
Giuocatore, Il (The Gambler), 178, 257
Glasco, Kimberly, 111, 113, 118
Goethe, Johann Wolfgang von, 134–35
Goffman, Erving, 104
Gorsky, Alexander, 68
Goslee, Nancy Moore, 103
Gosselin, Louis-François, 156–58
Gossett, Philip, 63
Grahn, Lucile, 5, 15, 42, 138, 165,

174–75, 202, 229–30, 247, 250, 254
Grande Chaumière (school), 18, 59
Granzini, Carolina(?), 256
Grégoire, (?), 214, 218
Grekowski, Helena (*née* Szlancowska), 158
Grekowski, Mikołaj, 143, 153, 157
Grieg, Edvard, 11
Griffitts, Michael, 179
Grimm, Thomas, 104
Grisi, Carlotta, 15, 27, 46, 62, 138, 165, 172, 203, 205, 226–27, 232–33, 236–37, 239, 245, 247, 250, 254.
Grisi, Giuditta, 232
Grisi, Giulia, 170, 232
grotteschi, 4, 184. *See also* Italian dance
Guerra, Antonio, 187–88, 192, 195, 229, 247
Guerre de Jugurtha, La, 235
Guest, Ivor, 9–10, 23, 44–45, 54, 56–60, 65, 83, 89, 91, 102, 129, 174, 180, 194, 246–48
Guillaume Tell, 13–14, 23–24, 245
Guimard, Marie, 122
Guindorf, Reine (also known as Marie-Reine), 85, 90
Gundberga, 194
Gusman, Rosina, 255
Gustave III, 23, 219, 245, 246
Gutwirth, Madelyn, 86
Guy-Stéphan, Marie, 245, 247
gypsy dances, 13–14, 16, 245, 249, 250
Gyrowetz, Adalbert, 249

Hammond, Sandra Noll, 56, 65
Hansell, Kathleen Kuzmick, 170, 174, 179
Harding, Cathryn, 102
harem, 7, 67, 69, 71, 73–76, 79–84, 87, 129, 206, 210–11, 217
Hauke, Mons., 150
Heine, Heinrich, 44, 46, 66, 108, 119, 233–34, 241
Henley, Nancy M., 104
Henry, Louis (also known as Luigi), 135, 184, 187, 226–27

Herder, Johann Gottfried von, 11, 30, 32–34, 36, 57, 63
Hernani, 91, 133
Herold, Ferdinand, 9
Hertel, Peter Ludwig, 9
heterogeneity, 107–08, 119
Highland Fling, 96
Hindu dancing girls. *See* bayadères, *devadasis*, Indian dancers
Hindustan dance. *See* Indian dance
Hirszel, (?), 153
historiography, 12, 13, 45, 51–53
Hoeskick, Ferdynand, 155, 162
Hongroise (dance), 39
hornpipe dance, 248
Hubbe, Nikolaj, 104
Huckenpahler, Victoria, 87, 89
Hugo, Victor, 11, 44, 108, 133, 217
Huguenots, Les, 13–14, 230, 245, 246
Hungarian dance, 27, 248, 250
Hus, Pierre, 184

iconography, 1, 15, 16, 42–43, 62, 129
Ifigenia in Aulide (Iphigenia in Aulis), 195–96
Ile des pirates, L', 227
Ileria, 256
Illusioni di un pittore, Le (The Illusions of a Painter), 173, 253
Imperial Ballet (St. Petersburg), 7, 9, 162
Imperial Ballet Academy (La Scala), 138
impresario, 183–84. *See also* Barbaja, Domenico, and Jacovacci, Vincenzo
Indes galantes, Les, 75, 87
Indian dances, 37, 41–42, 48, 50.
Indian dancers, 60, 66, 189. *See also* bayadères, *devadasis*
Ines de Castro. *See Pietro di Portogallo*
Ingres, Jean-Auguste-Dominique, 74, 240, 241
internationalism, 1–2, 8, 11–68
Ippomene. *See Atalanta ed Ippomeme*
Isaura o la bellezza fatale (Isaura,

or The Fatal Beauty), 256
Isolano, L' (The Islander), 175, 254
Italian ballet, 131–41, 165–80, 184
Italian dance, 36, 37, 41
Ivanov, Lev, 9
Izzo, Filippo, 170–71, 253

Jacobs, Joseph, 103
Jacovacci, Vincenzo, 9, 167, 168
Jagielska, (?), 147
Janin, Jules, 5, 26–27, 46, 70, 86–87, 100, 155–56, 197–241, 246
Jasiński, Jan (Seweryn), 148–50, 156, 158
Jeppesen, Lis, 104
jig (Scottish), 24, 43, 46, 47, 249, 250, 251
Joan of Arc, 70, 86
Johnson, Mary Durham, 88
Jolie Fille de Gand, La, 20, 241, 250
Joly, Anténor, 246
Jones, Alan, 55, 56, 68
jouissance, 110, 118
Journal des Débats, Le, 197–98
Jovita, ou les Boucaniers, 251
Jowitt, Deborah, 53, 62, 67
Juive, La, 14, 24
July Monarchy, 1, 70
Jürgensen, Knud Arne, 54, 60, 194
Jurkiewicz, Eugenia, 163
Justament, H., 42, 65

Kain, Karen, 116,
Karska, Jozefa, 148
Kaya ou l'Amour voyageur, 45, 250
Kazmierzak, Janusz, 26, 62
Kchessinsky, Felix. *See* Krzesiński, Feliks
Kchessinska, Mathilde, 144, 162
Keet, Marina, 68
Kelly, Joan, 88
King, Giovannina, 175–76, 254, 255
Kleinbaum, Abby, 75, 87
Koegler, Horst, 67
Koonz, Claudia, 88
Kosicka, Jadwiga, 162
Koss, Eugenia, 144

Kossak, Juliusz, 150–51
Kowalska, Ludwika, 161
Kowalski, Mons., 150
krakowiak (dance), 26, 62
Kraszewski, Jozef Ignacty, 145, 162
Kristeva, Julia, 7, 107, 109–19
Kronstam, Henning, 104
Krzesińska, Maria, 143, 148
Krzesińska, Matylda, 143, 146
Krzesiński, Feliks Adam Walerian (Felix Kchessinsky), 143–44, 148–149, 161–62
Kuhne, Ludwik, 143
Kunzle, David, 126, 130
Kwiatkowski, Antoni, 147–48

Labarre, Théodore, 61, 251
Lacotte, Pierre, 67
Lady Henriette, 241
Laitière suisse, La. *See Nathalie, ou la Laitière suisse*
Lalla Rookh, 23, 41, 65, 251
Lami, Eugène, 129
Lamoureux, Louise, 173
Lanari, Antonio, 167
language, 21, 32, 33, 107, 109; of dance, 4, 37–44, 65, 131
Lanner, Katti, 8, 10, 159
La Scala (Milan), 5, 7, 9, 61, 132–33, 135, 138, 141, 176, 183, 187–88, 194
Lasina, Giovanni Battista, 176, 256
Lasina, Giuseppe, 176
Laskowska, Honorata, 148
Lassalle, Louis, 211
Lecomte, Hippolyte, 127
Lendvai, Yseult, 117
Légende, La, 206
Léon, Pauline, 75
Lepaulle, (François) Gabriel Guillaume, 99
Lepri, Giovanni, 138, 140–41, 256
Leroux, Pauline, 79, 157, 223, 225
Lesueur, Jean-François, 154
Lévi-Strauss, Claude, 95
Levinson, André, 52–53, 56, 67, 103
Levy, Darlene, 75, 88
lezghinka (Caucasian dance), 34
libretti, 1, 21, 27, 69, 182–83, 188, 190, 195
Lichtenthal, Peter, 60

Lifar, Serge, 66
Lightbody, Charles Wayland, 86
linzer tanz, 248
Little Humpbacked Horse, The, 6
lituana (dance), 37, 39, 247
Liuzzi, Concetta, 254, 255
Lives of the Saints, 207
Locke, Ralph, 68
Lopoukov, Andrei, 67
Lormier, Paul, 129
Louis XV of France, 213
Lovenskjold, Baron Hermann
 Severin, 67, 93
Luca e Lauretta (Luke and
 Lauretta), 184
Lucilla ossia la figlia del torrente
 (Lucille, or The Daughter of
 the Torrent), 256
Lucrezia Borgia, 133

Mabille, Auguste, 245, 250
Macbeth, 176, 207
Madoglio, Luigi, 257
Mademoiselle de Maupin, 218
Maglietta, Luigi(?), 187
Magri, Gennaro, 31, 63
Maillot, (?), 124
Malakhov, Vladimir, 117
male body, 5, 139
male dancers, 2, 5, 58, 72, 131,
 135–39, 176–77, 204, 213,
 218–219, 231–32; male sylph, 5,
 131–41. *See also* cross-dressing,
 danseur noble, gender
male gaze, 119, 124
Maleuvre, (?), 78, 79
Malibran, Maria, 170
manola (Spanish dance), 27, 250
Manola, La, 253
Manning, Susan, 119
Manon Lescaut, 61–62, 87
Manzotti, Luigi, 179
Marchak, Catherine, 110, 120
Marché des Innocents, Le, 45
Marco Visconti, 191
Margherita di Scozia (Margaret of
 Scotland), 256
Mariquita, Madame, 8
Marivaux, Pierre Carlet de
 Chamblain de, 75, 88
Markova, Alicia, 124
Marliani, Marco Aurelio, 249
Marmet, Melina, 255
Marocchesi, Francesco, 178, 257

marriage, as theme, 7, 72, 80–81,
 91–92, 94–96, 98, 100, 102; and
 ballet dancer, 143, 145, 147–49
Marsh, Carol, 65
Martin, John, 211, 212
Masaniello (also known as *Il
 Pescatore di Brindisi* [The
 Fisherman from Brindisi]), 175,
 249
Massaro, Maria Nevilla, 180
Matis, Domenico, 253
Matrimonio in un festino, Un, 255
Maywood, Augusta, 138, 256, 257
Mazeppa, 255
Mazilier, Joseph, 104, 205,
 249–51, 254, 257
mazourka. *See* mazurka
mazur. *See* mazurka
mazurka, 3, 4, 6, 13–15, 17–18,
 20, 24–25, 27, 34, 38, 44–46, 66,
 144, 154–55, 158, 249, 250
Mazzarelli-Astolfi, Fanny. *See*
 Astolfi, Fanny
Megilla, 193
Meglin, Joellen A., 7, 54, 67,
 69–90, 276
Memmi, Ottavio, 178, 257
Manzeli, Elizabeth, 8, 10
Mérante, Louis, 192
Mereguita, 255
Meunier, Hipolit, 143, 148
Meyerbeer, Giacomo, 212, 218,
 230, 245, 256
Mierzyńska, Julia, 143, 144, 148
Mierzyński, Andrzej, 143
Milon, Louis, 126, 127, 199, 220,
 224, 227
Milton, John, 206–08, 212
mime, 20–21, 114–15, 132, 165,
 172, 176, 182, 184. *See also*
 narrative ballet, pantomime
mind-body dichotomy, 198
minuet, 42, 47, 250
mirletons (shepherds and
 shepherdesses), 18, 59
Mirza, 87
Mochi, David, 177, 254, 256
Mohicans, Les, 227–29
Moi, Toril, 115, 120
Moïse (*Mosè in Egitto*), 226–27
Moncada, Filippo, 254, 255
Monplaisir, Ippolito, 138, 139
Monsieur Chalumeaux, 176, 254
Montagu, Lady Mary Wortley,
 210, 212

Montesquieu, Charles de
 Secondat, Baron de, 70, 75, 87
Montessu, Pauline (*née* Paul),
 210, 212, 223
Montez, Lola, 246
Moore, Lillian, 173
Moorish dances, 41–42
Morlacchi, Guiseppina, 8, 10
Morosini, Livio, 176–77, 254,
 256
Mort d'Adonis, La, 204
Mort de Tasse, La, 127
Mose in Egitto. See Moïse
Moses, Claire Goldberg, 86
movement, 22, 29, 32. *See also*
 language of dance
Mozart, Wolfgang Amadeus, 245
Muette de Portici, La, 14–15, 19,
 23, 60, 175, 245, 246
Murat, Joachim, 181
music, ballet, 1, 24–25; and
 national dance, 21–22, 25–26,
 43, 46–49
Mussi, Antonio, 257

Nabucco, 133
Nadaud, J.B., 245
Naples, 5, 181–96
Napoleon (Emperor of France),
 122, 181
Napoli, 183
narcissism, 109, 114
narrative ballet, 13, 20–30, 44,
 107, 108–09, 113–18. *See also*
 pantomime
Natalini, Giovanna, 179
Natarova, Anna Petrovna, 58
Nathalie, ou la Laitière suisse,
 221, 224
national dance, 3–4, 6, 11–68, 161,
 245–52; categories of, 36–42; in
 operas, 245–46; in divertissements, benefit performances
 and entr'actes, 247–48; in
 ballets, 249–52. *See also*
 character dance, folk dance,
 and specific national dances:
 anglaise, bolero, cachucha,
 cosaque, cracovienne,
 fandango, Indian, jig, mazurka,
 minuet, polka, polonaise,
 saltarello, sicilienne, Styrian,
 tarantella, tyrolienne,
 varsovienne, waltz, zapateado

nationalism, 1, 6, 11, 31–32, 132–33

native dance. *See* national dance

native dancers, 34–35

Natural History of the Ballet Girl, The, 14

naturalism, 2, 27, 29, 30

neoclassicism, 199–200

Neapolitan dance, 14

Neapolitanischen fischer, Die. See Le Pêcheur napolitain

Negri, Angiolina, 256

Negro, Silvio, 166, 179

Neumann, L.T., 134

Nicholas I (Tsar of Russia), 145

Nicolas, (?), 214, 218

Niedermeyer, Louis, 245

Nijinsky, Vaslav, 140, 173

Nina, ou la Folie par amour, 199–200, 205, 220–24

Nirstein, Daniel, 160

Noblet, Félicité, 15, 59, 224, 229–30. *See also* Dupont, Mme. Alexis

Noblet, Lise, 15, 58, 200, 202, 210–12, 215–16, 218, 224, 229–30, 247

Noces de Pélée et de Thétis, Les, 105

Noce di Benevento, Il, 135

Nodier, Charles, 92, 103

Noja, Duke di, 185, 186

Nordic dance, 36

Norwegian dance, 250

Nourrit, Adolphe, 92, 223, 224

Nouveau Robinson, Le, 205

Noverre, Jean-Georges, 52, 75, 88, 131–32, 197–98, 204, 225

Nuit de bal, Un, 247

Nuits florentines, Les, 66

Nureyev, Rudolf, 55

Nutcracker, The, 20, 56, 62, 68

Obizzo di Malaspina (Obizzo of Malaspina), 175, 255

Obuchowska, Paulina, 147

odalisque, 48, 74, 212

O'Donoghue, 158

Offen, Karen M., 90

Oliwińska, Józefa, 149

Olympie, 128

Ondine, 6, 23, 26, 44, 46, 65, 94, 250

opera, 7, 13, 21, 26, 29, 61, 68,

132; and ballet, 175, 211; balls, 17–18, 59

Orfa, 156

Orgie, L', 60, 249, 251

oriental, dance, 53; costume, 127–28. *See also* Indian dances

Orientales, Les, 11

orientalism, 67–68, 70, 74–75, 211, 225

Orłowski, Antoni (also known as Antek), 157

Otranto liberata (Otranto Liberated), 185

Ozaï, 62, 251, 252

Page inconsistant, Le, 249

Pages du Duc de Vendôme, Les, 249

Palczewska, Antonina, 143–44, 148, 153–54

Palczewska, Teresa, 143–44, 148

Pallerini, Antonia, 255

Pandora, 186

pantomime, 20–22, 29, 53, 65, 69, 74, 77–78, 93, 140, 158, 191, 197–99, 214

Paolo e Virginia, o sia i due creoli (Paul and Virginia, or The Two Creoles), 184

Papillon, Le, 8

Pâquerette, 46, 251

Paquita, 250, 257

Paradol, Mme., 226–27

Parfum et les Echarpes, Le (Perfume and Scarves) dance, 42

Paria, Il (The Pariah), 188

Paris Opéra (Académie Royal de Musique), 1, 3, 5, 7–9, 13–16, 19–20, 23, 26, 35, 45, 58–59, 61, 64, 69, 74, 82–83, 89, 91, 108, 120, 124, 126–28, 139, 153–54, 156–58, 183–84, 194, 200, 202–03, 205, 208, 210–11, 218–19, 222–23, 224, 227–29, 245, 249–51

Parker, Roger, 68

pas de caractère. *See* character dance

pas de Chibouque, 41–42

pas de l'abeille. *See* bee dance

Paskiewicz, Teodor, 146

Pasta, Giuditta, 170

patriarchy, 72, 82, 86, 119

patrons, 166–67

Paul, Mons. (Antoine), 214, 218

Pavlova, Anna, 173

Pêcheur napolitain, Le (*Die neapolitanischen fischer*), 15, 46, 65, 247

Pedoni, Ludovico, 168, 154, 256, 257

Peer Gynt, 11

Penco, Francesco, 177, 254–57

Peri, La (La Péri), 254

Péri, La, 27, 42, 47, 62, 129, 211, 250, 252

Perrault, Adelaide (Mme. Taglioni), 184, 189

Perrot, Jules, 3, 7, 9, 13, 15, 23, 40–41, 44–51, 54, 58, 61, 65, 67–68, 88, 140–41, 159, 170, 173–74, 211, 218–19, 226–27, 230, 232–33, 237, 241, 245–48, 250–51, 254

Perrot-Grisi, Mme., 230. *See also* Grisi, Carlotta

Pescatore di Brindisi, Il (The Fisherman of Brindisi), 175, 254

Pesci, U., 140

Peshkov, Nikita, 34

Pestelli, Giorgio, 179

Petipa, Lucien, 7, 9, 14, 235

Petipa, Marius, 4, 7, 9, 34, 45, 55–56, 64, 139

Petit, Anatole, 249

Petrobelli, Pierluigi, 68

Petrov, Oleg, 55, 68

Philtre, Le, 13, 14

Pietra filosofale, La (The Philosopher's Stone), 193

Pietro di Portogallo (Pedro of Portugal) (also known as *Ines de Castro*), 188

Piglia, Clara, 179

Pion, Maurice, 67, 144, 152–53

Pius IX (Cardinal Giovanni Maria Mastai Ferretti), 172

Plunkett, Adeline, 35, 250

Pochini, Carolina, 256

Podczaski (brothers), 146

Poesio, Giannandrea, 5, 131–41, 276

Poggiolesi, Ettore, 256

pointe, 1, 3–6, 8. 10, 53, 56, 91, 124–25, 137, 139, 141, 198, 215. *See also* costumes

Poland, 3–4, 6, 24–25, 143–64

Poliak, Zuzanna, 148
Polish dances, 38–39, 60, 62, 248
politics, and ballets, 165–68, 193
polka, 3, 14–15, 18–19, 247, 150
polonaise, 4, 17, 18
polska, 37
Pontecchi, Egisto Napoleone, 254, 255
Popiel, Helena, 148, 161
Popiel, Jan, 147–48
Portughesi nelle India, I (The Portuguese in the Indies) (also known as *La conquista di Malacca* [The Conquest of Malacca]), 188–89
Powers, Harold, 63
Pratesi, Gaspare, 254
Prévost, Hippolyte, 201, 205
Priora, Egidio, 177, 255
Priora, Olimpia, 177, 255
Prisco, Gaetano, 253, 255, 256
Prisco, Raffaella Santalicante, 177, 253, 255, 256, 257
Promessi sposi, I (The Betrothed), 191
Prophete, La, 245, 246
Proserpine, 122
prostitution, 6–7, 79, 81–2, 86; of ballerinas, 145–47
Przyborowski, Walery, 146, 162
Pudełek, Janina, 6, 7, 46, 54, 143–64, 276
Pugni, Cesare, 61, 250–53
"pure dance", 52, 53, 55, 182. *See also* abstract ballet

Quadrille of the Four Parts of the World, 250, 251
quadrilles, 17, 18
quadrille-mazurka, 17
queer desire, 111–12

Rabine, Leslie Wahl, 86
Rabinowitz, Stanley, 67
Racine, Jean, 212, 226
Radiciotti, Giuseppe, 172, 173
Radziwiłł, Prince Michał, 146
Ramaccini (Blasis), Annunziata, 255
Ramaccini, Antonio, 254
Ramaccini, Francesco, 175–76, 254
Rameau, Jean-Philippe, 75, 87

Rautenstrauch, General Józef, 144–45
Ravaglia, Rosina, 254
Razzanelli, Assunta, 255
Read's Characteristic National Dances, 27
realism, 23, 62, 210. *See also* authenticity
Reber, Henri, 250
Récamier, Jeanne, 122
redowa, 18, 245, 250
Regli, Francesco, 183–84
Renato d'Arles (Renato of Arles), 177, 255
Reppe, Ludwika, 149
reviews, 16, 21, 191–92. *See also* critics
Révolte au sérail, La (also known as *La Révolte des femmes*), 7, 21–2, 60, 69–90, 203–05
Revolt of the Workhouse, The, 83, 89
Reyna, Ferdinand, 66
Richardson, Philip J.S., 58
Rignier, (?), 149
Rinaldi, Mario, 174, 180
Ritorni, Carlo, 135, 140
Robert le Diable, 14, 23, 58, 92, 199, 223–25, 228, 230
Robin-Challan, Louise, 9
Rob Roy, 11
Roesler, Franz,, 166
Rolland, Enrico, 253
romaneque (dance), 250
Romanow, 247
romantic ballet, aesthetic of, 11; definition of, 51–52
Romanticism, 1, 3, 5, 8, 91–105, 133, 181, 199
Rome, 5, 165–80
Ronzani, Domenico, 5, 171–74, 253, 254
Ropiquet, Louise, 205
Rosati, Carolina, 139
Rosselli, John, 179
Rosiera, La (The Crown of Roses), 255
Rossi, Adelaide, 257
Rossi, Luigi, 141, 180
Rossi, Raffaele, 256, 257
Rossini, Gioacchino, 24, 167, 217, 227, 237, 245
Rota, Giuseppe, 165, 171–72, 176, 178–79, 257
Rotondi, Sergio, 179

Rosselli, John, 194
Rouvroy, Claude Henri de, Comte de Saint-Simon, 69
Royal Danish Ballet, 9, 104
Royer, Adolphe, 156
Roøniecki, Gabriel, 148, 159, 161
Ruffin, Elena, 176, 180
Russian ballet, 4, 68
Russian dances, 31, 34
Russlan and Ludmilla, 34

Saint-Aubaire, (?), 214
Saint-Léon, Arthur, 41, 65, 68, 168–70, 205, 245, 247, 250–51, 253
Saint-Léon, Michel, 15, 25, 43, 58, 65, 68
Saint-Saëns, 68
Saint-Simonian movement, 7, 69–72, 77, 79–80, 84–86
Saïs, Le, 42
Sala, Emilio, 61
saltarello, 13, 14, 44, 68, 245, 250, 252
Saltimbanco, Il (The Juggler), 256
Saluste, Guillaume de, 235, 241
Samengo, Paolo, 125
Samson et Dalila, 68
Sand, Georges, 155
Sangalli, Rita, 10
Saqui, Marguerite-Antoinette Lalanne, 214
sarabande, 249
Scafidi, Nadia, 9
Scaramelli, G.A., 256
scarf dance, 23
Scherzo di gioventù di Enrico V re d'Inghilterra (The Youth of Henry V, King of England), 254
Schiano, Vincenzo, 254
Schiedel, Susan I., 193
schottish, 18
Schneitzhoeffer, Jean-Madeleine, 24, 67, 91, 249
Scott, Joan Wallach, 80, 89
Scott, Sir Walter, 11, 92, 103, 235
Scottish dances, 31, 247; in *La Sylphide*, 96–97. *See also* Highland Fling and jig
Second, Albéric, 83
Segarelli, Costanza, 255
Segarelli, Domenico, 253, 255

Seguaci di Bacco, I (The Followers of Bacchus), 185
semiotics, 107, 109–10, 112, 114–15, 117–18
Sennato, Marina, 179
Serafini, Giacomo, 172
seraglio, 145, 147. *See also* harem
Serenade, 3
Sergeyev, Nicholas, 9
Serral, Dolores, 15, 19, 30, 34, 37, 39
Servante justifiée, La, 129
Sesostri (Sesostris), 188, 191
Sette reclute, Le (The Seven Recruits), 255
sexuality, 79–80, 82, 92, 100, 102, 111–12, 116. *See also* gender
Shakespeare, William, 132
Shiriaev, Alexander (also Shirayev), 54, 67
Sibilska, Joanna, 64
Sicilien, Le, 59, 249, 251
sicilienne (dance), 41, 68
Silfide, La (La Sylphide), 171, 254. *See also* La Sylphide
Simon, François, 207, 212
Slavic dances, 37, 39, 43, 251. *See also* specific dances
Sleeping Beauty, The, 3, 4
Smetana, Bedrich, 11
Smith, Albert, 58
Smith, B.F., Jr., 173
Smith, Marian, 3, 11–68, 119, 245–52, 276
smolenska, 247
social order, 113–19
social dance, 4, 13–20
Sogno, Il (The Dream), 176, 256
Sogno della vita ossia la bella fanciulla di Gand, Il (The Dream of Life, or The Beautiful Maid of Ghent), 254
Soirée de carnaval, Une, 247
Somnambule, La, 223, 225, 241
Sor, Fernando, 249
Soul, Victor, 59
Souritz, Elizabeth, 68, 140
"Souvenirs de jeunesse," "Les," 18
Spanish dance, 3, 4, 12–16, 18–19, 31, 35–37, 39–41, 43, 54–55, 58–60, 63, 67–68, 245, 247, 249, 250. *See also* bolero, cachucha, and fandango

Springer, Ludwika, 152
Stefańska, Kamila, 157, 158, 159
Stella, 61, 256
Stolpe, Alojzy, 148
stories, 115. *See also* narrative ballet
Stradella, 245, 246
Straus, Anna, 143, 144, 148
Straus, Karolina, 143, 144, 147
Straus, Paulina, 143, 144
Styrian dance, 20, 39–40, 245, 247, 249
supernatural, 1, 5, 91, 103, 124, 133, 165
Surmeyan, Hazaros, 112
Sventura in un sogno, La (The Dreamed Mishap) (also known as the *La sventura in sogno, ovvero la bella fanciulla di Gand* [The Dreamed Mishap, or The Beautiful Maid of Ghent]), 176, 254
Swan Lake, 3, 4, 20, 55–56, 68
Swiss dance, 248
Sylphide, La, 1, 3, 7, 9, 15–16, 24, 28, 46–47, 52–53, 67, 73, 81, 91–105, 129, 135, 197, 199, 205, 216, 218, 223–25, 241, 249, 251, 252
sylphs, 8, 54, 92, 94–95, 99, 101, 124, 129, 182, 199; male, 5, 131–41
Sylvain, James, 40
symbolism, 107, 110, 112, 114–15, 117
Szczepańska, Olimpia, 152
Szczepański, Kornel, 152
Szlancowska, Helena. *See* Grekowski, Helena

tableaux, 22–23, 26, 29–30, 61, 69–70, 78
Tadei, Abbé, 191
Taglioni, Amalia (*née* Galster), 218
Taglioni, Carlo, 183
Taglioni, Filippo, 7. 61. 67, 69–70, 72, 75, 86, 91–92, 104, 135, 181, 183, 199, 220–21, 224–25, 245, 249, 254
Taglioni, Luigia, 183
Taglioni, Luisa, 183, 184
Taglioni, Marie, 2, 5–8, 12, 16, 20,

24, 34, 56, 52, 54, 59, 69, 87, 91–93, 102–03, 125, 127, 139, 157, 165, 172, 181, 184, 198–99, 201–03, 205, 210, 212–20, 223–26, 228, 232, 236, 245, 249, 251, 254
Taglioni, Paul, 9, 183, 217, 218
Taglioni, Salvatore, 5, 181–96, 259–61
Talamo, (?), 187
Talismano, Il (The Talisman), 193
Talma, François-Joseph, 223, 225
tarantella, 6, 15, 17, 20, 26, 31, 41, 43–44, 46, 227, 247–50, 252
Tarantola, La (The Tarantula), 254
Tarentule, La, 22, 26–28, 47, 219, 220, 247, 249, 252
Tardival, E.C., 64
Tarnowski, Aleksander, 143, 153
Tarnowski, Antoni, 143, 150
Teatro Argentina (Rome), 5, 167–68, 171–72, 174–76, 178–79, 253–57
Teatro di Apollo (formerly Teatro di Tordinona) (Rome), 167, 253–57
Teatro di San Carlo (Naples), 5, 158, 181–87, 193–94
Teatro Fondo (Naples), 183, 187
Teatro Tordinona (Rome), 179
technique, ballet, 133, 136–38
Télémaque (Telemachus), 184
Tempête, La, 9, 205
Teniers, David, 212
Tennant, Veronica, 112
Tentation, La, 22, 205–12, 217
Termanini, Filippo, 171–72, 253, 255, 256
Terziani, Eugenio, 256
Théâtre de la Renaissance, 130
Théâtre des Italiens (Paris), 155
Théâtre des Variétés, 35
Theaters. *See* specific names
Thébaïde, La, 212
Théleur, E.A., 59
Thierry, Louis, 144
Thomas, Ambroise, 249
Tintori, Giampiero, 194
Tipoo-Saeb (Tipu Sahib), 189–91, 195
Tiricanti, Giulio, 179
Tibullus, Albius, 209, 212
Tolbecque, Jean-Baptiste, 251

Torlonia, Alessandro, 166–68
Torlonia, Giovanni, 166–67
Torrelli, Vincenzo, 191
Toschi, Andrea, 9, 179
training, in ballet, 6–8, 133, 136, 138–39, 143–44; in character dance, 55
travesty dancer, 9, 87. *See also* cross-dressing
Trawna, Julia, 143, 147
Tribune des Femmes, 69, 72, 81, 84–86, 89–90
Trionfo dell'innocenza, Il (The Triumph of Innocence), 178, 257
truandaise, 250. *See also* bolero
Tudesq, André-Jean, 89
Turczynowicz, Konstancja (*née* Damse), 143, 148–49, 153–56
Turczynowicz, Konstanty, 149
Turczynowicz, Leon, 149
Turczynowicz, Maria, 149
Turczynowicz, Roman, 144, 148, 150–51, 153–56
Turkułł, Ignacy, 146, 147
tutus, 3, 129, 182, 194
Tyrolean dances, 13–14, 24, 31, 245, 248

Ultimo fiorno di Pompei, L', 61
Urban, Chrétien, 240, 241
utopian socialism. *See* Saint-Simonian movement

Vagon, Mlle. (?), 22, 224
Vaillat, Léandre, 34, 59, 184, 194
Valette, C., 235
Valois, Ninette de, 67
vampirism, 112, 192
Vampiro, Il (The Vampire), 192
Van Gennep, Arnold, 104
Varennes, Julia de, 202, 210, 212, 215, 218

Varin, Elise, 205, 220, 222–24
varsovienne (dance), 38–39, 247
Vecchio della Foresta, Il (The Old Man of the Forest), 192
Vendetta d'amore, La (Love's Revenge), 253
Venturi, David, 254
Verdi, Guiseppe, 63, 133, 167, 175–76
Veret, Désirée (Jeanne-Désirée), 90
Vernoy de Saint-Georges, Jules-Henri, 9, 66, 109, 233, 240–41
Véron, Dr. Louis, 74, 78, 82–83, 87, 89, 219
Vert-Vert, 19, 251
Vestris, Auguste, 126, 199
Victor Emmanuel (King of Italy), 181
Vic-Wells Ballet, 9
Vienna, Lorenzo, 256
Viennese dancers, 248
Viganò, Salvatore, 131–32, 135, 176, 184, 198
Vincita al lotto, La (Win at the Lottery), 253
Viotti, Emanuele, 176, 178–79, 256, 257
Virginia, 254
Virginie, Mlle., 126
Vivandiera ed il Postiglione, La, 68
Vivandière, La, 250
Viviani, Luigi Maria, 254, 255
Voilquin, Suzanne, 90
Voltaire, 70, 233
Volynsku, Akim, 67
Vuillier, Gaston, 123

waltz, 18, 37, 46–47, 49, 250–51
War of the Women, 251
Warsaw Courier, 157–63

Warsaw Ballet, 54, 67, 143–64
Watteau, 208
Weber, Carl Maria von, 46
Weiss, Josephine, 248
Wendt, Karolina, 143
Wielki Theater (Warsaw), 6, 143–64
Wierzbicka, Józefa, 147
Wild, Nicole, 61
Wiley, Roland John, 62, 63, 68
Wilis. *See* Giselle
William Tell, 167
Willis, N.P., 59
Winter, Marian Hannah, 60
witches, in *Les Sylphides*, 98–100
women, 4–8, 69–70, 75–76, 84, 107. *See also* La Révolte au sérail
Woodcock, Sarah, 129
working class, 80–82, 107
Woroniecki, Mikołaj, 148
Wuthier (Casati), Margherita Gottier, 177

yodeling, 24, 43

Zabò, Adelaide, 256
Zaleski, W., 145, 162
Zalewski, Antoni, 161
zapateado, 15, 28, 56, 211
Zapolska, Gabriela, 148
Zelt, Józef, 153
ziguerrerena, 245
zinganka, 251
Zingaro, 58, 141, 205, 218, 230–32, 245
Żółkowski, Alojzy, 150
Zorn, Friedrich Albert, 38, 64
Zuleika, 256
Zurkowski, Jan, 161

Library of Congress Cataloging-in-Publication Data

Rethinking the sylph : new perspectives on the Romantic ballet /
    edited by Lynn Garafola.
        p.   cm. — (Studies in dance history)
    Includes bibliographical references (p.   ) and index.
    ISBN 0–8195–6325–0 (cloth : alk. paper). — ISBN 0–8195–6326–9
(pbk. : alk. paper)
    1. Ballet—Europe—History—19th century.   I. Garafola, Lynn.
II. Series: Studies in dance history (Hanover, N.H.)
GV1643.R48   1997
792.8'094'09034—dc21   97–21728